Teacher's
Resource Book

Lewis Lansford

B1 >

Business
Partner

Student's Book contents

Contents

Overview

Business Partner is a flexible course designed for a variety of learners. It is suitable for students with mixed abilities, requirements and interests and for varied class sizes where the common requirement is to learn professional English language and develop key skills for the workplace.

When talking to learners, their reasons for studying business English almost always relate to their employability. Many tertiary students want to maximise their chances of finding a job in an international environment, while in-work professionals want to communicate more effectively in their workplace and improve their future career prospects. Other learners may simply need to study and pass a business English exam in order to complete their overall degree.

In all three cases, teachers need to be able to engage and motivate by providing learning materials which:

- are interesting and relevant to their life experiences.
- match their learning needs and priorities.
- are appropriate for the amount of study time available.

Business Partner has been designed to enable teachers to meet these needs without spending many hours researching their own materials. The content and structure of the course is based on three key concepts: **employability**, **flexibility** and **learner engagement**.

Course aims and key concepts

Employability

Balance between language and business skills training

In order to achieve their employability goals, learners need to improve their knowledge of English language as it is used in the workplace and also develop key skills for the international workplace. *Business Partner* provides this balance.

In addition to building their vocabulary and grammar and developing their writing skills, *Business Partner* trains students in Communication and Business skills. Language being only one aspect of successful communication, students also require an understanding of different business situations and an awareness of different communication styles, especially when working across cultures.

- 'Communication skills' (Lesson 3) provides the soft skills needed in order to work effectively with people whose personality and culture may be different from your own. These include dealing with disagreement, responding to customer concerns and managing conversations.
- 'Business skills' (Lesson 4) provides the practical skills needed in different business situations, such as taking part in meetings, presentations and negotiations.

Flexibility

The modular approach means that *Business Partner* can be adapted to suit a variety of teaching requirements from extensive lessons to intensive short courses. In addition to the Coursebook, a wide variety of additional optional activities and resources are provided which can be used to focus on and extend material which is most useful to learners' needs.

Extra activities and extra grammar points

You can extend your lessons or focus in more depth on certain areas by using the large bank of extra activities in MyEnglishLab (clearly signposted for you throughout the Coursebook). These include extra vocabulary and grammar practice exercises for use in class as well as activities which draw attention to useful language in reading texts.

 Teacher's resources: extra activities

These are PDFs in MyEnglishLab that you can download and print or display on-screen.

 The email contains examples of adverbs of degree. Go to MyEnglishLab for optional grammar work.

Business Partner offers a flexible approach to grammar depending on whether you want to devote a significant amount of time to a grammar topic or focus on consolidation only when you need to. There is one main grammar point in each unit, presented and practised in Lesson 2.

In addition, the Writing section (Lesson 5) includes a link to an optional second grammar point in MyEnglishLab, where students can watch short video presentations of the grammar points and do interactive activities.

 page 112 See Pronunciation bank Pronunciation activities are included at the back of the book. This allows teachers to focus on aspects of pronunciation which are most useful for their students.

Teacher's Resource Bank: Photocopiables, Writing bank, Reading bank and Functional language bank

You can use these resources as and when needed with your classes. The Photocopiables further activate and practise vocabulary from Lesson 1 and grammar from Lesson 2 as and when needed.

The Reading bank for each unit gives students more reading practice and can be also used for self-study. The activity types reflect those found in a range of business English exams. The Writing bank provides supplementary models of professional communication and the Functional language bank extends useful phrases for a range of business situations.

Learner engagement

Video content: We all use video more and more to communicate and to find out about the world and we have put video at the heart of *Business Partner*. There are two videos in every unit with comprehension and language activities:

- an authentic video package in Lesson 1, based on real-life video clips and interviews suitable for your learners' level of English.
- a dramatised communication skills training video in Lesson 3 which follows characters in an international team as they deal with different professional challenges.

Authentic content: Working with authentic content really helps to engage learners, and teachers can spend many hours searching for suitable material online. *Business Partner* has therefore been built around authentic videos and articles from leading media organisations such as the *Financial Times* and news channels. These offer a wealth of international business information as well as real examples of British, U.S. and non-native-speaker English.

Relevance for learners without work experience: Using business English teaching materials with learners who have little or no work experience can be particularly challenging. *Business Partner* has been carefully designed to work with these students as well as with in-work professionals. In the case of collaborative speaking tasks and roleplays, the situation used will either be:

- one that we can all relate to as customers and consumers; OR
- a choice of situations will be offered including a mix of professional and everyday situations.

Both will allow learners to practise the skill and language presented in the lesson, but in a context that is most relevant to them.

Business workshops: Learners have the opportunity to consolidate and activate the language and skills from the units in 8 business workshops at the end of the book. These provide interesting and engaging scenarios where students simulate real-life professional situations such as roleplaying meetings, negotiations or presentations.

Approach to language and skills

Business Partner offers fully integrated skills, including the essential critical thinking and higher-order thinking skills, which are built into the activities.

Vocabulary and video The main topic vocabulary set is presented and practised in Lesson 1 of each unit, building on vocabulary from the authentic video. Teachers are given lots of opportunities to use the vocabulary in discussions and group tasks, and to tailor the tasks to their classroom situations.

Functional language (such as giving advice, summarising, dealing with objections) supports learners' capability to operate in real workplace situations in English. Three functional language sets are presented and practised in every unit: in Lessons 3, 4 and 5. You will be able to teach the language in group speaking and writing tasks. There is a Functional language bank at the back of this Teacher's Resource Book which students can also find in MyEnglishLab so that they can quickly refer to useful language support when preparing for a business situation, such as a meeting, presentation or interview.

Listening and video The course offers a wide variety of listening activities (based on both video and audio recordings) to help students develop their comprehension skills and to hear target language in context. All of the video and audio material is available in MyEnglishLab and includes a range of British, U.S. and non-native-speaker English. Lessons 1 and 3 are based on video (as described above). In four of the eight units, Lesson 2 is based on audio. In all units, you also work with significant audio recordings in Lesson 4 and the Business workshop.

Grammar The approach to grammar is flexible depending on whether you want to devote a significant amount of time to grammar or to focus on the consolidation of grammar only when you need to. There is one main grammar point in each unit, presented and practised in Lesson 2. There is a link from Lesson 5 to an optional second grammar point in MyEnglishLab – with short video presentations and interactive practice. Both grammar points are supported by the Grammar reference section at the back of the Coursebook (p.118). This provides a summary of meaning and form, with notes on usage or exceptions, and business English examples.

Reading *Business Partner* offers a wealth of authentic texts and articles from a variety of sources, particularly the *Financial Times*. Every unit has a main reading text with comprehension tasks. This appears either in Lesson 2 or in the Business workshop. There is a Reading bank at the back of this Teacher's Resource Book which students can also find in MyEnglishLab and which has a longer reading text for every unit with comprehension activities.

Speaking Collaborative speaking tasks appear at the end of Lessons 1, 3, 4 and the Business workshop in every unit. These tasks encourage students to use the target language and, where relevant, the target skill of the lesson. There are lots of opportunities to personalise these tasks to suit your own classroom situation.

Writing *Business Partner* offers multiple opportunities to practise writing. Lesson 5 in every unit provides a model text and practice in a business writing skill. The course covers a wide range of genres such as reports, proposals, note-taking and emails, and for different purposes, including formal and informal communication, summarising, invitations, replies and project updates. There are also short writing tasks in Lesson 2 which provide controlled practice of the target grammar. There is a Writing bank at the back of this Teacher's Resource Book which students can also find in MyEnglishLab and which provides models of different types of business writing and useful phrases appropriate to their level of English.

Pronunciation Two pronunciation points are presented and practised in every unit. Pronunciation points are linked to the content of the unit – usually to a video or audio presentation or to a grammar point. The pronunciation presentations and activities are at the back of the Coursebook (p.112), with signposts from the relevant lessons. This section also includes an introduction to pronunciation with British and U.S. phonetic charts.

Approach to Communication skills

A key aspect of *Business Partner* is the innovative video-based communication skills training programme.

The aims of the Communications skills lessons are to introduce students to the skills needed to interact successfully in international teams with people who may have different communication styles from them due to culture or personality. Those skills include teamwork, decision-making and influencing.

These lessons are based on videos that provide realistic examples of work situations. This is particularly important for pre-service learners who may not have direct experience of the particular situations they are about to see. In each of these videos students watch two possible scenarios (Option A and Option B) in which a different communication style is used. These options give students the opportunity to engage in critical viewing of each option and gain awareness of the impact of different communication styles.

Approach to testing and assessment

Business Partner provides a balance of formative and summative assessment. Both types of assessment are important for teachers and learners and have different objectives. Regular review and on-going assessment allows students to evaluate their own progress and encourages them to persevere in their studies. Formal testing offers a more precise value on the progress made on their knowledge and proficiency.

Formative assessment: Each Coursebook lesson is framed by a clear lesson outcome which summarises the learning deliverable. The lesson ends with a self-assessment section which encourages students to reflect on their progress in relation to the lesson outcome and to think about future learning needs. More detailed self-assessment tasks and suggestions for further practice are available in MyEnglishLab. (See also section on the Global Scale of English and the Learning Objectives for Professional English.)

The Coursebook also contains one review page per unit at the back of the book to recycle and revise the key vocabulary, grammar and functional language presented in the unit; they are structured to reflect the modularity of the course.

Summative assessment: Unit tests are provided and activities are clearly labelled to show which section of the unit they are testing to reflect the modular structure of the course. The tests are available in PDF and Word formats so that you can adapt them to suit your purposes. They are also available as interactive tests that you can allocate to your students if you wish to do so.

These Unit tests are based on task types from the major business English exams (BEC, BULATS, PTE Professional) and task types are clearly labelled. There is also an additional LCCI writing task for professional English for every unit. This approach familiarises learners with the format of the exams and gives them practice in the skills needed to pass the exams.

MyEnglishLab also contains additional interactive PTE Professional exam practice activities to help students prepare for this exam. The content and level of the exam tasks matches the Coursebook so it can also be used as additional revision material.

The Global Scale of English

The Global Scale of English (GSE) is a standardised, granular scale from 10 to 90 which measures English language proficiency. The GSE Learning Objectives for Professional English are aligned with the Common European Framework of Reference (CEFR). Unlike the CEFR, which describes proficiency in terms of broad levels, the Global Scale of English identifies what a learner can do at each point on a more granular scale – and within a CEFR level. The scale is designed to motivate learners by demonstrating incremental progress in their language ability. The Global Scale of English forms the backbone for Pearson English course material and assessment.

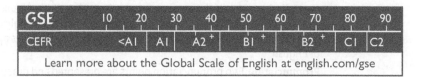

Business Partner has been written based on these Learning Objectives, which ensure appropriate scaffolding and measurable progress. Each Lesson outcome in each lesson in the Coursebook encapsulates a number of specific Learning Objectives which are listed in this Teacher's Resource Book in the Teaching notes. These Learning Objectives are also listed in the Self-assessment sheets available to students in MyEnglishLab. (See also Self-assessment above in Approach to testing and assessment.)

Course structure

Business Partner is an eight-level course based on the Global Scale of English (GSE) and representing the CEFR levels: A1, A2, A2+, B1, B1+, B2, B2+, C1.

	For the teacher	For the student
print	Teacher's Resource Book with MyEnglishLab	Coursebook with Digital Resources Workbook
blended	Active Teach	Coursebook with MyEnglishLab

Business Partner is a fully hybrid course with two digital dimensions that students and teachers can choose from. MyEnglishLab is the digital component that is integrated with the book content.

Access to MyEnglishLab is given through a code printed on the inside front cover of this book. As a teacher, you have access to both versions of MyEnglishLab, and to additional content in the Teacher's Resource folder.

Depending on the version that students are using, they will have access to one of the following:

Digital Resources includes downloadable Coursebook resources, all video clips, all audio files, Lesson 3 additional interactive video activities, Lesson 5 interactive grammar presentation and practice, Reading bank, Functional Language bank, Writing bank and My Self-assessment.

MyEnglishLab includes all of the **Digital Resources** plus the full functionality and content of the self-study interactive workbook with automatic gradebook. Teachers can also create a group or class in their own MyEnglishLab and assign workbook activities as homework.

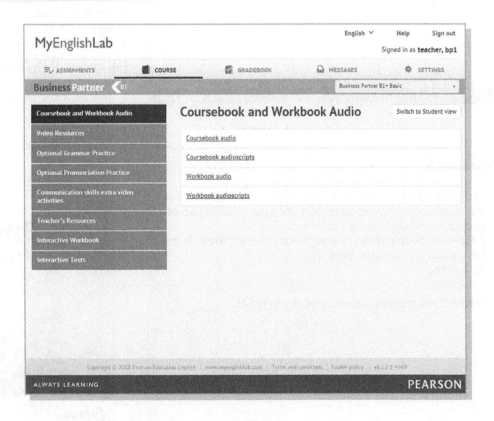

Coursebook
(with access code for MyEnglishLab)

- Eight units, each containing five lessons (see pages 2–3 for unit overview)
- Eight Business workshop lessons relating to each of the eight units
- A one-page Review per unit to revise key language and grammar
- A Pronunciation section which practises two points from each unit
- A Grammar reference with detailed explanations and examples
- Videoscripts and audioscripts
- A glossary of key business vocabulary from the book

Coursebook video and audio material is available on MyEnglishLab.

MyEnglishLab digital component

Accessed using the code printed on the inside cover of the Coursebook. Depending on the version of the course that you are using, learners will have access to one of the following options:

Digital resources powered by MyEnglishLab
- Video clips
- Audio files and scripts
- Extra Coursebook activities (PDFs)
- Lesson 3 extra interactive video activities
- Lesson 5 interactive grammar presentation and practice
- Reading bank
- Writing bank
- Functional language bank
- PTE Professional™ exam practice
- My Self-assessment
- Workbook audio files and scripts

Full content of MyEnglishLab
- All of the above
- Interactive self-study Workbook with automatic feedback and gradebook

Workbook

- Additional self-study practice activities, reflecting the structure of the Coursebook. Activities cover vocabulary, grammar, functional language, reading, listening and writing.
- Additional self-study practice activities for points presented in the Coursebook Pronunciation bank.
- Answer key
- Audioscripts

Workbook audio material is available on MyEnglishLab.

Teacher's Resource Book (with access code for MyEnglishLab)

- Teaching notes for every lesson including warm-ups, background/ culture notes and answer keys
- Business brief for every unit with background information on the unit topic and explanations of key terminology; it gives teachers an insight into contemporary business practices even if they have not worked in these particular environments.

- Photocopiable activities – two per unit with teaching notes and answer keys
- Reading bank – an extended reading text for every unit with comprehension activities (+ answer keys)
- Writing bank – models of different types of business writing with useful phrases
- Functional language bank – useful phrases for different business situations, e.g. meetings, interviews
- Videoscripts and audioscripts

MyEnglishLab digital component

Accessed using the code printed on the inside cover of the Teacher's Resource Book.

Coursebook resources

- Video clips and scripts
- Audio files and scripts
- Extra Coursebook activities (PDFs)
- Lesson 3 extra interactive video activities for self-study
- Lesson 5 interactive grammar presentation and practice for self-study
- PTE Professional™ exam practice
- My Self-assessment: a document that students can use to record their progress and keep in their portfolio

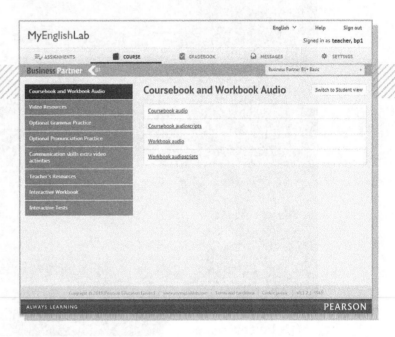

Workbook resources

- Self-study interactive version of the Workbook with automatic feedback and gradebook
- Teachers can assign Workbook activities as homework
- Workbook audio files and audioscripts

Teacher's Book resources

- Alternative video (Unit 4) and extra activities
- Photocopiable activities + teaching notes and answer keys
- Reading bank + answer keys
- Writing bank
- Functional language bank

Tests

- Unit tests (PDFs and Word), including exam task types (BEC, BULATS, LCCI)
- Interactive Unit tests, with automatic gradebook
- Tests audio files
- Tests answer keys

ActiveTeach

- Digital version of the Teacher's Resource Book
- Digital version of the Coursebook with classroom tools for use on an interactive whiteboard
- Video clips and scripts
- Audio files and scripts
- Extra Coursebook activities (PDFs)

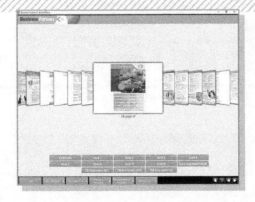

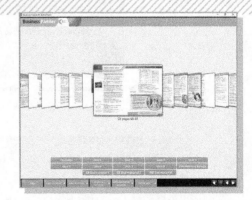

A unit of the Coursebook

Unit overview page >

(1) A well-known or provocative quote related to the unit topic is provided as a talking point. There are suggestions for how to use the quote in the Teacher's Resource Book notes for each unit.

(2) The Unit overview summarises the contents of each lesson as well as the lesson outcomes.

(3) Content at the back of the book which extends the unit is highlighted: the Business workshop, Review, Pronunciation bank and Grammar reference.

Customer service 7 >

(1) *'Customer service is not a department, it's everyone's job.'*
Anonymous

(2) > Unit overview

7.1 >	Airline customer service	Video: Customer service in the airline industry
	Lesson outcome: Learners can use vocabulary related to customer service.	Vocabulary: Customer service
		Project: Design a premium service

7.2 >	Hanging on the telephone	Listening: Complaint about a service
	Lesson outcome: Learners can use a range of verbs taking *to*-infinitive or *-ing*.	Grammar: Verb + *to*-infinitive or *-ing*
		Writing: A complaint on a company forum

7.3 >	Communication skills: Responding to customer concerns	Video: Solving customer problems
	Lesson outcome: Learners can use a range of expressions to manage customer relationships and support a colleague.	Functional language: Responding to customer concerns
		Task: Deal with customer complaints

7.4 >	Business skills: Generating and presenting ideas	Listening: Training day on customer service
	Lesson outcome: Learners can use a range of expressions to generate and present ideas.	Functional language: Discussing and presenting ideas
		Task: Generate and present ideas

7.5 >	Writing: External 'thank you' email	Model text: A 'thank you' email
	Lesson outcome: Learners can write an email expressing thanks.	Functional language: Opening, giving details and closing a 'thank you' email
		Grammar: *some (of), any, all (of), most (of), no, none (of)*
		Task: A 'thank you' email

(3) > Business workshop 7: p.100 | Review 7: p.110 | Pronunciation: 7.2 Unstressed syllables at the end of a sentence 7.4 Introducing a topic p.117 | Grammar reference: p.124

Lesson 1 ⟩

The aims of this lesson are:

- to engage students with the unit topic through a video based on authentic material.
- to present and practise topic business vocabulary, drawing on vocabulary from the video.
- to encourage students to activate the language they have practised in a group project.

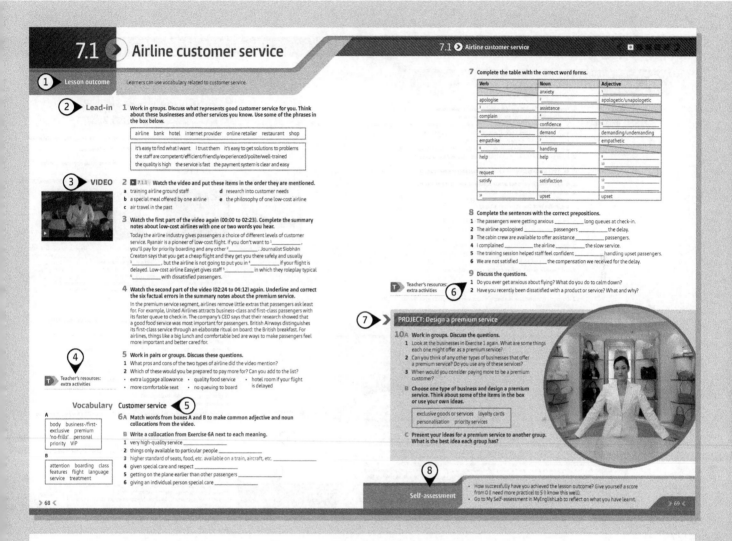

①⟩ The Lesson outcome defines a clear learning outcome for every lesson. Each Lesson outcome encapsulates a number of specific Learning Objectives for Professional English which are listed in this Teacher's Resource Book in the Teaching notes.

②⟩ Every lesson begins with a short Lead-in activity to engage learners with the lesson topic on a personal level.

③⟩ Lesson 1 is based on an authentic video of about 4 minutes with comprehension activities.

④⟩ **T** Teacher's resources: extra activities   Extra activities are clearly signposted. These are PDFs in MyEnglishLab to display on-screen or print. They can be used to extend a lesson or to focus in more depth on a particular section.

⑤⟩ The main unit vocabulary set is presented and practised in Lesson 1, building on vocabulary from the video. Extra activities are available in MyEnglishLab.

⑥⟩ Follow-up questions provide an opportunity for personalisation.

⑦⟩ The Project at the end of Lesson 1 is a collaborative group task with a strong emphasis on communication and fluency building. It can be done in class or in more depth over several weeks in and out of class.

⑧⟩ Every lesson ends with a short Self-assessment section which encourages learners to think about the progress they have made in relation to the lesson outcomes. More detailed self-assessment tasks and suggestions for extra practice are available in MyEnglishLab.

Lesson 2 ▶ Reading or Listening

The aims of this lesson are:

- to provide students with meaningful reading or listening skills practice based on engaging, relevant and up-to-date content.
- to present and practise the unit grammar point, drawing on examples from the text.
- to encourage students to activate the grammar point they have practised through communicative speaking or writing activities.

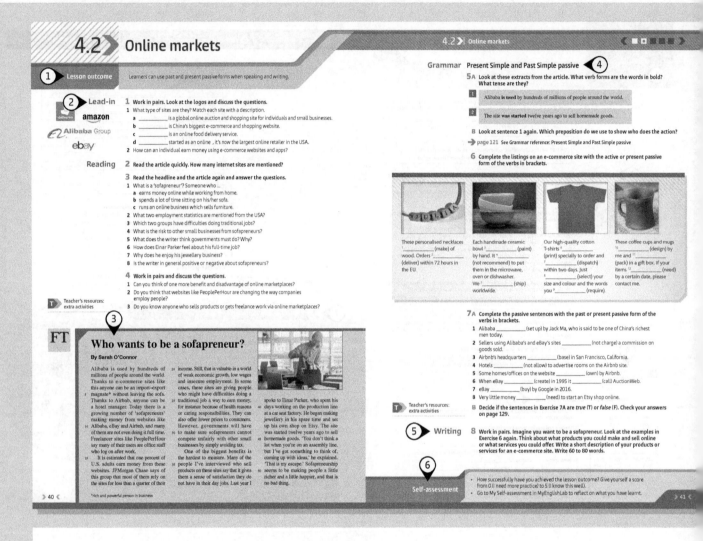

1. ▶ The Lesson outcome defines a clear learning outcome for every lesson.

2. ▶ Every lesson begins with a short Lead-in activity to engage learners with the lesson topic on a personal level. This section includes pre-teaching of vocabulary needed for the reading or listening to come.

3. ▶ The reading text is generally an article, often from the *Financial Times*. The text focuses on a particular aspect of the unit topic which has an interesting angle, and it contains examples of the grammar point presented.

4. ▶ There is one grammar point in each unit, presented in Lesson 2. In general a guided discovery (inductive) approach has been taken to the presentation of grammar. The grammar is presented with reference to examples in the reading (or listening) text, followed by controlled practice.

5. ▶ Discussion questions and communicative practice of vocabulary and grammar is provided in the final Speaking or Writing section of this lesson.

6. ▶ Every lesson ends with a short Self-assessment section which encourages learners to think about the progress they have made in relation to the lesson outcomes.

Lesson 3 ⟫ Communication skills

The aims of this lesson are:

- to introduce students to the skills needed to interact successfully in international teams.
- to encourage students to notice different communication styles and the misunderstandings that can arise as a result, by watching the scripted skills training video.
- to present and practise functional language associated with the communication skill in the lesson.

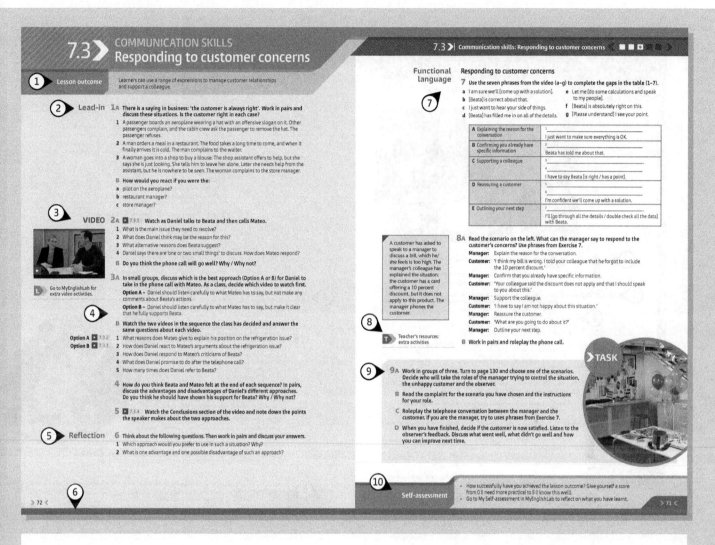

① The Lesson outcome defines a clear learning outcome for every lesson.

② Every Communication skills lesson begins with a short Lead-in activity to engage learners with the lesson topic on a personal level and to set-up the video which follows.

③ The Communication skills training video introduces learners to the skills needed to interact successfully in international teams, with people who may have different communication styles due to culture or personality. There is a storyline running through the eight units, with the main characters appearing in different situations. Note: Each clip, however, can be watched separately and each lesson done independently without the need to watch the preceding video clips.

④ In each Communication skills lesson, you will:
- **a** watch a set-up video which introduces the main characters and challenge of the lesson;
- **b** watch the main character approach the situation in two different ways (Options A and B);
- **c** answer questions about each approach (Option A and Option B) before watching the conclusion.

⑤ Students work alone on a short reflection activity. The approach to this reflection activity may change to suit each lesson. The idea is to encourage students to think about communication styles and their implications.

⑥ The lesson to this point works as a standalone lesson for teachers who have a limited amount of time to work on communication skills. In other teaching situations, the lesson can be extended using the activities on functional language.

⑦ This page presents and practises a set of useful functional language from the video in the Communication skills lesson.

⑧ 🅣 Teacher's resources: extra activities   The optional extension activities for this lesson provide controlled practice of the functional language.

⑨ The lesson ends with a collaborative group task designed to practise the functional language and the communication skill presented in the lesson. There is a scenario or scenario options which pre-work students can relate to, as well as an element of personalisation in the scenario to help with mixed-ability classes.

⑩ Every lesson ends with a short Self-assessment section which encourages learners to think about the progress they have made in relation to the lesson outcomes.

Lesson 4 ⟫ Business skills

The aims of this lesson are:

- to give students exposure to a functional business skill or sub-skill using a listening comprehension, encouraging them to notice successful and unsuccessful techniques.
- to present and practise relevant functional language drawing on examples from the listening.
- to encourage students to activate the skill and language they have practised by collaborating on a group task.

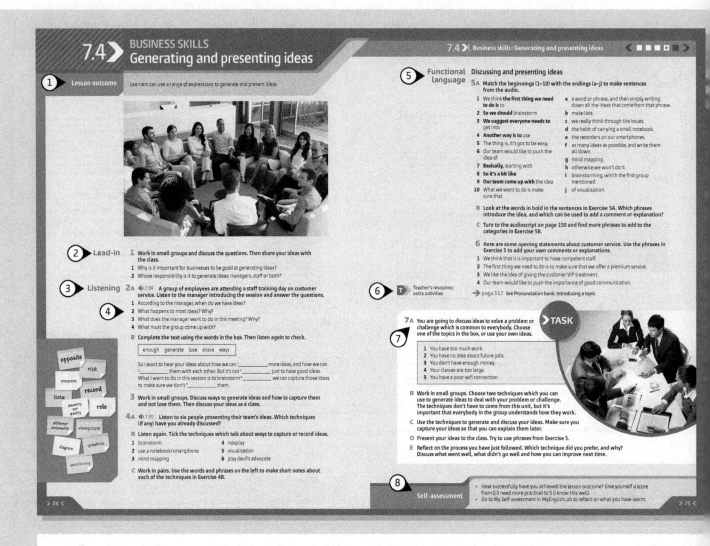

1. ▶ The Lesson outcome defines a clear learning outcome for every lesson.
2. ▶ Every Business skills lesson begins with a short Lead-in activity to engage learners with the lesson topic on a personal level.
3. ▶ An original listening comprehension introduces the business skill and related key techniques and key functional language.
4. ▶ Listening comprehension activities check that students have understood the meaning of key concepts or vocabulary, and move on to listening for detail.
5. ▶ The section on Functional language offers presentation and practice of a set of useful functional language related to the business skill of the lesson. The language exponents come from the audioscript, and common tasks include gap-fill activities.
6. ▶ **T** Teacher's resources: extra activities The optional extension activities for this lesson provide controlled practice of the functional language and additional listening practice using the lesson listening text.
7. ▶ The lesson ends with a significant collaborative group task to practise the target business skill and provide an opportunity to use the functional language presented. A scenario or several scenario options are provided to help with mixed classes, and often include an opportunity for personalisation.
8. ▶ Every lesson ends with a short Self-assessment section which encourages learners to think about the progress they have made in relation to the lesson outcomes.

Lesson 5 ❯ Writing

The aims of this lesson are:

- to present and practise a specific aspect of business writing, focusing on either genre, function or register.
- to present and practise relevant functional language, drawing on examples from the model text.

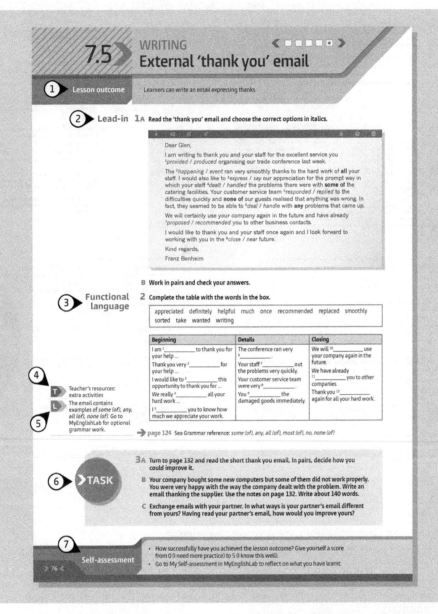

① The Lesson outcome defines a clear learning outcome for every lesson.

② Every Writing lesson starts with a writing model with an associated task. The task often requires students to notice or do something with the language within the model text. In specific cases, this section may also include an element of listening, if for example the writing skill refers to 'taking notes from a phone call or presentation', or 'summarising what a speaker or colleague says'.

③ The functional language is presented in a table summarising useful language associated with the target writing skill, and includes a related activity. The table is likely to be categorised according to the different sections of the writing model. Tasks include completing exponents in the table or identifying which ones are formal and informal.

④ **T** Teacher's resources: extra activities The optional extension activities for this lesson provide controlled practice of the functional language.

⑤ **L** The summary contains examples examples of *some (of), any, all (of), none (of)*. Go to MyEnglishLab for optional grammar work.

There is a signpost to the optional second grammar point. Some examples of the target language point are included in the writing model. The teacher's notes include instructions to focus students on the examples before directing them to the activities in MyEnglishLab if they choose to do so.

⑥ The lesson ends with at least two writing tasks, from controlled to freer practice.

⑦ Every lesson ends with a short Self-assessment section which encourages learners to think about the progress they have made in relation to the lesson outcomes.

Business workshops »

The aims of the Business workshops are:

- to simulate a real-life professional situation or challenge which is related to the theme of the unit.
- to provide multiple opportunities for free, communicative practice of the language presented in the unit.

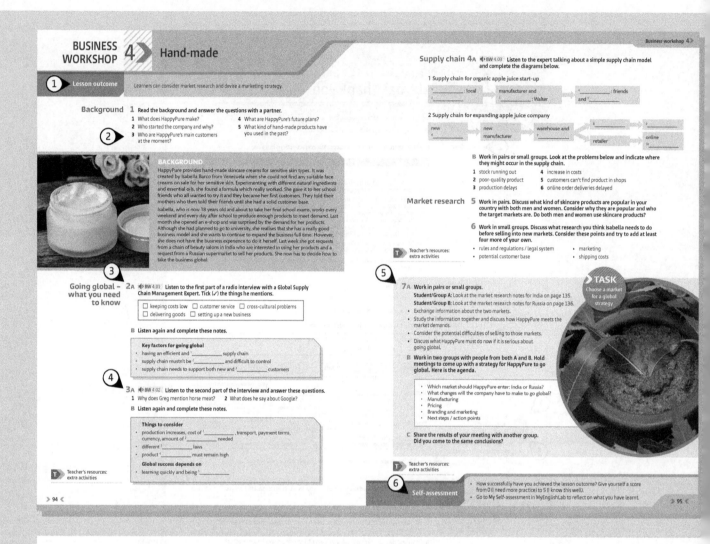

(1)► The Lesson outcome defines a clear learning outcome for every lesson.

(2)► The workshop begins by providing some background information on the company and the situation or challenge the scenario focuses on.

(3)► In units where Lesson 2 contains a reading text, the Business workshop contains a significant listening section, as in Business workshop 6 here. Where Lesson 2 contains a listening, the Business workshop contains a reading text.

(4)► This section includes an activity to check understanding.

(5)► The task is a practical, collaborative task which addresses the challenge set out in the background section. It focuses on speaking, but usually also includes an element of writing. The Business workshops provide a good variety of output task types.

(6)► Every lesson ends with a short Self-assessment section which encourages learners to think about the progress they have made in relation to the lesson outcomes.

Extra material ⟫

Extra Coursebook activities (PDFs)
⟩ go to MyEnglishLab, Teacher's Resources

Photocopiables (PDFs)
⟩ at the back of this Teacher's Resource Book, and on MyEnglishLab, in the Teacher's Resources

Resource Bank: Reading bank, Writing bank, Functional language bank (PDFs)
⟩ at the back of this Teacher's Resource Book, and on MyEnglishLab, in the Teacher's Resources

Unit tests, with audio files and answer keys (PDFs and Word documents)
⟩ go to MyEnglishLab, Teacher's Resources; also available as Interactive tests

1 > Career choices

Unit overview

	CLASSWORK	FURTHER WORK
1.1 > **Transferable skills**	**Lead-in** Students discuss the importance of life skills. **Video** Students watch a video which presents a guide to the skills and qualities needed to get a job and to survive once in the job market. **Vocabulary** Students look at vocabulary that describes professional skills that can be transferred from job to job as they move up the career ladder. **Project** Students research a job and identify the skills needed to do it, then use the language they have studied in this lesson to write a job description.	**MyEnglishLab:** Teacher's resources: extra activities **Pronunciation bank:** p.114 Word stress **Teacher's book:** Resource bank Photocopiable 1.1 p.132 **Workbook:** p.4 Exercises 1–3
1.2 > **Careers advice**	**Lead-in** Students talk about social media platforms. **Listening** Students listen to a phone-in programme host give advice about how to create an effective online profile and look at transferable skills. Students look at whether or not a programme host's advice was useful. **Grammar** Students learn how to give advice and make suggestions. **Speaking** Students practise using the language of giving advice and suggestions.	**MyEnglishLab:** Teacher's resources: extra activities; Reading bank **Grammar reference:** p.118 Advice and suggestions **Pronunciation bank:** p.114 Voice range **Teacher's book:** Resource bank Photocopiable 1.2 p.133 **Workbook:** p.5 Exercises 1–3, p.6 Exercises 1–3
1.3 > **Communication skills:** Building rapport	**Lead-in** Students explore ways of building rapport when they meet someone for the first time. **Video** Students watch a video about ways of building rapport when meeting people for the first time. **Reflection** Students reflect on the conclusions from the video and discuss their own approach to first-time meetings. **Functional language** Students look at questions that are commonly used when we meet people and help to build good working relationships. **Task** Students practise the functional language from the lesson by having a conversation and trying to build rapport with a partner.	**MyEnglishLab:** Teacher's resources: extra activities; Interactive video activities; Functional language bank **Workbook:** p.7 Exercise 1
1.4 > **Business skills:** Networking	**Lead-in** Students discuss careers events and tips for how to prepare for them. **Listening** Students listen to a recruiter giving advice about networking at a careers event. **Functional language** Students look at useful phrases for talking with other people. **Task** Students practise the functional language and ideas they have learnt about starting and finishing conversations and showing interest	**MyEnglishLab:** Teacher's resources: extra activities; Functional language bank **Workbook:** p.7 Exercises 2 and 3
1.5 > **Writing:** Emails –Introducing yourself	**Lead-in** Students look at how we introduce ourselves to new colleagues in an email, and also at formal and informal language. **Functional language** Students look at both formal and informal phrases for a written self-introduction. **Task** Students write an email of self-introduction.	**MyEnglishLab:** Teacher's resources: extra activities; Interactive grammar practice; Writing bank **Grammar reference:** p.118 Adverbs of degree **Workbook:** p.8 Exercises 1 and 2
Business workshop 1 > Global recruitment agency	**Reading** Students read a job listing and online candidate profiles. **Listening** Students listen to initial job interviews. **Writing** Students write an online professional profile. **Task** Students discuss job candidates.	**MyEnglishLab:** Teacher's resources: extra activities

Business brief

The main aim of this unit is to introduce students to the concept of a **career ladder**. A career ladder is the progression from an entry-level job to positions of higher pay, increased skill and more responsibility. Every field has a career ladder. In construction, workers might start out doing unskilled labour such as moving materials from place to place, but then progress to more skilled work such as using power tools and eventually to leading groups of other workers. In banking, workers may start out as clerks or phone-banking personnel and eventually move into positions of management.

The first step on the career ladder is education. At school, students learn **transferable skills** – planning and organisation, using maths, working in a team and so on. These are skills that are useful in almost any job and can be taken from education into work and from one job to the next. People usually continue to develop transferable skills as they move up the career ladder.

People often seek **careers advice** before leaving school. A good careers advisor can discuss work and educational possibilities. A student who does not enjoy academic work and is keen to enter the workforce and start earning might be guided straight into the **job market** or encouraged to take a **vocational-technical course** that focuses on **skilled work** such as hairdressing, plumbing, operating machinery or working in food service. Other students may choose to follow an academic path, studying for a **bachelor's degree** at university and then entering the job market or continuing on for even further study, with a **master's** or **doctoral degree**.

In the past, a career ladder could often be climbed within a single company, in a position of lifetime employment. However, around the world, the **portfolio career** is becoming more common. Rather than having a traditional **full-time job** with a single employer, many workers today work in multiple **part-time jobs**, including **freelancing** or **temporary jobs**, which, when combined, are the equivalent of a full-time position, but with more variety and flexibility.

Whichever career path your students are on, they should be aware of the benefits of developing transferable skills and of seeking careers advice. Communication skills such as **building rapport** at first meetings by using a range of appropriate questions, recognising verbal and non-verbal techniques for building rapport and being able to start, close and show interest in face-to-face communication are essential. Writing skills such as introducing yourself in an email are also important and transferable.

Career choices and your students

It is important that students are aware of the concept of a career ladder and of transferable skills. It is important for pre-service students to understand that the skills they are developing in their education will be useful at work no matter which field they choose to work in. It is especially important for them to understand that although they may think they are headed in a certain direction now, they may end up somewhere unexpected – but still be able to make use of the skills they have developed.

Unit lead-in

Elicit a brief description of the photo (hot-air balloons floating over mountains) and look at the quote with the class. Ask: *What is the connection between balloons and a career?* (When you develop the right skills and experience, your career can 'take off' like a balloon and carry you up to where you can see more of the world. We describe successful people as *high flyers.*) Check that students understand *attribute* (a quality or feature, especially one that is considered to be good or useful) and *sector* (a part of an area of activity, especially of business, trade, etc.). Ask: *How can we say this in simpler words, as advice?* On the board, write: *Workers should ...* and elicit ways to complete the sentence, e.g. *learn skills they can use in many different types of work so they can get better jobs.* Say: *We're going to learn more about these skills and qualities in this unit.*

1.1 ❯ Transferable skills

GSE learning objectives

- Can understand a large part of a video on a work-related topic.
- Can use language related to aptitude, ability, knowledge and skills.
- Can talk about skills needed to do tasks or jobs.
- Can give examples to demonstrate skills for the workplace.
- Can discuss how to develop skills.
- Can express opinions using simple language.
- Can write descriptions of familiar job roles and responsibilities.

Warm-up

Write the following question on the board: *What are you good at?* Say a couple of things you are good at, e.g. *I'm good at speaking English. I'm good at playing* a game). On the board, write: *Skills* and underneath write *speaking English, playing Candy Crush Saga.* Elicit skills from a few students and accept any answer as long as it's a skill (e.g. *skiing, playing the guitar, cooking*).

Lead-in

Students discuss the importance of life skills.

1 Go through the words in the box before students begin and get them to check the meanings of any unknown words in a dictionary. Students do the exercise individually, then, as feedback, go through the list quickly and ask students to raise their hand if they ticked a word.

2 Students do the activity in pairs. During the activity, help each pair as necessary. As feedback, ask a few groups to share their answers to question 2.

Video

Students watch a video which presents a guide to the skills and qualities needed to get a job and to survive once in the job market.

3A Tell students they are going to watch a short video about

skills that are useful when you climb the career ladder. Explain the meaning of *career ladder:* the progression from an entry-level job to positions of higher pay, increased skill and more responsibility. Ask them if any of the skills you discussed in the warm-up can be applied to a range of tasks and roles. Then get them to discuss the question in pairs. During the activity, monitor and help each pair as necessary. As feedback, ask each pair to share a couple of answers with the class. At this point, accept any reasonable answer. The answers from the video are in the key for Exercise 4A.

3B ▶ 1.1.1 The video mentions twenty different skills, abilities and qualities. The idea behind this flow of exercises is that students almost certainly will not in Exercise 3A name the exact twenty skills and characteristics that are in the video. In this exercise, they are just listening for their own ideas from Exercise 3A to be mentioned.

Play the video. Encourage students to listen just for the information they need to complete the task. Ask them to raise their hand each time they hear one of the skills they talked about in Exercise 3A. After watching the video, ask them to share some of the skills that were mentioned. At this point, accept any reasonable answers. The answers from the video are in the key for Exercise 4A.

4A ▶ 1.1.1 Before playing the video again, ask students to read the three questions. Play the video. Consider pausing the video briefly sometimes after answers are given, to allow students time to process the information and make notes.

> 1 the ability to work in teams / be a good team player, the ability to work well with other people, passion about the topic, the ability to think outside the box, the ability to set goals you can achieve, flexibility, critical thinking, problem-solving, communication skills, honesty, enthusiasm, being genuine, being authentic, working hard, determination, integrity, ability, being motivated, having a can-do attitude
>
> 2 in person, on paper, one-to-one, in small groups, in large groups
>
> 3 have skills that you can transfer from one job to another, be a good team player and don't forget that employers look at the person behind the resume

4B Students discuss their answers in pairs. Then check answers with the whole class.

Possible answers

lazy, dishonest, negative, not motivated / unmotivated, not a good team player, not able to set goals (You may wish to call attention to the negative forms of some of the adjectives: *dishonest, unmotivated, unable to think outside the box.*)

Extra activities 1.1

A This activity gives further practice of key vocabulary from the video. Ask students to complete it individually, then check answers with the class. Alternatively, play the video for students to check their answers individually.

> **1** performance **2** skills **3** tasks **4** teams
> **5** movement **6** person **7** skillset **8** teamworking

B ▶ 1.1.1 Students do this individually or in pairs.

> **1** tasks **2** performance **3** teams **4** teamworking
> **5** movement **6** skillset **7** person **8** skills

5 Put students in pairs or small groups to do the exercise. If they need help to get started, give an example or two using your own experience, e.g. *As a teacher, I need to be a good team player. I work closely with the other teachers and with the management to plan classes, organise activities, track students' progress and so on.* Check answers with the class.

Vocabulary: Transferable skills

Students look at vocabulary that describes professional skills that can be transferred from job to job as they move up the career ladder.

6 Explain that the words and phrases from the video are used to describe people. Note that the video says *think outside of the box* although the more usual expression is *think outside the box* (see Notes below). Ask students to match phrases 1–4 with the best description, then check answers as a class. Do the same again with words/phrases 5–8.

> **1** d **2** b **3** a **4** c **5** f **6** g **7** e **8** h

Notes

The expression *think outside the box* refers to the 'nine dots puzzle', which was popular with management consultants in the 1970s and 80s. It featured a grid of nine dots. The puzzle was to draw four straight lines that connected all nine dots without lifting your pencil. This required making lines outside of the box formed by the dots. This is one of many possible solutions:

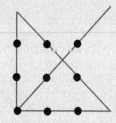

7 Put students in pairs and ask them to complete the tables. Go through the answers with the whole class.

> **1** adaptable **2** flexibility **3** motivated **4** confidence
> **5** dependable **6** resourcefulness **7** independent
> **8** ambition **9** passionate **10** enthusiasm **11** honest
> **12** authenticity

8 Tell the class that this is an opportunity to learn more vocabulary for describing transferable skills. Ask them to do the exercise in pairs or small groups. If possible, get them to stand and write their ideas on the board.

Possible answers

1 able to manage time well, able to lead others, able to meet deadlines, friendly, able to listen well, careful, able to write well, patient, hard-working
2 able to manage time well: get to class on time with work complete; able to lead others: join student government, become a sports team captain; able to meet deadlines: hand in work on time; friendly: become socially involved; able to listen well: pay attention to other people in groupwork situations; careful: complete assignments well by following the instructions; able to write well: write and edit papers; patient: keep working until you've mastered the material, when working with groups, give others time to understand; hard-working: do your work completely and on time

Extra activities 1.1

C Get students to do this individually as a quick vocabulary quiz. You could get them to compare answers in pairs before checking answers with the class.

> **1** flexible **2** critical thinking **3** communication
> **4** independent **5** confidence **6** adaptable
> **7** Dependability **8** passionate **9** integrity
> **10** critically **11** set goals **12** can-do attitude

❯ **Pronunciation bank**
p.114: Word stress

Warm-up

Write *flexible* and *communication* on the board. Get students to say the words and ask: *Which syllable is stressed?* Elicit the first syllable in *flexible* and underline it on the board. Elicit the fourth syllable in *communication* and underline it on the board. Refer students to the explanation in the box and drill the pronunciation of *performance*.

1 Ask students to complete the exercise individually and then compare answers in pairs. Do not confirm answers yet as students will check them in the next exercise.

> **1** passion, people **2** confident, flexible
> **3** computer, resourceful **4** adaptable, reliable
> **5** independent, motivation **6** adaptability, dependability

2 ◀)) P1.01 Play the recording for students to check their answers. Then play the recording a second time for students to listen and repeat.

3 Put students in pairs and ask them to do the exercise. During the activity, monitor to check that students are using the correct word stress.

Project: Writing a job description

Students research a job and identify the skills needed to do it, then use the language they have studied in this lesson to write a job description.

9 Go through the words in the box before students begin and get them to check the meaning of any unknown words in a dictionary. Working in pairs or small groups, students think of a few transferable skills that would be useful for each job. During the activity, monitor and help each pair as necessary. As feedback, ask a few groups to share their answers with the class.

> **Model answer**
>
> personal trainer – needs to meet students (be friendly, be confident), explain exercises, lead classes (be confident, be dependable), work with many different types of people (be flexible, motivate people), keep fit (set goals, be hard-working)

10A Students do the exercise in pairs. For a model answer, see Exercise 9. During the activity, monitor and help each pair as necessary.

10B Put students in pairs to write a job description. For stronger classes, ask students to do this individually. It may be assigned as homework.

> **Model answer**
>
> **Wanted: Personal trainer**
> We're looking for a friendly, confident personal trainer. You should be dependable and flexible and also hard-working and able to set goals. Responsibilities include meeting students, explaining exercises and leading classes. You need to keep fit and be able to work with many different types of people.

10C During the activity, monitor and help each pair as necessary.

10D After students have checked each other's work, if there is time, put the corrected job descriptions on the wall. Take a poll to find out which of the jobs is the most attractive.

MyEnglishLab: Teacher's resources: extra activities
Pronunciation bank: p.114 Word stress
Teacher's book: Resource bank Photocopiable 1.1 p.132
Workbook: p.4 Exercises 1–3

1.2 ❯ Careers advice

GSE learning objectives

- Can understand the main points of a simple podcast.
- Can make suggestions using *what about / how about* with verbs in the gerund.
- Can make offers and suggestions with *Why not / Why don't you/we ...* ?
- Can make offers and suggestions using *could*.
- Can make negative suggestions with *Let's not*.
- Can give informal advice on everyday matters, using a range of fixed expressions.
- Can identify the main points in a work-related meeting on a familiar topic.

Warm-up

Ask: *What's a good job? What's your dream job?* Accept any answer and help the class with words for jobs they want to talk about but may not know. If they are not sure, suggest *doctor, lawyer, CEO* and *film star* to get them started.

Lead-in

Students talk about social media platforms.

1 Write *social media platform* on the board and ask students for one or two examples (see Notes below). There is a list of platforms in the answer key to Exercise 1, question 1. Get students to work through the four questions in pairs or small groups, then share answers as a class.

> **1** Possible answers: Twitter, Facebook, WhatsApp, WeChat, Skype, QQ, LinkedIn, Instagram, Tumblr, Snapchat, Reddit
> **2** Employers may use social media to advertise jobs. People looking for work may try to find jobs on social media. Employers may try to use social media to find out about a job applicant's background.
> **3** a person's name, location, work experience, education and a profile statement
> **4** Too much personal information, embarrassing photos, anything that makes you look bad. These things may damage your chances of getting a job.

> **Notes**
>
> Online social networking began in the 1970s, when very early users of the internet created the first multi-user chatrooms – online forums where people could share messages with groups of people. However, the launch of the first social networking website as we know them today wasn't until 1997. It was called SixDegrees.com and it ran until 2001. The following year, the business-oriented social network LinkedIn was launched, followed by Facebook in 2004 and Twitter in 2006. Since that time, online social networking has become an increasingly important part of working life.

2 Students do the exercise in pairs and then share answers with the whole class. If you think your class may not have received formal careers advice, point out that most people have received some kind of advice from a family member or friend at some point. This could be something as simple as someone saying, 'You should study law. Lawyers make a lot of money!'

Listening

Students listen to a phone-in programme host give advice about how to create an effective online profile and look at transferable skills.

3 Ask students to read the sentence and the two questions, then discuss them in pairs or small groups. During the activity, monitor and help each pair or group as necessary. Any answer is acceptable at this point, but note that Jenny's actual advice is summarised in the Exercise 4 answer key.

4 🔊 1.01 Go through the instructions with students, then play the recording. Share answers as a class.

> The host recommends that the caller avoid over-used adjectives to describe himself, and instead show what's special about himself by giving details of experience.

5 🔊 1.01 Tell students to read the true/false questions and try to answer the questions from memory. Then play the recording again and get students to check which sentences are true or false. During the activity, monitor and check the answers. Play the recording again if necessary.

> **1** F **2** F **3** F **4** T **5** T **6** T **7** F **8** T

6 Students do the exercise in pairs. If they need help to get started, give them some examples, e.g. *I'm on a basketball team. That shows I'm a team player. I use a spreadsheet to do my personal financial planning. That shows I'm good with computers. I help plan activities for my local theatre group. That shows I'm organised.*

> ### Extra activities 1.2
>
> **A** 🔊 1.01 This activity gives further practice of vocabulary from the recording. Get students to complete the exercise individually and then check their answers in pairs before class feedback.
>
> > **1** graduate **2** interview **3** website **4** stand out
> > **5** profile **6** solving **7** issues **8** deal with

Grammar: Advice and suggestions

Students learn how to give advice and make suggestions.

7A You could do this as a quick whole-class exercise, checking answers as you go along.

> **1** Why not try **2** Why don't you **3** How **4** should
> **5** could **6** ought

7B Give students two minutes to identify the verb forms that come after the expressions of advice or suggestion. If they need help, write *bare infinitive* on the board and ask them to say which sentences use it (2, 4, 5). Then elicit the other two forms: *-ing* (1, 3) and *to*-infinitive (6).

> bare infinitive (2, 4, 5), *-ing* (1, 3), *to*-infinitive (6)

7C Get students to do this exercise individually. During the activity, monitor and help as necessary. When students have finished, get them to check answers in pairs.

> **1** send **2** setting up **3** research **4** making **5** to spend
> **6** think **7** asking

8 Refer students to the Grammar reference on page 118. Give them a few minutes to do the exercise individually. Monitor and if students are struggling with any of the items, write them on the board and go through them with the whole class.

> **1** You shouldn't ~~to~~ use words that explain the obvious – like *hard-working*.
> **2** Why don't you try~~ing~~ giving more details about your IT skills?
> **3** ~~Should you~~ **You should** show your transferrable skills rather than explaining them.
> **4** What about join**ing** some online groups to make more contacts?
> **5** Why not ~~to~~ **try** writing a blog about your experience?
> **6** You could ~~doing~~ some volunteer work, then add it to your profile.
> **7** How about ~~to include~~ **including** more information about your hobbies?
> **8** You ought **to** give some information about the languages you speak.

> ### Extra activities 1.2
>
> **B** This activity gives further practice in the grammar of advice and suggestions. Get students to complete the exercise individually and then check their answers in pairs before class feedback.
>
> > **1** Why don't you try making more online connections?
> > **2** How about sending a message to one of your contacts?
> > **3** You shouldn't update your status too often.
> > **4** Why not post some information about your English studies?
> > **5** What about adding some details about your artistic ability?
> > **6** You could try asking your online connections for advice.
> > **7** Why don't you consider doing an MBA?
> > **8** You should keep in touch with your university colleagues.

Listening

Students look at whether or not a programme host's advice was useful.

9 ◀ 1.02 Explain that a few weeks after the call in Listening 1, the caller phones again to tell Jenny how well her advice has worked. Get students to read the questions. Then play the recording. Answer the questions as a class.

> **1** Yes, it was useful. The caller got four job interviews and two job offers.
> **2** He can't decide which job offer to accept.

10A ◀ 1.02 Get students to do the exercise individually. Play the recording again and check answers with the class.

> **1** c **2** a **3** f **4** b **5** d **6** e

10B Do the exercise with the whole class or get students to work in pairs asking and answering the questions.

> **1** b **2** d **3** a **4** f **5** e **6** c

11A Get students to do this exercise in pairs. During the activity, monitor and help as necessary. Don't share answers with the class yet, as that will be part of Exercise 11B.

> **Possible answers**
>
> What would you spend the money on if you took the highly paid job? Would the highly paid job take all of your time or would you have time off to enjoy the money? Do you like expensive things – cars, holidays and so on? Could you take the highly paid job until your loans are paid off, then change to a more exciting job?

11B Explain that the purpose of the exercise is to continue the conversation between Jenny and the caller. During the activity, monitor and help as necessary. Have each pair share their conversation with another pair. If you have time, choose one or two pairs to share their conversation with the whole class.

> ❯ **Pronunciation bank**
> **p.114: Voice range**
>
> **Warm-up**
>
> Write *How are you?* on the board. Say it in a very flat, monotone way that sounds as though you don't want to know the answer. Ask: *Do I sound interested?* (Elicit negative answers: *No, you don't.*) Then say it with some expression, as though you're asking a friend who you care about. Ask: *Do I sound interested?* (Elicit affirmative answers: *Yes, you do.*) Refer students to the explanation in the box and drill the pronunciation of *How are you?* with interest and enthusiasm.

1 ◀ P1.02 Ask students to complete the exercise individually and then compare answers in pairs.

> **1** b **2** b **3** b

2 ◀ P1.03 Play the recording for students to listen and repeat.

3 Put students in pairs and ask them to do the exercise. During the activity, monitor to check that students are using a wide voice range.

Speaking

Students practise using the language of giving advice and suggestions.

12 Get students to read the online profile and list of information on page 126. Ask: *Does the profile follow Jenny's advice?* (no) *What does it do that Jenny recommends against?* (It describes the person using adjectives rather than showing what skills the person has by describing experiences.) Make it clear to students that the task here *isn't* to rewrite the profile, it's just speaking: giving advice to the profile-writer to improve it. They should think of as many sentences as possible. If possible, they should use all seven of the expressions that appear in Exercise 7B. Ask stronger classes to give reasons, when appropriate, to revise some of the vocabulary from 1.1 if you've done that section of the book. Suggestions are included in the answer key below.

> **Possible answers**
>
> You could explain that you have a degree in mathematics. (That shows you're good with numbers.)
>
> How about saying that you graduated with honours? (That shows you're smart and hard-working.)
>
> You ought to explain that you had a part-time job as a cleaner during your university studies. (It shows that you manage your time well.)
>
> You should include some information about your stories that were published in a university magazine. (This indicates that you have writing skills.)
>
> Why don't you say that you played for a city-league football team in secondary school? (That shows you're a team player.)
>
> Why not try saying that you hope to find a job in the financial services industry? (That would show that you're planning your career.)
>
> What about mentioning that you would consider working in other industries if a job looks interesting? (It would indicate that you're flexible.)

13A Put students in pairs. Ask them to decide who is Student A and who is Student B, and refer them to the relevant information on pages 126 and 128. Give them some time to read their instructions, and answer any questions they may have. There are two exercises in the roleplay. For Exercise 1, point out that Student A is giving advice and Student B is receiving it. The Student Bs can use real information about themselves or make it up, e.g. *When I was in school, I delivered papers six days a week, first thing in the morning. That shows I'm hard-working.* For Exercise 2, point out that Student B is the careers advisor and Student A is receiving advice. In this roleplay, Student A has three different skills to talk about, e.g. *I organised an after-school baking club when I was in year 9. This shows I'm a good leader.* During the activity, monitor and help as necessary.

13B For further practice, students do the roleplay again, with different partners. Again, as they work, monitor and help as necessary.

MyEnglishLab: Teacher's resources: extra activities; Reading bank
Grammar reference: p.118 Advice and suggestions
Pronunciation bank: p.114 Voice range
Teacher's book: Resource bank Photocopiable 1.2 p. 133
Workbook: p.5 Exercises 1–3, p.6 Exercises 1–3

1.3 ❯ Communication skills
Building rapport

GSE learning objectives

- Can listen and compare their ideas with the speaker's.
- Can identify phrases the speaker uses to build rapport.
- Can give or seek personal views and opinions in discussing topics of interest.
- Can use polite questions to build rapport in work-related social situations.

Warm-up

Ask: *How do you usually feel when you meet someone for the first time?* Elicit some answers (*confident, shy, nervous, interested*, etc.). Depending on your students' situation, you may want to refine the question and discuss how they feel meeting someone new in a business context, a social context or an educational context (teachers, other students). They may also say it depends on who the person is – someone older, someone younger, someone above or below them in the hierarchy. On the board, note down the feelings that are mentioned.

Lead-in

Students explore ways of building rapport when they meet someone for the first time.

1A Tell students that they are going to look at how we behave when we meet people for the first time and also how we can start off communicating well with people we meet. Put students in pairs and ask them to read the definition of *rapport* and discuss the question. Encourage them to think of different situations (meeting people at work, socially or in a class).

1B Elicit the definition of *verbal communication* (things we say) and *non-verbal communication* (see Notes below). Put students in small groups. Get them to think of two examples of each type of communication. As they work, monitor and help as necessary. Once students have discussed in their groups, ask a few groups to share their answers with the class.

Possible answers
Non-verbal
face the person you are speaking to; nod to show you are listening; maintain eye contact, but not too intensely; smile warmly; use open body language (no folded arms or crossed legs if sitting); keep personal space (not too close)

Verbal
ask questions; use positive sounds to show interest (e.g. *uh-huh*); use gentle humour if appropriate; use the person's name; don't interrupt; find something in common with the other person; use a friendly tone of voice

Notes
Non-verbal communication is how we move and behave. This includes body language (how we stand, whether we cross our arms or not, etc.), distance (how close we stand to other people when we talk), eye contact (whether or not we look other people in the eye), touch and also pauses in speech.

Video

Students watch a video about ways of building rapport when meeting people for the first time.

2 ▶ 1.3.1   In the first sequence, two people, Alex and Daniel, who work for a company called Evromed, meet a group of recent graduates for the first time. Alex and Daniel are running a meet-and-greet event where they, along with their CEO Jessica, will meet Beata, a new employee. Explain to students that they are going to watch a short video about some businesspeople who are going to meet each other for the first time. Tell students to read questions 1–4 and then play the video. Check answers with the class.

1 She sounded professional on the phone. She's a little older and has five years' professional experience.
2 She prefers people that are not overly confident.
3 He's been with the company for a year.
4 He uses humour.

3A Explain to the class the idea of Beata having two options when she meets Daniel and Alex and go through the details of Options A and B with the class. Make it clear to students that they can choose which option they want to see first on the video. Put students in small groups and ask them to discuss the two options, giving reasons for their answers. Elicit ideas from a few groups and as a class, decide which video to watch first.

3B ▶ 1.3.2   ▶ 1.3.3   Tell the class to answer the questions for Option A or B depending on their choice, and play the video. You could ask students to discuss the questions in their groups first, and then check the answers as a whole class. Do the same for the second video.

Suggested answers

Option A

1 Alex: smiles, engages in conversation about Japan; Jessica: makes eye contact, shakes hand, nods to show she is listening, smiles warmly

2 Alex: successful, they chat for a while about their time in Japan; Jessica: successful – she feels nervous, but Jessica thinks she sounds confident and not arrogant; she invites Beata to meet her in a few weeks to talk about her progress

3 Beata will be more easily assimilated into the team, and her positive connection with Jessica could have positive benefits in terms of her future career in the company.

Option B

1 Alex: doesn't try to build rapport with him, preferring to speak only to Daniel, folds her arms, turns away from him; Jessica: makes eye contact, shakes hand

2 Jessica: unsuccessful – her eye contact is too intense, she stands too close and doesn't respect Jessica's personal space; she sounds over-confident

3 Beata will find it more difficult to assimilate into the team and her negative connection with Jessica could even jeopardise her future career in the company.

4 Put students in pairs and give them 3–4 minutes to discuss the question. During the activity, monitor and help as necessary.

Possible answer

Listening can be an effective way to build rapport. In Option A, Beata had a quieter approach. Jessica reacted positively to her and they were able to bond. Beata also developed rapport with Alex as they discovered they shared a common interest in Japan. In Option B, Beata didn't listen as well and showed that not listening and being over-confident can damage rapport.

5 ▶ 1.3.4 Students should do this in the same pairs as Exercise 4. Explain that they are going to watch another video, which is a summary of the ideas they looked at in the previous videos. Play the video and give students 3–4 minutes to discuss and make notes, then discuss the main learning points with the whole class.

Good rapport makes it easier to get on well with someone or a group. Sometimes this happens naturally, but you can also use techniques to help you build rapport.
Verbal: find out what you have in common with the other person, ask about travel as this is an easy topic on which to find common interest.
Non-verbal: use eye contact (but not intense eye contact), smile, use an open posture.
Once you have built rapport with someone, you have to develop it and maintain it.

Reflection

Students reflect on the conclusions from the video and discuss their own approach to first-time meetings.

6 Allow students to work individually on this so that they can reflect on their own preferences and ideas. Ask them to think of their own answers to the questions and to make notes. Then put students in pairs to discuss their answers. Get brief feedback from the class.

Functional language: Asking questions to build rapport

Students look at questions that are commonly used when we meet people and help to build good working relationships.

7A Explain that this exercise highlights expressions from the video that we use when we meet people for the first time. Get students to do the exercise in pairs, then check answers as a class.

1 Where exactly	**2** Do you know	**3** How long
4 When were	**5** What did you	**6** What did you

7B Ask students to read the information in the grey box and ask: *Did Beata do this?* (Yes, in Option A she did this with Alex and discovered a common interest in Japan.) Point out that this exercise shows that there are categories of question. Rather than memorise exact questions, encourage students to remember the categories and to be able to form appropriate questions for each category. Get students to do the exercise individually. Then go through the answers with the class.

a 3 **b** 6 **c** 1 **d** 4 **e** 5

7C Do this as a whole-class activity.

1 c **2** b **3** a **4** d **5** e **6** a **7** e

8A Tell students that they are going to build up a conversation from some basic information they will be given. Put them in pairs and go through the instructions with them. Refer them to the role cards on pages 126 and 128. Ask them to assign roles. Each student has a role card with information about his/her own trip to Barcelona. Tell students to write questions about the location, purpose, timing, duration and likes of their partner's trip. Ask a few students to read a question out so that the class can check their answers.

Possible answers

Location: Where exactly did you stay? Which places did you visit?
Purpose: What were you doing there? What did you and your partner do while you were there?
Timing: When were you in Barcelona? When were you there?
Duration: How long did you stay? How long were you in Barcelona for? Did you stay long?
Likes: What did you like (best) about it?

8B Put students in pairs and get them to take turns to ask questions and answer them according to the role cards in the back of the book. If you have time, ask one or two pairs to perform the roleplay for the class.

Extra activities 1.3

A This activity gives further practice with the five categories of question. Get students to complete the exercise individually, then check answers in pairs. Go over the answers with the whole class.

> 1 Location 2 Purpose 3 Timing 4 Duration
> 5 Likes

B Students do this individually or in pairs. For stronger classes, ask them to try to reconstruct the conversation from memory. They probably won't be able to remember it word-for-word, but if they can remember the topics and flow of the conversation, it will help them remember the questions.

> 1 Have you ever been there?
> 2 How long did you stay?
> 3 So why did you go to Berlin?
> 4 What were you doing there?
> 5 Did you stay long?
> 6 What did you like about it?
> 7 What did you and your partner do while you were there?

Task

Students practise the functional language from the lesson by having a conversation and trying to build rapport with a partner.

9A Students will need to do a certain amount of preparation before they begin the task, so bear this in mind when you're planning this stage. Ask the class to read the four situations and to choose one they are interested in talking about. Give them 2–3 minutes to make some notes on what they will talk about.

9B Elicit a few natural ways to begin a conversation on each topic and write them on the board, e.g. *Your English is really good. I hear you went to a meeting in (place). I hear you've visited/lived in (place). I hear you went on holiday to (place).* Ask students to work in pairs. Before starting the conversation, each student should tell his/her partner the topic they have chosen to talk about. That way, they will be able to use one of the conversation openers on the board.

Ask students to start talking. During the activity, monitor and help as necessary. Remind students to focus both on what they say and what other students say, and at the same time note which conversations are the most successful.

9C When they have finished, ask a few students to say what they learnt about their partner. Then ask which conversations were the most successful and encourage them to discuss why they were successful or not.

9D Get students to discuss the questions they used, and what, if anything, they found difficult. Round off the task by asking how students will handle first meetings in the future. With stronger classes, get students to write three action points starting *In future first meetings I will …*

MyEnglishLab: Teacher's resources: extra activities; Interactive video activities; Functional language bank
Workbook: p.7 Exercise 1

1.4 ❯ Business skills
Networking

GSE learning objectives

- Can understand simple informal advice on a work-related situation.
- Can identify phrases and expressions used in professional networking.
- Can use phrases and fixed expressions to network at a work-related event.
- Can show interest in conversation using fixed expressions.
- Can initiate, maintain and close simple face-to-face conversations on familiar topics.

Warm-up

Ask: *How do people find jobs? How do employers find workers?* Accept any reasonable answers.
(Possible answers: advertisements, careers events, networking; sometimes people write letters and send CVs even though a job hasn't been advertised)

Lead-in

Students look at careers events and tips for how to prepare for them.

1A Focus attention on the photo. Ask: *What is a job fair?* (an event where companies with available jobs and people who are looking for jobs can get together) Put students in pairs and ask them to discuss questions 1–3. Then discuss as a class.

> 1 to find out about potential future employers and the opportunities currently available at a company or organisation
> 2 Employers are looking for potential candidates who are interested in their company.
> 3 Students' own answers

1B With the whole class, go through the list relatively quickly to make sure that everyone understands each item. Put students in pairs and ask them to choose the three most important tips. During the activity, monitor and help as necessary. When students have finished, put each pair with another pair and get them to explain their choices.

Listening

Students listen to a recruiter giving advice about networking at a careers event.

2A 🔊 1.03 Tell students they are going to listen to a recruiter giving advice about attending a careers event. Ask them to read the table so they know what they're listening for. In stronger classes, students could attempt to think of possible answers to the questions before they listen. Play the recording. Get students to check their answers in pairs. Then check answers with the whole class.

1 research the companies that will be interested in you; prepare a brief, thirty-second introduction; update your CV; think of questions for the recruiters
2 dress professionally / look professional; network; introduce yourself; shake hands; make eye contact; speak clearly and confidently; show communication skills; show you are adaptable, resourceful, ambitious, passionate; don't oversell yourself – be honest if you don't know something; ask for contact details
3 email recruiters / company representatives and thank them for their time; do this within five days; send an updated CV if necessary

2B Get students to do the exercise in pairs. During the activity, monitor and help as necessary. Discuss the ideas with the whole class.

3A ◀) 1.04   Tell students they are going to listen to two people talking to a recruiter. Play the recording. Ask: *Who was better prepared?* Elicit the answer.

Jamie

3B ◀) 1.04   Tell students to read the question. Stronger classes may be able to answer some of the questions without listening again. Play the recording. Answer the questions as a class.

1 She brought copies of her CV.
2 degree in marketing, enjoys travelling
3 The recruiter invited her to contact him with questions if necessary.
4 developed a marketing plan to promote UK tourism in Spain; presented the plan; speaks Italian
5 brought business cards, researched the company and the posts available, prepared questions for the recruiter
6 The recruiter will put him in touch with the person in charge of marketing projects.
7 Ella could have researched the company in more detail, thought about what department she would like to work in, prepared some questions for the recruiter. Jamie could have brought more copies of his CV, practised his introduction – he speaks a little too fast.

3C Get students to discuss the questions in pairs. During the activity, monitor and help as necessary. Ask a few pairs to share their answers with the class.

Functional language: Networking at a careers event

Students look at useful phrases for talking with other people.

4A Explain to students that these are questions and phrases from the previous conversations. Tell them to complete the sentences with the correct words. You could do this exercise with the whole class, checking answers as you go along.

1 in touch with, in charge of   2 tell me more   3 ask you a few questions   4 How are you   5 been nice talking
6 sounds   7 see   8 could I just ask   9 for your time
10 really

4B Get students to look at the three categories. Tell them that each sentence in Exercise 4A belongs in one of the three columns. Students do the exercise individually. Then check answers with the whole class.

Starting a conversation: 3, 4, 8
Showing interest: 2, 6, 7, 10
Closing the conversation: 1, 5, 9

4C Read the first phrase. Elicit which category it goes in (*Showing interest*). You could do this exercise with the whole class, checking answers as you go along.

Starting a conversation: 2, 7
Showing interest: 1, 5, 6
Closing a conversation: 3, 4

Extra activities 1.4

A ◀) 1.04   Get students to read the sentences. Then play the recording and get them to complete the exercise. Check answers with the class.

1 Assistant Recruitment
2 marketing (with a specialism in) tourism (at) Manchester (University)
3 promote (UK) tourism
4 business card
5 charge (of) marketing

B Get students to do the exercise in pairs. When they have finished, get them to read the conversation together. During the activity, monitor and help as necessary. Then get them to swap roles and read it again.

1 do you have a few minutes to talk about
2 That sounds very interesting.
3 Uh-huh
4 Oh, really
5 Yes, definitely
6 Could you put me in contact with
7 I really appreciate your time
8 very nice to have met you

Task

Students practise the functional language and ideas they have learnt about starting and finishing conversations and showing interest.

5A Put students in groups of three. Explain the task. There are three roles – a recruiter, a candidate and an observer – and three scenarios so that each student has the opportunity to play each role once. Allocate roles A, B and C and refer each student to the relevant page for their roleplay card (Student A: page 126; Student B: page 128; Student C: page 130). If you do not have the right number of students, give priority to having A and B roles.

5B Give students time to read their role instructions and ask you any questions if anything is not clear, and allow 4–6 minutes' preparation time. Then tell the observers they can take notes while listening, and set a time limit for each conversation. During the activity, monitor, but only help out if a group or student is completely stuck. It is important that students learn to deal with silences and not being sure about what to say.

5C The groups should stay together when they have finished their roleplays. It is now the observer's role to give feedback to the other two students. Try to keep in the background at this stage. Students A and B should also talk about their performance and their opinions about how to start, finish and show interest in conversations. You could do a whole-class round-up at the end if you feel that it would be useful. It is often good for students to hear the opinions of others to get a balanced perspective on their own performance and an objective view of the task as a whole.

MyEnglishLab: Teacher's resources: extra activities; Functional language bank
Workbook: p.7 Exercises 2 and 3

1.5 ▶ Writing
Emails – Introducing yourself

GSE learning objectives

- Can write an email to introduce self or others containing simple personal information.
- Can use appropriate openings and endings in simple informal emails.
- Can qualify adjectives with *really/quite/very*.
- Can use common quantifiers such as *a lot* and *much* as adverbs.

Warm-up

Ask: *When you introduce yourself to other people, what sort of information do you give? What are you interested in knowing about others?* Accept any reasonable answers. Usual answers might be what people do for work, what their interests are outside of work, where they come from and so on.

Lead-in

Students look at how we introduce ourselves to new colleagues in an email, and also at formal and informal language.

1A Ask: *Have you ever written an introduction email? Who was it to? What do you find difficult about writing emails in English?* Get students to look at the two emails. Explain that they are both self-introduction emails written by the same person, but that they are in two different styles. Students do the exercise individually. Then check answers in pairs, and finally go over them with the class.

> 1 Dear 2 myself 3 joined 4 wanted 5 for 6 if
> 7 meeting 8 Kind 9 studying 10 scary 11 all

1B Ask which email is more formal. You will look at this in more detail in the next exercise, so do not spend too much time analysing the formal and informal language at this point.

> Email A is more formal.

Functional language

Students look at both formal and informal phrases for a written self-introduction.

2A Tell students that you are now going to look more closely at formal and informal language. Check that they understand the meaning of *formal* (more polite and serious) and *informal* (more friendly and not as polite). Get them to complete the exercise in pairs. For this and the next exercise, you could copy the table onto the board and invite different students to come up and write answers in the correct column.

> (Answers in italics are answers to Exercise 2B.)
> **More formal**
> *Greeting:* Dear colleagues; *Opening:* I would like to introduce myself, *I'm sending this email to introduce myself; New job:* the new Account Executive, *I have been appointed as the new Marketing Manager; Previous job:* I was working in a similar position, *My previous job was as Customer Services Manager; Invitation:* Please feel free to contact me by email or phone; *Closing:* I very much look forward to meeting you all in person, *I hope to meet you all soon; Sign off:* Kind regards, *Yours*
> **Less formal**
> *Greeting:* Hi everyone, *Good morning Helen; Opening:* I'm Alexis Pinar, I want to introduce myself to you; *New job:* the new Assistant Designer; *I've just got the job of IT Supervisor; Previous job:* I was a Store Manager before; *Invitation:* Perhaps we can meet up over lunch today; *Closing:* I'm looking forward to working with you all, *I hope to meet you all soon; Sign off:* Bye for now, *Best wishes*

2B Get students do to do the exercise individually or in pairs. Then check answers with the class.

> See answers in italics in Exercise 2A above.

Extra activities 1.5

A This activity gives further practice of phrases to use in an email. Ask students to complete it individually and then get them to check answers in pairs before class feedback.

> 1 Dear 2 would 3 myself 4 appointed 5 Before
> 6 as 7 free 8 any 9 meeting 10 regards

Optional grammar work

The email in Exercise 1 contains examples of adverbs of degree, so you could use it for some optional grammar work. Refer students to the Grammar reference on page 118 and use the exercises in MyEnglishLab for extra grammar practice.

Task

Students write an email of self-introduction.

3A Put students in pairs and refer them to the email on page 126. Explain that they will be using this information to write their own email. Ask students to discuss the email: Is it formal or informal? Friendly or unfriendly? How could they improve it?

3B Set a time limit for the writing task and remind students to use the email from Exercise 3A and the phrases from Exercises 2A and 2B. They can write their emails individually and then come back together for Exercise 3C. Alternatively, they can write their emails in pairs and then work with a different partner for Exercise 3C.

Model answer

Dear colleagues,

I would like to introduce myself to you. My name is ... and I am the new HR Manager for the company. Before I joined this company, I was working for a manufacturing company. I am really excited to be working with you all here in this young, fast-growing company.

Please feel free to contact me any time if you have any immediate questions and I look forward to meeting you all very soon.

Kind regards,

3C In their pairs, students evaluate and discuss each other's answers. Monitor and make a note of any errors/points to highlight during feedback.

MyEnglishLab: Teacher's resources: extra activities; Interactive grammar practice; Writing bank
Grammar reference: p.118 Adverbs of degree
Workbook: p.8 Exercises 1 and 2

Business workshop >1
Global recruitment agency

GSE learning objectives

- Can understand duties and responsibilities listed in job descriptions.
- Can understand information in advertisements for jobs and services.
- Can describe skills and abilities using simple language.
- Can write a short online profile.

Background

Students learn about a global recruitment agency that has a database of job-seekers and a database of vacancies.

1 Ask students to read the background and discuss the questions in pairs. Check answers with the class. For students who are already in work, you could get a few to explain how they found their current job.

---

1   It's a global recruitment agency and matches jobs with job-seekers.
2–3 Students' own answers

A job vacancy

Students read a job listing and some information about degrees, professional experience and other interests and activities that might match the job.

2A Refer students to the job listing. Confirm that they understand that this has been written by an employer who wants to hire someone. Check that they understand *medical insurance* (a product that you pay into each month that will pay your medical expenses if you need help), *product writer* (a person who produces the written material that explains an insurance product), *internal* (inside the company), *customer-facing* (dealing with customers) and *website copy* (the writing that appears on a website). Ask students to read the job listing. Answer any questions they have.

Refer students to the three categories. Explain that in each category, they will choose the one item that they think best fits the job. Point out that there may be more than one correct answer, but that they should be able to explain their choice.

Possible answers

Degrees

I chose a degree in medicine because the company sells medical insurance.
I chose a degree in economics and finance because insurance is a financial product.
I chose a degree in English because writing is important, and also the job is based in London, so fluent English is probably important.
I didn't choose engineering or fine art because they don't seem connected with the job.

Professional experience

I chose nursing because the company sells medical insurance.
I chose insurance sales because that is directly related to the job.
I chose freelance writing because that is directly related to the job.
I didn't choose retail sales or accounting because they don't seem connected with the job.

Other interests and activities

I chose playing team sports because they need someone to work with several departments.
I chose volunteering in a local hospital because the product is medical insurance.
I didn't choose cooking, travel or reading and going to the movies because they don't seem connected with the job.

2B Once students have discussed in their pairs, you could broaden this into a class discussion.

3A ◆ BW 1.01 Tell students that they are going to listen to three people who are applying for the medical insurance writer job. Before playing the recording, get students to read items a–f so they know what to listen for. Play the recording once and check answers with the class.

1 b, c **2** a, d **3** e, f

3B Get students to discuss the question in pairs. Then check answers with the class.

> **Possible answers**
>
> Agata's study of economics would be useful in the insurance business. Her interest in sports shows that she's a team player. She has medical experience through her volunteer job in the hospital.
> Taro's writing experience would be useful in the job.
> Maria's medical experience and experience managing a clinic would both be useful in the job.

> **Extra activities Business workshop 1**
>
> **A** ◆) BW 1.01 Get students to read the questions. Then play the recording and get them to complete the exercise. Check answers with the class.
>
> > **1** forty-two
> > **2** fifteen years
> > **3** because she's exhausted
> > **4** twenty-two
> > **5** playing football and volunteering at a hospital
> > **6** thirty-two
> > **7** travel writing
> > **8** He hasn't earned much.

Online professional profiles

Students read three online professional profiles and consider each person's suitability for an advertised job.

4 Ask the class if they use LinkedIn or any other online professional networking site. Ask a few students what sort of information they have there about themselves. Get students to read the first profile. Ask: *What information does Agata give about her studies?* (She is studying economics. She loves her classes.) *What other activities does she do?* (football, volunteering at a children's hospital). *What does she want for the future?* (a job in the finance sector, preferably internationally) Get students to do the exercise individually, then check answers in pairs.

> **Taro**
> Activity or experience: degree in English, travelling the world, travel writing for newspapers and magazines
> Item mentioned in the vacancy listing: degree in a related field, confident, can-do attitude, willingness to try new things, creative
>
> **Maria**
> Activity or experience: medical degree, opened a clinic, hired two partners
> Item mentioned in the vacancy listing: degree in a related field, good team-worker, confident, can-do attitude, willingness to try new things

Task: Discuss job candidates

Students choose one job applicant to interview from three possibilities.

5A Put students in groups of three and go through the instructions and checklist with them. Teach or elicit the meaning of *pros* (good or positive things) and *cons* (bad or negative things). Answer any questions they may have and allow 4–6 minutes for the activity. During the activity, monitor and help each pair as necessary.

5B Put students in new groups of three to explain the decision of their previous group. During the activity, monitor and help each group as necessary.

5C Say the name of each candidate, asking students to hold up their hand to vote for that person for the job. If there is a clear winner, ask the people who chose that person why they voted the way they did.

6 Refer students back to the three online profiles in Exercise 4 and get them to write one about themselves. The three examples in Exercise 4 all serve as model answers. During the activity, monitor and help as necessary.

> **Extra activities Business workshop 1**
>
> **B** Get students to do the exercises individually. Check answers with the class.
>
> > **1** London **2** will graduate in six months
> > **3** about twelve weeks **4** didn't return
> > **5** Immediately **6** weeks
>
> **C** Ask students to look back at the online profiles in Exercise 4 on page 89. Go through the checklist with them, then ask them to write their own profile, including all the information in the checklist.
>
> **D** After students have written their profiles, ask them to exchange profiles with a partner. Ask them to check that their partner's profile includes the three elements in the checklist.

MyEnglishLab: Teacher's resources: extra activities

Review ◀1

> **1** **1** attitude **2** player **3** determination **4** thinking
> **5** outside **6** goals **7** integrity **8** communication
> **2** **1** adaptable **2** resourceful **3** Dependability
> **4** confidence **5** flexibility **6** ambitious **7** passionate
> **8** independence
> **3** **1** write **2** go **3** giving **4** send **5** using **6** list
> **7** to find
> **4** **1** long **2** Where **3** know **4** What **5** When
> **5** **1** Could you tell me more about your experience?
> **2** Can you put me in touch with the person in charge?
> **3** I'd like to ask you a few questions about the company.
> **4** Thank you for your time.
> **5** How are you enjoying your new job?
> **6** Could I give you a call next week?
> **6** **1** would like to **2** appointed as **3** similar position
> **4** hope to meet **5** feel free **6** by email
> **7** any questions **8** to meeting you

2 Business sectors

Unit overview

	CLASSWORK	FURTHER WORK
2.1 ❯ **Japan's economy**	**Lead-in** Students share their knowledge of Japan. **Video** Students watch a video that shows the history of the automotive and electronic industries in Japan. **Vocabulary** Students look at vocabulary related to different areas of business. **Project** Students research and write about different areas of business.	**MyEnglishLab:** Teacher's resources: extra activities; Reading bank **Teacher's book:** Resource bank Photocopiable 2.1 p.134 **Workbook:** p.9 Exercises 1–3
2.2 ❯ **The energy industry**	**Lead-in** Students look at compound nouns used to discuss the energy industry. **Reading** Students read a newspaper article about a French oil company diversifying into renewable energy. **Grammar** Students learn how to use the Past Simple and Past Continuous. **Writing** Students write a short story from their own life.	**MyEnglishLab:** Teacher's resources: extra activities **Grammar reference:** p.119 Past Simple and Past Continuous **Pronunciation bank:** p.114 Stress in compound nouns and noun phrases **Teacher's book:** Resource bank Photocopiable 2.2 p.135 **Workbook:** p.10 Exercises 1–3, p.11 Exercises 1–3
2.3 ❯ **Communication skills:** Dealing with interruptions	**Lead-in** Students talk about ways of taking turns and interrupting in meetings. **Video** Students watch a video about preparing for an induction meeting. **Reflection** Students reflect on the conclusions from the video and discuss their own approach to interruptions in meetings. **Functional language** Students look at questions that are commonly used to ask permission to interrupt, accept an interruption and go back to an earlier point. **Task** Students roleplay a meeting to discuss a controversial proposal.	**MyEnglishLab:** Teacher's resources: extra activities; Interactive video activities **Pronunciation bank:** p.114 Stress in phrases for turn taking **Workbook:** p.12 Exercise 1
2.4 ❯ **Business skills:** Voicemail messages	**Lead-in** Students look at the language we use when we leave voicemail messages. **Listening** Students listen to a voicemail message received by the office of a Human Resources Manager. **Functional language** Students look at useful phrases for leaving a voicemail message. **Task** Students leave a voicemail message.	**MyEnglishLab:** Teacher's resources: extra activities; Functional language bank **Workbook:** p.12 Exercise 2
2.5 ❯ **Writing:** Emails – Action points	**Lead-in** Students listen to a meeting between three colleagues and complete a list of action points. **Functional language** Students look at useful language for writing an email that includes action points. **Task** Students write an email outlining action points from a meeting.	**MyEnglishLab:** Teacher's resources: extra activities; Interactive grammar practice; Writing bank **Grammar reference:** p.119 *will* and *going to* **Workbook:** p.13 Exercises 1 and 2
Business workshop 2 ❯ Investing your money	**Listening** Students listen to a conversation about investment possibilities. **Speaking** Students exchange information about charts and find out about a company before investing in it. **Task** Students choose a company to invest in.	**MyEnglishLab:** Teacher's resources: extra activities

Business brief

The main aim of this unit is to introduce students to the concept of **sectors** and **industries**. The two terms are often used interchangeably to describe groups of companies that are in the same type of business. However, the two terms have slightly different meanings.

An **economic sector** is a large section of the economy, while an **industry** is a more specific group of companies that are in the same business. There are three economic sectors. The **primary sector** is concerned with **raw materials** and includes the **agriculture**, **forestry**, **fishing** and **mining industries**. The **secondary sector** is **manufacturing**, sometimes known as **production**. This includes all industries which process raw materials: **food production**, the **textile** and **clothing industries** and the **automotive industry**, among many others. The **tertiary sector** is **sales and services**. This includes **retail sales**, **transportation** and **entertainment**. Some economists now talk about a fourth sector, the **quaternary sector**, to include the **knowledge-based** part of the economy such as **information technology**, **research and development** and **financial planning**. However, most economic models class those industries as part of the tertiary sector.

The above economic model is the one presented in this unit. However, you may also encounter the Global Industry Classification Standard (GICS), which was developed in 1999 for the global financial community. It divides the economy into eleven sectors (energy, materials, industrials, consumer discretionary, consumer staples, healthcare, financials, information technology, telecommunications services, utilities, real estate), twenty-four industry groups, sixty-eight industries and 157 sub-industries. When **investors** and **financial advisors** talk about sectors and industries, this is most likely the terminology they will use.

When investors and financial advisors consider **shares** to buy, they often focus on investing in certain sectors because they think some sectors may be better than others for reaching their financial goals. Shares in more **volatile** industries tend to go up and down in value quickly. This means the potential to earn or lose money in a short amount of time is very high. The energy industry, healthcare and automobile industries all tend to be volatile. On the other hand, the least volatile industries are **utilities** (gas, electricity and water companies), **drug manufacturing** and **packaged foods**. Share prices in these industries tend to change more slowly, so they are seen as safer investments.

Business sectors and your students

It is important that students are aware of the concept of sectors and industries. It is helpful for pre-service students to begin anticipating which sector and industry they may work in in the future, and for in-work students to be able to talk about how their own company and work fit into the larger economy.

Unit lead-in

Elicit a brief description of the photo (an oil refinery – a place where oil from the ground is turned into petrol and other products) and then look at the quote with the class. Check that students understand *rate of change* (how fast things are becoming different). Give them two minutes to discuss in pairs or small groups: What industries are changing the most quickly now? (Cars and computers are changing a lot, but other industries are too.) Accept any reasonable answers and discuss different ideas.

2.1 ⟩ Japan's economy

GSE learning objectives

- Can understand a large part of a video on a work-related topic.
- Can contribute to a group discussion if the discussion is conducted slowly and clearly.
- Can use language related to industry.
- Can express opinions using simple language.
- Can give a simple presentation about a familiar topic.
- Can search the internet for specific everyday or work-related information.

Warm-up

Ask: *What do you think represents your country? Think of food, language, clothing, art, manufacturing, and so on.* Elicit answers or start by sharing ideas from your own country, e.g. *I'm from the UK. When people think of my country, they think of big red buses, the Queen and Manchester United Football Club.* After a few people have shared their ideas, say: *Today we're going to talk about Japan.*

Lead-in

Students share their knowledge of Japan.

1 Get students to look at and briefly describe the photos. If you can locate them, show the class some more iconic images from Japan, e.g. samurai, geisha, kimono, Shinto shrines, temples, sumo wrestling, sushi bar, packed Tokyo metro, Doraemon eating dorayaki, street in Electric Town Tokyo, robots (e.g. ASIMO).

> **A** Mount Fuji, cherry blossoms and a pagoda
> **B** Pepper robot – created by SoftBank Robotics. It has the ability to read emotions as it can analyse expressions and tone of voice.

2 Do this exercise with the class. For question 3, mention some key brands if students need help, e.g. Nintendo, Sony. See question 4 in the key below for more companies. If you have time, after going through the four questions, ask: *What Japanese products do you have or would you like to have? What do you like about these products?* Discuss the answers.

Possible answers

1 From Exercise 1, students can talk about the traditional aspects of Japanese culture and society (e.g. sumo wrestling, temples) and the more modern aspects such as robots.

2 Many childhood crazes of the past thirty years come from Japan (Transformers, Power Rangers, Tamagotchi, Pokémon, Manga, anime, etc.) and become popular in different sectors: cartoons, comics, toys, films, fashion, video consoles/games and music.

3 Students' own answers

4 These large corporations have several businesses. These are some of the most well-known for each company:
Canon: specialised in the manufacture of imaging and optical products, including cameras, camcorders, photocopiers, computer printers and medical equipment
Mitsubishi: cars, consumer electronics, satellites, banking
Nikon: cameras, microscopes, optical equipment
Nintendo: gaming consoles, video games, toys
Softbank: telecommunications and internet corporation
Softbank Robotics makes and markets humanoid and programmable robots.
Sony: consumer electronics, smartphones, PlayStation, films, music, TV shows and financial services
Toyota: cars, vans, hybrid vehicles

Video

Students watch a video that shows the history of the automotive and electronic industries in Japan.

3A Go through the list of industries and make sure students understand *agriculture* (farming), *energy* (producing electricity and also fuel for cars, planes, etc.) and *finance* (banks).

3B ▶ 2.1.1 Play the video. Ask: *Which industries from Exercise 3A does it mention?*

> The video focuses mainly on cars and consumer electronics, although it also mentions finance.

4 ▶ 2.1.1 Before playing the video again, ask students to read the statements. Make sure they understand *internet technology sector* (both information technology companies, like Apple, and telecommunications companies, like Virgin Media) and *industrialised economy* (a country with a lot of manufacturing). Also, teach or elicit the meaning of the verb *pioneer* (be the first to do, invent or use something). Play the video. Consider pausing the video briefly after answers are given, to allow students time to process the information and make notes. For statement 2, point out that the largest is the USA and the second largest is China.

> **1** T
> **2** F – It was the second largest in the 1960s. It's the third largest today.
> **3** T
> **4** F – It used robots before other countries.
> **5** F – The cars were popular in the USA and Europe and exports were high.
> **6** T
> **7** F – It was small and portable; people could listen to music 'on the go/move'.
> **8** T

5 Get students to answer the questions in pairs, then check answers with the class. If they are interested and have a good enough level, ask: *Which countries are Japan's main competitors in the car and consumer electronics industries today?* (cars: China, the USA, Germany, South Korea; consumer electronics: China, the USA, South Korea, Germany)

> **1** By pioneering the use of robots in manufacturing, which enabled them to produce to a high standard very efficiently. Also, by exporting their cheap, reliable cars to European and U.S. markets from the 1970s onwards.
> **2** the Toyota Prius, the first and best-selling mass-produced hybrid car ever, and Nissan's Leaf, the world's first all-electric car
> **3** The Sony Walkman made it possible for people to listen to music while 'on the move'.

> **Extra activities 2.1**
>
> **A** ▶ 2.1.1 This activity gives further practice of key vocabulary from the video. Ask students to complete it individually, then check answers with the class. Alternatively, play the video for students to check their answers individually.
>
> > **1** luxury goods **2** global players **3** pioneered
> > **4** reliable **5** market share **6** breakthrough
> > **7** sustainable **8** innovative **9** released, portable
> > **10** handheld

Vocabulary: Sectors and industries

Students look at vocabulary related to different areas of business.

6 Make sure that students understand *retail* (selling to the public, through shops and stores or online) and *service sector* (tourism, healthcare, etc.). Get them to complete the exercise individually, then check answers in pairs.

> **1** service sector **2** retail **3** transportation
> **4** manufacturing **5** automotive

7 Make sure that students understand *raw materials* (basic products such as wood or metals that other materials are made from). Teach or elicit the meaning of *primary* (first), *secondary* (second) and *tertiary* (third). In business, these words are used to talk about economic sectors – different areas of business and the economy. Put students in pairs and ask them to do the exercise. Go through the answers with the whole class.

> **A** 3 **B** 1 **C** 2

8 Go through the industries and make sure students understand what they all are. Then do the exercise as a class. Point out that the industries in question 7 are all very high-tech and use a lot of advanced technology. If you have time, after you have completed the exercise, ask students if they can think of companies that they know in some of the sectors.

> **1** financial services – service/tertiary sector
> **2** the tourism industry – service/tertiary sector
> **3** manufacturing – secondary sector
> **4** extraction of raw materials – primary sector
> **5** agriculture – primary sector
> **6** transportation – service/tertiary sector
> **7** manufacturing – secondary sector
> **8** retail – service/tertiary sector

9 Discuss the questions as a class.

> **Extra activities 2.1**
>
> **B** Get students to do this individually as a quick vocabulary quiz. You could get them to compare answers in pairs before checking answers with the class.
>
> > **1** automotive **2** raw **3** mining **4** crop
> > **5** construction **6** manufacturing **7** retail **8** plant
> > **9** textile **10** primary **11** secondary **12** service

Project: Research sectors and industries

Students research and write about different areas of business.

10A Read through the four bullet points and elicit some ideas of what students need to find out for each point:

- a description of the industry: which sector it is in; what it processes, produces or provides; who its customers are
- the size of the industry: the amount it processes or produces; the number of customers it serves
- the number of employees
- its economic impact on the country: the amount of money it earns

Guide students to official and credible websites such as central and local government sources (e.g. the UK Office for National Statistics), as well as recognised news sources. Many EU governments provide these economic indicators in English. Make sure students look for the most up-to-date figures they can find online and quote their sources for facts and figures.

Encourage students to use relevant images in their presentations as well. These presentations could be in PowerPoint. Refer students to the sample on page 126. Ask a few questions to focus their attention on it: *What is Spain's main primary sector activity?* (agriculture) *What specific examples of products does the presentation give?* (olives, cereal, grapes, oranges and lemons, vegetables, pig and chicken farming, olive oil) Ask each member of the pair or group to prepare their own 100–120-word presentation, so that each student has a chance to speak.

10B Get students to practise their presentations in their pairs or groups before giving them to the class. Ask audience members to take notes and after each presentation, ask the class a couple of questions about it to check comprehension.

10C After watching all of the presentations, discuss which industries have the biggest impact on the economy.

MyEnglishLab: Teacher's resources: extra activities; Reading bank
Teacher's book: Resource bank Photocopiable 2.1 p.134
Workbook: p.9 Exercises 1–3

2.2 ❯ The energy industry

GSE learning objectives

- Can generally understand straightforward factual texts on familiar topics.
- Can make simple inferences based on information given in a short article.
- Can scan short texts to locate specific information.
- Can use *when* to link clauses in the Past Simple and Past Continuous.
- Can use *while* with the Past Simple and Past Continuous to refer to past actions and states.
- Can make offers and suggestions using *could*.
- Can write a story with a simple linear sequence.
- Can write a simple story or description of an event using basic time expressions.
- Can narrate a story.

Warm-up

Write *energy* on the board. Ask: *What do you do every day that uses energy?* (Possible answers: turn on the lights, cook, drive a car, use a mobile phone; almost anything we do these days uses energy, because even if I don't use energy putting my clothes on, a lot of energy was used to produce and transport the clothes, and to wash and possibly dry them.) Say: *Today we're going to talk about the energy industry.*

Lead-in

Students look at compound nouns used to discuss the energy industry.

1 Write *climate* on the board and elicit the word from the second circle that often goes with it to make a compound noun (*change*). Students do the exercise in pairs, then check answers as a class. If they are unable to form all of the compound nouns, help them out. Elicit the meanings to make sure everyone understands them (see answer key below).

climate change: a general warming or cooling of average temperatures on earth, and large-scale changes to weather
electricity bill: a statement that shows how much you must pay for electricity you have used
fossil fuel: coal, oil, natural gas
global warming: a general warming or cooling of average temperatures on earth
greenhouse gases: pollution in the air that contributes to global warming
renewable energies: wind, solar, wave – anything that doesn't use up a resource
solar panels: equipment that turns the sun's energy into electricity or hot water

2A Students do the exercise individually and then share answers with the class.

1 renewable energy   **2** solar panels   **3** fossil fuel
4 climate change / global warming

2B Put students in groups. For stronger classes, ask if any students have any direct experience with any of the energy sources – a house with solar panels, for example, or a geothermal energy plant they may know about.

1 Examples of traditional energy include electricity, gas and oil. Some examples of renewable energy sources are solar energy, wind energy, hydropower, geothermal energy and biomass energy.
2 Some suggestions are lower electricity bills and fewer greenhouse gas emissions.
3 Wood is considered a renewable energy as it is not fossilised and trees can be replanted.
4 Students' own answers

❯ **Pronunciation bank**
p.114: Stress in compound nouns and noun phrases

Warm-up
Write the following compound nouns on the board: *oil company, green energy*. Get students to say the compound nouns and ask: *Which word is stressed?* Elicit the first word in *oil company* and underline it on the board. Elicit the second word in *green energy* and underline it on the board. Refer students to the explanation in the box and drill the pronunciation of *climate change* and *fossil fuel*.

1 Ask students to complete the exercise individually and then compare answers in pairs. Do not confirm answers yet as students will check them in the next exercise.

backup power   electricity bill   energy supply
global warming   greenhouse gases   power cut
solar panel   wind energy

2 ◆ P2.01   Play the recording for students to listen and check, and then again for them to listen and repeat.

3 Put students in pairs and ask them to do the exercise. During the activity, monitor to check that students are using the correct stress.

Reading

Students read a newspaper article about a French oil company diversifying into renewable energy.

3 Ask students to read the social media post and answer the question. Ask them if they have ever had this experience and if they knew what the cause of it was.

During a snow storm, the electricity went out in Mark's home. He says this is something that often happens.

Students' own predictions about his solution to the problem

4 Students read the first paragraph. Draw attention to the word *blackout* and get them to work out the meaning from the context. (In this context, it is a period of darkness caused by a failure of the electricity supply. A synonym is *power cut*.) Also note the phrasal verb *went out / go out* (of lights: suddenly stop working).

Mark decided to install solar panels on the roof of his house as a backup system in case of blackouts / power cuts.

5 Ask students to read the article and answer the questions. Alternatively, you could assign different questions to pairs of students and get them to skim the article to find the answer to their question. During the activity, monitor and help as necessary. Check answers with the class.

Possible answers

1 The article headline uses the colours to represent different types of energy industries. Black represents the oil industry and green represents renewable energies – in this case, solar power. It symbolises the story about a large oil company, Total, buying a solar energy company in the USA, SunPower.
2 He will cut his electricity bill by 50 percent and he will get a tax deduction from the government.
3 It's a large oil company.
4 It has spent more than any other large oil or gas company on a renewable energy business.
5 The risks are stricter regulations on emissions, and more competition from the renewable energies industries.
6 To stay only in the oil and gas industry because demand will continue for decades or to move into the renewable energy business as well.

6 Get students to do the exercise in small groups. During the activity, monitor and help as necessary. Discuss answers as a class. If there is interest, continue the discussion by asking: *Are the big oil and gas companies the best industry to lead the transition to renewable energies? Why / Why not?*

Possible answers

1 Good business sense: to do this at a time when oil prices are low, renewable projects look like good long-term investments, and it is still cheap to buy green businesses now. Also, governments, environmental groups and shareholders are asking for action on climate change from big oil and gas companies. It's good publicity for the big oil and gas companies to invest in green energy. Bad business sense: there is still a storage problem with renewable energies – the process of keeping sun and wind energy for later use. Companies have to invest a lot of money in finding storage solutions.
2 Some suggestions: the fossil fuels industry has grown for over one hundred years and still dominates as the global source of energy. According to the *Financial Times*, oil, gas and coal together account for eighty-six percent of energy used for transport, heat and power worldwide. This is likely to continue for many reasons; the demand for petrol-driven cars is increasing globally, especially in developing countries. In addition, oil is hard to substitute in trucks, ships and planes. Another reason is the high cost of investment, research and development of renewable energies.

Extra activities 2.2

A This activity gives further practice in vocabulary from the reading. Learning synonyms is a good way for learners to increase their vocabulary. Get students to complete the exercise individually and then check their answers in pairs before class feedback.

1 b 2 a 3 g 4 c 5 j 6 i 7 h 8 e 9 f 10 d

Grammar: Past Simple and Past Continuous

Students learn how to use the Past Simple and Past Continuous.

7A Do this as a quick whole-class exercise. After eliciting the answers, write the forms on the board so you can refer back to them when you do Exercise 8.

Past Continuous
it **was snowing**
we **were** just **watching**
I **was sitting**
form: *was/were* + verb + *-ing*

Past Simple
the electricity **went** out
I **thought**
form: regular verbs: infinitive + *-ed*; many of the most frequently used verbs have an irregular form, e.g. *think – thought, go – went*

7B Make sure students understand the concept of *background* in question 1 (see Notes below). Get them to do the exercise individually, check answers in pairs and then as a class.

Notes

Background: details about the circumstances or situation at the time when the main story or event happens, e.g. weather, location. These details establish the setting for the main events to come.

1 Past Continuous 2 Past Continuous 3 Past Simple
4 Past Simple, Past Continuous

8 Refer students to the Grammar reference on page 119. Give them a few minutes to do the exercise individually. Monitor and if students are struggling with any of the items, refer back to the forms you wrote on the board when you did Exercise 7A. You could also write any items the students find difficult on the board and go through them with the whole class.

1 was studying, started 2 told, were having
3 was presenting, went out 4 were getting, decided
5 were you doing, tried 6 was thinking, phoned
7 started, were sitting 8 got, was already working

9A To set the scene, ask students if they have used Airbnb and WhatsApp or if they know anyone who has. Explain that they are going to read about the story of each company. Divide the class into Student As and Student Bs. Refer Student As to the text on page 21 and Bs to page 127 and ask them to do the exercise individually.

Airbnb
1 were sharing 2 were both looking 3 heard
4 decided 5 found 6 were waving 7 wasn't making
8 flew 9 were having 10 took

WhatsApp
1 met 2 was studying 3 was also working 4 grew
5 was watching 6 became 7 were using 8 were living
9 was thinking 10 bought

9B Ask: *What is the most important information in any story?* Elicit *who, what, when, where, why* and *how*. Ask students to make brief notes (see Notes below) about the company they read about, answering each of those questions. Then tell them to use the notes to tell their partner about the company. Encourage them to speak naturally rather than reading the notes.

Notes

When we ask students to *make brief notes*, we expect them to write words and phrases rather than whole sentences. For Airbnb, they might write:
who: Job Gebbia / Brian Chesky
what: cheap accommodation
when: 2007
where: New York City
why: hotels fully booked
how: website
This is the most basic information, but it is enough to remind them of the main ideas of the article.

Extra activities 2.2

B This activity gives further practice with the Past Simple and Past Continuous. Students do it individually and check answers in pairs before class feedback.

1 Silvia arrived ✓ while they ~~had~~ ✗ **were having** dinner.
2 It was raining ✓ so we ~~were taking~~ ✗ **took** a taxi back to the hotel.
3 I ~~had~~ ✗ **was having** a job interview when my mobile phone ~~was ringing~~ ✗ **rang**. It was a bit embarrassing!
4 He was living ✓ with his parents when he ~~was making~~ ✗ **made** his first million.
5 A: What were you doing ✓ at ten o'clock?
   B: We were negotiating ✓ a new contract with the suppliers.
6 They ~~were having~~ ✗ **had** coffee first and then they started ✓ the meeting.
7 He ~~was breaking~~ ✗ **broke** his leg when he fell down ✓ the stairs.
8 She ~~was meeting~~ ✗ **met** her business partner while she was working ✓ as an intern.

Writing

Students write a short story from their own life.

10A Get students to look at the short story framework and example story on page 127. Ask: *What is the background of the story?* (It was in March a few years ago. The writer was working late at the office.) *What details does the writer give?* (It was snowing. The writer decided to go home, but driving was impossible and the trains were cancelled. The writer walked to a metro.) *What was the conclusion?* (The writer felt lucky to have returned home safely.)

Give students time to write their short stories. Make sure they use the Past Continuous as well as the Past Simple. Exercise 10A could be set for homework and followed up with Exercise 10B in the next class.

10B Put students in pairs. Remind them of the technique of note-taking in Exercise 9B and encourage them to tell their story naturally rather than read it out. During the activity, monitor and help as necessary. Encourage students to ask at least one question about their partner's story.

MyEnglishLab: Teacher's resources: extra activities
Grammar reference: p.119 Past Simple and Past Continuous
Pronunciation bank: p.114 Stress in compound nouns and noun phrases
Teacher's book: Resource bank Photocopiable 2.2 p.135
Workbook: p.10 Exercises 1–3, p.11 Exercises 1–3

2.3 ❯ Communication skills
Dealing with interruptions

GSE learning objectives

- Can identify the main points in a work-related meeting on a familiar topic.
- Can give detailed accounts of experiences, describing feelings and reactions.
- Can give or seek personal views and opinions in discussing topics of interest.
- Can respond to interruptions in a meeting using fixed expressions.
- Can express limited opinions and arguments during work-related meetings.

Warm-up

Write *meeting* on the board. Ask: *How would you define a meeting?* (when two or more people get together to discuss a particular topic. It's usually planned in advance.) Say: *Think about your last meeting.* For pre-work students, this would most likely be with other students or with a teacher or school counsellor. For in-work students, it would probably be a business meeting, team meeting, planning meeting, etc. Ask different students to answer a question or two about their meeting: *How long did it last? How many people were there? Did you mostly talk or mostly listen? Was it boring or interesting? Was it face-to-face or online?*

Lead-in

Students talk about ways of taking turns and interrupting in meetings.

1A Put students in pairs and ask them to discuss whether interrupting in a meeting is positive or negative in their country (see Notes below). If you want to extend the discussion, ask: *Is it ever important to interrupt?* (If there was an emergency, yes.) *Can you interrupt someone without being rude?* (Yes, if you have a good reason and you are polite.)

> ### Notes
>
> Whether or not interrupting is considered positive or negative generally depends on the individuals and contexts involved rather than the wider culture. If someone occasionally interrupts a semi-formal meeting to make an important contribution or to ask for clarification that most of the group needs, then that is generally not a problem. However, interrupting a formal presentation is rarely appropriate. And if someone constantly interrupts without trying to be polite about it, the behaviour will generally be seen as negative.

1B In the same pairs, students discuss the five statements. During the activity, monitor and help as necessary. Once students have discussed in their groups, have a few groups share their answers with the class. There may be more than one view, especially on statements 3 and 4. For 3, in an ideal situation, you should prepare your contribution in advance, but in some situations, that may be impossible because your contribution will be a response to what others in the meeting say. You cannot completely prepare for that. For statement 4, ideally, we should not have to interrupt someone, but if they are dominating the meeting, taking too much time or giving incorrect information, it is probably appropriate to interrupt. At times, it can also be important to ask for clarification of what a speaker is saying.

Video

Students watch a video about preparing for an induction meeting.

2A ▶ 2.3.1 In the first sequence, we see Beata preparing for her day at work by doing some research about Evromed. Then we see her arriving at the office to meet Jessica, the CEO of the company, who will be giving Beata and other new starters an introduction to the Diabsensor, one of the company's products. Explain to students that they are going to watch a short video about a business meeting. Tell students to read questions 1–4 and then play the video. Check answers with the class.

> **1** family business **2** 145 **3** Europe **4** hospital

2B Discuss the questions with the whole class.

> **1** She is happy to answer questions at any time during the presentation.
> **2** The trainees might interrupt her constantly as she speaks.

3A Explain to the class the idea of Beata having two options in the meeting and go through the details of Options A and B with the class. Make it clear that they can choose which option they want to see first on the video. Put students in small groups and ask them to discuss the two options, giving reasons for their answers. Elicit ideas from a few groups and as a class, decide which video to watch first.

3B ▶ 2.3.2 ▶ 2.3.3 Ask the class to answer the questions for Option A or B depending on their choice, and play the video. You could ask students to discuss the questions in their groups first, and then check the answers as a whole class. Do the same for the second video.

> **Option A**
> **1** She asked several questions, demonstrated her knowledge of the product.
> **2** The other trainees were annoyed by her continually interrupting. She didn't consider them, but dominated the conversation. They decided not to speak to her after the presentation. She did not create a good rapport with the team.
> **3** She was tolerant and remained polite, but finally decided to invite questions from other interns; she didn't discourage Beata, but tried to make her understand it was important that other people had the chance to ask questions.
> **4** She felt she asked too many questions, but didn't think the other trainees were interested in the presentation/ product. She realised that she had annoyed Jessica a little and would be careful not to do the same thing at the next meeting.
>
> **Option B**
> **1** She didn't interrupt; instead asked for permission to speak, only asked a question to clarify a point she wasn't sure about.
> **2** One of the trainees thanked her for asking an important question about glucose. At the end of the presentation there is a positive atmosphere as the trainees chat together, Beata included.
> **3** She responds well and answers her questions.
> **4** She felt there was a relaxed friendly atmosphere. She'd wanted to ask a lot of questions but realised she needed to let others speak.

4 Put students in pairs to discuss the question. During the activity, monitor and help as necessary.

5 ▶ 2.3.4 Students should do this in the same pairs. Explain that they are going to watch another video, which is a summary of the ideas they looked at in the previous videos. Play the video and give students 3–4 minutes to discuss and make notes, then discuss the main learning points with the whole class.

> Option B is a more effective way to participate in meetings. It's important to listen and show respect to the speaker and the other participants. We should watch the other participants and the speaker to find the right moment to interrupt and ask permission before asking a question. We should not ask direct or accusatory questions.

Extra activities 2.3

A ▶ 2.3.3   This activity gives practice with the product description that Jessica gives in the video. Students complete the exercise individually, then check answers in pairs. Do a final check by showing the video.

> **1** small   **2** handheld   **3** grams   **4** glucose   **5** skin
> **6** manage

Reflection

Students reflect on the conclusions from the video and discuss their own approach to interruptions in meetings.

6 Allow students to work individually on this so that they can reflect on their own preferences and ideas. Ask them to think of their own answers to the questions and to make notes. Then put students in pairs to discuss their answers. Get brief feedback from the class.

Functional language: Interrupting and dealing with interruptions

Students look at questions that are commonly used to ask permission to interrupt, accept an interruption and go back to an earlier point.

7A Explain that this exercise highlights expressions from the video that we use to interrupt and to respond to interruptions. Get students to do the exercise in pairs, then check answers as a class.

> **a** Please go ahead   **b** Sorry to interrupt
> **c** So, as I was saying

7B Do this question as a quick whole-class activity.

> Jessica invites questions from other members of the audience: 'But maybe someone else has a question?'

7C Get students to do this individually, then check answers in pairs. Answer any questions if there is any disagreement about the correct answers.

> **a** 3, 6, 10   **b** 1, 2   **c** 4, 5, 7   **d** 8, 9

8 Tell students that they are going to build up a conversation from some basic information that they will be given and the phrases from Exercise 7. Divide the class into Students A, B and C and get them to form groups of three. There are no role cards for this situation. After students have chosen which scenario they want to practise, tell them to work together to make notes for each speaker before they do the roleplay. During the activity, monitor and help as necessary.

Extra activities 2.3

B–C These activities give more practice with the turn-taking phrases from the video. Students do them individually and check answers in pairs.

> **1** h (B)   **2** d (A)   **3** e (C)   **4** c (C)   **5** g (D)   **6** f (A)
> **7** a (C)   **8** b (B)

> **Pronunciation bank**
> **p.114: Stress in phrases for turn taking**
>
> **Warm-up**
> Write on the board: *Can I just finish my point?* Ask: *When do you say this?* (when someone interrupts you) Get students to say the phrase and ask: *Which syllables are stressed?* Elicit *fin*ish and *point* and underline them on the board. Refer students to the explanation in the box and drill the pronunciation of *Sorry to interrupt*.

1 Ask students to complete the exercise individually. Do not confirm answers yet as students will check them in the next exercise.

2 ◀》 P2.02   Play the recording for students to listen and check, and then again for them to repeat.

> **1** <u>Please</u> con<u>tin</u>ue.
> **2** <u>As</u> I was <u>say</u>ing, ...
> **3** The <u>point</u> I was <u>mak</u>ing ...
> **4** Ex<u>cuse</u> me for inter<u>rup</u>ting.
> **5** <u>Please</u> go a<u>head</u>.

Task

Students roleplay a meeting to discuss a controversial proposal.

9A Put the class in groups of three or four and ask them to read the three scenarios and to choose one they are interested in talking about or to come up with their own.

9B Give students 3–4 minutes to make some notes about arguments for or against the proposal they have chosen. Refer them to page 127 for some example arguments. To make the exercise work, there needs to be disagreement, so make sure that they understand that even if they do not actually agree with a certain position, for the sake of the argument, at least one person should choose a different side from the others.

9C Tell each group to choose a chair for the meeting. This person will be responsible for starting the meeting and keeping it moving. The chair should make sure that each point of view is heard. Remind students to use the phrases in Exercise 7. During the activity, monitor and help as necessary.

9D Tell students to discuss the language they used and what, if anything, they found difficult. Round off the task by asking how students will handle interruptions in the future. With stronger classes, get students to write three action points starting *In future meetings I will …*

MyEnglishLab: extra activities; Interactive video activities
Pronunciation bank: p.114 Stress in phrases for turn taking
Workbook: p.12 Exercise 1

2.4 ❯ Business skills

Voicemail messages

GSE learning objectives

- Can understand the main information in a simple work-related phone message.
- Can note key information from a voicemail message.
- Can leave a polite voicemail message including key information.

Warm-up

Ask for a show of hands: *Who in this class uses voicemail?* If necessary, elicit or explain the meaning of *voicemail*. Ask where they use voicemail (on a mobile phone, landline at home, office phone, etc.) and then ask: *How many voicemails do you record or receive each day?* Find out who is the heaviest voicemail user in the class. Finally, ask if anyone receives or leaves voicemail messages in English.

Lead-in

Students look at the language we use when we leave voicemail messages.

1A Ask: *Do you ever need to listen to voicemail messages more than once?* Get students to answer the question in pairs. Take a poll to find out how many times, on average, students listen to voicemail.

1B Put students in small groups and ask them to complete the exercise. During the activity, monitor and help as necessary. Invite groups to share answers with the class.

Possible answer

The caller speaks too fast / too quietly.
There is background noise.
The speaker has a strong accent.
You don't understand the context of the message.
The caller doesn't leave their full name and contact details.

1C Get students to do the exercise in pairs, sharing their feelings about leaving messages. After they have finished, you can turn this into a class poll. Write the numbers 1 to 5 on the board, then read the numbers one at a time and ask students to hold up their hands to show their answer.

Listening

Students listen to a voicemail message received by the office of a Human Resources Manager.

2A 🔊 2.01   Tell students they are going to listen to three voicemail messages. Draw attention to the grid and point out that they simply need to tick the correct column to describe the speaker. Play the recording. Get students to check their answers in pairs. Then check answers with the whole class.

Caller 1: speaks too fast   Caller 2: is unclear
Caller 3: sounds annoyed

2B 🔊 2.02   Get students to do the exercise individually, then compare answers in pairs. It is likely that students will have heard and understood different parts of the message. Point out that collaborative listening is an authentic listening skill. If you did not hear something, the person next to you may have.

1 Emma Newman   2 Mark Thomas   3 logistics   4 called
5 call him back on his mobile   6 44 7623 911 129
7 until 4 p.m. today   8 send email

3A 🔊 2.03   Tell students they are going to listen to a fourth message. Ask them to look at gaps 1–3 and point out that all they have to do is decide which of these describe the aims of the message. Play the recording. Check answers as a class.

1, 3

3B 🔊 2.03   Ask students to read the question and checklist. For stronger groups, get them to do the exercise and then listen to check. Play the recording, then check answers with the class.

The caller did everything except repeat her contact details.

3C Put students in pairs. During the activity, monitor. Ask a few pairs to share their answers with the class before comparing with the sample on page 128.

Sample answer

Daniella Rossi called re terms of new contract. Please call back on 07654 322 187 before 2 p.m. today or leave message with Elliot Barber, Ext. 5238. Also, please resend copy of contract.

Extra activities 2.4

A 🔊 2.01   Get students to look at the blank message form. Then play the recording, which is message 2 from Exercise 2A, and get them to complete the exercise. Check answers with the class.

1 don't know   2 Carla   3 wants to talk about interview candidates   4 called   5 no action required   6 no number left   7 none   8 none

Functional language: Leaving a voicemail message

Students look at useful phrases for leaving a voicemail message.

4A Explain to students that these are questions and phrases from the fourth voicemail message in the listening. Ask them to complete the sentences with the correct words. You could do this exercise with the whole class, checking answers as you go along.

> 1 This is Daniella Rossi, R-O-S-S-I.
> 2 Emma asked me to contact her to discuss …
> 3 Can she also re-send a copy of my new contract?
> 4 In case she doesn't have my number, I'm on 07654 322 187.
> 5 Maybe she can leave a message with my assistant, Elliot Barber.
> 6 I'm available to talk until 2 p.m. today.
> 7 I hope to hear from you soon.

4B Get students to look again at the seven categories in Exercise 4A. Tell them that each sentence/question in Exercise 4B matches a category. Get them to do the exercise individually. Then check answers with the whole class.

> **1** g **2** b, e, j **3** a, f **4** c, d **5** k **6** i **7** h

Extra activities 2.4

B Get students to do the exercise in pairs. Point out that this is message 3 that they listened to in Exercise 2A. Remind students to follow steps 1–7 so that their message is complete and correct. During the activity, monitor. Then get students to compare their rewritten messages with another pair.

Model answer

Good morning. This is Zhanna Petrovna – I'll spell that for you: Z-H-A-N-N-A , P-E-T-R-O-V-N-A. I'm calling from the Logistics department. This is a message for Emma Newman. Please ask her to call me back on extension 4385 – that's 4-3-8-5. I'd like to discuss the references for one of the shortlisted candidates. Could she call me back by the end of the day as it's very urgent? She can also call me on my mobile number: 0777 9345 299 – that's 0777 9345 299.

Task

Students leave a voicemail message.

5A Put students in pairs. Allocate roles A and B and refer them to the relevant page. Explain that each student is given a name, phone number, reason for calling and action required. Each student reads the information and makes notes to prepare the voicemail message. Remind them to review the useful phrases in Exercise 4. If possible, get them to practise their voicemail message aloud.

5B If students can record their voice on their phone, tell them to record their voicemail for their partner to listen to. If you prefer, this could be done as homework. Get students to play back their voicemail while their partner writes a message. If they cannot record their message, ask them to say it as their partner writes the message.

5C Students use the checklist to check their message. During the activity, monitor and help as necessary. Then ask students to swap roles. By a show of hands, find out how many messages in the class included all seven points.

MyEnglishLab: Teacher's resources: extra activities; Functional language bank
Workbook: p.12 Exercise 2

2.5 ➤ Writing
Emails – Action points

GSE learning objectives

- Can take simple notes at meetings and summarise action points.
- Can write a simple summary of action points in a meeting.
- Can express personal plans and intentions for the future using *going to*.

Warm-up

Write *Priorities for this week* on the board. Elicit or explain the meaning of *priorities* (the most important things) and then give a few examples from your own life, e.g. *mark some exam papers, take my car to the mechanic's, buy a new shirt.* Ask students to share a few of their own priorities for the week.

Lead-in

Students listen to a meeting between three colleagues and complete a list of action points.

1A ◀) 2.04   Ask: *Have you ever had to take notes at a meeting?* Make sure students know what *action points* are (priorities, things you have to do) and point out that the purpose of many meetings is to identify action points. Get students to look at the email. Tell them that the action points are a summary of the meeting, so they will not hear the list exactly as it appears in the email. Play the recording, then get students to check their answers in pairs. Ask: *What was the meeting about?* (preparations for building a factory in Indonesia) If students found the exercise difficult, play the recording again.

> **1** Investment **2** month **3** open **4** location **5** register
> **6** permissions **7** site manager **8** flights

1B Refer students to the audioscript on page 148 to check their answers. For weaker classes, ask them to underline the part of the script where each answer is given.

Functional language

Students look at useful language for writing an email that includes action points.

2 Tell students that you are now going to look closely at the language for writing an email with action points. Get them to complete the exercise in pairs. You could copy the table onto the board and invite different students to come up and write answers in the correct column.

> **1** we are going to build a factory in Indonesia next year … we had a meeting with our Indonesian partner yesterday
> **2** get licence, visit Indonesia, open bank account
> **3** imperatives – get, visit, open, choose, register, organise, interview, book
> **4** Matthew
> **5** by tomorrow

Extra activities 2.5

A ◀》 Ext 2.01   This activity gives further practice of phrases to use in an email. Play the recording. Ask: *What was the meeting about?* (problems last week with late deliveries, the possibility of finding new suppliers, the need for more factory staff, problems with equipment, customer complaints) Ask students to complete the exercise individually and then get them to check answers in pairs before class feedback.

> **1** problems   **2** new/alternative   **3** week
> **4** advertise   **5** candidates   **6** Wednesday   **7** Aiko
> **8** Filipo   **9** strategy   **10** this week

Optional grammar work

The email in Exercise 1A contains examples of *will* and *going to* for the future, so you could use them for some optional grammar work. Refer students to the Grammar reference on page 119 and use the exercises in MyEnglishLab for extra grammar practice.

Task

Students write an email outlining action points from a meeting.

3A ◀》 2.05   Put students in pairs and refer them to the list of action points on page 128. Get them to read through the points. They will number them in the order that they come up in the meeting and delete any points that are not mentioned. Play the recording and ask students to do the exercise individually, then check answers with a partner.

> • letter to employees explaining situation – 3
> • ~~get customer feedback~~
> • meeting with all staff – 2
> • ~~ask staff for their opinions~~
> • contact with individual customers – 4
> • email inviting staff to meeting – 1
> • press release – 5

3B Set a time limit for the writing task and remind students to use the corrected action point list from Exercise 3A and the phrases from Exercise 2. Students can write their emails individually and then come back together for Exercise 3C. Alternatively, they can write their emails in pairs and then work with a different partner for Exercise 3C.

Model answer

To: CEO
From: Kenzo
Subject: Meeting about Indonesian factory

As you know, we had a meeting to discuss the best way to inform staff and customers about the possible takeover of our company by Bines plc. We feel it is important to inform them of the situation before they hear it from the press. We think we should meet the staff to explain the situation and also that we should contact our biggest customers as soon as we know the takeover is going ahead.

Key action points:
• send email inviting staff to meeting
• have meeting with all staff
• send staff a letter outlining the situation
• contact biggest customers
• issue press release after speaking to biggest customers

3C Remind the class about the meaning of *formal* (more polite) and *informal* (more friendly). Get them to answer the questions. During the activity, monitor and help as necessary.

MyEnglishLab: Teacher's resources: extra activities; Interactive grammar practice; Writing bank
Grammar reference: p.119 *will* and *going to*
Workbook: p.13 Exercises 1 and 2

Business workshop ➤2
Investing your money

GSE learning objectives

• Can extract key details from conversations between colleagues about familiar topics.
• Can answer basic questions about information presented in graphs and charts.

Background

Students learn about three friends who set up an investment club.

1 Ask students to read the background and discuss the questions in pairs. Check answers with the class.

> **1** They want to invest their own money in the stock market.
> **2** because they didn't have enough money (to make investments alone)
> **3** you don't need to have a lot of money; sharing knowledge and ideas; making joint decisions; sharing risk
> **4** They are researching the best industries.

Investment possibilities

Students listen to a conversation about possible investments and complete notes.

2A ◀) BW 2.01   Write *graphite* on the board and ask if anyone knows what it is. (It is used in the writing part of pencils, and the raw material comes from mines.) Ask which sector graphite mining is in (primary, because it's a raw material). Then write *graphene* (a new material made from graphite) and ask if anyone has heard of it. Ask which sector graphene production is in (secondary, because it's manufactured). Explain that the friends are talking about the best industry to invest in. Get them to read the five statements. Elicit or teach *nuclear waste* (dangerous unwanted material from the nuclear power industry). Play the recording. Students listen and complete the exercise individually. Check answers with the class.

> **1** T   **2** T   **3** T   **4** F   **5** F

2B ◀) BW 2.01   For stronger classes, get students to try to complete the exercise before listening again. Otherwise, play the recording and get students to complete the notes. Check answers with the class.

> **1** graphite   **2** steel   **3** heat   **4** tablet   **5** charge

3A ◀) BW 2.02   Tell students that they are going to listen to Toni explaining her research to Melanie and Franco. Explain or elicit the meaning of *package holiday* (a vacation that includes the travel, accommodation and sometimes food for one price), *spa* (a place where people go to relax) and *profit* (the money a company keeps after it has paid all of its costs). Point out that the exercise is to identify things that Toni *doesn't* mention. Play the recording. Students complete the exercise individually, then check answers in pairs.

> camping , train travel, cooking

3B ◀) BW 2.02   Check or elicit the meaning of *mega-resort* (a very large hotel with lots of entertainment and sports facilities). Play the recording again. Students complete the exercise individually, then check answers in pairs.

> **1** tourism   **2** online   **3** chains

4 ◀) BW 2.03   Tell students that they are going to listen to Franco talking about his research. Get them to read the questions. Then play the recording. Check answers as a class.

> **1** the food industry   **2** healthy snack market
> **3** companies new to the industry   **4** because it is growing faster than other markets in the food industry

Extra activities Business workshop 2

A ◀) BW 2.03   In this exercise students will listen more closely to what Franco says. Play the recording and get them to complete the exercise. Check answers with the class.

> **1** do you think, go   **2** margins   **3** proper meals
> **4** Companies new, making, profits   **5** free-from
> **6** packaging   **7** ideal, working   **8** beating

5A Ask students which words and phrases they know for trends (e.g. *go up, rise, increase; go down, fall, decrease, drop; remain stable/steady, level*). Get them to look at the data in the charts again and decide which industry looks like the best investment. Remind them of the use of comparatives for describing graphs, e.g. *Sales were lower this year than last year. Prices rose more this year than last year.*

5B Groups make a decision.

5C Have weaker classes do this as a group. Stronger classes could do it individually, possibly as homework.

> **Model answer**
>
> To all club members
> I think that it would be best to invest in the food industry, in particular, healthy snacks. This is because more and more people are eating snacks, but they also want to keep fit and eat less sugar, salt and fat, etc. I therefore think that this market has great potential for expansion.

Company investment checklist

Students discuss what they would like to know about a company before investing in it.

6A Put students in groups. Elicit or teach the meaning of *sales figures* (the amount of money a company earns by selling its product or service). Do not check answers yet as Exercise 6B will answer the question.

6B ◀) BW 2.04   Get students to read the notes. Answer any questions they have about vocabulary. Then play the recording. Students check answers in pairs.

> **1** history   **2** set, up, when   **3** reports   **4** worth
> **5** strengths and weaknesses   **6** Management
> **7** experience   **8** employees   **9** Future   **10** risky
> **11** social

6C In pairs or small groups, students formulate questions. During the activity, monitor and help as necessary. See the answer key to Extra activity B for possible answers.

Extra activities Business workshop 2

B This activity gives more practice with question formulation. You could assign each student a question, then check answers as a class. Alternatively, get students to complete the exercise individually, then check answers in pairs.

1 How many people work for the company?
2 Where is the company based?
3 When did you start the business?
4 Did the company make a profit in the first year?
5 When did you start exporting to Thailand?
6 How much was the factory producing last year?
7 What are your future plans for the company?
8 Who is the CEO of the company?
9 Have you got much experience in the industry?
10 Why did you decide to move into the mining industry?

Task: Choose a company to invest in

Students discuss three companies and choose one to invest in.

7A Put students in groups. Explain the task. There are descriptions of three companies. Allocate roles A, B and C and refer each group to the relevant page for their company. Teach or elicit some of the vocabulary that may be new to students: *company vision* (an idea of what top managers think a business should be like, including the sort of product they want to produce, the level of quality they want to provide, how they want consumers to see them and so on), *current product range* (the products that a company makes at this time), *financial performance* (how much money a company earns), *additional factors* (one of several things that influence or cause a situation). Encourage them to use their dictionaries for any other words they do not understand. Each group follows the four steps. During the activity, monitor and help as necessary.

7B Groups take turns to present their company to the class, following the four bullet points. Help as necessary by guiding with questions.

7C Do the exercise as a class.

MyEnglishLab: Teacher's resources: extra activities

Review ◀2

1 1 financial, card, tertiary 2 primary, agriculture
 3 manufacturing, secondary 4 automotive 5 retail
 6 extraction, drilling
2 1 was studying 2 had 3 was working 4 met
 5 was explaining 6 was 7 owned 8 offered
 9 didn't hear 10 repeated 11 was waiting
 12 interrupted
3 1 sorry to interrupt 2 before we speak 3 just say
 something 4 Going back to 5 for interrupting
 6 Can I 7 I was making
4 1 this 2 message 3 returning 4 call me back 5 get
 6 hearing
5 1 know 2 involve 3 meeting 4 decide 5 organise
 6 by

3 > Projects

Unit overview

	CLASSWORK	FURTHER WORK
3.1 > **Project management**	**Lead-in** Students discuss the importance of schedules and budgets. **Video** Students watch a video about the construction of London's Millennium Bridge. **Vocabulary** Students look at project management vocabulary. **Project** Students do a project debriefing.	**MyEnglishLab:** Teacher's resources: extra activities; Reading bank **Pronunciation bank:** p.115 Stress in derived words **Teacher's book:** Resource bank Photocopiable 3.1 p.136 **Workbook:** p.14 Exercises 1–3
3.2 > **Large-scale projects**	**Lead-in** Students discuss shipping canals. **Listening** Students listen to information about the construction of three of the world's most important canals. They also listen to three people explain the service their company can offer and how much it will cost. **Grammar** Students learn how to use comparatives and superlatives. **Speaking** Students discuss and decide on a bid.	**MyEnglishLab:** Teacher's resources: extra activities **Pronunciation bank:** p.115 Weak forms in comparisons **Grammar reference:** p.120 Comparatives and superlatives **Teacher's book:** Resource bank Photocopiable 3.2 p.137 **Workbook:** p.15 Exercises 1 and 2, p.16 Exercises 1 and 2
3.3 > **Communication skills:** Giving instructions	**Lead-in** Students explore ways of leading and instructing others. **Video** Students watch a video of a discussion about a change to a delivery schedule. **Reflection** Students reflect on the conclusions from the video and discuss their own approach to giving and responding to instructions, and standing their ground. **Functional language** Students look at phrases that are commonly used to give and respond to instructions and to stand your ground. **Task** Students roleplay a scenario where a leader needs to direct the group but group members need to stand their ground and resist what they are being instructed to do.	**MyEnglishLab:** Teacher's resources: extra activities; Interactive video activities **Workbook:** p.17 Exercise 1
3.4 > **Business skills:** Meetings: Updates and action	**Lead-in** Students look at the language we use when we give and receive updates and discuss follow-up action items. **Listening** Students listen to a meeting where everyone is standing up and they take turns by throwing a ball to a person who then speaks. **Functional language** Students look at language for asking for and giving updates. **Task** Students do a roleplay where they ask for and give updates.	**MyEnglishLab:** Teacher's resources: extra activities; Functional language bank **Workbook:** p.17 Exercise 2
3.5 > **Writing:** Email requesting an update	**Lead-in** Students read an email asking for a project update, then correct the spelling mistakes in it. **Functional language** Students look at the language of requesting a project update. **Task** Students write an email requesting an update.	**MyEnglishLab:** Teacher's resources: extra activities; Interactive grammar practice; Writing bank **Grammar reference:** p.120 (not) enough **Workbook:** p.18 Exercises 1 and 2
Business workshop 3 > The grand opening	**Reading** Students read a meeting agenda and a project priority box. **Speaking** Students analyse meeting minutes and follow-up emails. **Task** Students hold a project meeting.	**MyEnglishLab:** Teacher's resources: extra activities

Business brief

The main aim of this unit is to introduce students to the concept of **projects** and **project management**. A project is a carefully planned piece of work, intended to build or produce something new or to deal with a problem. The result of a project is often called a **deliverable**. Project management is the work of coming up with ideas, planning, controlling and finishing the job.

A project has a clear **goal** or desired **outcome**, which is to be achieved within four main constraints:

1 the **schedule**, which usually includes not only a target date for completion, but also **deadlines** along the way.
2 the **budget**, which usually specifies how much money can be spent on a project, and also specifically what the money is spent on and often when it can be spent.
3 the **scope**, which is the understanding of exactly what is and isn't included in the project.
4 **quality**, which, in business, means the fitness for purpose of a product or service. This also includes how a product or service compares with competing products or services in the marketplace, and possibly the degree to which it is produced correctly or conforms to any regulations relating to the product.

One big challenge of project management is balancing these four constraints, which are often in direct competition with one another. For example, it might be desirable for a project to take months to develop a high-quality product, but the reality of the budget may be that a medium-quality product has to be produced in weeks. The constraints of a project are usually explained in some kind of **project documentation**, often a brief that includes a schedule, a budget, a scope-of-work statement, along with other details about exactly what will be produced.

Though some small business projects are carried out by individuals, most are the work of **teams**. In addition to managing the constraints mentioned above, a project manager must also manage the work of teams who are often from a variety of disciplines. There are several different ways of approaching project management.

The traditional '**waterfall**' approach breaks the project into a set of four clear process areas, typically:

1 initiation.
2 planning and design.
3 execution.
4 completion or closing.

A fifth process area is monitoring and controlling, which connects with and oversees areas 2 and 3 above.

While the above works well for small, well-defined projects, it often does not work for larger, more complex projects – for example, **civil engineering projects** such as building road networks or canals. In such cases, an **iterative and incremental** approach is taken, where there is an ongoing and repeating cycle of planning, analysis, testing and evaluation that eventually leads to a deliverable. This sort of approach is much more effective for large, multi-company projects, projects with requirements that may change quickly and projects with a lot of financial risk. In the world of software development, this iterative approach is called the **agile** model, where a product **emerges** over time through the collaboration of different teams. This approach allows projects to **evolve** and to respond quickly to change.

Projects and your students

It is important that students are aware of projects and project management. There is project work in almost any industry or professional environment, and also in formal educational contexts. Having a better understanding of projects and project management, and understanding the basic concepts and terminology has immediate practical applications for everyone.

Unit lead-in

Ask students to look at the photo and quote. The International Space Station is a huge, complex project built by the space agencies of Canada, Europe, Japan, Russia and the USA. Planning began in 1984, and construction started in 1998 and was completed in 2011. Check that students know the meaning of *riot* (a situation in which a large crowd of people are behaving in a violent and uncontrolled way, especially when they are protesting about something). Ask if anyone knows anything about Groucho Marx. He was an American comedian, writer and actor who lived from 1890 to 1977, and is considered by many to be one of the greatest American comedians ever. Discuss the quote. Do students agree? Why / Why not?

3.1 ❭ Project management

GSE learning objectives

- Can understand a large part of a video on a work-related topic.
- Can express belief, opinion, agreement and disagreement politely.
- Can give straightforward descriptions on a variety of familiar subjects.
- Can give a simple update on a work-related project.
- Can show a basic direct relationship between a simple problem and a solution.

Warm-up

Write the following words on the board and teach or elicit their meanings: *schedule* (a plan that includes dates and times), *budget* (a plan for how much money you can spend on something). Ask: *What in your life has a schedule? What has a budget?* Elicit answers. (Example answers: *schedule* – work or classes, public transport, holidays, mealtimes, television shows, projects; *budget* – household bills and expenses, saving for something, holidays)

Lead-in

Students discuss the importance of schedules and budgets.

1 These comments are meant to activate students' ideas about or experiences of schedules and budgets, as well as of the story the video tells. After students have discussed in pairs, take a vote for which comments are the most agreed with.

Video

Students watch a video about the construction of London's Millennium Bridge.

Notes

Built between 1998 and 2000, the Millennium Footbridge is the thirty-third bridge over the Thames in the Greater London Area. It links the Bankside Gallery, Tate Modern art museum and the Globe Theatre on the south of the river with St Paul's Cathedral on the north side. On the day that it opened in June 2000, people who used it complained that it moved from side to side as they walked across it, and it was closed after being open for only two days. Engineers discovered that the motion was harmless, but spent the next two years modifying the bridge to eliminate the unwanted movement.

2A Do this exercise with the class and discuss any guesses students may have. The actual answer is that the bridge was closed because it moved from side to side when people walked over it, and the builders feared it might be dangerous, but you don't need to tell the class that at this point, as it will be revealed in the video.

2B ▶ 3.1.1 Before playing the video, encourage students to listen out for the ideas they discussed in Exercise 2A.

> The bridge moved from side to side when people walked over it. They fixed the problem by attaching additional parts to stop movement.

3 ▶ 3.1.1 Ask students to read through the statements. Teach or elicit the meaning of *nightmare* (literally a very bad dream, but in this context, a very bad situation). With stronger groups, get students to try the exercise first and then check their answers by watching.

> **1** F **2** T **3** T **4** F **5** T **6** T **7** T **8** F

4 Put students in pairs or small groups to do the exercise. For question 1, if students need help getting started, give them a recent or historical example, such as the Volkswagen diesel emissions scandal in 2015, the sinking of the *Titanic* in 1912, BP's Deepwater Horizon disaster in 2010 or the Rio Olympics, all of which were plagued by problems. For question 2, there is no clear correct answer. On the one hand, the problems with the bridge will always be part of its story, but they were fixed, which can be seen as a great success.

Extra activities 3.1

A ▶ 3.1.1 This activity gives practice with the skill of understanding cause and effect, and of summarising. Students complete the exercise individually, then check answers in pairs. Do a final check by showing 02:18–02:52 of the video again.

> **a** 5 **b** 2 **c** 4 **d** 1 **e** 3

Vocabulary: Managing projects

Students look at project management vocabulary.

5 Check that students understand *anticipating* (expecting, preparing for), *milestones* (points in a project that you plan to reach at a certain time), *risk register* (a list of common risks to look out for) and *setback* (a problem that causes a delay). Get them to complete the exercise individually, then check answers in pairs.

> **1** budget **2** risk management **3** anticipating
> **4** setback **5** milestones **6** project managers **7** predict
> **8** risk register

Extra activities 3.1

B This activity gives practice with more vocabulary from the video. Students complete the exercise individually, then check answers in pairs.

> **1** c **2** d **3** a **4** f **5** b **6** e

Word building – verbs and nouns

6 Explain that in English, words or parts of words are sometimes used in different parts of speech (see Notes below). Put students in pairs and ask them to do the exercise. Go through the answers with the whole class.

Notes

Manage is a verb, but has the noun form *management*, which is the work of managing, and also *manager*, a person who manages. Noticing that *-ment* and *-ion* often appear on the end of nouns can help students guess the meaning of words they have never met before.

1 construction 2 suspension 3 move 4 investigate
5 communication 6 identification 7 solve 8 addition
9 attach 10 decision

7A Do the exercise as a class.

1 construction, management 2 investigate, identify, solution 3 attached, movement

7B Put students in pairs or small groups to discuss the questions. During the activity, monitor and help as necessary. Check answers by having a few pairs/groups share their ideas with the class.

Possible answers

1 Because if something goes wrong, many people could be injured or killed.
2 Probably yes. The problem was very complicated and it was important for the engineers to find the correct solution. A lot of money had already been spent on the project, so they needed to fix it properly.
3 They could have removed the bridge and started again. As the bridge was safe, they could have opened it again and talked about the wobble as a feature rather than a problem.

> **Pronunciation bank**
> **p.115: Stress in derived words**
>
> **Warm-up**
> Write the following words on the board: *arrange – arrangement, imagine – imagination.* Get students to say the words and ask: *Which syllable is stressed in each word?* (ar*range* – ar*range*ment, i*ma*gine – imagi*na*tion) Ask: *What's the difference between the pairs of words?* (In the first pair, the stress is on the same syllable in both words, but in the second pair, the stress moves to a different syllable in the second word.) Refer students to the explanation in the box and drill the pronunciation of the four words there.

1 Ask students to complete the exercise in pairs and then check answers with the class. Do not confirm answers yet as students will check them in the next exercise.

2 🔊 P3.01 Play the recording for students to check their answers. Then play the recording a second time for students to listen and repeat.

add → ad*di*tion – moves
con*struct* → con*struc*tion – stays the same
in*ves*tigate → investi*ga*tion – moves
sus*pend* → sus*pen*sion – stays the same

3 Put students in pairs and ask them to complete the exercise. Check answers with class.

Possible answers

at*tach* – at*tach*ment
com*mu*nicate – communi*ca*tion
des*cribe* – des*crip*tion
*de*tail – *de*tailed
*hap*py – *hap*piness
i*den*tity – i*den*tify – identi*fi*cation
*in*terest – *in*terested – *in*teresting
move – *move*ment
per*form* – per*for*mance
*per*son – *per*sonal
pre*sent* – presen*ta*tion
*rea*son – *rea*sonable

Project: A project debriefing and lessons learnt

Students do a project debriefing.

8A Check that pre-work students understand that they have experience working on projects in school or as a hobby (saving for, buying and learning to play a guitar, for example). Students read and answer the questions individually. During the activity, monitor and help as necessary.

Possible answers

1 I created a presentation for biology class. I explained the animals and plants of the Sahara Desert.
2 I worked with two classmates.
3 The research went very well. We enjoyed that part of the project, and we had a lot of interesting facts and information as well as pictures.
4 The biggest challenge was the presentation. We all felt very nervous and when we spoke, we were too quiet. The content of the talk was interesting, but the presentation was too quiet and boring.
5 Next time I would practise more.

8B Explain the meaning of *debrief* (discuss a project after completion in order to discover what went well and what could be improved next time). Make it clear that students are asking each other questions and writing down their partner's answers on the form rather than their own. During the activity, monitor and help as necessary.

Possible answers

Project description: biology presentation
Team members: Tomas and two classmates
Successes: good research and interesting content
Challenges: the presentation – speakers were nervous and the talk was too quiet and boring
Lessons learnt / Improvements for next time: practise speaking to give a good, interesting presentation

9A Do this exercise as a class. You could invite individual students to come to the board and write their ideas to build up the list.

Model answer

Don't
• try to do too much.
• make an unreasonable schedule.
• expect other people to do all the work.
• forget to share information with everyone on the team.
• try to do everything yourself.

Do
• plan carefully.
• communicate with the team.
• make a clear schedule.
• practise presentations.
• share the work equally.

MyEnglishLab: Teacher's resources: extra activities
Pronunciation bank: p.115 Stress in derived words
Teacher's book: Resource bank Photocopiable 3.1 p.136
Workbook: p.14 Exercises 1–3

3.2 › Large-scale projects

GSE learning objectives

• Can extract key factual information such as dates, numbers and quantities from a presentation.
• Can make comparisons using (*not*) *as ... as* with adjectives and adverbs.
• Can use all forms of comparatives and superlatives of adjectives.
• Can make direct comparisons between two or more people or things using known adjectives.

Warm-up

Write *ships* on the board. Ask students what big ships they have ever seen or been on. Ask: *Why are ships important in today's economy?* (They transport raw materials and goods all over the world.) *What do they carry?* (Everything! Oil and gas, minerals, cars, toys – almost anything you can think of.)

Lead-in

Students discuss shipping canals.

1A Get students to discuss the questions in pairs or groups or, for weaker groups, do the exercise with the whole class. If necessary, teach or elicit some of the jobs created by this sort of large-scale building project (see Notes below).

Notes

Large-scale engineering projects generally require workers from a wide range of fields. Here are a few examples:
• **accountant:** someone whose job is to keep and check financial accounts, calculate taxes, etc.
• **designer:** someone whose job is to make plans, roads, buildings, etc.
• **engineer:** someone whose job is to design or build roads, bridges, machines, etc.
• **labourer:** someone whose work needs physical strength, e.g. building work
• **manager:** someone whose job is to manage part or all of a company or other organisation

Possible answers

1 easier trade, shorter journeys for ships, revenue from charging canal users
2 engineers, labourers, cooks to feed the workers, specialised machine operators
3 some of the longest shipping canals in the world: Qaraqum Canal, Russia; Saimaa Canal, Finland; Eurasia Canal, Russia; Erie Canal, USA; Nara Canal, Pakistan; Rhone–Rhine Canal, France; Gota Canal, Sweden

1B Ask students to locate Egypt, the Mediterranean Sea, the Red Sea, the Atlantic Ocean, the Pacific Ocean and China on the map. Do the exercise as a class.

a Suez Canal **b** Panama Canal **c** Grand Canal

Listening

Students listen to information about the construction of three of the world's most important canals.

2 ◀) 3.01 Explain that students are going to hear about the three canals. Give them time to read items a–f so they know what they need to listen for. Do the exercise individually, then check in pairs.

1 d, a **2** e, b **3** c, f

3 ◀) 3.01 Go over the information that students need to listen for. For weaker classes, write the answers on the board in random order so that students can see the figures they need to use. Teach or elicit the meaning of *minimum width* (the distance from one side to the other, at the narrowest point) and *minimum depth* (in a canal, the distance from the top of the water to the bottom of the canal). Point out that not every person will hear every answer, so after they listen, get them to check answers in pairs. Then quickly go over the answers with the class. If necessary, play the recording again for students to listen out for the answers.

1 1,700 **2** 1,700 **3** Five **4** four **5** 4 **6** 30,000
7 1,900 **8** 190 **9** 55 **10** 77 **11** 4 **12** 375 **13** 33 **14** 12

Extra activities 3.2

A 🔊 3.01 This activity practises vocabulary from the listening. Explain that a *collocation* is two or more words that are often used together. For weaker classes, get students started by doing the first item together. Get students to complete the exercise individually, then play the recording for them to check their answers before class feedback.

> 1 e 2 d 3 f 4 a 5 b 6 c

B This activity uses the collocations from Exercise A. Get students to do the exercise individually, then go over the answers with the whole class.

> 1 missed, target 2 come in under budget
> 3 begin work 4 fell behind schedule
> 5 run out of money 6 ran over budget

C This exercise focuses on *depth, width* and *length*. You could introduce it by drawing a simple diagram of a swimming pool on the board, with a 5 to indicate depth, a 10 to indicate width and a 15 to indicate length. Ask: *What is the pool's depth? How deep is it?* (5 m) *What is the pool's width? How wide is it?* (10 m) *What is its length? How long is it?* (15 m) Get students to do the exercise individually, then go over the answers with the whole class.

> 1 deep, depth 2 length, long 3 wide, width

Grammar: Comparatives and superlatives

Students learn how to use comparatives and superlatives.

4A 🔊 3.02 Tell students that they are going to listen again to some extracts from the listening and focus on the grammar. Teach or elicit *time-consuming* (taking a lot of time). Play the recording as students complete the exercise. Check answers in pairs.

> 1 longest 2 more amazing 3 hardest 4 later
> 5 most important 6 shorter 7 less difficult 8 harder
> 9 as straightforward as 10 least challenging

4B Complete the grammar rules as a class.

> 1 comparative 2 superlative

5 Refer students to the Grammar reference on page 120. Give them a few minutes to do the exercise individually. Monitor and if students are struggling with any of the items, write them on the board and go through them with the whole class.

> 1 not as long as 2 the least profitable 3 the least modern 4 not as expensive as / less expensive than 5 not as large as 6 later than

Extra activities 3.2

D This activity gives further practice with comparatives and superlatives. Give students a few minutes to do the exercise individually. Monitor and if students are struggling with any of the items, write them on the board and go through them with the whole class.

> 1 the biggest 2 more popular than 3 as easy as
> 4 the least expensive 5 the most important
> 6 less experienced than / not as experienced as
> 7 less quickly 8 least difficult 9 more urgently than 10 the most clearly

Pronunciation bank
p.115: Weak forms in comparisons

Warm-up
Write on the board: *I'm taller than him.* Get students to say the sentence. Do not comment on their pronunciation yet. Refer them to the explanation in the box. Then get them to say the sentence, paying attention to the pronunciation of *taller* and *than*.

1 Ask students to complete the exercise in pairs. During the activity, monitor and help as necessary. Note that students will listen and check their pronunciation in the next exercise.

2 🔊 P3.02 Play the recording for students to check their pronunciation. Then play the recording a second time for students to listen and repeat.

Listening

Students listen to three people explain the service their company can offer and how much it will cost.

6A 🔊 3.03 Explain that the listening is still about projects, but considers a very different type of project: the installation of a computer network in a shipping company. Explain that in business, many projects are put out to bid (see Notes below). Say: *We're going to listen to three bids for a new computer network.* Refer students to the two questions so they know what to listen for. Play the recording. Get students to check answers in pairs, then go over them with the class.

Notes
A bid is an offer to do work or provide services for a specific price. Often, when a company needs a product or service, it will ask several possible suppliers to bid for the job or product. At a minimum, this will include a price, schedule and budget. After considering several bids, a company will usually choose one and sign a contract with that supplier.

> 1 Bid B 2 Bid C

6B 🔊 3.03   Teach or elicit the meaning of *technician* (a person who looks after certain processes or equipment) and *guarantee* (an agreement to fix any problems that arise with a product or service, usually within a given time, such as a year). Play the recording. Check answers in pairs.

Bid A	Bid B	Bid C
February 20	February 13	March 6
five days	one day	three weeks
yes	no	yes
no	yes	yes
three years	one year	two years
€13,000	€17,000	€11,000

Speaking

Students discuss and decide on a bid.

7A Students write sentences comparing the bids individually. During the activity, monitor and help as necessary.

7B Put students in small groups to discuss the three bids, using the sentences they made in Exercise 7A. Encourage each group to reach a consensus. At the end, ask groups to share their decision.

MyEnglishLab: Teacher's resources: extra activities
Pronunciation bank: p.115 Weak forms in comparisons
Grammar reference: p.120 Comparatives and superlatives
Teacher's book: Resource bank Photocopiable 3.2 p.137
Workbook: p.15 Exercises 1 and 2, p.16 Exercises 1 and 2

3.3 ❯ Communication skills
Giving instructions

GSE learning objectives

- Can understand instructions delivered at normal speed and accompanied by visual support.
- Can infer speakers' opinions in conversations on familiar everyday topics.
- Can give or seek personal views and opinions in discussing topics of interest.
- Can give simple instructions to complete a basic task, given a model.
- Can respond to opinions and instructions in a work situation.
- Can give simple, clear instructions and allocate tasks.

Warm-up

Ask: *Who tells you what to do?* If students need help getting started, you could say, e.g. *My boss tells me to come to meetings. My partner tells me to help out with dinner.* Ask: *Do you ever tell people what to do? Or do you ask nicely?*

Lead-in

Students explore ways of leading and instructing others.

1A Put students in pairs and ask them to discuss the statements. Get a few opinions and discuss ideas as a class.

1B Students discuss in pairs, then compare answers as a class.

Video

Students watch a video of a discussion about a change to a delivery schedule.

2A ▶ 3.3.1   In the first sequence, we see Daniel introduce Clarice and Beata. The three then have a meeting together. Daniel explains that he is leaving Beata in charge of the Diabsensor project. Play the video from 00:00 to 01:15 and do the matching exercise with the whole class.

> **1** b **2** c **3** a

2B Discuss the questions with the whole class. Teach or elicit the meaning of the expression *handle it* (deal with a situation or problem by behaving in a particular way and making particular decisions).

> Beata feels confident. She says she has the required work experience and she says she can 'handle it' and that she can get support from Daniel.

2C ▶ 3.3.1   Explain that Beata has a problem with components for the Diabsensor. This part of the video shows Beata and Clarice discussing this issue. Get students to look at the questions so they know what to listen for. Then play the next part of the video while students do the exercise in pairs.

> **1** The problem is that Beata needs the components earlier than planned.
> **2** 17 April **c**   9 May **d**   10 May **b**   28 May **a**

3A Get students to think about possible solutions to the problem. Ask how they would handle a conversation with a supplier. Explain the idea of Beata having two options in her conversation with Clarice and go through the details of Options A and B with the class. Make it clear to students that they can choose which option they want to see first on the video. Put students in small groups and ask them to discuss the two options, giving reasons for their answers. Elicit ideas from a few groups and as a class, decide which video to watch first.

3B ▶ 3.3.2   ▶ 3.3.3   Tell the class to answer the questions for Option A or B depending on their choice, and play the video. You could ask students to discuss the questions in their groups first, and then check the answers as a whole class. Do the same for the second video.

Possible answers

Option A
1 There is no solution. Clarice will have to find one.
2 Beata simply tells Clarice that she has to find the solution.
3 We do not know, but we can sense that she is not satisfied with the situation.
4 We do not know, but it is likely that this has not helped the two women build a strong relationship.

Option B
1 The solution is that Beata may be able to transport the consignment via another supplier.
2 Beata and Clarice arrive at the solution together.
3 Clarice seems pleased with this solution.
4 We do not know, but it is likely that this has helped the two women build a strong relationship.

4 Put students in pairs and give them 3–4 minutes to discuss the questions. During the activity, monitor and help as necessary.

5 ▶ 3.3.4 Students should do this in the same pairs as Exercise 4. Explain that they are going to watch the last section of the video, which is a summary of the ideas they looked at in the previous videos. Play the video and give students 3–4 minutes to discuss and make notes, then discuss the main learning points with the whole class.

Possible answers

You should remember that you can take different approaches (use your authority or use a more collaborative approach) depending on the situation. You should think about how the other person will feel and how this will affect your working relationship. Flexibility and the ability to see the other person's point of view are important skills.

Reflection

Students reflect on the conclusions from the video and discuss their own approach to giving and responding to instructions, and standing their ground.

6 Allow students to work individually on this so that they can reflect on their own preferences and ideas. Ask them to think of their own answers to the questions and to make notes. Then put students in pairs to discuss their answers. Get brief feedback from the class.

Functional language: Giving and responding to instructions, standing your ground

Students look at phrases that are commonly used to give and respond to instructions and to stand your ground.

7A Explain that this exercise highlights expressions from the video that we use to give and respond to instructions, and to stand our ground. If it has not already come up, teach or elicit the meaning of *manoeuvre* (movement, adjustment). Get students to do the exercise in pairs, then check answers as a class.

1 h **2** c **3** f **4** a **5** b **6** d **7** g (e is extra)

7B Students do this individually, then check answers in pairs.

a 1, 4 **b** 2, 6 **c** 3, 5, 7

7C Get students to do this individually, then check answers in pairs. If necessary, teach or elicit the meaning of *flexibility* (ability to move or change) and point out that *my hands are tied* is a metaphor – a figure of speech that is not literally true (see Notes below).

Notes

Tie literally means *fasten things together or hold them in a particular position using a piece of string, rope, etc.* It is used in a lot of expressions that can be useful in business contexts.
• *tie in with something*: be similar to another idea, statement, etc.
• *be tied to/by something*: be restricted by a particular situation, job, etc., so that you cannot do exactly as you want
• *tie-in*: a product such as a record, book or toy that is related to a new film, TV show, etc. used to help promote the film, etc.
• *break a tie*: end a relationship with a person or organisation

a 3, 4 **b** 2, 6 **c** 1, 5, 7

8 Tell students that they are going to build up a conversation from some basic information that they will be given and the phrases from Exercise 7. Divide the class into Students A and B and get them to form pairs. Give them 2–3 minutes to look through the phrases in Exercise 7 and to make sure they understand the situation and their roles. For weaker classes, get students to work together to make notes for each speaker before they do the roleplay. During the activity, monitor and help as necessary.

Extra activities 3.3

A This activity gives more practice with the phrases for giving and responding to instructions. Students do the exercise individually and check answers in pairs

1 Can you bring Clarice **up** to speed?
2 You need **to** meet this new deadline.
3 I'm sorry, there's no flexibility **on** this deadline.
4 I'd like you to change **the** delivery date.
5 I would **like** to help you, but I can't.
6 I'm afraid I'm just **not** that flexible.
7 I have no room **for** manoeuvre on this.

Task

Students roleplay a scenario where a leader needs to direct the group, but group members need to stand their ground and resist what they are being instructed to do.

9A This works best with groups of three. If you have more than three people in a group, either share a scenario between two people or choose an observer, who will make notes and give feedback about the approach the leader chooses to take. Students will need to do a certain amount of preparation before they begin the task, so bear this in mind when you are planning this stage. Put the class in groups of three and have each group choose one of the three scenarios and decide who will be the leader.

9B Refer the non-leaders to the information on page 129 and make sure they look only at the information for the scenario their group has chosen. Tell the leaders that they need to think about how they will deal with the situation. During the activity, monitor and help the leaders as necessary. Allow 3–4 minutes for everyone to think and make some notes about what they will need to say.

9C Ask groups to do the roleplay. During the activity, monitor and help as necessary.

9D Tell students to discuss the language they used and what, if anything, they found difficult. Round off the task by asking how students will handle giving and responding to instructions and standing their ground in the future. With stronger classes, get students to write three action points starting *In future meetings I will …*

MyEnglishLab: Teacher's resources: extra activities; Interactive video activities

Workbook: p.17 Exercise 1

3.4 ❯ Business skills

Meetings: Updates and action

GSE learning objectives

- Can give clear work-related instructions.
- Can summarise the main ideas in a meeting using simple language.
- Can ask for a simple update on a work-related project.
- Can give a simple update on a work-related project.
- Can describe future plans and intentions using fixed expressions.
- Can show a basic direct relationship between a simple problem and a solution.

Warm-up

Write *to-do list* on the board. Explain or elicit that this is a list of things you need to do. Some people keep an actual written-down list or maybe an app that keeps track of things they need to do, while others have a *mental to-do list* – a list that they keep in their mind, but do not actually write down. Ask: *Who has a to-do list?* Then ask: *Where do you keep it?* Find out how students keep track of things they need to do.

Lead-in

Students look at the language we use when we give and receive updates and discuss follow-up action items.

1A Go over the definitions. If you like, you could point out that English is full of words that are both nouns and verbs: *aim, break, cover, dream, guess, shop,* etc. With pre-work students, make it clear that they still have updates and action items each week. Updates could be related to school work, checking in with family, following the performance of a sports team and so on. Action items are anything that a person needs to do. Put students in pairs to discuss the questions.

1B Especially for pre-work students, explain that they can talk about both formal and informal meetings, including get-togethers with friends and family. Students complete the exercise in their pairs. During the activity, monitor and help as necessary. Ask different pairs to share their answers with the class.

Listening

Students listen to a meeting where everyone is standing up and they take turns by throwing a ball to a person who then speaks.

2A ◀ 3.04 Get students to read the instructions, then play the recording. Answer the question quickly as a class.

> a stand-up meeting

> ### Notes
>
> In a stand-up meeting, all of the participants remain standing for the entire meeting. The idea is that if people are not completely comfortable, they will not waste time talking about unimportant matters, and meetings will be short and efficient. Stand-up team meetings are an essential feature of agile software development. In a project management framework called *scrum*, small teams of developers have a daily fifteen-minute stand-up meeting to co-ordinate their work.

2B Go through the questions so that students know what they are listening for. Teach or elicit the meaning of *impediment* (something that stops you from doing what you want or need to do; a blocker). Play the recording. Get students to do the exercise individually, then compare answers in pairs. Then ask: *What do you think of this type of business meeting?* Some students may think it is a great idea, others may think it is silly.

> 1 fifteen minutes
> 2 to bring everyone up to date about what is going on in the team
> 3 every morning
> 4 9 a.m.
> 5 to decide who speaks
> 6 what they did yesterday, what they plan to do today, any impediments
> 7 The team leader will discuss follow-up action with individuals as necessary.

3A 🔊 3.05 Tell students that they are going to listen to the next part of the meeting. Ask them to look at the table. With weaker groups, you could assign some students to listen and note only *Yesterday*, others to note down only *Today* and a third to note only *Problems/Impediments*. They could then compare answers in pairs. Play the recording, then check answers with the class.

> **Jack**
> worked on contract for China project; meeting with lawyers, complete draft contract; lawyers have limited time
>
> **Sal**
> sub-supplier meeting followed by lunch; write summary of meeting, brief production team leader; none
>
> **Tom**
> discussed logo ideas with department heads, met designer; work on logo designs, meet with remaining department heads; not all department heads available

3B 🔊 3.05 For stronger groups, get students to answer the question first and then listen to check. Play the recording, then check answers with the class.

> Students' own answer, but a likely answer is Tom because his speech wasn't very well organised and didn't follow the same sequence as Jack and Sal.

4 Explain that the point of the exercise is to make Tom's speech follow the rules of the meeting better. Get students to do the exercise in pairs. During the activity, monitor and help as necessary.

> **Possible answer**
> Yesterday I spent most of the day discussing ideas for the new logo with different departments. I also met with one of the new designers who will be working on this project until the end. Today I'm planning to work on the designs for the new logo. I'll be discussing them with the departments I missed yesterday. A possible impediment is that not everyone will be available to see me.

5 🔊 3.05 Play the recording again. If students struggle to answer the question, ask: *Which two speakers are facing possible problems?* (Jack and Tom) *What are they?* (Jack may have a scheduling/time problem with the lawyers and Tom isn't sure he'll be able to see the managers he needs to see.) Point out that the team leader might want to follow up where there are potential impediments.

> **Possible answer**
> The manager will probably want to speak to Jack about lawyer availability, and to Tom about department head availability.

6 🔊 3.06 Explain that this is a listening and speaking exercise. Students will hear questions from the team leader's manager. Write the questions on the board:

1 *How are we doing with the redrafting of the China contract?*
2 *What about Sal's meeting with the sub-suppliers yesterday? What's happening with the deadlines?*
3 *Where are we with the logo?*
4 *Can you bring me up to date on the programme for today?*
5 *What's the latest on the new schedule? Can you give me an update on the plans?*
6 *When will you be able to bring me up to speed on the factory shutdown?*

Students will need to refer back to the notes they made in Exercise 3. Discuss the answers as a class. Then do the exercise with the whole class. Tell students not to worry about saying exactly what their classmates say, but to say their answers loudly and confidently. For weaker classes, you may want to pause the recording after each question to give them more time to answer.

> **Possible answers**
> 1 Jack is handling that. He's meeting with the lawyers today, and is hoping to finish the draft today too.
> 2 They agreed some new deadlines, but I haven't seen them yet. I'm sure they'll be OK.
> 3 Tom's working hard on that. He's going round the departments getting feedback, and he's meeting with the designers. It's all in hand.
> 4 Jack is doing the contract, Sal is writing up yesterday's meeting and doing some briefings, and Tom is working on the logos. I'll be focusing on the new schedule and the factory shutdown.
> 5 Yes, I can do that now if you like.
> 6 I should be in a position to do that this afternoon.

Extra activities 3.4

A 🔊 3.04 Explain that the text explains how to have a stand-up meeting. Get students to do the exercise individually, then play the recording again for them to check their answers. Go over the answers as a class.

> 1 start 2 gives 3 did 4 plan 5 see 6 throw
> 7 answers 8 spoken 9 follow up 10 Catch

Functional language: Asking for and giving updates

Students look at language for asking for and giving updates.

7 Explain to students that these are questions from the listening. You could do this exercise with the whole class, checking answers as you go along.

> 1 b 2 d 3 g 4 c 5 f 6 a 7 e

8A These sentences are all from the listening. Get students to do the exercise individually, then check answers in pairs.

> 1 worked 2 progress 3 impediment 4 agreed
> 5 followed up 6 finish 7 see 8 work on 9 spent

8B Get students to look at the three questions, which are basically categories. Tell them that each sentence in Exercise 8A matches a category. Get them to do the exercise individually. Then check answers with the whole class.

> **a** 1, 4, 5, 9 **b** 2, 6, 8 **c** 3, 7

9A 🔊 3.06 Put students in pairs to do the exercise. Then play the recording for students to check their answers.

> **Possible answers**
> See possible answers for Exercise 6.

9B Students do the exercise in pairs. During the activity, monitor and help as necessary.

> **Extra activities 3.4**
>
> **B** Revise the meaning of *preposition* (see Notes below) and get students to do the exercise individually, then check answers in pairs. Answer any questions. For many of these, there is no rule that determines which preposition is used; students just have to develop a feel for what people usually say.
>
> > **1** with, of **2** with **3** with **4** up **5** on **6** on
> > **7** up, on

> *Notes*
>
> A preposition is a word that is used before a noun, pronoun or gerund to show place, time, direction, etc. In the phrase *the trees **in** the park*, *in* is a preposition.

Task

Students do a roleplay where they ask for and give updates.

10A Put students in small groups and explain the task. Students read the notes and think about what they would say in a stand-up meeting in each situation. They may want to make notes about which information is *Yesterday*, *Today* and *Impediments* for each scenario.

10B Remind students to review the useful phrases in Exercises 7 and 8 to ask for and give updates. Make sure that someone in each group has the job of noting down action points. During the activity, monitor and help as necessary.

10C Tell students to discuss the language they used and what, if anything, they found difficult. Round off the task by asking how students will handle updates and action points in the future. With stronger classes, get students to write three action points starting *In future meetings I will …*

MyEnglishLab: Teacher's resources: extra activities; Functional language bank
Workbook: p.17 Exercise 2

3.5 ❯ Writing
Email requesting an update

> **GSE learning objectives**
>
> - Can request a simple update on a work-related project or task.
> - Can give a simple update on a work-related project or task.
> - Can qualify adverbs, adjectives and nouns with *enough*.

> **Warm-up**
>
> Write *deadline* on the board. Elicit or remind students of the meaning (a specific time for completing something). Ask: *Who has a deadline soon?* Ask students to raise hands and ask one or two for more details. Then ask: *When you have a deadline, how do you usually work? Do you wait until just before the deadline, then work all night? Or do you try to finish ahead of the deadline so you can relax?* Discuss answers.

Lead-in

Students read an email asking for a project update, then correct the spelling mistakes in it.

1A Teach or elicit the meaning of *CFO* (Chief Finance Officer – the person who is responsible for money in a company) and *funds* (available money). Focus attention on the rubric and get students to read the email to answer the question. Answer the question as a class.

> update him on deadlines and cost details and meet him tomorrow

1B Ask: *Did anyone notice any spelling mistakes in the email?* If so, elicit the misspelt words and write them on the board in their misspelt form. Do not write the correct spelling yet. If students do not say all eight mistakes, ask them to read the email again and underline the misspelt words.

> **1** orignal – original **2** curent – current
> **3** shedule – schedule **4** sevral – several
> **5** aditional – additional **6** whether – weather
> **7** asistant – assistant **8** reguards – regards

1C Students check their answers with their partner. Complete the list of eight words on the board, then ask students to provide the correct spellings.

Functional language

Students look at the language of requesting a project update.

2 Tell students that you are now going to look closely at the language for writing an email asking for an update. Get them to complete the exercise individually, then check answers in pairs. They may ask what the difference is between using a statement and using a question. For an answer, see Notes below.

Notes

Generally, when asking for information, statements seem a little more direct and authoritative, while questions feel a little less direct. But a lot depends on the context – the other sentences in the message – and the overall tone.

1 if **2** grateful **3** appreciate **4** help **5** request **6** what **7** to **8** mind **9** possible **10** possibly

Extra activities 3.5

A This activity gives further practice of phrases used to ask for information. Get students to complete the exercise individually and then check answers in pairs before class feedback.

1 f **2** j **3** a **4** h **5** i **6** c **7** g **8** b **9** e **10** d

Optional grammar work

The email in Exercise 1A contains examples of adjective/adverb + *enough* and *enough* + noun/*to*, so you could use them for some optional grammar work. Refer students to the Grammar reference on page 120 and use the exercises in MyEnglishLab for extra grammar practice.

Task

Students write an email requesting an update.

3A Put students in pairs and refer them to the information on page 129. Get them to read through the points and discuss in more detail what they want to find out.

Possible answers

Are you going to meet the deadline? If not, when (do you think you'll finish)?
What work did you complete? / Have you completed all the work?
What work didn't you complete / haven't you completed?
Why didn't you complete the work?
Is the new furniture ready?
Have you ordered the new furniture and equipment?
What other problems did you have?
What problems do you think you might have?

3B Set a time limit for the writing task and remind students to use their ideas from Exercise 3A and the phrases from Exercise 2. Students can write their emails individually and then come back together for Exercise 3C. Alternatively, they can write their emails in pairs and then work with a different partner for Exercise 3C.

Model answer

To: Yolanda, Project Leader
From: Lydia
Subject: Request for update on refurbishment of Head Office

Dear Yolanda,

I'd like to know how the refurbishment of Head Office is going and if we are going to be able to move in on schedule. Could you possibly let me know what the current state of the project is?

If you are not going to meet the deadline, I'd appreciate it if you could let me know when the new finish date will be. Also, please could you give me details of what work you have completed and the work which isn't yet finished? I'd also be grateful if you could outline the reasons for any delays.

Would you also let me know if you have ordered all the new furniture and equipment and that it is ready to go into the offices?

Finally, I'd like a list of all the problems so far and information about any problems that you think might happen in the future.

Thanks for your help.

3C Get students to do the exercise in pairs. Encourage them to suggest corrections if they think there is an error in their partner's email. During the activity, monitor and help as necessary.

MyEnglishLab: Teacher's resources: extra activities
Grammar reference: p.120 (not) enough
Workbook: p.18 Exercises 1 and 2

Business workshop ➤ 3
The grand opening

GSE learning objectives

- Can scan short texts to locate specific information.
- Can write simple minutes for a meeting on a familiar work-related topic.
- Can express limited opinions and arguments during work-related meetings.

Background

Students learn about a new hotel that is planning a grand opening.

1 Ask students to read the background and discuss the questions in pairs. Check answers with the class.

1 It's a boutique hotel.
2 Because people are more and more interested in environmentally friendly businesses.
3 Students' own answers

Understanding project priorities

Students read a meeting agenda and a project priority box.

2A ▶ BW 3.01   Teach or elicit the meaning of *agenda* (a list of items to discuss in a meeting) and *wind turbines* (see the inset photo on page 92 – equipment for producing wind energy; they look like fans on top of poles). Get students to read the agenda. Ask: *What is the date of the meeting?* (1 August) *What is the date of the grand opening of the hotel?* (1 October) Play the recording, then check answers with the class.

> **1** a **2** d **3** b **4** c

2B Teach or elicit the meaning of the verb *delegate* (assign a job to another person). Get students to do the exercise, then check answers with the class.

> ### Notes
>
> The project priority box is sometimes called the *Eisenhower matrix* or *Eisenhower method*. It gets its name from former U.S. President Dwight D. Eisenhower. He is quoted as saying, 'I have two kinds of problems: the urgent and the important. The urgent are not important and the important are never urgent.' He did not claim to have invented the idea, but said it came from 'a former college president'.

> 1) 'Save the date' invitations to guest list – 2
> 2) Contract with actress Lana Gabler-Jones – 1
> 3) Engineer to explain wind turbines – 4
> 4) Food order for the event – 3

> ### Extra activities Business workshop 3
>
> **A** ▶ BW 3.01   In this exercise, students will listen more closely to Lily and Carlos's phone call. Play the recording and get them to complete the exercise. Check answers with the class.
>
> > **1** She has to leave for the airport.
> > **2** Lana's agent
> > **3** 1 July – a month ago
> > **4** the fabulous hotel
> > **5** Sam's Sandwiches & More

Analysing meeting minutes

Students look at the minutes of a meeting.

3A Teach or elicit the meaning of *meeting minutes*. Refer students to the minutes on page 134. Ask: *What do LJ and CE mean?* (They are the initials of Lily and Carlos. J and E stand for their surnames, which we don't know.) Answer the question as a class.

> It was written after the meeting because it gives information about what Carlos and Lily discussed at the meeting.

3B Get students to do the exercise in pairs. Point out that the things Carlos needs to do are action points.

> **1** Yes, they did.
> **2** email to guest list, email to Lana Gabler-Jones, cancel engineer, ask Sarah to order food

Analysing follow-up emails

Students look at emails following up a meeting.

4A Tell students that the three emails are all related to the Casa Paradiso grand opening. Assign each student only one email to read and match with an item in the minutes on page 134, so that roughly a third of the class reads each email. Check answers with the class. Then ask: *Which agenda item has not yet been taken care of?* (1 – 'Save the date' invitations)

> **A** ('Dear Constance') 2   **B** ('Hi Sarah') 4   **C** ('Dear Jim') 3

4B Get students to work in groups of three – one person who read each email. Quickly go through the answers with the whole class.

> **1** T
> **2** F – He wants to speak with Constance.
> **3** T
> **4** T
> **5** F – He spoke with Jim a few weeks ago.
> **6** F – He doesn't need anything from Jim now.

> ### Extra activities Business workshop 3
>
> **B** In this activity, students will look more closely at the three emails in Exercise 4A. Get them to do the activity in pairs or small groups. Check answers with the class.
>
> > **1** The message to Sarah. He starts with *Hi* and ends with *Cheers*.
> > **2** I hope you're well; You may recall that ... ; We'd like to ... ; I know you're busy, but would it be possible ... ; Could we perhaps ...
> > **3** Could we perhaps have a phone call? Let me know if you have any questions.
> > **4** The message is direct and business-like, so there's nothing wrong with it. If he wanted to be a bit more polite, he could begin with *I hope you're well*, like in his email to Constance. He could say *Thank you for taking the time to talk with me a few weeks ago about possibly ...* He could say *I'm afraid the owners have decided ...* to soften that sentence.

Task: Hold a project meeting

Students hold a meeting to discuss a project.

5A As a reminder, ask: *What is M&PR's role in the Casa Paradiso grand opening?* (They're a marketing and public relations firm, and they're handling all of the arrangements for the event.) Put students in pairs and ask them to choose who is Student A and who is Student B, and to turn to the appropriate role card. Give them a couple of minutes to read their role card, then get them to work through the agenda and share the information they have. During the activity, monitor and help as necessary.

5B Get the groups to summarise the information that came up in the meeting. Then get them to discuss the two questions. During the activity, monitor and help as necessary. Then ask a few pairs to explain what they have decided to do.

5C Students do the exercise individually. If you think they will struggle, get them to do it in pairs. During the activity, monitor and help as necessary.

Possible answers

Project: Casa Paradiso Grand Opening
Meeting date: 15 September
Event date: 1 October

1) Progress of hotel construction
   Discussion: The project is behind schedule. The hotel won't be ready until 15 October.
   Decision: Change party date to 16 October.
   Action: Send an email to guests explaining the change.

2) Update on guest list
   Discussion: 125 people would like to attend, but Casa Paradiso want to host 100.
   Decision: Reduce guest list to 100.
   Action: Choose 100 guests and confirm that they can attend on 16 October.

3) Special celebrity guest
   Discussion: Lana Gabler-Jones signed the contract but leaves for China on 2 October. If we change the date, she won't be able to attend.
   Decision: We need to cancel her contract and find another celebrity.
   Action: Contact Lana and try to cancel the contract. Search for another celebrity.

4) Music
   Discussion: Can choose DJ or band.
   Decision: Choose the band, if possible.
   Action: Contact band and confirm date.

5) Food
   Discussion: The food order wasn't placed in time and now the caterers aren't available.
   Decision: Food can be rearranged for 16 October.
   Action: Contact the caterers to check their availability for 16 October.

6) AOB
   Information discussed: Wind-power electric system working well.
   Decision: Send pictures to guest list.
   Action: Include pictures in email with date change.

5D Put students in groups to compare their work. During the activity, monitor and help as necessary.

Extra activities Business workshop 3

C Students write an email that explains a change in plans. Remind them to follow the structure given in the checklist and to try to make the email as positive as possible even though the change of date may be bad news.

Model answer

Dear Travel Professional,

On 2 August we invited you to come to a fabulous grand opening event for specially selected travel industry professionals to introduce the area's newest boutique hotel right on the beach – Casa Paradiso. We originally invited you for 1 October, but we need a little more time to prepare, so we've changed the date to 16 October. We hope you can still make it to our magical poolside evening event, which will include live music, a welcome from a special celebrity guest and a delicious buffet and open bar. There will be tours of the luxurious new hotel throughout the evening.

We look forward to seeing you on 16 October!

The Casa Paradiso Team

MyEnglishLab: Teacher's resources: extra activities

Review ❮3

1 1 milestone 2 setback 3 anticipate 4 predict
  5 risk
2 1 decision 2 construction 3 identify 4 solution
  5 addition 6 suspend 7 investigate
  8 attachment(s)/attached
3 1 biggest 2 less quickly 3 as experienced
  4 more experienced 5 as hard 6 larger
  7 least expensive
  8 as good 9 longer 10 better
4 1 up to speed 2 need you to meet 3 no problem
  4 like you to think about 5 compromise on
  6 there's no flexibility 7 can do it 8 Leave it
5 1 in progress 2 Where 3 latest 4 an update
  5 doing 6 impediments 7 finish
6 1 d 2 g 3 e 4 a 5 b 6 f 7 h 8 c

4 > Global markets

Unit overview

	CLASSWORK	FURTHER WORK
4.1 > One size fits all	**Lead-in** Students talk about adapting international brands to local tastes. **Video** Students watch a video about how Starbucks, Jaguar and Volvo have customised some of their products for China. **Vocabulary** Students look at vocabulary that describes global markets and marketing. **Project** Students plan the best way to change a product to make it market-appropriate.	**MyEnglishLab:** Teacher's resources: alternative video and extra activities; Reading bank **Teacher's book:** Resource bank Photocopiable 4.1 p.138 **Workbook:** p.19 Exercises 1–3
4.2 > Online markets	**Lead-in** Students discuss logos of online businesses. **Reading** Students read about Alibaba, eBay and Airbnb – companies that make it easy for people to run small online businesses. **Grammar** Students learn how to use passives. **Writing** Students write a description of a product they could make and sell online to become a sofapreneur.	**MyEnglishLab:** Teacher's resources: extra activities **Grammar reference:** p.121 Present Simple and Past Simple passive **Teacher's book:** Resource bank Photocopiable 4.2 p.139 **Workbook:** p.20 Exercises 1–3, p.21 Exercises 1–3
4.3 > Communication skills: Managing conversations	**Lead-in** Students explore ways of changing topic and staying on track in meetings. **Video** Students watch a video about the importance of changing topic and staying on track. **Reflection** Students reflect on the conclusions from the video and discuss their own skills of changing topic and staying on track. **Functional language** Students look at questions and statements that are commonly used to change the topic of a conversation or to stay on topic. **Task** Students roleplay a scenario where they have a meeting to discuss an app that a supplier has just produced.	**MyEnglishLab:** Teacher's resources: extra activities; Interactive video activities **Pronunciation bank:** p.115 Pronunciation of -(e)s endings **Workbook:** p.22 Exercise 1
4.4 > Business skills: Building consensus	**Lead-in** Students discuss the challenges of building consensus. **Listening** Students listen to a manager running a meeting about how to build consensus. **Functional language** Students practise using expressions for reaching agreement. **Task** Students choose a topic to discuss and try to reach agreement.	**MyEnglishLab:** Teacher's resources: extra activities; Functional language bank **Pronunciation bank:** p.115 Consonant–vowel linking between words **Workbook:** p.22 Exercise 2
4.5 > Writing: Letter confirming an order	**Lead-in** Students read and complete an order confirmation letter. **Functional language** Students look at the language of confirming an order. **Task** Students assess an order confirmation letter and then write their own.	**MyEnglishLab:** Teacher's resources: extra activities; Interactive grammar practice; Writing bank **Grammar reference:** p.121 Verbs + prepositions **Workbook:** p.23 Exercises 1 and 2
Business workshop 4 > Hand-made	**Listening** Students listen to an expert talking about key factors for global business. **Speaking** Students discuss market research. **Task** Students choose a market for a global strategy.	**MyEnglishLab:** Teacher's resources: extra activities

Business brief

The main aim of this unit is to introduce students to the concept of **global markets**. Increasingly, brands that used to sell within the borders of their home country are expanding their scope of business to include a variety of countries around the world.

Though many famous brands sell throughout the world, it is not uncommon for companies to **adapt** their products to the needs, tastes and desires of their markets. The Swedish carmaker Volvo, for example, sells a model exclusively for the high-end Chinese market with no front passenger seat, for added luxury in the back, and Starbucks in China focuses on tea more than coffee. Not all brands adapt, though. IKEA successfully **exports** its flat-pack furniture to more than forty countries. However, the company does heavily adapt its marketing to meet local needs and expectations.

Global markets mean that more than ever, companies operate across borders, time zones and languages. Employees who work with colleagues around the world need not only good language skills, but also an understanding of different cultures and the ability to recognise and react to different **communication styles**. This includes such subskills as understanding contexts and key details in meetings, and of building consensus among an international team.

Other practicalities of international business include the consideration of cost of production in various countries and an understanding of **transport** and all other aspects of a **supply chain** – the entire sequence of steps and processes necessary to **produce** and **distribute** a product. In addition, some understanding of **payment terms**, **currencies** and **trading laws** in an international business context is useful.

A **global marketing strategy** requires an understanding of potentially very different markets around the world. This means that **market research** may require the assistance of firms with good knowledge of the local markets in question and, as mentioned above, an understanding of the potential need to **localise** both products and advertising.

The internet has made a profound contribution to the globalisation of business. Companies such as Amazon, Uber, Airbnb and Alibaba have built **global brands** using the internet, and paved the way for people around the world to become '**sofapreneurs**' – people who earn money from often small online businesses without ever leaving their own home.

Global markets and your students

Everyone – not just people working in business – should have a basic understanding of global markets. Even if we are not involved in doing business globally, we are almost certainly consumers of products from global companies, and it is useful to understand and be able to speak about the global nature of business.

Unit lead-in

Look at the photo with the class and elicit what it shows (a floating fruit and vegetable market in Indonesia). Ask: *Is this a local market or a global market?* (local) *Where do the fruit and vegetables probably come from?* (nearby) *Who probably buys it?* (people who live nearby) Then look at the quote with the class and check that students understand *open, global marketplace* (the situation where people and companies all over the world are able to buy and sell products and services with people from many different countries). Explain that Procter & Gamble is an American multinational that produces consumer goods, including soap, shampoo, toothpaste and many other personal care products. Ask: *What do you think Pritchett means by 'the full impact of the global marketplace'? What effects has globalisation caused?* Accept any reasonable answers. Some ideas may include a huge variety of products being available worldwide, increased competition between very small businesses and multinational rivals, and the growth of very powerful corporations.

4.1 > One size fits all

GSE learning objectives

- Can identify the main point of TV news items reporting events, accidents, etc. where the visual supports the commentary.
- Can make and respond to suggestions.
- Can give a simple effective presentation about a familiar topic.

Warm-up

Ask: Which multinational brands and products are popular in your country? What makes them popular? Discuss why foreign brands are popular. Then ask: What local products are the most popular in your country? Are they popular outside of your country?

Lead-in

Students talk about adapting international brands to local tastes.

1 Refer students to the lesson title *One size fits all* and elicit or explain what it means (that something is considered suitable for every person). Do this exercise either in small groups or with the class.

Video

Students watch a video about how Starbucks, Jaguar and Volvo have customised some of their products for China.

2 Refer students to the photos. At this point, accept and discuss any reasonable suggestions.

3 ▶ 4.1.1 Play the video. If you like, you could pause the video any time one of the students' predictions is mentioned and get them to confirm it. You might also like to mention that Starbucks made other changes for the Chinese market not mentioned in the video (see Notes below).

Volvo's car does not have a passenger front seat but it has extra luxuries / 'luxury features'.
Starbucks coffee stores adapted their logo (removed the brand name) and sell (speciality) teas as well as coffee.

Notes

Starbucks has adapted itself to China in many ways:
1 They have bigger stores with more seating space. Chinese customers do not want coffee-to-go like U.S. customers. They expect to sit there all afternoon because of the price of the coffee.
2 Management makes an effort to get to know employees' families. The company said in a statement that 'family forums have been held for parents of store partners to hear managers discuss gratifying career paths at Starbucks'.
3 They sell traditional Chinese desserts, like moon cakes.

4 ▶ 4.1.1 Teach *rich elite* (very wealthy people), *middle class* (the social class that includes people who are educated and work in professional jobs, e.g. teachers or managers), *chauffeur* (a person whose job is to drive someone else's car). Get students to read through the questions and answer any they can. Then play the video as they complete the exercise.

1 middle class **2** is **3** Volvo's **4** with a chauffeur **5** slight **6** name **7** teas **8** thinks

5 Get students to do the exercise in pairs. You could extend the exercise with some more questions, e.g.

1 *Who gets the extra legroom if there are two important passengers?*
2 *Where does the bodyguard sit?*
3 *Would a successful Chinese tea shop chain be successful abroad?*
4 *Would the (e.g.) Italians change their tastes and start drinking tea?*
5 *Would you like to be an agent for a Chinese tea chain?*
6 *How would you win customers?*

1 Volvo wanted to target wealthy consumers who have drivers, so they removed the front passenger seat to give passengers in the rear more legroom.
Starbucks decided to only use the logo and not the brand name because many people in China might not be familiar with the Latin alphabet. Also, as the Chinese are generally tea-drinkers, they had to adapt and introduce more teas in their shops.
2 Possible answers: cruise control, seat heater, automatic transmission, DVD video / TV screens in the back, sunroof, sat nav, leather seats, parking sensors, cameras to replace rear-view mirrors, high-quality music system, reclining seats, bar, fridge, coffee machine, voice-activated doors and windows
3 Possible answers: use famous Chinese sports personalities, film and pop stars to promote coffee; introduce special offers and free gifts
4 Possible answers: have more speciality teas that interest different markets; open trendy tea shops to attract customers; introduce beverages with some tea in them, e.g. smoothies; promote the health benefits of certain teas, e.g. green tea

Extra activities 4.1

A ▶ 4.1.1 This activity gives further practice of key vocabulary and main ideas from the video. Teach or elicit the meaning of *appetite* (literally the feeling of being hungry, but also generally when you want something). Ask students to complete the exercise individually, then check answers with the class. Alternatively, play the video for students to check their answers individually.

> **1** b **2** f **3** c **4** a **5** e **6** d

B Get students to do this individually, as a quick vocabulary quiz. You could get them to compare answers in pairs before checking answers with the class.

> **1** Western goods **2** range **3** launched **4** sedan
> **5** removing (Note that *removed* appears in item 3 in Exercise A.) **6** room **7** packed **8** luxury features
> **9** the wealthy **10** high-end, premium

Vocabulary: Global markets: adjective and noun collocations; word building

Students look at vocabulary that describes global markets and marketing.

6A Go through the words with the class and make sure they understand the meaning of each (*consumer* – a person who buys and uses something; *local* – in a certain area, e.g. a country, city or neighbourhood; *luxury* – not necessary and usually expensive; *marketing* – the work of letting possible customers know about a product or service; *target* – something you want to reach or do; *product* – something made by a company; *brands* – names of companies or products; *customisation* – the process of changing or making something for a special purpose; *goods* – things that people buy; *preferences* – likes and dislikes; *strategy* – a plan for how to do something; *territories* – areas). For lower-level students, ask them to make a list of the collocations here which they can then use in Exercise 6B (consumer brands, local preferences, luxury goods, marketing strategy, product customisation, target territories).

6B Make sure that students understand *multinationals* (companies that do business in more than one country). Students do the exercise individually, then check answers in pairs.

> **1** target territories **2** marketing strategy
> **3** local preferences **4** product customisation
> **5** luxury goods **6** consumer brands

7 Elicit or remind students of the meaning of *verb* (a word that describes an action, state or something that happens), *noun* (a person, place or thing) and *adjective* (a word that describes a noun). Remind them that the three types of word can be closely related. Write *adaptation/adaptability* on the board and elicit its part of speech (noun); then write *adaptable* (adjective) and finally elicit the verb form (*adapt*). Students do the exercise individually, then check answers in pairs.

> **1** adapt **2** appeal **3** consumption **4** customisation
> **5** customised **6** grow **7** growth **8** preference
> **9** product **10** specialise **11** standard **12** target

8A Elicit or teach the meaning of *aspirational* (describing something that people see as a sign of success or higher social class). Students do the exercise individually, then check answers in pairs. Ask a few extension questions, e.g. *Why were Chinese consumers confused by IKEA?* (because the prices were low; they expected aspirational Western products to be expensive) *What two things did it have to adapt?* (its products and its marketing strategy) *What didn't it change?* (its low prices)

> **1** customised **2** preferences **3** consumers **4** targeted
> **5** adapted **6** appealing **7** production **8** growing

8B Discuss the questions as a class. This leads into the project in Exercise 9.

Extra activities 4.1

C This activity gives further practice of key vocabulary related to global markets. Ask students to complete it individually, then check answers with the class.

> **1** consumer brands **2** luxury goods **3** appealing
> **4** adaptation **5** specialises **6** targeting
> **7** customisation **8** standard, preferences

Project: Adapt to a new market

Students plan the best way to change a product to make it market-appropriate.

9A This project can be done as a twenty-minute activity at the end of class or as an extended project over two classes. Students can do research online to find out about local preferences in other countries for homework. Then they compare their findings and prepare a marketing presentation in the next class.

Put students in pairs or groups. Read through the bullet points and make sure students understand the task. Make sure they understand the meaning of *profile* (a description of the country's needs – its demographic, what consumers want, etc.). During the activity, monitor and help as necessary. When everyone's profile is more or less complete, move on to Exercise 9B.

9B As students discuss the questions, monitor and help as necessary.

9C Groups take turns giving their presentations. After watching all of the presentations, discuss which products would be the easiest and most difficult to adapt for a different market.

MyEnglishLab: Teacher's resources: extra activities; Reading bank; alternative video and worksheet
Teacher's book: Resource bank Photocopiable 4.1 p.138
Workbook: p.19 Exercises 1–3

4.2 > Online markets

GSE learning objectives

- Can scan short texts to locate specific information.
- Can use the Past Simple passive.
- Can write a short simple description of a familiar device or product.

Warm-up

Ask: *How many times each day do you use the internet?* Get a few students to answer. Then ask: *What devices do you use to go online? Mobile phone? Laptop? Tablet? Desktop computer? What apps do you use the most often?*

Lead-in

Students discuss logos of online businesses.

1 Tell students to look at the logos. Ask: *Have you visited any of these websites? Why? How often? Can you name any other e-commerce websites?* Get students to do the exercise in pairs.

> **1 a** eBay **b** Alibaba **c** Deliveroo **d** Amazon
> **2** Suggested answers: by selling second-hand goods they don't want; by making goods and selling online; by becoming a distributor and selling online; by becoming an 'influencer'; by renting out rooms via Airbnb

Reading

Students read about Alibaba, eBay and Airbnb – companies that make it easy for people to run small online businesses.

2 Ask students to do the exercise individually and then share answers with the whole class. Ask: *How is PeoplePerHour different from the other four?* (It matches freelancers and jobs.)

> Five websites are mentioned in the article, in this order: Alibaba; Airbnb; eBay; PeoplePerHour, a freelance employment site; Etsy, an online marketplace where people can sell homemade goods.

3 Write *health reasons* and *caring responsibilities* on the board. Ask students for examples of health problems that may make it difficult for someone to work at a usual job (e.g. someone with a chronic condition like arthritis, asthma, diabetes or back pain) and examples of caring responsibilities (e.g. people looking after very young children and/or old/sick/disabled family members or those with mental illnesses). Students do the exercise individually, then check answers in pairs.

> **1** a
> **2** One percent of U.S. adults earn money from websites and these people earn less than a quarter (25 percent) of their income from these sites.
> **3** people who can't work in traditional jobs for health reasons and people with caring responsibilities
> **4** that they will compete unfairly offering lower prices because they don't pay taxes
> **5** Governments have to make sure they pay taxes / don't avoid paying taxes.
> **6** He says, 'You don't think a lot', which suggests he finds it easy and boring.
> **7** It gives him something to think about. It's his escape from his job.
> **8** She seems more positive from her concluding sentence.

4 Put students in pairs to do the exercise. During the activity, monitor and help as necessary.

> **Possible answers**
> **1 Benefits:** It's a cheap and quick way to sell online.
> **Disadvantages:** There's global competition on e-commerce sites which drives prices down. Freelance sites offer low-paid, temporary work and you have to compete with people in other parts of the world. There are no workers' rights in terms of pensions, sick pay, holiday pay, etc.

Extra activities 4.2

A This activity gives further practice with vocabulary from the reading. Get students to complete the exercise individually and then check their answers in pairs before class feedback.

> **1** c **2** b **3** a **4** c **5** a **6** b **7** a **8** b **9** b **10** a
> **11** c **12** c

Grammar: Present Simple and Past Simple passive

Students learn how to use passives.

5A Get students to do this individually, then check answers in pairs. After eliciting the answers, write the forms on the board.

> **1** Present Simple passive   **2** Past Simple passive

5B Do this as a quick whole-class activity.

> In sentence 1, the agent is mentioned and *by* indicates it.

6 Refer students to the Grammar reference on page 121. Give them a few minutes to do the exercise individually. Monitor and if students are struggling with any of the items, write them on the board and go through them with the whole class.

1 are made 2 are delivered 3 is painted
4 is not recommended 5 ship 6 are printed
7 (are) dispatched 8 select 9 require 10 are designed
11 packed 12 are needed

7A Explain that these sentences give information about the websites students have been talking about, but that some of the information is not true. In Exercise 7B, students will correct the false statements.

1 was set up 2 are not charged 3 is based
4 are not allowed 5 are owned 6 was created, was called 7 was bought 8 is needed

7B Do the exercise as a class to see how much students know about these companies. Students can check their own answers on page 129.

1 T
2 F – If your item sells, eBay charges 9 percent of the selling price to a maximum of $50.00. Alibaba charges a commission of 2–5 percent for each transaction.
3 T
4 F – Hotels are allowed to list on Airbnb as long as they don't hide the fact.
5 T
6 T
7 F – eBay does not belong to Google.
8 T (It currently costs $0.20 to publish a listing to the marketplace. A listing lasts for four months or until the item is sold.)

Extra activities 4.2

B This activity gives further practice with the Present and Past Simple passive. There are two parts to the exercise. First, get students to complete the questions individually. Then get them to answer the questions as pairs. Check answers with the whole class.

1 are, assembled 2 are estimated 3 was, founded
4 are employed 5 is, based 6 are sold
1 a (Most of Apple's iPhones are assembled in Shenzhen, China by contractors Foxconn.)
2 c (And it is rising.)
3 b (In 2016 Amazon was the world's largest e-commerce company by revenue.)
4 c
5 c (It is the largest e-commerce site in Japan and among the world's largest by sales.)
6 b

Writing

Students write a description of a product they could make and sell online to become a sofapreneur.

8 Put student in pairs. Encourage them to draw a picture or include a photo of their product with the description. If they need inspiration, get them to look at etsy.com or a similar site. During the activity, monitor and help as necessary.

Model answer

These handmade multi-coloured cushion covers were inspired by my children's drawings. There are three patterns: birds, leaves and butterflies. The covers are made of high-quality 100 percent cotton. They are printed on one side only. The back of the cover is a light grey colour. Available in three sizes: 40x40, 45x45 and 50x50 cm. Handwash in cold water with mild detergent. Orders are dispatched on the same day as payment is received.

Teacher's resources: Teacher's resources: extra activities
Grammar reference: p.121 Present Simple and Past Simple passive
Teacher's book: Resource bank Photocopiable 4.2 p.139
Workbook: p.20 Exercises 1–3, p.21 Exercises 1–3

4.3 › Communication skills
Managing conversations

GSE learning objectives

- Can extract key details from conversations beween colleagues about familiar topics.
- Can infer speakers' opinions in conversations on familiar everyday topics.
- Can give or seek personal views and opinions in discussing topics of interest.
- Can respond to opinions expressed by others.
- Can respond to interruptions in a meeting using fixed expressions.

Warm-up

Write *multitasking* on the board and teach or elicit the meaning (doing several things at one time. Ask: *Who in this class multitasks?* and elicit a show of hands. Then ask students who raised their hand to give examples of the things they do when they multitask.

Lead-in

Students explore ways of changing topic and staying on track in meetings.

1A Teach or elicit the meaning of *national culture* (the customs and traditions of a country). Put students in small groups to discuss the five differences. Ask a few groups to share with the class the things they discussed.

1B Do this exercise in small groups or, as a class.

Video

Students watch a video about the importance of changing topic and staying on track.

2A ▶ 4.3.1 In the first sequence, we see Beata talking with Alex about Beata's forthcoming trip to Brazil. Before playing the video, go over the questions with the class so they know what to listen for. Teach or elicit the meaning of the two expressions: *He/She likes the sound of his/her own voice.* (He/She talks a lot and is very confident.) and *He/She goes with the flow.* (He/She is very relaxed and does whatever is the easiest.) Then play the video. Answer the questions as a class.

1 Yes, he has.
2 He has met him twice, on trips with Daniel.
3 He means that Mateo likes to talk about other topics.
4 She has done some background reading.
5 He says that Mateo likes the sound of his own voice and can be domineering at times. He tells her that the trip will be just like any other trip. He also warns her that Mateo likes to multitask. He suggests she 'goes with the flow'.

2B ▶ 4.3.1 Ask the question in the rubric. If students know the answer, play the video for them to check that they are right. If not, play it for them to find the answer. Check as a class.

> She feels it may be difficult and that there won't be enough time to learn about the market, get to know Mateo and establish a good working relationship.

3A Explain the idea of Beata having two options when she meets Mateo and go through the details of Options A and B with the class. Make it clear to students that they can choose which option they want to see first on the video. Put students in small groups and ask them to discuss the two options, giving reasons for their answers. Elicit ideas from a few groups and as a class, decide which video to watch first.

3B ▶ 4.3.2 ▶ 4.3.3 Ask the class to answer the questions for Option A or B depending on their choice, and play the video. You could ask students to discuss the questions in their groups first, and then check the answers as a whole class. Do the same for the second video.

> **Option A**
> 4 We see him take a phone call during the meeting.
> 1 They talk about family and Mateo's previous trips to Poland.
> 2 She tries to change the subject at every chance she gets.
> 3 He ignores them or tells her they will discuss the Diabsensor later.
> 5 She does not manage to get Mateo to talk about the Diabsensor.
>
> **Option B**
> 4 We see him take a phone call during the meeting.
> 1 They talk about family and Mateo's previous trips to Poland.
> 2 She answers his questions and asks her own.
> 3 No, she doesn't. She goes with the flow and waits for Mateo to turn the discussion towards the Diabsensor.
> 5 She goes with the flow. She does not try to get Mateo to talk about the Diabsensor.

4 Put students in pairs and give them 3–4 minutes to discuss the questions while you monitor and help as necessary.

> **Possible answers**
> 1 Beata does not get to discuss her agenda. Beata might build a better relationship with Mateo.
> 2 Beata's attempts to bring the conversation back to the Diabsensor affected the relationship. Mateo seems to be less friendly towards Beata in Option A than in Option B.

5 ▶ 4.3.4 Students should do this in the same pairs as Exercise 4. Explain that they are going to watch another video, which is a summary of the ideas they looked at in the previous videos. Play the video and give students 3–4 minutes to discuss and make notes, then discuss the main learning points with the whole class.

> **Possible answer**
> Going with the flow might help build a better relationship with the business partner, but will take more time, whereas focusing on the task might save time, but may affect the relationship.

Reflection

Students reflect on the conclusions from the video and discuss their own skills of changing topic and staying on track.

6 Allow students to work individually on this so that they can reflect on their own preferences and ideas. Ask them to think of their own answers to the questions and to make notes. Then put students in pairs to discuss their answers. Get brief feedback from the class.

Functional language: Changing the subject and staying on track

Students look at questions and statements that are commonly used to change the topic of a conversation or to stay on topic.

7 Explain that this exercise highlights phrases from the video that we use to change the subject and stay on track. Ask students to do the exercise in pairs, then check answers as a class.

> **1** S **2** C **3** C **4** S **5** C **6** S **7** C **8** C

8 Give students time to fill in the gaps individually. Then put them in pairs to practise reading the conversation. After reading through it once, encourage them to try to say it more naturally, looking down but not speaking when they read, then saying the conversation out loud, but not reading at the same time.

> 1 can we move to
> 2 this a good moment to start talking about the
> 3 get to the
> 4 in a moment
> 5 reminds me
> 6 will be plenty of time for that later

9A Tell students that they are going to build up a conversation from some basic information that they will be given and the phrases from Exercise 7. After students have chosen which scenario they want to practise, tell them to work together to make notes for each speaker before they do the roleplay. During the activity, monitor and help as necessary.

9B Students now work in pairs to complete the exercise, this time trying to make the language in the dialogue as accurate and correct as possible. Monitor and help as necessary.

Extra activities 4.3

A This activity gives practice of the language of changing the subject and staying on track. Ask students to complete the exercise individually, then check answers in pairs.

1 That ~~remind~~ **reminds** me.
2 Can we ~~moved~~ **move** to the next item on the agenda?
3 ~~That~~ **There** will be plenty of time for that later.
4 Is this **a** good moment to start talking about the delivery schedule?
5 We'll get to the details in ~~the~~ **a** moment.
6 I really think we should get ~~on~~ **to** the next point now.
7 Before I ~~forgot~~ **forget**, let me tell you what happened to Mike this morning.

B This activity gives practice of the language in the video script. Ask students to write the sentences with errors individually first, then swap sentences with a partner.

❯ **Pronunciation bank**
p.115: Pronunciation of -(e)s endings

Warm-up
Write *pen* and *lunch* on the board. Ask: *What's the plural?* (*pens, lunches*) and write the words on the board. Ask: *Which word has two syllables?* (*lunches*) Refer students to the explanation in the box and drill *go – goes* and *age – ages*.

1 Get students to do the exercise in pairs. Do not confirm answers yet as students will check them in the next exercise.

extra syllable: bus → buses, choice → choices, manage → manages, office → offices
no extra syllable: agenda → agendas, client → clients, decide → decides, talk → talks

2 ◀) P4.01 Play the recording for students to check answers. Then play it again so they can listen and repeat.

3 Students do the exercise in pairs. During the activity, monitor and help as necessary. Ask a few pairs to share one or two of their sentences.

Task

Students roleplay a scenario where they have a meeting to discuss an app that a supplier has just produced.

10A Put students in pairs and ask them to read the scenario and choose roles. Refer Student S to page 128 and Student C to page 131. Answer any questions they may have.

10B Get students to have their meeting. During the activity, monitor and help as necessary. Remind them to use phrases from Exercise 7.

10C Students do this in their pairs first, then with another pair, in groups of four. Tell students to discuss the language they used and what, if anything, they found difficult. After a couple of minutes, ask a few groups to share their ideas, and find out if there were similar challenges for everyone.

10D Students form new pairs. During the activity, monitor and help as necessary. Round off the task by asking how students will handle interruptions in the future.

MyEnglishLab: Teacher's resources: extra activities; Interactive video activities
Pronunciation bank: p.115 Pronunciation of -(e)s endings
Workbook: p.22 Exercise 1

4.4 ❯ Business skills
Building consensus

GSE learning objectives

- Can extract key details from a presentation if delivered slowly and clearly.
- Can derive the probable meaning of simple unknown words from short, familiar contexts.
- Can express belief, opinion, agreement and disagreement politely.
- Can express attitude and agreement with *agree/think* (*that*) + complement clause.
- Can use language related to agreement or disagreement.
- Can make and respond to suggestions.

Warm-up
Think of a question that not everyone in the class will agree on the answer to (e.g. *Who thinks football is the best sport? What about basketball? What about tennis?*). Ask for a show of hands, identify a majority and say: *Ten people think football is the best, five think it's basketball and only two say tennis. So, the majority of people like football.* 'Majority' means 'the most'. It's an important idea when groups of people are trying to make a decision.

Lead-in

Students discuss the challenges of building consensus.

1 Put students in small groups and ask them to complete the exercise. Ask groups to share answers with the class.

Listening

Students listen to a manager running a meeting about how to build consensus.

2 ◀) 4.01 Tell students they are going to listen to a manager leading a meeting with some employees. Tell them to read the two questions first, so they know what they are listening for. Get students to do the exercise individually, then compare answers in pairs.

1 The speaker aims to focus on ways of building consensus.
2 finding what the group wants to do, not what each individual wants to do

3 🔊 4.01 Get students to read the sentences. Teach or elicit the meaning of *of equal weight* (the same importance). Get them to do the exercise individually, then play the recording again. Check answers as a class.

1 involved, chance 2 respected, important

4 🔊 4.02 Tell students that they are going to listen to the next part of the meeting. Focus their attention on the question, then play the recording.

Possible answer

They haven't reached a consensus. The manager says, 'So we are already narrowing down the options and moving towards consensus. Not everybody has spoken, so I would like to hear what the rest of us have to say.'

5 🔊 4.02 Get students to read the questions so they know what they are listening for. With stronger groups, you might try to elicit some answers before playing the recording again. Go over the answers with the class.

1 staying as one large group, breaking into small groups, working in pairs
2 a way of controlling who speaks
3 The manager uses *process* to talk about 'how' they achieve consensus.
4 The manager uses *narrowing down* to mean 'getting closer to consensus by removing one of the options'.

Extra activities 4.4

A This activity practises some of the expressions from the recording. Get students to complete the exercise individually, then check answers in pairs before class feedback.

1 building consensus 2 middle ground
3 talking sticks 4 equal weight 5 meet halfway

Functional language: Reaching agreement

Students practise using expressions for reaching agreement.

6 🔊 4.02 Explain to students that this is part of the conversation they just listened to. Go through the first two lines, which are already numbered 1 and 2, showing how the second line follows naturally from the first, while none of the other lines do. Elicit the third line (*Tanya: I'm afraid I disagree. …*). Get students to do the exercise individually, then play the recording so they can check their answers

1 **Manager:** Yes, Jose? What do you think?
3 **Tanya:** I'm afraid I disagree. It will be much better in smaller groups. That way everyone gets much more talking time.
5 **Dorothy:** Yes, I agree, too. We can be much more efficient if we work in small groups.
11 **Dorothy:** So we need to find consensus about the number of sticks before we can even start a real discussion?
6 **Jose:** Well, I don't think my idea is that bad. I agree that in a big group one or two people could dominate, but that is easy to fix. We use talking sticks.
2 **Jose:** So I think we should stay as one big group. There are not so many of us, and it will be easy for everyone to be heard.
8 **Jose:** Each person has two sticks. This gives them the right to talk twice. Each time they say something, they must give up a stick. When they have no more sticks, they cannot talk. That way everyone has the same chance.
10 **Jose:** That was just an example. Of course we need to decide how many sticks to use.
4 **Sam:** I agree with Tanya. Much better. With a big group one or two people always dominate.
7 **Sam:** What are talking sticks?
9 **Sam:** Actually that's not a bad idea. But we will need more than two sticks.

7A Point out the phrases in bold in the conversation in Exercise 6. Explain that each phrase belongs in one of the four categories in the table. Get students to do the exercise individually. Then check answers with the whole class.

Expressing agreement: Yes, I agree too., I agree that, I agree with
Expressing disagreement: I'm afraid I disagree.
Making a suggestion: I think we should
Reacting to a suggestion: So we need to, I don't think, that's not a bad idea

7B Get students to do the exercise individually, then check answers in pairs.

Expressing agreement: 1
Expressing disagreement: 2, 5
Making a suggestion: 3, 6
Reacting to a suggestion: 4

Extra activities 4.4

B This exercise gives more practice in the language of reaching consensus. Get students to do it quickly, then check answers in pairs.

1 e 2 a 3 f 4 c 5 b 6 d

Pronunciation bank
p.115: Consonant–vowel linking between words

Warm-up

Write *his office* on the board. Get students to say it a couple of times. Ask: *What do you notice about the two words when you say them quickly?* (They join together.) Refer students to the explanation in the box.

1 ◆ P 4.02   Do the exercise as a class.

2 Get students to do the exercise in pairs.

> 1 meet_again next week
> 2 just_an_example
> 3 not_a bad_idea
> 4 I'm_afraid_I disagree
> 5 I want to remind_everybody
> 6 decide_as_a group
> 7 listed_on the board
> 8 narrow it down_if possible

3 ◆ P 4.03   Keep students in pairs and play the recording for them to listen and check, and then again to listen and repeat.

4 Get students to do the exercise in pairs. Walk round and monitor to check that students are linking the consonants and vowels correctly.

Task

Students choose a topic to discuss and try to reach agreement.

8A Put the class in groups of three or four and ask them to read the three topics and, as a group, to choose one they are interested in talking about, or they could come up with their own. Teach or elicit the meaning in this context of *maximum* (the greatest number) and *minimum* (the smallest number). Give them 3–4 minutes to make some notes individually about their ideas for the topic they have chosen.

8B Ask students to follow the four steps during their discussion. To check comprehension, ask: *What do you do when you aren't speaking?* (listen and make notes) *What will you list on the board?* (everyone's preferences) Get them to start talking. During the activity, monitor and help as necessary. If groups are slow to reach consensus, give them a time limit, maybe 2–3 more minutes. End the exercise when most of the groups have reached agreement.

8C Get the groups to discuss questions 1–4 and then to share answers with the class.

MyEnglishLab: Teacher's resources: extra activities; Functional language bank

Pronunciation bank: p.115 Consonant–vowel linking between words

Workbook: p.22 Exercise 2

4.5 ❯ Writing
Letter confirming an order

> **GSE learning objectives**
>
> Can write a simple email requesting work-related information, emphasising the most important points.

> **Warm-up**
>
> Write *confirmation* on the board and teach or elicit the meaning (making sure that something is true or correct). Ask: *When do you usually receive confirmation?* (when you book a hotel or flight, when you order something online, etc.) *What information does a confirmation usually contain?* (key information like time, date, place, cost and so on)

Lead-in

Students read and complete an order confirmation letter.

1 Before students complete the exercise, ask this question and tell them to find the answers in the letter: *What information does the letter confirm?* (the item that was ordered, the delivery schedule, the price including discount) Teach or elicit the meaning of *hesitate* (wait before doing something). Get students to do the exercise in pairs, then check answers as a class.

> 1 order 2 received 3 agreed 4 Payment 5 enclose
> 6 thank 7 hesitate 8 sincerely

Functional language

Students look at the language of confirming an order.

2 Tell students that you are now going to look closely at the language for writing an order confirmation. Teach or elicit the meaning of *attached* (connected to an email so that you can send them together), *enclosed* (included inside an envelope as well as a letter) and *enclosures* (other information or paperwork that is sent in the same envelope with the letter). Get them to do the exercise in pairs. During the activity, monitor and help as necessary. Some terms may need to be explained: *cash on delivery* (goods must be paid for immediately), *payment in advance* (goods must be paid for before they are delivered), *details of our new range are enclosed* (with this letter we have included information about our new products), *Yours faithfully* (a standard formal way to close a letter – see Notes on the next page).

> *Notes*
>
> When you do not know the name of the person you are writing to, you begin your letter with *Dear Sir/ Madam* and close with *Yours faithfully*. When you write to someone by name, you close your letter with *Yours sincerely*.

Greeting: Dear Mr Chahal, Dear Sir/Madam

Opening: we are writing to you to confirm your order; this is to confirm your order; we are pleased to confirm your order

Order details: order number 674190 for 1,000 123/XC units a week for 12 weeks; order no 01 for five chairs

Delivery details: to your factory in Mumbai; the first delivery will be on 05/11; we will deliver the goods to your head office

Payment terms: Payment terms are $4,000 monthly; 30 days after the date of the invoice; cash on delivery; payment in advance

Enclosures: We enclose full terms and conditions for your records; details of our new range are enclosed

Ending: We thank you for your business and look forward to working with you. If you have any queries, please do not hesitate to contact us; we look forward to supplying you again in the future

Closing: Yours sincerely, Yours faithfully

Extra activities 4.5

A This activity gives further practice of phrases to use in a confirmation letter. Elicit or explain the meaning of *unit* (one of a particular thing – so an order of fifty chairs would be fifty units). Get students to complete the exercise individually and then get them to check answers in pairs before class feedback.

1 Dear 2 writing 3 discussed 4 confirm 5 price
6 of 7 terms 8 enclose 9 appreciate 10 queries
11 sincerely

Optional grammar work

The letter in Exercise 1 contains examples of verbs + prepositions, so you could use it for some optional grammar work. Refer students to the Grammar reference on page 121 and use the exercises in MyEnglishLab for extra grammar practice.

Task

Students assess an order confirmation letter and then write their own.

3A Put students in pairs and refer them to the letter on page 129. Get them to read through the letter. Ask: *How is it different from the examples we've looked at?* (It doesn't use formal language. It doesn't contain specific information.) Get them to discuss specific ways to improve it.

3B Get students to look at the order form on page 130. Set a time limit for the writing task and remind students to use the language in Exercise 2 and the information in the order form. Students can write their letters individually and then come back together for Exercise 3C. Alternatively, they can write their emails in pairs and then work with a different partner for Exercise 3C.

Model answer

Dear Ms Liang,

We are writing to confirm your order number WT3488 for 100 PR765 printers, which we received this morning. The unit price of the printers is €230. I am pleased to confirm that, as we agreed at our meeting last week, there is a discount of 8 percent for any orders over 80 units. We will deliver the goods to your warehouse in Felton Business Park on 5 May.

We confirm that our payment terms are 30 days after the date of the invoice. We enclose our business terms and conditions for your records.

We thank you for your business and look forward to supplying you again in the future.

If you have any queries, please do not hesitate to contact us.

3C If students wrote their letters in pairs, put them in new pairs for this exercise. If they did the writing task individually, put them in the same pairs as Exercise 3A. Get them to exchange letters and discuss the questions. During the activity, monitor and help as necessary.

MyEnglishLab: Teacher's resources: extra activities; Interactive grammar practice; Writing bank
Grammar reference: p.121 Verbs + prepositions
Workbook: p.23 Exercises 1 and 2

Business workshop ❯4
Hand-made

GSE learning objectives

- Can follow the main points in a simple audio recording aimed at a general audience.
- Can extract the key details from a presentation if delivered slowly and clearly.
- Can express limited opinions and arguments during work-related meetings.
- Can convey simple information of immediate relevance and emphasise the main point.

Background

Students read about a small but growing skincare cream maker.

1 Ask students to read the background and discuss the questions in pairs. Check answers with the class. Students may want to know the meaning of *essential oil* (a liquid made from a plant, usually with a strong, pleasant smell).

1 skincare creams for sensitive skin types
2 Isabella Barco because she couldn't find suitable products for her sensitive skin
3 friends and mothers of friends
4 HappyPure may go global
5 Students' own answers

Going global – what you need to know

Students listen to a supply chain management expert talk about key factors for going global with a small business.

2A 🔊 BW 4.01 Write *supply chain* on the board and ask students if they can explain what it is (the steps and processes necessary to make a product and deliver it to consumers). Call their attention to the items in the box and make sure they understand *cross-cultural problems* (communication challenges or difficulties caused when people from different countries work together, as a result of different styles of thinking, ways of doing things or ideas about what is 'normal'). Play the recording, then check answers with the class.

> keeping costs low, customer service

2B 🔊 BW 4.01 For stronger classes, ask students to try to complete the exercise before listening again. Otherwise, play the recording and ask students to complete the notes. Check answers with the class.

> **1** effective **2** too long **3** existing

3A 🔊 BW 4.02 Tell students they are going to listen to more information about supply chains. Explain or elicit the meaning of *tumble dryer* (a machine that uses hot air to dry laundry). Play the recording, then check answers with the class.

> **1** because it was discovered in some food products in the UK, which caused a scandal
> **2** It started in a garage.

3B 🔊 BW 4.02 Get students to read through the notes so they know what they are listening for. Teach or elicit the meaning of *currency* (type of money, e.g. U.S. dollar, Japanese yen, euro). Play the recording again. Students complete the exercise individually, then check answers in pairs.

> **1** distribution **2** stock **3** trading **4** quality
> **5** organised

Extra activities Business workshop 4

A 🔊 BW 4.01 In this activity, students will listen more closely to what Greg says. Play the recording and get them to complete the exercise. Check answers with the class.

> **1** F **2** T **3** F **4** F **5** T **6** T **7** F **8** T

Supply chain

Students listen to an expert talking about supply chains.

4A 🔊 BW 4.03 Tell students a bit about supply chains (see Notes below). Get them to look at the two models. Ask: *What is at the beginning of a supply chain, on the left?* Teach or elicit *raw materials* (the things the product is made from – steel, for example, is made from iron ore, which comes from a mine). Ask: *What is at the end of a supply chain, on the right?* (consumers – people who buy and use products) Play the recording, then check answers with the class.

Notes

The supply chain is relevant for many different businesses and is something which can make or break a company. Failings along the chain could lose the business customers and credibility. The diagrams in the book show a very simple supply chain first – one that only involves a few people right at the beginning of a business's life, while the second one is slightly more complex as more people are involved. Bigger companies sometimes have very complex supply chains.

> **1** supplier **2** farmer **3** retailer **4** customers
> **5** neighbours **6** suppliers **7** distribution **8** wholesaler
> **9** shops **10** consumer

4B Teach or elicit the meaning of *stock* (the supply of a product, or something you use to make a product). Put students in small groups and get them to do the exercise. During the activity, monitor and help as necessary. Discuss the answers as a class.

Possible answers

> **1** warehouse (poor organisation,) distribution (not enough trucks), manufacturer (can't get supplies to produce enough, not enough production capacity, staffing issues), supplier (can't supply enough raw material)
> **2** supplier (inferior quality materials), manufacturer (problem on production line, poor quality control)
> **3** supplier (can't supply materials), manufacturer (problems with equipment or staff)
> **4** supplier (raw material prices increased), manufacturer (staffing costs increased), warehousing and distribution (staffing or premises costs increased, transportation – fuel costs increased), wholesaler (wants bigger profit margin)
> **5** wholesaler and distribution (not enough stock, late deliveries), retailer (not enough retailers stocking product)
> **6** warehouse and distribution (poor communication and organisation, low stock levels)

Market research

Students discuss market research for HappyPure skincare products.

5 Put students in pairs. As they are discussing the question, monitor and help as necessary. Get a few pairs to share their ideas with the class.

6 Explain that students are going to plan market research for HappyPure, Isabella Barco's company, as it prepares to go global. Get them to complete the exercise in small groups. If you have enough board space, get them to stand up and write their additional ideas on the board, then go over the lists with the whole class.

Possible additional ideas

> what customers want from a face cream, competitors, branding, visit the country, find out more about the culture

Task: Choose a market for a global strategy

Students read about Russia and India and decide which market would be best for HappyPure.

7A Put stronger classes in pairs and weaker classes in groups of 4–6. Students working in pairs each take a role: Student A or Student B. For students working in groups, assign half of each group either Group A or Group B. Explain the task. Refer them to the research notes on two possible markets for HappyPure on page 135 (India) and 136 (Russia). Check that students understand the task. First, each student/group reads their information. Then they work through the four bullet points in the exercise. With weaker groups, you could have the whole class work on a single bullet point at a time and note a few main ideas from each point on the board. Allow stronger classes to work at their own pace. As they work, monitor and help as necessary.

7B Explain that students are now going to have a meeting to create a marketing strategy for HappyPure. Remind students of the meaning of *agenda* (a plan for a meeting) and call their attention to the agenda on the page. Teach or elicit the meaning of *branding* (the process of creating a name and image for a product). Give students 6–8 minutes to hold their meeting. During the activity, monitor and help as necessary.

7C Groups take turns to present their ideas to each other. Ask a few groups to share a couple of their ideas with the class.

Extra activities Business workshop 4

B This activity is based on a summary of a meeting about the Russian and Indian markets. It acts as a model or a follow-up to the meetings that students hold in Exercise 7B and gives more practice with the language of global marketing. Assign this as homework or, if you have time, do it in class.

1 detail 2 added 3 discussion 4 focus 5 order
6 make 7 Increased 8 Consequently 9 strategy
10 meet 11 range 12 competitors 13 brand
14 review 15 target

MyEnglishLab: Teacher's resources: extra activities

Review ◀ 4

1 1 target territories 2 marketing strategy 3 luxury goods 4 local preferences 5 consumer brand
2 1 consumption 2 specialise 3 preferable 4 standardise 5 growth
3 1 are sold 2 was founded 3 were employed 4 was expanded 5 was built 6 were, exported 7 were shipped 8 were opened 9 are employed 10 is produced
4 1 wonder if we could 2 a good moment 3 come to that 4 reminds me 5 I forget
5 1 should 2 with 3 don't 4 bad 5 sure 6 about
6 1 This 2 deliver 3 unit 4 discount 5 payment 6 enclose 7 thank 8 supplying 9 queries 10 hesitate

Design and innovation

Unit overview

	CLASSWORK	FURTHER WORK
5.1 › Innovative product design	**Lead-in** Students discuss their lunchtime habits. **Video** Students watch a video about a new type of restaurant in San Francisco. **Vocabulary** Students look at vocabulary for discussing and describing developments in technology. **Project** Students think about how businesses could use technology to change the way they work.	**MyEnglishLab:** Teacher's resources extra activities; Reading bank **Pronunciation bank:** p.116 Numbers of syllables in words **Teacher's book:** Resource bank Photocopiable 5.1 p.140 **Workbook:** p.24 Exercises 1–3
5.2 › Product testing	**Lead-in** Students discuss products and the job of product testing. **Reading** Students read and discuss an article in which a video games tester explains how he got his job and what it is like playing games for a living. **Grammar** Students learn how to talk about things that have and have not happened. **Speaking** Students talk about their day.	**MyEnglishLab:** Teacher's resources: extra activities **Grammar reference:** p.122 Present Perfect Simple with *just*, *already* and *yet* **Pronunciation bank:** p.116 Contrastive stress **Teacher's book:** Resource bank Photocopiable 5.2 p.141 **Workbook:** p.25 Exercises 1–3, p.26 Exercises 1 and 2
5.3 › Communication skills: Managing information	**Lead-in** Students explore ways of asking for information. **Video** Students watch a video about the importance of asking for information. **Reflection** Students reflect on the conclusions from the video and discuss their own ability to manage information and ask questions. **Functional language** Students look at how to ask questions to get short, simple answers and questions where there are many possible answers. **Task** Students roleplay a scenario where they have to give each other feedback on their presentation skills.	**MyEnglishLab:** Teacher's resources: extra activities; Interactive video activities **Workbook:** p.27 Exercise 1
5.4 › Business skills: Selling a product	**Lead-in** Students look at the language we use to describe the features and benefits of a product. **Listening** Students listen to two sales representatives describing a product. **Functional language** Students look at useful phrases for talking about products and what they can do. **Task** Students research a product and describe its features and benefits.	**MyEnglishLab:** Teacher's resources: extra activities; Functional language bank **Workbook:** p.27 Exercise 2
5.5 › Writing: Product review	**Lead-in** Students read and complete a product review. **Functional language** Students look at language that is commonly used in product reviews. **Task** Students read and improve a product review and then write a review of a product they have recently bought.	**MyEnglishLab:** Teacher's resources: extra activities; Interactive grammar practice; Writing bank **Grammar reference:** p.122 Order of adjectives before nouns **Workbook:** p.28 Exercises 1 and 2
Business workshop 5 › Smart fabric	**Reading** Students read texts about market research. **Listening** Students listen to conversations about product development and marketing. **Task** Students choose a product to develop.	**MyEnglishLab:** Teacher's resources: extra activities

Business brief

The main aim of this unit is to introduce students to the concepts of **design** and **innovation**. Design, which is a part of almost every industry and field of business, is the creation of a plan for an object, system or even a human interaction. Examples include plans for machines, buildings, roads, electrical networks, computer user interfaces, clothes, corporate identities, business processes and many, many others. Innovation in a business context means creating or improving processes and products to improve quality, shorten production schedules, lower costs or respond to changes in markets.

The traditional design process has four main stages:

1 **Pre-production design:** In this stage, a **design brief** sets out the goals of the project. **Research** may be carried out into similar designs and into the market, and a **specification** – a list of details of the design – will be started. Generally, this stage will result in a **design presentation**, in which the work so far is presented to **stakeholders** (people who have a financial interest in the project).

2 **Design during production:** This is the stage where **product development** and **testing** take place. Often, a **prototype** or series of prototypes will be created, tested and improved upon. At the end of this stage, the product (or service) will be produced and introduced into the market.

3 **Post-production design feedback:** After the design has been used for its intended purpose, the designers will evaluate its performance, often with the input of **end users**. Any **constructive criticism** will be taken on board for future improvements.

4 **Re-design:** In this stage, any or all of the above three stages are repeated, with changes or improvements made as necessary.

The traditional model is not the only approach, however. Many companies and designers do not actually work this way. Computer software developers often use an approach called **agile software development**, where the final design of a product **emerges** over time through the collaboration of **cross-functional teams** – groups of people from different disciplines who are all working towards the same goal. For example, when developing a smartphone game, game designers decide how the game works and develop the concept, software engineers write computer code to make the game function, and artists provide the characters or other visual elements. Where the traditional model identifies the problems and solution in step 1 and then works in a linear way, the agile model encourages design solutions to **evolve** and to be responsive to change. That means that if the game designers decide to introduce a new element to the game after several months of testing and development, the software engineers need to make it work and the artists need to provide additional visual material.

In business, innovation and design are often directly related to marketing. The promise of success in the market is the only reason it makes sense to spend money designing a product. One traditional model of marketing is the **4 Ps** – product, price, promotion and place. The first two, product and price, are major considerations of the design process: what are we making and how much will consumers be willing to pay for it? A similar marketing model is the **4 Cs** – consumer, cost, communication and convenience. This model places slightly more emphasis on the consumer and less on the product itself.

Design and innovation and your students

Design and innovation are fundamental concepts in all areas of business. No matter where your learners are working or intend to work, they will find an understanding of the basic concepts of design and innovation – and the ability to speak about them – useful.

Unit lead-in

Elicit a brief description of the photo. Ask: *What year do you think the photo was taken?* Elicit answers, then explain that the photo was taken around 1910, but that the exact place and date are unknown. It shows a triplane – a plane with three wings – and was first published in *Berliner Illustrirte Zeitung* in Germany in November 1910. Look at the quote with the class. Ask: *How have designers made airplanes better since 1910?* (They are safer; they are larger so they can carry more people and things; they are faster.) *How do you think designers will improve airplanes in the future?* (They will use less fuel; they will travel further and faster; they may take passengers to space.) If you want to broaden the discussion, ask students for ideas of things that have improved over time, e.g. cars, phones, houses.

5.1 ❯ Innovative product design

GSE learning objectives

- Can follow the main points in TV programmes on familiar topics if delivered in clear standard speech.
- Can identify a simple chronological sequence in a recorded narrative or dialogue.
- Can give straightforward descriptions on a variety of familiar subjects.
- Can make and respond to suggestions.

Warm-up

Write *design* on the board. Say: *Design is a noun and also a verb.* Teach or elicit the meaning of the verb (make a drawing or plan of something that will be made or built; plan or develop something for a specific purpose). Ask: *What kinds of thing do people design?* (The list is endless. A few ideas: buildings, computers, cars, roads, books, furniture – almost any object we can put our hands on in modern life, but also interactions, such as the way a computer and its user interact.) Then teach or elicit the meaning of the noun (a plan, e.g. a set of drawings showing how a house will be made, but also the way something looks: *This chair has an unusual design.*). Ask: *What things do you know of that have a nice or interesting design?* (Accept and discuss any reasonable answers.)

Lead-in

Students discuss their lunchtime habits.

1A Explain that this lesson is about how technology is changing our eating habits in some parts of the world. Get students to read through the statements, then do the exercise.

1B Students do the exercise. You could quickly say just the item numbers and ask students to raise their hands for each item they ticked, to see if there is a most popular answer.

Video

Students watch a video about a new type of restaurant in San Francisco.

2A Draw students' attention to the photos. At this point, accept and discuss any reasonable suggestions. Eatsa is a cafeteria (see Notes below).

Notes

A cafeteria is a restaurant where customers serve themselves from a choice of food at a counter and pay before eating. This sort of food service is common inside office buildings and factories around the world, and has the advantage of offering both speed and choice.

Possible answer

They use a computer to order their food; they don't talk to anyone. They pick up their food when it's ready by opening a small door.

2B ▶ 5.1.1 For more advanced classes, get students to read the question and the statements in Exercise 3 before watching the video. Then get them to do both exercises and watch the video again to check their answers. For other classes, just play the video for them to check their answers to Exercise 2A.

Possible answers

Eatsa customers don't order their food from people, and people don't bring the food to the table. The customers don't see the people who prepare the food. The food is prepared more quickly than the food in a traditional restaurant. In a traditional cafeteria, food is often served by staff and customers' money is usually taken by a person.

3 ▶ 5.1.1 Teach or elicit the meaning of *accurate* (correct; as expected, needed or requested), *cashier* (a person whose job is taking your money when you pay in a shop or restaurant). Get students to read through the questions and answer any they can. Then play the video as students complete the exercise.

1 T
2 F – The order is prepared by chefs.
3 F – less than two minutes
4 T
5 F – He's not sure it's the best thing.
6 T
7 T
8 F – They aren't as 'designed' – they use machines for ordering and a system with tickets.

4 ▶ 5.1.1 Teach or elicit the meaning of *consumer* (someone who buys and uses products and services), *patience* (the ability to continue waiting or doing something for a long time without becoming angry or anxious), *unprecedented* (never having happened before) and *precise* (exact, clear and correct). Get students to do the exercise individually, then check answers as a class by watching 00:14–00:41 in the video again.

a 3 **b** 5 **c** 1 **d** 2 **e** 6 **f** 4

5A Get students to do this exercise in pairs. If you have enough board space, get pairs to think about and discuss their answers, then write them on the board. During the activity, monitor and help as necessary. Then go over the answers as a class.

> **Possible answers**
> **Positive:** *fast*, order is correct, you don't have to talk to a person, gives people new jobs
> **Negative:** *no human contact*, inconvenient if something goes wrong, you can't make special requests

5B This can be a quick whole-class question. Get a few students to share their answers with the class.

> **Extra activities 5.1**
>
> **A** ▶ 5.1.1 This activity gives further practice of key vocabulary and main ideas from the video. Ask students to complete it individually, then check answers with the class. Alternatively, play the video for students to check their answers individually.
>
> > **1** f **2** a **3** g **4** c **5** h **6** b **7** e **8** d
>
> **B** Get students to do this individually, as a quick vocabulary quiz. You could get them to compare answers in pairs before checking answers with the class.
>
> > **1** fully automated restaurant **2** computer store
> > **3** touch-screen menu **4** freshly made meals
> > **5** lunch hour **6** quick, healthy lunch
> > **7** social interaction

Vocabulary: Technological innovation

Students look at vocabulary for discussing and describing developments in technology.

6 In the video, Mike Peng says that ordering food through an app *is really gonna disrupt the current food business today*. Mike is referring to a current business buzzword: *disruptive innovation* (see Notes below). Get students to do the exercise individually, then check answers in pairs. Encourage them to use a dictionary if necessary.

> *Notes*
>
> The term *disruptive innovation* was coined by business expert Clayton Christensen in his 1997 book *The Innovator's Dilemma*. It refers to innovations that quickly change traditional ways of doing business. One example is the way ride-sharing apps have changed the taxi business. Where taxis in many place have traditionally been driven by professional drivers working for taxi companies, ride-sharing apps allow anyone with a car to carry passengers. Shared rides are generally cheaper than traditional taxis, so ride-share apps have taken market share away from taxi companies.

> **1** innovation **2** disrupt **3** interact **4** automated
> **5** swipe **6** customise **7** place **8** choice **9** magical

Describing innovative products

7A Make sure that students use their dictionaries to check the meaning of any terms they do not understand. Get them to do the exercise individually, then check answers in pairs.

> **1** e **2** b **3** a **4** c **5** d **6** h **7** f **8** i **9** g

7B Students do the exercise in pairs. For stronger groups, get them to try to think of two or three items for each adjective. During the activity, monitor and help as necessary.

7C With smaller groups, this could also be done as a whole-class activity.

> **Extra activities 5.1**
>
> **C** This activity gives further practice of key vocabulary related to technological innovation. Ask students to complete it individually, then check answers with the class.
>
> > **1** automated **2** advanced **3** top-of-the-range
> > **4** stylish **5** well designed **6** choice **7** customise
> > **8** interact

> **Pronunciation bank**
> **p.116: Numbers of syllables in words**
>
> > **Warm-up**
> > Write *friendly* and *idea* on the board. Get students to say the words and ask: *How many syllables does each word have?* (They both have two.) Refer students to the explanation in the box and drill the pronunciation of the example words.
>
> **1** Ask students to complete the exercise individually and then compare answers in pairs. Do not confirm answers yet as students will check them in the next exercise.
>
> **2** ◀ P5.01 Play the recording for students to check their answers. Then play the recording a second time for students to listen and repeat.
>
> > **1** one **2** two **3** two **4** four **5** two **6** three
> > **7** two **8** two
>
> **3** Put students in pairs and ask them to complete the exercise. Check answers with the class.
>
> > **1** restaurant **2** delivering **3** similar
> > **4** necessary
>
> **4** ◀ P5.02 Play the recording for students to listen and check their answers. Answer any questions they may have.

Project: Innovation in business

Students think about how businesses could use technology to change the way they work.

8A Get students to read the example. If they feel uncertain, work through another example on the board: *Supermarket: I check the food I have in the house. I make a shopping list. I drive the car to the supermarket. I do my shopping. I pay. I return home. I put my shopping away.* Then get students to make a similar list for another business.

8B Use your example for Exercise 8A to provide an example here: Say: *I could have a fridge that automatically checks the products inside and makes a list for me. I could order my food on the internet and have it delivered. I could pay using online banking.* As students discuss their own ideas, monitor and help as necessary.

8C Get pairs to take turns presenting their ideas to other pairs and making suggestions for actions. During the activity, monitor and help as necessary. To wrap up, ask a couple of pairs to talk about the ideas of the pair that they partnered with.

MyEnglishLab: extra activities; Reading bank
Pronunciation bank: p.116 Numbers of syllables in words
Teacher's book: Resource bank Photocopiable 5.1 p.140
Workbook: p.24 Exercises 1–3

5.2 ≫ Product testing

GSE learning objectives

- Can scan short texts to locate specific information.
- Can use the Present Perfect with *just, yet* and *already.*
- Can ask questions about someone's professional experience.
- Can give detailed accounts of experiences, describing feelings and reactions.

Warm-up

Ask for a show of hands: *Who plays games on their mobile phone?* Elicit which games people play. Ask: *What types of game do you like? What makes a game fun to play?* Elicit answers. Ask if anyone knows about the video games industry. *Who creates games? How are they developed? What jobs are involved?* Accept any answer. Then say: *In this lesson, we're going to look at one job in the video games business.*

Lead-in

Students discuss products and the job of product testing.

1A Write *Quality Assurance Tester* on the board. Elicit or explain that this is a job where people try out products to make sure they work properly. Explain that almost everything that is manufactured goes through some sort of product testing. Refer students to the examples. Then get them to go through the list in pairs.

1B Get students to do the exercise in pairs, then ask the class to share a few ideas.

2 Get students to do the exercise in pairs, then ask the class to share a few ideas. If students find this difficult, get them started with some questions. *Would you want to test perfume? What if you had to, for your job? Would it be fun to test cleaning products over and over again? Do you think testers pay for the products they use?* (almost certainly not)

Possible answer

The worst part of being a product tester might be having to try the same product over and over again. Even if you love snack food, tasting something all day long might get boring. Also, there might be flavours you don't like that you have to taste. The best part might be getting to use products you love as part of your job. If you love motorcycles, being a motorcycle test driver would be a perfect job.

Reading

Students read and discuss an article in which a video games tester explains how he got his job and what it is like playing games for a living.

3 Get students to do the exercise individually and then check answers with the class.

1 It's about being a video games tester.
2 **Possible good points:** It's fun. He's always enjoyed gaming. He's happy in his current job and the money is OK.
   Possible bad points: Doesn't play games like a normal person. It's hard work. There's a lot of administrative work. Playing games outside work is now too much like work.

4 Assign half the class items 1–3 and the other half 4–6. Then tell them to get together in pairs, with one person from each half of the class, and share answers.

1 People think I play video games all day, but that isn't what I do. (line 1)
2 ... but it's also hard work. (line 8)
3 TestPilot has worked as a Quality Assurance Tester in the video games industry for about six years. (line 12)
4 I never expected to get a job in the industry. (line 15) / It was a total surprise! (line 18)
5 They've just made me Quality Assurance Manager. (line 26)
6 ... he doesn't often play games for fun now. 'It's too much like work.' (line 31)

5A Students do the exercise individually. During the activity, monitor and help as necessary.

Possible answers

(though not all students will necessarily agree on pros and cons)
Pros: It's fun. The money is OK. It isn't boring.
Cons: You don't get to play the games in a normal way. It's hard work. There's a lot of administrative work. The money isn't great.

5B Put students in pairs to do the exercise. Then ask a few pairs to share their ideas with the class.

Extra activities 5.2

A This activity gives further practice of vocabulary from the text. Get students to complete the exercise individually and then check their answers in pairs before class feedback.

> **1** b **2** e **3** a **4** f **5** c **6** d **7** h **8** g

Grammar: Present Perfect Simple with *just, already* and *yet*

Students learn how to talk about things that have and have not happened.

6 Do this as a quick whole-class exercise. After eliciting the answers, write the forms on the board.

> **1** b, d **2** c, f **3** a, e

7 Get students to do the exercise individually, then check answers in pairs.

> **1** already tested **2** just paid it **3** yet **4** just **5** yet
> **6** Has he started his new job already?

8 Refer students to the Grammar reference on page 122. Give them a minute or two to do the exercise individually. During the activity, monitor and help as necessary.

> **Possible answers**
> **1** had breakfast / done any homework / made a phone call
> **2** finished three reports / had five meetings / worked fifty hours
> **3** arrived at the office / written sixteen emails / been on the phone with colleagues in Shanghai

Extra activities 5.2

B This activity gives further practice of the Present Perfect with *just, already* and *yet*. Get students to complete the exercise individually and then check their answers in pairs before class feedback.

> **1** I've **just** had lunch.
> **2** Have you talked to Alberto **yet**?
> **3** They've **already** started the meeting. / They've started the meeting **already**.
> **4** She hasn't finished her training **yet**.
> **5** He has **already** left the office. / He has left the office **already**.
> **6** We've **just** seen Alicia.

Pronunciation bank
p.116: Contrastive stress

> **Warm-up**
> Write the following on the board: *It's not my car. It's his car.* Ask: *Which words are stressed?* (*my* and *his*) Refer students to the explanation in the box and drill the pronunciation of the example sentences.

1 ◀》 P5.03 Ask students to complete the exercise individually and then compare answers in pairs.

> **1** People think I spend all my time <u>playing</u> the games, but I'm actually <u>working</u> all the time.
> **2** I've never really <u>played</u> the games – I try to find <u>problems</u> with them.
> **3** It's <u>fun</u>, but it's also hard <u>work</u>.
> **4** I've always <u>enjoyed</u> gaming, but I never expected to get a <u>job</u> in the industry.

2 Put students in pairs and ask them to complete the exercise. During the activity, monitor to check that students are using the correct word stress.

3 Ask students to complete the exercise in pairs. Do not confirm answers yet as students will check them in the next exercise.

4 ◀》 P5.04 Play the recording for students to check their answers. Then play the recording a second time for students to listen and repeat.

> **1** What do you think is the <u>worst</u> and the <u>best</u> part of being a product tester?
> **2** I was surprised to hear that he's <u>left</u> his new job. He only <u>started</u> it last week!
> **3** I haven't become <u>bored</u> with it yet – in fact I still <u>love</u> it.

Speaking

Students talk about their day.

9A Get students to do the exercise individually for about a minute, then gather a few ideas and write them on the board.

> **Possible answers**
> have lunch, write reports, make schedules, do research, talk to colleagues, update social media

9B Get students to do the exercise individually. Monitor and help as necessary. Ask a few students to share their ideas with the class.

> **Possible answers**
> Have you had lunch yet? Have you written a report yet? Have you made a schedule yet? Have you done research yet?

9C Students do the exercise in pairs. Monitor and help as necessary. Round off the exercise by asking students to raise their hands to answer a few questions, e.g. *Who has written ten emails today? Who has been for a run?*

MyEnglishLab: Teacher's resources: extra activities

Grammar reference: p.122 Present Perfect Simple with *just*, *already* and *yet*

Pronunciation bank: p.116 Contrastive stress

Teacher's book: Resource bank Photocopiable 5.2 p.141

Workbook: p.25 Exercises 1–3, p.26 Exercises 1 and 2

5.3 ❯ Communication skills
Managing information

GSE learning objectives

- Can infer speakers' opinions in conversations on familiar everyday topics.
- Can suggest pros and cons when discussing a topic, using simple language.
- Can give or seek personal views and opinions in discussing topics of interest.
- Can ask open questions to encourage longer answers.
- Can ask questions about the content of a presentation or lecture aimed at a general audience, using simple language.

Warm-up

Ask: When you're lost, do you prefer asking someone for directions or do you prefer to find your own way? Elicit answers. Ask: If you are confused about something in your work or school work, do you ask for help immediately or do you prefer to take some time to figure it out yourself? Elicit answers. Say: Today we're going to talk about managing information and asking for information.

Lead-in

Students explore ways of asking for information.

1A Get students to read and discuss the comment in pairs. After a minute or two, elicit a few answers. In general, businesspeople need to know about their market in order to sell anything, about their colleagues in order to work well together, about their work assignment in order to carry it out properly and so on. In almost any situation, asking questions will help people get the information they need. That is why questions are the key to success. The same is true of education. Students can learn a great deal by asking questions and thinking critically: *Why has my teacher given me this assignment? What is the author's reason for writing this text? Who would benefit from this change in the law?* and so on.

1B Do this as a quick whole-class exercise.

> 1 Students' own answers
> 2 to clarify information, to get more information, to show interest

Video
Students watch a video about the importance of asking for information.

2A ▶ 5.3.1 In the first sequence, Beata shares her impressions of Mateo. If your students watched the video in Lesson 4.3, ask: *From the video in Lesson 4.3, do you remember what the meeting was like?* (Mateo talked a lot, multitasked and didn't stick to one topic.) Before playing the video, go over the question with the class so they know what to listen for.

> 1 He was not focused and asked lots of personal questions.
> 2 She's not sure how much to tell Daniel about the meeting. She's also worried about his reaction to the situation.

2B Discuss the question as a class. Accept any reasonable answers.

3A Explain to the class the idea of Beata having two options when she has the video conference call with Daniel and Clarice, and go through the details of Options A and B with them. Make it clear to students that they can choose which option they want to see first on the video. Put students in small groups and ask them to discuss the two options, giving reasons for their answers. Elicit ideas from a few groups and as a class, decide which video to watch first.

3B ▶ 5.3.2 ▶ 5.3.3 Tell the class to answer the questions for Option A or B depending on their choice, and play the video. You could ask students to discuss the questions in their groups first, and then check the answers as a whole class. Do the same for the second video.

Option A

> 1 She gave a lot of information, including unimportant details such as information about who they did the market research on and the questionnaire. But the key information that she passed on is that Mateo had issues with the colour of the Diabsensor, a possible problem with storage, and the design of the packaging.
> 2 He asks for specifics, e.g. 'What does Mateo want to change exactly?', 'What does he want exactly?', 'Are you sure?'
> 3 Yes, he did, for the most part. However, he did not ask about the storage problem.
> 4 She felt happy that she had shared all the information with them.

Option B

> 1 The key information that she passed on is that Mateo had issues with the colour of the Diabsensor, a possible problem with storage, and the design of the packaging. She omitted the details such us who they did the market research with.
> 2 He asks for specifics: 'The colour of the Diabsensor or the packaging?'
> 3 Yes, he did for the most part. However, he did not ask about the storage problem and at the end asked, 'Really? Nothing else?', which gives the impression he was expecting more information.
> 4 She feels happy that she has given them enough information and that if Daniel wanted to know more, he would have asked.

4 Put students in pairs and give them 3–4 minutes to discuss the question. During the activity, monitor and help as necessary.

> **Possible answers**
> **Option A**
> **Pros:** Beata provides a lot of detailed information. We learn there is a problem with the storage.
> **Cons:** The information she provides is often unnecessary. Daniel has to ask Beata specific questions in order to obtain the exact information he needs. He often has to clarify information. Beata mentions the storage problem. The meeting is longer.
>
> **Option B**
> **Pros:** Beata's overview means the discussion is much shorter than in Option A. We learn there is a problem with the storage.
> **Cons:** Beata doesn't provide any details about the storage problem. Daniel doesn't ask the exact nature of the problem.

5 ▶ 5.3.4 Put students in pairs. Explain that they are going to watch another video, which is a summary of the ideas they looked at in the previous videos. Play the video and give students 4–6 minutes to discuss and make notes, then discuss the main learning points with the whole class.

> It's important to ask questions to get more information or to stay on track. Giving more details doesn't necessarily mean that the meeting is more informative as not all of these details translate into action points.

Reflection

Students reflect on the conclusions from the video and discuss their own ability to manage information and ask questions.

6 Allow students to work individually on this so that they can reflect on their own preferences and ideas. Ask them to think of their own answers to the questions and to make notes. Then put students in pairs to discuss their answers. Get brief feedback from the class.

Functional language: Asking open and closed questions

Students look at how to ask questions to get short, simple answers and questions where there are many possible answers.

7A Explain that this exercise highlights open and closed questions from the video. Get students to do the exercise in pairs, then check answers as a class.

> **1** d **2** e **3** b **4** a **5** c

7B Do this as a quick whole-class exercise.

> **1** a **2** b **3** b **4** a

8A Get students to do the exercise in pairs. The question *Why did they spend so much time on this?* appears to be an open question asking for detailed information, and students should write it in that space. But in the video, Clarice is actually asking a rhetorical question (see Notes below). Her meaning is: *He has wasted our time.*

> *Notes*
>
> A **rhetorical** question is a question that you ask as a way of making a statement, without expecting an answer. For example, if someone asks you, 'Who stole your car?' you might respond, 'Who knows?' You do not expect an answer – it is another way of saying, 'I don't know.' Rhetorical questions can also be used to offer criticism. For example, when Clarice asks, 'And that's what he asked them about? The colour? Seriously? Why did they spend so much time on this?' she isn't trying to obtain information. She asks these questions to express her disapproval of Mateo's work. She is criticising him for wasting time.

> **Encouraging someone to speak:** Tell us about your meeting with Mateo.
> **Asking for confirmation:** Have you ever met him? Can we change the colour?
> **Asking for information:** What does Mateo want to change exactly? Why did they spend so much time on this?

8B Students now work in pairs to complete the exercise. Refer them to the videoscript on page 142. During the activity, monitor and help as necessary.

> **Extra activities 5.3**
>
> **A** This activity gives further practice of the language in the video script. Get students to complete both conversations individually, then check answers in pairs.
>
> **Conversation 1**
> **1** what does Mateo want
> **2** what do you think
> **3** we change the colour
> **4** tell us about
>
> **Conversation 2**
> **1** Is it possible to
> **2** How long will it take
> **3** Can you get back to us
> **4** Monday

Task

Students roleplay a scenario where they have to give each other feedback on their presentation skills.

9A Students will need to do a certain amount of preparation before they begin the task, so bear this in mind when you are planning this stage. Put students in pairs and ask them to read the scenario and to decide who is A and who is B. Refer Student A to page 136 and Student B to page 133. Answer any questions they may have.

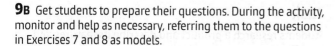

9B Get students to prepare their questions. During the activity, monitor and help as necessary, referring them to the questions in Exercises 7 and 8 as models.

9C Students take turns asking each other questions and asking for clarification as necessary. Student A asks mainly closed questions, and Student B asks mainly open questions. During the activity, monitor and help as necessary.

9D Students do the exercise in their pairs. Tell them to discuss the language they used, and what, if anything, they found difficult. After a couple of minutes, ask a few groups to share their ideas, and find out if there were similar challenges for everyone. Round off the task by asking how students will handle asking questions in the future. With stronger classes, get students to write three action points starting *In future meetings I will …*

MyEnglishLab: Teacher's resources: extra activities; Interactive video activities

Workbook: p.27 Exercise 1

5.4 ❯ Business skills
Selling a product

GSE learning objectives

- Can extract key details from a presentation if delivered slowly and clearly.
- Can extract key factual information such as dates, numbers and quantities from a presentation.

Warm-up

Ask: *What's a product you don't own that you would love to buy?* Allow students to share a few answers. Ask: *What's a product you don't own that you would never buy?* Allow students to share a few answers. Say: *Today we're going to talk about products and why people buy them.*

Lead-in

Students look at the language we use to describe the features and benefits of a product.

1A Put students in small groups and ask them to complete the exercise. During the activity, monitor and help as necessary. Invite groups to share their answers with the class.

1B Read through the comments with the class. Ask: *Why do people buy oranges?* (Because they're delicious and healthy.) Write *Features* on the board and elicit some features of an orange (e.g. round, orange coloured, citrus fruit). Then write *Benefits* and elicit some benefits of an orange (e.g. delicious, source of vitamin C, good for your health).

> 1 Features   2 Benefits

Listening

Students listen to two sales representatives describing a product.

2A 🔊 5.01   Focus students' attention on the instructions so they know what they are listening for. Ask them to think about what kind of chair the ZX3 Hot-Seat might be. Accept any answer, as the correct answer will be revealed in the recording. Play the recording.

> features: Kendra; benefits: Paolo

2B Put students in pairs to discuss the questions. If necessary for weaker classes, play the recording again.

> 1 a portable, heated chair
> 2 Possible answers: sports fans, concert-goers, campers, people sitting in their garden – because it would make them warmer and more comfortable in cooler conditions

3A 🔊 5.02   Teach or elicit the meaning of these words: *dimensions* (the size of something, especially when this is given as its length, height and width. They are often measured in millimetres – abbreviated *mm* – or centimetres – abbreviated *cm*. We use *by* (the *x* symbol) to separate dimensions – 10 mm x 30 mm x 20 mm), *memory foam* (a soft material used for making seats comfortable), *water-resistant nylon mesh* (a fabric that does not get wet), *heavy-duty rubber* (a very strong substance used to make tyres, boots, etc.). Draw a box on the board and arrows showing height 10 mm, width 30 mm and depth 20 mm, and say: *The box is ten millimetres by thirty millimetres by twenty millimetres.* Get students to read through the table so they know what information they are listening for, then play the recording. Get students to complete the table individually, then check answers in pairs.

> 1 940   2 1,050   3 blue, green   4 seat   5 cover
> 6 handles

3B 🔊 5.03   Read through the list and make sure students understand the meanings of the words. Then play the recording. Check answers as a class.

> 1, 3, 5, 7 and 8

Functional language: Describing features and benefits

Students look at useful phrases for talking about products and what they can do.

4A Explain to students that this is part of the recording they just listened to. Teach or elicit the meaning of the words *retractable* (able to fold up or fold in) and *arms* (the part of a chair where you rest your arms). Get students to do the exercise individually, then check answers in pairs.

> 1 comes with   2 measures   3 weighs   4 made of
> 5 comes in

4B Draw attention to the Tip box. Ask: *What's a smart phone used for?* Elicit: *A smartphone is used for making phone calls, surfing the internet and running apps* or similar answers. Ask: *What's a smartphone designed for?* Elicit: *It's designed for carrying easily in your pocket or bag.* or similar answers. Teach or elicit the meaning of *stadium* (a large, usually open building with a playing field and seats, for sports events and concerts) and *optional* (not necessary; something you can choose). Get students to do the exercise individually. Then check answers with the whole class.

1 means that you can	**2** allow you to	**3** lets you
4 so it's easier to	**5** make it easier to	

5A Teach or elicit the meaning of *military* (the army; a group of people trained to fight) Put students in pairs to do the exercise.

A 1, 4 a,	(e) f
B 3, 6	b, e
C 2, 5	c, d

5B Students continue working in the same pairs. Remind them to use the phrases in Exercise 4.

Model answers

The military-style rucksack is made of washable fabric so it's easier to keep clean. It also comes with additional side pockets, which means that you have a place for your student or work ID or keys.

The smartphone comes with a 5G internet connection which allows you to use it abroad while you're on holiday or a business trip. In addition, it comes with a dual SIM, which means there's no need to carry two phones.

The newly opened supermarket provides shoppers with a home delivery service. This makes it easier to shop online, and there is no need to interrupt your busy schedule. It also offers weekly discounts on fresh products to allow you to save money.

Extra activities 5.4

A This activity gives practice of the language of describing features and benefits. Get students to complete the exercise individually, then check answers in pairs.

1 is made of	**2** is designed	**3** made of	**4** comes in
5 measures	**6** weighs		

B This activity gives students further practice of describing features and benefits. Make sure that they know what each product is: a personal fitness tracker (a watch that monitors and records your exercise), a portable barbecue (a metal frame for cooking food on outdoors). With weaker groups, brainstorm features and benefits before they write their description.

Task

Students research a product and describe its features and benefits.

6A Say: *We're going to talk about printers*. Teach or elicit the meaning of *print resolution* (the quality of a printed image), *pixel* (the unit for measuring resolution – short for *picture element*) and *touch sensitive* (a type of screen, as on a tablet, that has buttons and other controls you can control with your fingers). Put students in pairs. Get them to read the instructions and the three steps before turning to page 131. Exercise 6B will work better if half the class chooses one printer and half the class chooses the other, so assign half the pairs the Officejet Pro 2 Printer and half the Instata Print. Remind them to use the language in Exercise 4 for their presentation. During the activity, monitor and help as necessary.

6B Put each pair with another pair who worked on a different printer to give their presentations. Remind them to note down questions to ask at the end of the presentation. During the activity, monitor and help as necessary. At the end of the exercise, find out how many students chose to buy the Officejet Pro 2 and how many chose the Instata Print.

6C After a couple of minutes, ask a few groups to share their ideas, and find out if there were similar challenges for everyone. Round off the task by asking how students will handle describing features and benefits in the future. With stronger classes, get students to write three action points starting *In future meetings, when discussing features and benefits, I will …*

MyEnglishLab: Teacher's resources: extra activities; Functional language bank
Workbook: p.27 Exercise 2

5.5 > Writing
Product review

GSE learning objectives

- Can discuss product features in a business setting, using simple language.
- Can write a short, simple description of a familiar device or product.

Warm-up

Write *product review* on the board. Teach or elicit its meaning (the opinion of people who have bought and used a product – usually written, often seen online, e.g. on Amazon). Ask: *When you're thinking of buying something, do you read product reviews?* Say: *Today, we're going to learn how to write a product review.*

Lead-in

Students read and complete a product review.

1A Before students complete the exercise, ask a few questions and get them to skim the review for answers: *What kind of product is the review for?* (a phone) *Does the review give any good points about the product?* (yes) *Any bad points?* (yes) Get students to do the exercise individually.

> **1** as **2** The **3** which **4** to **5** by/with **6** is **7** off **8** If

1B Students check their answers in pairs. Ask: *Based on this review, would you buy the phone?* Elicit a few answers and also the reasons for the answers.

Functional language

Students look at language that is commonly used in product reviews.

2 Tell students that you are now going to look closely at the language for writing a product review. Get them to do the exercise individually. During the activity, monitor and help as necessary. Get students to check answers in pairs.

> **1** chose **2** said **3** decided **4** included **5** Another **6** impressed **7** particularly **8** most **9** downside/problem **10** problem/downside **11** thing **12** worst

Extra activities 5.5

A This activity gives further practice of phrases to use in a product review. Elicit or explain the meaning of *kitchenware* (the things you use in a kitchen to prepare food – bowls, spoons, etc.). Get students to complete the exercise individually and then check answers in pairs before class feedback.

> **1** decided **2** because **3** said **4** particularly **5** most **6** impressed **7** Another **8** downside **9** included **10** recommend

Optional grammar work

The review in Exercise 1 contains examples of the order of adjectives before nouns, so you could use them for some optional grammar work. Refer students to the Grammar reference on page 122 and use the exercises in MyEnglishLab for extra grammar practice.

Task

Students read and improve a product review and then write a review of a product they have recently bought.

3A Put students in pairs and refer them to the online product review on page 129. Ask: *How is it different from the examples we've looked at?* (It lists information but doesn't give any details.) Get them to discuss specific ways to improve it.

Model answer

The XB Watch promises to track all your activity during the day: walking, running, exercising in the gym as well as monitoring your sleep. It also syncs with a fitness app on your phone.

What I like most about this watch is the long-lasting battery, which doesn't need to be charged every few hours like some of the major competitors' watches. Another good thing is that it really is waterproof so I can go swimming with it on my wrist. Finally, I was also impressed by the easy-to-use phone app, which is full of very useful advice.

The main downside for me is the size of the watch. It's far too big and not very attractive at all. In fact, I think it's quite ugly.

However, the watch does what it promises, so if you are not worried about the design and want an inexpensive activity watch, I can recommend this one.

3B Get students to do this exercise individually. If there is no time to do it class, assign it as homework.

3C Get students to answer the questions. During the activity, monitor and help as necessary.

MyEnglishLab: Teacher's resources: extra activities; Interactive grammar practice; Writing bank

Grammar reference: p.122 Order of adjectives before nouns

Workbook: p.28 Exercises 1 and 2

Business workshop ❯5
Smart fabric

GSE learning objectives

- Can follow the main points of extended discussion around them if in standard speech.
- Can discuss product features in a business setting using simple language.

Background

Students learn about a British textile company called eFAB and a new 'smart fabric' that it is developing.

1 Write *smart* on the board and teach or elicit technology words that it modifies: *smartphone, smart watch, smart TV, smart card* (a credit card with a chip in it). Ask: *What does 'smart' mean in these expressions?* (They all connect to other devices or to the internet. *Smart* means that they aren't just a phone, a watch, a TV or a card.) Ask: *What smart devices do you have?* Discuss answers. Teach or elicit the meaning of *fabric* (cloth; the material used to make clothes). Then ask: *What do you think 'smart fabric' is?* Accept any answers at this point, then say: *We're going to read about smart fabric.* Ask students to read the background and discuss the questions in pairs. Check answers with the class. Check the meaning of *smart fabric* (looks and feels like normal cloth, but includes a very thin electronic element, allowing it to change colour, to display a variety of designs and even to light up).

1 a textile manufacturer
2 a fashion design company
3–4 Students' own answers

Market research

Students read about a company's market research into a product they might produce with smart fabric.

2A In business, innovation and design are often directly related to marketing. If you cannot sell a product, there is no point in manufacturing it. This means that before designing a product, companies need to think long and hard about who will buy it and what exactly people want to buy. Teach or elicit the meaning of *focus groups* (see Notes below). Get students to do the exercise individually, then check answers as a class.

> ### Notes
>
> Marketing people get focus groups to share their opinions about a product or an idea for a product with representatives from the manufacturer. They are usually paid for their time and given free use of the products they are reviewing.

1 teens and early 20s who love technology
2 €35 – not cheap, but OK for a premium product
3 carry out more detailed market research, test the product with focus groups

2B ◆ BW 5.01 Tell students that they are going to listen to a focus group discussing a smart-fabric T-shirt. Get them to read the three sentences so they know what to listen for. Play the recording and get students to complete the exercise individually, then check answers in pairs.

1 have already 2 think 3 have a few

2C ◆ BW 5.01 For stronger classes, get students to try to complete the exercise before listening again. Otherwise, play the recording and get students to complete the notes. Check answers with the class.

Positive feedback: looks amazing, really cool, good for being seen (cycling)
Negative feedback: feels like rough plastic, really uncomfortable, smells strange/weird, difficult to wash
Suggestions: good for safety clothing, curtains, wallpaper

The marketing mix

Students look at the four elements that define a target market.

3A For a business to succeed, having an innovative product is not enough. The product needs to sell. This means setting the right price, placing the product in the right shops and letting people know it's there. The combination of product, price, place and promotion is called the *marketing mix*. Teach or elicit the meaning of *promotion* (telling potential customers that your product or service exists). Then get students to look at the diagram and do the exercise. Get them to check answers in pairs.

1 place 2 product 3 target market 4 promotion
5 price

3B Get students to do the exercise in pairs.

1 product 2 promotion 3 price 4 target market
5 place

Considering options

Students listen to eFAB's Product Developer and Marketing Manager and make notes about how the fabric will be placed in the market.

4A ◆ BW 5.02 Write the following words on the board and explain or elicit their meanings: *Product Developer* (a person whose job is creating and improving products), *Marketing Manager* (a person whose job is organising product promotion). Tell students that they are going to listen to a conversation between these two people. Get them to read the instructions. Then play the recording.

a safety vest for cyclists

4B ◆ BW 5.02 Get students to look at the five pieces of information they are supposed to listen for. For stronger classes, get students to try to complete the exercise before listening again. Otherwise, play the recording and get students to complete the notes. Check answers with the class.

Product: cycling safety vest
Target market: not serious racing/sport cyclists – people who cycle to work
Promotion: lifestyle magazines, online, social media
Place: online, in bike shops, department stores
Price: more than forty euros

Extra activities Business workshop 5

A In this activity, students will look more closely at some of the vocabulary from the listening. Get them to complete the exercise individually and check answers in pairs. Help with any vocabulary students are not sure about.

1 potential   2 commuters   3 lifestyle magazines
4 Distribution   5 retail price   6 premium product

B 🔊 BW 5.02   Get students to read the statements so they know what they are listening for. Teach or elicit the meaning of *shop displays* (in a store, the arrangement of a product so it looks good; sometimes the manufacturer provides special displays to go in shops). Play the recording. Get students to complete the exercise individually and check answers in pairs.

1 T
2 F – At the moment, there isn't a safety vest for cycling that's also fashionable. In the market, *safe* and *fashionable* are two very different ideas.
3 T
4 F – Distribution is expensive – shipping is getting more expensive all the time.
5 T

Task: Choose a product to develop

Students consider possible products to develop and then choose one.

5A Put students in pairs and get them to choose who is Student A and Student B. Explain the task. There are notes on the marketing mix for two possible products. Students must ask and answer questions to exchange information. Refer Students A to page 133 and Students B to page 129.

5B Explain that students are now going to choose a product for eFAB to develop. Remind them that they heard the Product Developer and Marketing Manager talking about the cycling vest, and students discussed the other two products in Exercise 5A. Give students 4–6 minutes to hold their meeting. During the activity, monitor and help as necessary.

6 This exercise could be assigned as homework. Remind students to use the email in Exercise 2A as a model. Get them to compare emails and go through the points below. Did their emails cover all of the points? Get them to work together to suggest any improvements to their own or their partner's email. Remind them to:
• define the target market.
• explain where the product will be placed.
• name the price.
• say something about promotion.

Model answer

After detailed consideration of the marketing mix of several possible products, we have decided to carry out further market research on a smart wallpaper. We have identified the target market as designers and decorators who help people with home decoration and design. We can price it at €48 per roll, so while it isn't cheap, it will be popular as a premium product. We plan to make it available in high-end department stores and to promote it in home decoration magazines. The next step will be to test the product with focus groups.

MyEnglishLab: Teacher's resources: extra activities

Review ⟨5

1 1 automated   2 innovation   3 choice   4 interacting
  5 customised
2 1 stylish   2 advanced   3 friendly   4 well-designed
  5 dependable
3 1 We've already built three factories this year.
  2 They haven't exported to the USA yet.
  3 Mr Kite has just become Sales Manager of the Year.
  4 Have you finished the designs for the new product line yet?
  5 Has Liam just got a new job?
  6 The boss has just sent me an email.
  7 I haven't started my new job yet.
  8 She has already finished the report.
4 1 O   2 C   3 O   4 C   5 O   6 C   7 O   8 O
5 1 d   2 e   3 g   4 a   5 f   6 b   7 c
6 1 chose   2 performed   3 impressed   4 Another
  5 what   6 One   7 downside   8 recommend

6 Safety and security

Unit overview

	CLASSWORK	FURTHER WORK
6.1 > **Safety at work**	**Lead-in** Students test their knowledge of international safety symbols. **Video** Students watch a video about how a London waste disposal company manages safety. **Vocabulary** Students look at health and safety vocabulary. **Project** Students conduct a survey to find out about their group's experience of accidents and injuries.	**MyEnglishLab:** Teacher's resources: extra activities **Teacher's book:** Resource bank Photocopiable 6.1 p.142 **Workbook:** p.29 Exercises 1–3
6.2 > **Being security-conscious**	**Lead-in** Students share their knowledge about typical security measures. **Listening** Students listen to descriptions of security measures in three different workplaces. **Grammar** Students look at the grammar often used to say what you can't or must do. **Writing** Students write an email to colleagues about a security measure.	**MyEnglishLab:** Teacher's resources: extra activities; Reading bank **Grammar reference:** p.123 Modal verbs of prohibition, obligation and no obligation **Pronunciation bank:** p.116 Phrasing and pausing **Teacher's book:** Resource bank Photocopiable 6.2 p.143 **Workbook:** p.30 Exercises 1–3, p.31 Exercises 1–3
6.3 > **Communication skills:** Dealing with disagreement	**Lead-in** Students explore confidence in speech and body language. **Video** Students watch a video about different ways of dealing with disagreement. **Reflection** Students reflect on the conclusions from the video and discuss their own skills in dealing with disagreement. **Functional language** Students look at phrases that are commonly used to explain rules and requirements. **Task** Students roleplay a scenario where there is some disagreement.	**MyEnglishLab:** Teacher's resources: extra activities; Interactive video activities **Workbook:** p.32 Exercise 1
6.4 > **Business skills:** Dealing with conflict	**Lead-in** Students look at conflicts within teams and the possible reasons for them. **Listening** Students listen to a conversation about a problem at work. **Functional language** Students practise using language for dealing with disagreement. **Task** Students roleplay a scenario where they have to deal with a conflict.	**MyEnglishLab:** Teacher's resources: extra activities; Functional language bank **Pronunciation bank:** p.116 Stress in phrases **Workbook:** p.32 Exercise 2
6.5 > **Writing:** Instructions and warnings	**Lead-in** Students complete warnings and instructions for using equipment. **Functional language** Students look at the language of dos, don'ts and warnings. **Task** Students read information about how to lift heavy loads or what to do in a fire and create guidelines.	**MyEnglishLab:** Teacher's resources: extra activities; Interactive grammar practice; Writing bank **Grammar reference:** p.123 Linking words for time **Workbook:** p.32 Exercise 2
Business workshop 6 > Visitor safety	**Reading** Students read a report about safety and security procedures. **Listening** Students listen to an interview about risk assessment in offices. **Task** Students prepare a visitor safety and security report.	**MyEnglishLab:** Teacher's resources: extra activities

Business brief

The main aim of this unit is to introduce students to the concept of **safety** and **security**. Safety is the state of being protected from danger. In business, safety generally refers to keeping workers and visitors from getting hurt in the workplace. It is often discussed in terms of **health and safety**, an area of government and law concerned with people's health and safety, especially at work, including regulations and procedures that are put in place to reduce accidents in the workplace or in public environments. Security refers to the measures that are taken to keep someone or something safe. In business, this means keeping buildings and computer systems safe from intruders.

The concept of **risk** is closely associated with safety and security. Risk is the possibility that something bad, unpleasant or dangerous might happen. Most companies carry out a **risk assessment** of their workplaces or for any special event that they put on. This is the systematic process of identifying and evaluating **hazards** – things that can cause harm – and weighing the risk, from low to high, of a hazard actually causing someone harm.

Standards organisations such as the European Food Safety Authority, the European Committee for Standardisation and the International Organisation for Standardisation set safety standards for food, manufacturing, workplaces and so on. They define and publish safety standards, including everything from the **personal protective equipment** that workers should use in various work environments to **warning signs and notices** and recommendations for food transport and storage. These standards allow consumers to know that the products they buy are safe, and let companies and workers know exactly what measures should be taken to keep people safe on the job. Most countries also have laws that ensure workplace safety.

Workplace security varies from sector to sector and from site to site. Some workplaces have no security, others require employees to carry an **ID badge** and some have more robust arrangements, with **security guards**, **fingerprint scanners** and even **metal detectors**. Other security measures may include **CCTV**, rules forbidding the use of mobile phones or **bag checks** at building entrances. In the retail industry, security is focused on keeping employees safe from aggressive customers, but also on preventing **shoplifting**. This may involve low-tech solutions, such as security guards, or more high-tech ones, such as the use of **radio frequency ID chips** that allow retailers to track products electronically and set off alarms if someone tries to take something without paying.

Safety and security and your students

It is important that students are aware of safety and security. There are safety and security issues in every industry or professional environment, so it is useful to understand and be able to discuss the concepts and use the basic terminology. Having a better understanding of safety and security has practical applications in the studies of pre-work learners as well because the same concepts apply to places of study that apply to places of work.

Unit lead-in

Ask students to look at the unit title and photo. Ask: *What are the people doing?* (They're paragliding – a sport in which you jump off a hill or out of a plane and use a parachute to get you safely back down to the ground.) *Are they addressing safety in any way?* (They appear to be wearing helmets and gloves.) Though these people are parachuting for fun, some pilots, particularly those in the Armed Forces, still wear a parachute as a safety device so that they can leave the plane in case of emergency. Look at the quotation. Make sure students understand the meaning of *asset* (something that a company owns). Ask: *Why is safety an asset rather than a cost?* Discuss ideas. (Possible answers: When workers are injured on the job, it costs them personally and can often cost the company a lot of money for lost work, sick pay, and maybe even legal costs. Investing in safety avoids injuries and can save companies a lot of money.)

6.1 > Safety at work

GSE learning objectives

- Can follow the main points in TV programmes on familiar topics if delivered in clear standard speech.
- Can contribute to a group discussion if the discussion is conducted slowly and clearly.
- Can use language related to diseases, accidents and injuries.
- Can carry out a prepared structured interview with some spontaneous follow-up questions.

Warm-up

Write *safety* on the board and teach or elicit the meaning (the state of being protected from danger, risk or injury). Ask: *What things keep us safe?* and elicit ideas (e.g. seat belts in cars, fire alarms, handrails on stairs). Say: *Today we're going to talk about safety at work.*

Lead-in

Students test their knowledge of international safety symbols.

1A This quiz is meant to activate students' knowledge of safety signs and symbols. Make sure they understand *square*, *rectangular*, *triangular* and *circular* by drawing each shape on the board and asking students to identify them. Then teach or elicit the meaning of *prohibited* (not allowed) and *obligatory* (necessary to do). Get students to do the exercise in pairs. Check answers as a class.

> **1** d **2** e **3** a **4** b **5** c

1B Do the exercise as a class.

Video

Students watch a video about how a London waste disposal company manages safety.

2A Do this exercise with the class and discuss any guesses students may have. The actual answer is that the company is a waste disposal firm, but you don't need to tell the class that at this point, as it will be revealed in the video.

2B ▶ 6.1.1 Before playing the video, encourage students to listen out for the ideas they discussed in Exercise 2A. For more background information, see Notes below.

> O'Donovan (Waste Disposal) is a (skip) company which collects waste and recycles it.

> *Notes*
> You can look at O'Donovan Waste Disposal's website at http://www.odonovan.co.uk. The company, founded in 1959, offers a full range of waste management solutions.

3 ▶ 6.1.1 Get students to read the sentences so they know what they are listening for. Alternatively, get them to try to complete the exercise based on what they recall, then watch the video to check.

> 1 O'Donovan Waste Disposal is based in ~~Manchester~~ **London**.
> 2 Paul Neal is the company's ~~Factory~~ **Logistics** Supervisor.
> 3 The company collects waste and ~~burns~~ **recycles** it.
> 4 Protecting the ~~environment~~ **public** is a priority for the company.
> 5 In order to protect cyclists, vehicles are ~~smaller~~ **lower** so the drivers can see more.
> 6 The company has also put ~~alarms~~ **cameras** and electronic sensors on vehicles.
> 7 The ~~police~~ **head office** can view the images from truck cameras if there are problems.
> 8 ~~Senior staff~~ **Everyone / All staff / All employees** at the recycling centre **is/are** given protective clothing and training.
> 9 Whenever there is an accident, it is recorded in ~~a database~~ **an accident book** and investigated.

4 Put students in pairs or small groups to do the exercise. For question 1, if students need help, you could suggest some of these ideas: If workers are safe, then they do not miss work because of injuries. If a company is safe, it will have a good reputation. While students are talking, monitor and help as necessary. Ask a few groups to share their answers before moving on.

Extra activities 6.1

A ▶ 6.1.1 This activity gives more practice of words and phrases from the video. Get students to complete the exercise individually, then check answers in pairs.

> 1 law **2** busy **3** early stage **4** side guards
> 5 the sides **6** wide variety **7** off site **8** dusty
> 9 investment **10** benefit

Vocabulary: Health and safety

Students look at health and safety vocabulary.

5 Teach or elicit the meaning of *health and safety* (an area of government concerned with regulations and procedures designed to reduce accidents in the workplace or in public environments) and *risk* (the possibility that something dangerous might happen). Get students to complete the exercise in pairs, then check answers as a class.

> **1** b **2** f **3** a **4** e **5** c **6** d
>
> fit – put on
> handle – carry, work with
> pose – create, be
> issue (someone with) – give (someone)
> hold – do, have
> record – write down

6A The correct technical term for *personal safety equipment and clothing* is *personal protective equipment (PPE)*. Get students to do the exercise individually, then check answers in pairs.

> **1** high-visibility clothing **2** steel toe-cap boots
> **3** hard hat **4** ear defenders **5** cut-resistant gloves
> **6** face mask **7** goggles

6B Do the exercise as a class.

7A Do the exercise as a class. Note the similarities between the verbs *injure*, *hurt* and *damage* for talking about harming someone (see Notes below). As you do the exercise, elicit past tense forms of the verbs and drill pronunciation before Exercise 7B.

> **Notes**
>
> While *injure* and *hurt* essentially mean the same thing, *damage* suggests a more serious problem. Also, *damage* can be used for things such as cars or equipment, while *injure* and *hurt* generally refer to people.

bleed:	lose blood, especially because of an injury
break:	damage a bone in your body by making it crack or split
cut:	injure yourself on something sharp that breaks the skin and makes you bleed
damage:	cause physical harm to something or to part of someone's body
drop:	stop holding or carrying something so that it falls
fall:	suddenly go down onto the ground after you have been standing, walking or running, especially without intending to
hit:	move a part of your body quickly against something accidentally, causing pain
hurt:	injure yourself or someone else
injure:	hurt yourself or someone else, e.g. in an accident
slip:	slide a short distance accidentally and fall or lose your balance slightly

7B Get students to do the exercise individually, then check answers in pairs.

> **1** dropped, broke **2** cut, bled **3** slipped, fell, hurt
> **4** damaged **5** hit **6** injured

8 If there are any expert first aiders in the group, get them to give a demonstration or tips about some basic first aid.

> **Extra activities 6.1**
>
> **B** This activity gives further practice of vocabulary from the lesson. Get students to complete the exercise individually, then check answers in pairs.
>
> > **1** issue **2** hold **3** handle **4** gloves **5** hard hat
> > **6** goggles **7** injure **8** hit **9** drop **10** first aid

Project: Accident questionnaire

Students conduct a survey to find out about their group's experience of accidents and injuries.

9A If possible, put students in groups of four or more. Make sure they understand the meaning of *bone* (the hard, white material in the centre of our arms, legs, etc.), *scar* (a mark that remains on the skin after a cut has healed) and *survey* (questions asked to a group of people to learn about how people are similar and different).

9B Get students to make a question for each statement, following the example. During the activity, monitor and help as necessary.

9C If you are working one-to-one or students are in pairs, get them to use appropriate phrases, e.g. *neither of us, one of us, both of us*.

9D Pre-teach the phrase *accident prone* (likely to have accidents more often than is usual). Get groups to present to other groups. Go over a few of the items with the class, asking for a show of hands, e.g. *Hold up your hand if you've ever broken a bone*.

MyEnglishLab: Teacher's resources: extra activities
Teacher's book: Resource bank Photocopiable 6.1 p.142
Workbook: p.29 Exercises 1–3

6.2 ❯ Being security-conscious

> **GSE learning objectives**
>
> - Can follow familiar topics if the speaker is clear and avoids idiomatic usage.
> - Can understand conversations about rules or regulations related to the workplace.
> - Can express belief, opinion, agreement and disagreement politely.
> - Can use a range of modal verbs in the past and present to talk about prohibition, obligation and no obligation.
> - Can write a simple email giving details of work-related events, facts or plans.

Warm-up

Write *security* on the board and teach or elicit the meaning (ways of keeping people and places safe). Ask: *Where do you often see a lot of security?* (in airports, office buildings, factories, etc.)

Lead-in

Students share their knowledge about typical security measures.

1A Draw students' attention to the lesson title *Being security-conscious* and elicit or teach the meaning, along with the meaning of *security measures* (see Notes below). Get students to do the exercise individually, then check answers in pairs.

Notes

When you are conscious of something, it means you think a lot about it or are concerned about it (e.g. *fashion-conscious, health-conscious, environmentally conscious*), so if you are **security-conscious**, you think about how to keep people and places safe.

Security measures: a measure is an action, especially an official one, which is intended to deal with a particular problem (e.g. *security measures, safety measures, preventive measures*).

A security tags   **B** x-ray machine / metal detector   **C** CCTV

1B Get students to work in pairs. Encourage them to think about examples of security they might typically see in the street (e.g. CCTV cameras as shown in photo C, speed cameras), at home (e.g. alarm system, front door lock), the place where they work or study (e.g. ID badges, security guards), in shops (e.g. security tags on clothes as shown in photo A). Ask if they think there are more security systems now than in the past and why that might be. Avoid too much discussion of cyber security as it is not the focus of the lesson. Ask a few pairs to share their ideas with the class.

Listening

Students listen to descriptions of security measures in three different workplaces.

2 🔊 6.01   Get students to look at the exercise. Explain that they are going to hear about security measures in three different settings. Make sure that they know they are listening for the most and least security measures.

Paul, who works in a university, seems to have the lowest level of security and Aisha, who works in an IT company, has the most security.

3 🔊 6.01   Go over the information students need to listen for. After they listen, get them to check answers in pairs. Then quickly go over the answers with the class.

1 b **2** c **3** a **4** c **5** b **6** a

4 Get students to do the exercise in pairs or small groups. During the activity, monitor and help as necessary. Ask a few pairs or groups to share their ideas with the class.

Possible answers

1 The university probably needs to employ a security guard or another person on reception to help with access control; security cameras were also suggested by the speaker; staff, student and visitor ID cards would also be useful.
2 **low tech:** in-room safe, receptionist, warning signs in classrooms, locks on doors, lockers
high tech: house alarm system, room key cards to operate lifts, CCTV, RFID badges for door/building access, printing and scanning, fingerprint scanners, facial recognition
3 Students' own answers

Extra activities 6.2

A 🔊 6.01   This activity gives further practice of vocabulary from the listening. For weaker classes, pause the recording after the first item and get them started by doing it together. Get students to complete the exercise individually and then check their answers in pairs before class feedback.

Jenn: 1, 3, 7
Paul: 2, 4, 5, 8, 9
Aisha: 6

B This activity uses the vocabulary from Exercise A. Get students to do the exercise individually, then go over it with the whole group.

1 commit a crime **2** valuables **3** theft **4** safe
5 on duty **6** vandalism **7** keep an eye on
8 unattended **9** warning **10** locker **11** locking
12 setting

Grammar: Modal verbs of prohibition, obligation and no obligation

Students look at the grammar often used to say what you can't or must do.

5A 🔊 6.02   Get students to do the exercise individually. Play the recording for them to check answers. Point out that for item 2, in addition to *don't have to*, you could also use the synonym *don't need to*. Similarly, for item 5, both *didn't need to* and *didn't have to* are possible.

1 need to **2** don't have to **3** has to **4** mustn't
5 didn't need to **6** must

5B Complete the grammar rules as a class. There are five other examples of these modal verbs in the audioscript, which you could ask students to find:
- *whenever she **needs to** go somewhere*
- *lecturers **have to** remember to lock the staffroom door*
- *We **need to** leave our mobile phones with the guard*
- *you **have to** use for checking into and out of the building*
- *you **have to** use it to print or scan anything as well*

> **a** mustn't   **b** need to, has to, must   **c** don't have to
> **d** didn't need to

6 Refer students to the Grammar reference on page 123. Give them a few minutes to do the exercise individually. Monitor, and if students are struggling with any of the items, write them on the board and go through them with the whole class.

> **1** S – All sentences have the same meaning – this is an obligation.
> **2** S – Sentences b and c have the same meaning – there is no obligation.
>   D – Sentence a means there is an obligation to do this.
> **3** S – All sentences have the same meaning – they are asking a question about an obligation in the present or in general.
> **4** S – Sentences a and c have the same meaning – they refer to something that was not necessary to do in the past.
>   D – Sentence b refers to a prohibition in the present.

7 Assign this as homework or get students to do it individually, then check answers in pairs.

> **1** had to / needed to
> **2** didn't have to / didn't need to
> **3** must / have to / need to
> **4** mustn't
> **5** has to / needs to / must
> **6** mustn't
> **7** must / has to / needs to
> **8** doesn't have to / doesn't need to

Extra activities 6.2

C This activity gives further practice of modal verbs of prohibition, obligation and no obligation. Give students a few minutes to do the exercise individually. Monitor, and if students are struggling with any of the items, write them on the board and go through them with the whole class.

> **1**   All visitors must ~~to~~ report to reception on arrival.
> **2**   They needed **to** leave early to catch their flight.
> **3**   ✔
> **4**   Staff **didn't have to pay** for the meal. It was courtesy of the company.
> **5**   ✔
> **6**   ✔
> **7**   **Did you have to** show your ID to the security guard?
> **8**   ✔
> **9**   ✔
> **10** My door is always open. You **don't have to** make an appointment to see me.

> **Pronunciation bank**
> **p.116: Phrasing and pausing**
>
> **Warm-up**
> Say the following as quickly as possible and without pausing: *Hello everyone I'm happy to see you and now we're going to talk about pronunciation.* Ask: *Did you understand what I just said?* (probably not) *Why not?* (It was too fast. It all ran together.) Repeat the sentence, this time with good phrasing and pausing: *Hello, everyone. I'm happy to see you. And now, we're going to talk about pronunciation.* Ask: *Was that easier to understand?* (yes) *Why?* (Because it wasn't too fast. There were pauses.) Refer students to the explanation in the box.

1 ◆ P6.01   Ask students to complete the exercise individually and then compare answers in pairs. Check answers with the class.

> b

2 ◆ P6.02   Play the recording for students to do the exercise.

> Retail theft, / also known as shoplifting, / is a major problem for shops. / In the past, / prevention measures were more personal / and low-tech. / Shopkeepers / and employees / had to watch customers closely / and the security system didn't need to be any more sophisticated than that.

3 Put students in pairs and ask them to do the exercise. During the activity, monitor to check that students are using effective phrasing and pausing.

Writing

Students write an email to colleagues about a security measure.

8A Get students to read the instructions, including the bullet points. Give them a few minutes to think and make notes about their emails. During the activity, monitor and help as necessary.

> **Model answer**
> Hello everyone,
>
> This is to inform you about new ID cards which we're introducing due to some thefts in the building recently. All staff must go to the HR department to prepare these by the end of this month. From 1 July, employees have to show their ID cards at reception when they enter the building. You do not have to wear the badge at all times but you must show it to any member of staff if requested.
>
> Regards,

8B Students can provide feedback in pairs or you can collect their work for marking and later feedback. As an optional round-up, ask and elicit answers to these questions: *What was the most interesting/surprising information you learnt about security in this lesson? In what situations could you typically use the modal verbs when speaking and writing?*

MyEnglishLab: Teacher's resources: extra activities; Reading bank
Grammar reference: p.123 Modal verbs of prohibition, obligation and no obligation
Pronunciation bank: p.116 Phrasing and pausing
Teacher's book: Resource bank Photocopiable 6.2 p.143
Workbook: p.30 Exercises 1–3, p.31 Exercises 1–3

6.3 ❯ Communication skills
Dealing with disagreement

GSE learning objectives

- Can tell when speakers agree or disagree in a work-related discussion.
- Can suggest pros and cons when discussing a topic, using simple language.
- Can give or seek personal views and opinions in discussing topics of interest.
- Can explain rules and requirements.
- Can discuss rules and requirements in a meeting or negotiation.

Warm-up

Write *confident* on the board and teach or elicit the meaning (feeling or showing that you can deal with a situation successfully). Ask: *How does someone who isn't confident behave?* (They don't speak up; they may try to hide; they may not speak clearly; they may often say things such as *I'm not sure, but* …) Say: *Today we're going to talk about confidence.*

Lead-in

Students explore confidence in speech and body language.

1A Put students in pairs and ask them to discuss the quotation. Get a few opinions and discuss ideas as a class.

1B Discuss in pairs, then compare answers as a class.

Possible answers

tone of voice
posture (sitting straight, standing)
positive body language (don't fold your arms), smile, eye contact (not intense)
speak slightly more slowly and clearly

Video

Students watch a video about different ways of dealing with disagreement.

2 ▶ 6.3.1   In the first sequence, Beata talks about her upcoming meeting with Mateo and explains how she feels about it. Play the video and answer the questions with the whole class.

1 nervous, worried
2 She finds Mateo increasingly difficult to work with, he doesn't want to follow regulations, she will have to negotiate and it won't be easy.
3 She wants to maintain a good relationship and make a good impression on Daniel. She wants Mateo to accept the storage regulations.
4 Students' own answers

3A Explain to the class the idea of Beata having two options in her meeting with Mateo and go through the details of Options A and B. Make it clear to students that they can choose which option they want to see first on the video. Put students in small groups and ask them to discuss the two options, giving reasons for their answers. Elicit ideas from a few groups and as a class, decide which video to watch first.

3B ▶ 6.3.2   ▶ 6.3.3   Tell the class to answer the questions for Option A or B depending on their choice, and play the video. You could ask students to discuss the questions in their groups first, and then check the answers as a whole class. Do the same for the second video.

Option A
1 It must be refrigerated at 5°C.
2 at room temperature
3 She first tries to explain why the regulations are important, but Mateo doesn't allow her to do this.
4 Beata and Mateo don't agree on the storage requirements. Beata tells Mateo that Daniel will call him to explain the situation.
5 She believes Mateo doesn't respect her but she managed to keep things professional.

Option B
1 It must be refrigerated at 5°C.
2 at room temperature
3 She firmly states the company's position on storage requirements.
4 Beata and Mateo don't agree on the storage requirements. She says she can't approve delivery. She tells Mateo that Daniel will call him to explain the situation.
5 She is frustrated but knows she couldn't agree to the delivery. She is worried what Daniel may think about how she handled the situation.

4 Put students in pairs and give them a couple of minutes to discuss the questions. During the activity, monitor and help as necessary.

Option B had the most positive outcome for the company. In Option B, Beata was not able to maintain good relations with Mateo on a personal level, but she remained strong on the company's policy regarding storage regulations. In Option A, as her main aim was to maintain good relations with Mateo, she allowed him to think that ignoring the regulations was possible.

5 ▶ 6.3.4   Explain that students are going to watch another video, which is a commentary on the communication issues they have seen in the previous videos. Play the video and give students 3–4 minutes to discuss and make notes, then discuss the main learning points with the whole class.

Possible answers

Use a lower voice and use pauses to punctuate your speech and indicate important information.
Use positive body language to show authority.
State your position strongly and explain rules and requirements.
Show you understand the other person's situation to help you build or maintain a good professional relationship with him/her.

Reflection

Students reflect on the conclusions from the video and discuss their own skills in dealing with disagreement.

6 Allow students to work individually on this so that they can reflect on their own preferences and ideas. Ask them to think of their own answers to the questions and to make notes. Then put students in pairs to discuss their answers. Get brief feedback from the class.

Functional language: Explaining rules and requirements

Students look at phrases that are commonly used to explain rules and requirements.

7A Explain that this exercise highlights expressions from the video that we use to explain rules and requirements. Teach or elicit the meaning of *EU rules* (laws set by the European Union). Get students to do the exercise in pairs, then check answers as a class.

---

1 g **2** i **3** h **4** a **5** d **6** c **7** f **8** e **9** b

---

7B Get students to do this individually, then check answers in pairs.

---

1 B **2** A **3** C **4** B **5** C

---

8 Tell students that they are going to build up a conversation from some basic information that they will be given and the phrases from Exercise 7. Divide the class into Students A and Students B and get them to form pairs. Get Students A to look at page 134 and Students B to look at page 138. For weaker classes, get them to work together to make notes for each speaker before they do the roleplay. During the activity, monitor and help as necessary.

Model answers

1 I appreciate you've already done a lot of work. But it needs to be finished by the end of the week. As I explained, it's a question of keeping to the schedule.
2 I can see you've not had a holiday for two years. I understand the tickets for Australia are expensive. However, I'm not comfortable agreeing to your holiday without speaking to the HR Director first. I hope you understand the situation. It's important that we can hire someone to cover your work while you're on holiday.

Extra activities 6.3

A This activity gives more practice of the phrases for dealing with disagreement. Get students to do the exercise individually and check answers in pairs.

---

1 j **2** h **3** f **4** a **5** e **6** d **7** b **8** i **9** c **10** g

---

B Get students to read the information next to the activity. Point out that in addition to making you sound more confident, pausing can also make you easier to understand. Get students to do the exercise in pairs.

Model answer

I can assure you, [P] the product needs to be refrigerated. [P] This is a question of patient safety. [P] I understand this is difficult for you. [P] And you've already done so much to help promote the product. [P] But my position is clear. [P] We can't go ahead with the delivery [P] unless the necessary storage measures are in place. [P] I have no doubt [P] that Daniel will say the same thing. [P] I'm sure we want the same outcome, Mateo. [P] But either we find a compromise [P] or I can't approve the delivery.

C Tell students that they are going to practise reading the text now. Have them work in pairs and read it a couple of times each, helping each other with posture and pace.

Task

Students roleplay a scenario where there is some disagreement.

9A Students will need to do a certain amount of preparation before they begin the task, so bear this in mind when you are planning this stage. Put students in groups of three and get them to decide who takes each role in the scenario.

9B Ask all three students in each group to read the information on page 133. Refer Student C also to page 131. As observer, Student C will listen to the conversation between Students A and B, make notes and give feedback. Allow 3–4 minutes for everyone to think and make some notes about what they will need to say. Remind them to try to use the phrases from Exercise 7.

9C The groups do the roleplay. During the activity, monitor and help as necessary.

9D Ask students to discuss the language they used, and what, if anything, they found difficult. Round off the task by asking how they will handle giving and responding to instructions and standing their ground in the future. With stronger classes, get students to write three action points starting *In future meetings I will …*

MyEnglishLab: Teacher's resources: extra activities; Interactive video activities
Workbook: p.32 Exercise 1

6.4 ❯ Business skills
Dealing with conflict

GSE learning objectives

- Can extract key details from conversations between colleagues about familiar topics.
- Can suggest a resolution to a conflict in a simple negotiation using fixed expressions.
- Can make and respond to suggestions.

Warm-up

Write *conflict* on the board and teach or elicit the meaning (disagreement, argument, fighting). Ask for some examples of conflict (any kind of argument between friends, 'road rage' when people get angry at other drivers, war, an argument between friends about what movie to see, etc.). Accept any reasonable answers, but point out that the word *conflict* can describe something simple like already having an appointment at a time that someone wants to meet you (*Sorry, I have a scheduling conflict.*), all the way up to a war.

Lead-in

Students look at conflicts within teams and the possible reasons for them.

1A Get students to look at the pictures and elicit what each one shows (left: a boss handing over a large quantity of work to an employee; middle: a pile of washing-up in an office kitchen; a spillage on a factory/workshop floor). Students do the exercise in pairs. Elicit other possible conflicts that people might have, but be careful to keep it light and avoid discussion of serious conflict that may be difficult to talk about.

1B Give students a chance to read the four sentences first and to tick the ones they agree with before explaining their choices to a partner. Ask a few pairs to share their ideas with the class.

1C As students do the exercise, monitor and help as necessary. If you would like to get the class up and moving, get the groups to do the exercise by writing their ideas on the board or a flip chart.

Possible answers

Begin by asking why your colleague is unhappy.
Don't focus on the person or their personality, focus on the problem.
Listen actively.
Encourage open communication/discussion.
Accept that conflict is part of life.
Don't interrupt when the other person is expressing their opinion.
Treat the other person and their opinions with respect.
Don't impose (force) your personal beliefs on the other person.

Listening

Students listen to a conversation about a problem at work.

2A 🔊 6.03 Get students to read the instructions, then play the recording. Answer the question quickly as a class.

> Picture 3 – a spillage on a factory floor

2B 🔊 6.03 Get students to read the items so that they know what they are listening for. Teach or elicit the meaning of *apprentice* (a worker who has little experience and is learning the job). Play the recording again. Get students to do the exercise individually, then compare answers in pairs.

> 1 T
> 2 F – Tony's apprentices are not responsible for cleaning.
> 3 F – The cleaner only works in the evenings.
> 4 T
> 5 T

2C Students do the exercise in pairs. During the activity, monitor and help as necessary. Then discuss ideas with the whole class.

2D 🔊 6.04 Get students to read the items so that they know what they are listening for. Ask them to do the exercise individually, then compare answers in pairs. Check answers with the whole class.

> 1 The company will provide slip-resistant shoes for the apprentices.
> 2 He agrees but is still concerned about repairing the machine.
> 3 yes
> 4 She will speak to the management team, suggests that she and Tony review the issue at the end of the week, and will send an email to summarise their decision.

Functional language: Resolving a conflict

Students practise using language for dealing with disagreement.

3A Explain to students that these are sentences from the listening. You could do this exercise with the whole class, checking answers as you go along.

> 1 appreciate, difficult 2 understand, saying 3 see, both
> 4 proceed 5 come 6 suggestion 7 check, happy

3B Get students to do the exercise individually, then check answers in pairs.

> 1 a 2 a, b 3 a 4 b 5 c 6 c 7 d

3C Get students to do the exercise individually, then check answers in pairs. Check answers with the whole class.

> 1 a 2 c 3 d 4 c 5 a 6 d 7 b 8 b

Extra activities 6.4

A ◀) 6.03   ◀) 6.04   This exercise gives students more practice of the language from the listening. Get them to do the exercise individually, then check answers in pairs. Answer any questions students may have.

1 I understand what you're saying
2 how do we proceed
3 what's your solution
4 my suggestion is to
5 sounds like a good idea
6 what about
7 Can I just check

❯ **Pronunciation bank**
p.116: Stress in phrases

Warm-up

Write the following on the board: *What are you doing?* Get students to say the phrase and ask: *Which syllables are stressed?* Elicit *What are you doing?* and underline them on the board. Refer students to the explanation in the box and drill the pronunciation of the example phrases.

1 Ask students to complete the exercise in pairs. Do not confirm answers yet as students will check them in the next exercise.

2 ◀) P6.03   Play the recording for students to check their answers.

1 It's important to a<u>void</u> <u>con</u>flict.
2 Now it's <u>over</u> to <u>you</u>.
3 Believe me, I <u>know</u> how you <u>feel</u>.
4 OK, then, <u>what's</u> the so<u>lu</u>tion?
5 Let's do the job as <u>quick</u>ly as <u>pos</u>sible.
6 I think we can <u>come</u> to a <u>com</u>promise.
7 So, <u>what</u> do <u>you</u> sug<u>gest</u>?
8 So, <u>how</u> do we pro<u>ceed</u>?

3 Put students in pairs and ask them to do the exercise. During the activity, monitor to check that students are stressing the correct syllables.

Task

Students act out a scenario where they have to deal with a conflict.

4A Put students in pairs and get them to read the scenario.

4B Get students to decide on roles. Refer them to the role cards on pages 132 and 134. Give them two or three minutes to read the cards. Answer any questions they may have. Remind them to review the useful phrases in Exercise 3.

4C As students do the roleplay, monitor and help as necessary.

4D Ask students to discuss the language they used and what, if anything, they found difficult. Round off the task by asking how students will handle conflict in the future. With stronger classes, get students to write three action points starting *In future conflicts I will …*

MyEnglishLab: Teacher's resources: extra activities; Functional language bank
Pronunciation bank: p.116 Stress in phrases
Workbook: p.32 Exercise 2

6.5 ❯ Writing
Instructions and warnings

GSE learning objectives

- Can write guidelines that clearly convey information.
- Can write basic instructions with a simple list of points.
- Can use a range of prepositions of time such as *before, during, since, till/until.*

Warm-up

Write *car* on the board. Ask: *What are some safety instructions and warnings for using a car?* Discuss any reasonable answers. (Possible answers: Wear a seat belt. Don't drive too fast. Don't text and drive at the same time. Wear your glasses or contact lenses when you drive.)

Lead-in

Students complete warnings and instructions for using equipment.

1A Revise or elicit the meaning of *protective clothing* (clothes that make you safe in a dangerous place, e.g. clothes that do not burn, that are difficult to cut, that protect your head). Focus attention on the instructions and warnings and ask: *Where do you see this sort of notice?* (probably in a factory) Get students to do the exercise individually. During the activity, monitor and help as necessary.

1 Put   2 Follow   3 Make   4 Report   5 touch   6 remove
7 Watch   8 Be

1B After students check answers in pairs, go over them quickly with the whole class. Point out that we often talk about *dos and don'ts* in all kinds of contexts – things you should and shouldn't do.

Functional language

Students look at the language of dos, don'ts and warnings.

2 Teach or elicit the meaning of *trip hazards* (things on the floor that may cause you to fall, e.g. electrical wires) and *forklift truck* (a vehicle for lifting heavy things, often used in a warehouse – a place where products are stored). Get students to do the exercise individually, then check answers in pairs. Point out that a warning usually uses an expression such as *beware of, be careful* of or *watch out for.*

1 DT   2 D   3 W   4 D   5 D   6 D   7 DT   8 W

Extra activities 6.5

A This activity gives further practice of phrases used for dos, don'ts and warnings. Get students to complete the exercise individually and then get them to check answers in pairs before class feedback.

1 forget **2** must **3** allowed **4** Watch **5** Don't
6 mustn't **7** sure **8** Beware **9** Leave **10** careful

Optional grammar work

The guidelines and instructions in Exercises 1 and 2 contain examples of linking words for time, so you could use them for some optional grammar work. Refer students to the Grammar reference on page 123 and use the exercises in MyEnglishLab for extra grammar practice.

Task

Students read information about how to lift heavy loads or what to do in a fire and create guidelines.

3A Put students in pairs. Ask them to choose who is Student A and who is Student B, and refer them to their information on pages 132 and 134. Give them some time to read their information, and answer any questions they may have. With weaker classes, spend some time going through the information, as there is a lot to take in. Get them to look at the headings and explain that the first task is simply to read and think about the information and how it might fit under the headings. They will write the guidelines in the next exercise.

3B Set a time limit for the writing task and remind students to use their ideas from Exercise 3A and the phrases from Exercises 1 and 2. Students write their guidelines in pairs.

Model answers

HANDLING HEAVY LOADS

Before lifting
- check size and weight of load
- check destination
- plan route
- check route for potential obstacles
- clear potential obstacles from route
- check available equipment to help move load

Lifting
- stand with feet apart
- keep knees and hips relaxed
- bend your knees
- take hold of load at the bottom
- lift steadily and smoothly keeping back straight
- keep load close to your body

Putting down
- follow the above instructions in reverse

Never
- twist your body while carrying heavy loads
- lift anything that is too heavy for one person

FIRE EMERGENCY

You must
- know where the fire exits and assembly points are

If you find a fire
- keep calm and leave the office with other staff
- sound the fire alarm
- only use an extinguisher if you are trained

How to escape
- close the door when everyone is out
- check doors are not hot before opening them
- if there's smoke, cover mouth and nose and keep close to floor level
- leave the building by the nearest exit
- meet at the assembly point outside

If you cannot leave office
- block any door gaps to stop fire and smoke entering
- open windows and shout for help

Never
- take personal items with you
- use the lifts
- return to the building until it is officially safe

3C Get students to do the exercise in new pairs, each made of one Student A and one Student B. Encourage them to suggest corrections if they think there is an error in their partner's guidelines. During the activity, monitor and help as necessary.

MyEnglishLab: Teacher's resources: extra activities; Interactive grammar practice; Writing bank

Grammar reference: p.123 Linking words for time

Workbook: p.28 Exercises 1 and 2

Business workshop >6
Visitor safety

GSE learning objectives

- Can scan short texts to locate specific information.
- Can contribute to a group discussion if the discussion is conducted slowly and clearly.
- Can write a short report on a work-related task or event.

Background

Students read about a company that needs to address security and safety issues.

1 Teach or elicit the meaning of *accessories for electronic devices* (extra products that usually do not come with the device when you buy it, e.g. cases, extra batteries, a selfie stick for a mobile phone). Ask students to read the background and discuss the questions in pairs. Check answers with the class.

1 It's a company which designs and produces accessories for electronic devices.
2 The company is going to move into a new office building and factory.
3 Possible answers: Maybe they have grown too quickly and not had time. Maybe they forgot or didn't think it was necessary.
4 Possible answers: He/She might bring in more up-to-date digital technology. He/She will be able to make sure that everyone follows the rules.
5 Students' own answers

Safety and security

Students discuss potential hazards in a factory.

2A Focus attention on the signs and elicit the meaning of each (A: You must wear goggles / eye protection. B: Take extra care / Be careful on the stairs. C: Be careful! Slippery/Wet floor/ground). Put students in small groups to do the exercise. During the activity, monitor and help as necessary. Share answers with the whole class.

> **Possible answers**
> machines or material that could damage the eyes; stairs; wet or slippery floors; machines that could catch clothing or fingers; smoke or dangerous gases; noise from machines; forklifts or other vehicles; danger from things falling on you

2B Students choose one of the ideas from Exercise 2A and work in pairs to design a sign. Point out that the example signs in Exercise 2A do not include any words. During the activity, monitor and help as necessary. Get students to put their work up on the wall to see if others can correctly understand the meaning of the sign.

3A Refer students to the report on page 137 and get them to do the exercise individually. Check answers with the whole class.

3B The report mentions risk assessment but is not a risk assessment document. That will be covered in Exercise 4. Teach or elicit the meaning of *risk assessment* (see Notes below). Get students to do the exercise in pairs.

> 1 equipment; chemicals; poor ventilation; heat; staff remove safety guards and fail to replace them; staff leave things on the floor
> 2 robots never forget; they always follow procedures; they don't daydream or get distracted; they are never tired, angry or bored; they are never late for work or sick; they are always reliable, therefore profitable
> 3 incorrectly installed/programmed; maintenance requirements
> 4 quick
> 5 easy to hack; privacy

> **Notes**
> A **risk assessment** is an examination of the possible risks involved in doing something, so that organisations can decide whether something is worth doing and how they can reduce the possibility that people will be injured. Risk assessments must be done in places such as schools and care homes, and also for events such as concerts or school field trips.

Extra activities Business workshop 6

A In this exercise, students will look more closely at some of the language in the report. Check answers with the class.

> 1 e 2 h 3 a 4 g 5 b 6 c 7 d 8 f

B In this exercise, students look at word families, e.g. *face* and *facial*. Get them to complete the exercise individually. Check answers with the class.

> 1 facial 2 identification/identity 3 privacy
> 4 installation 5 scanners 6 recognition
> 7 criminals 8 hazardous 9 Protective 10 reliable

Risk assessment

Students listen to an interview with a risk-assessment expert and complete notes.

4A ◀》 BW 6.01 Teach or elicit the meaning of *trailing wires* (electrical wires that are hanging down, not attached to a wall or ceiling) and *absenteeism* (the situation of people missing work). Play the recording. Students do the exercise and check answers in pairs.

> 1 Identify 2 carpet 3 noise 4 lighting 5 backache
> 6 Evaluate

4B Get students to work in pairs or groups of three. If necessary, get them started by asking: *What is dangerous about heavy boxes?* (They can hurt you when you lift them; they can fall on you or crush your hands or feet.) Get them to continue thinking of ideas. During the activity, monitor and help as necessary.

4C Explain that this basic risk assessment form is typical in many work situations. Before students do the exercise, teach or elicit some of the vocabulary they might need: *first aider* (someone who is trained to give first aid – simple medical treatment that is given as soon as possible to someone who is injured or who suddenly becomes ill), *accident record sheet* (a document where workers write details of injuries received at work), *run somebody over* (to hit someone or something with a vehicle and drive over them), *knock somebody over* (to hit someone with a vehicle while you are driving, so that they are hurt or killed), *beep* (if a forklift beeps when it reverses, it makes a series of short, loud sounds). Get students to take their ideas about lifting heavy boxes from Exercise 4B and complete the form. Then get them to complete a risk assessment for forklift trucks and ladders.

Possible answers

1 *Lifting heavy boxes*
2 Injuries to back / Dropping boxes on feet
3 *Warehouse staff*
4 There is training for staff and signs in the warehouse showing them how to lift correctly.
5 *People might forget to lift properly* (and cause injuries to themselves and others – quite likely to happen)
6 Call company first-aider, call ambulance and take to hospital; complete accident record sheet

1 Working near forklift trucks
2 Could be knocked over / Vehicle could run over feet
3 Warehouse staff
4 Training, warning signs and all vehicles must beep continually while they are moving
5 Someone might turn off the warning beep so workers are not aware of vehicle – unlikely to happen
6 Call company first-aider, call ambulance and take to hospital; complete accident record sheet

1 Using ladders
2 Falling from ladder / Ladder falling or slipping because no one is holding it / Dropping things on workers below
3 Warehouse staff
4 Train staff about using ladders and put up signs reminding them of the procedures
5 Staff often use the ladder without someone holding it and they can easily fall or ladder can slip – could happen
6 Call company first-aider, call ambulance and take to hospital; complete accident record sheet

Visitor information for factory visits

Students discuss why visitors to a factory are more likely than workers to have an injury.

5A Often, visiting business people are given a factory tour. While they may be given a hard hat, eye protection and maybe ear protection, they are rarely given full personal protective equipment. Put students in small groups. Get them to read the statement and do the exercise.

Possible answers

Visitors may not be aware of the hazards in a factory and may not be trained to look out for them. They may not have full protective clothing. They may not be trained in how to deal with hazards (e.g. washing chemicals out of eyes).

5B Get students to do this in their same small groups. If necessary, get them started by asking: *What do factory visitors need to know about equipment?* (They need to know what they can and can't touch, which equipment may catch their hair or clothing, which machines may be very hot, etc.)

Task: Prepare a visitor safety and security report

Students discuss possible hazards for visitors to a factory and create a report for management.

6A For smaller classes, put students in two groups, A and B. For larger classes, you may want several A groups and several B groups of 3–5 students each.

6B Point out that this exercise has two steps: first, they come up with procedures that should be put in place and second, with a list of signs they recommend. For the first step, they should use all the ideas they discussed in Exercises 5B and 6A.

Possible answers

Group A: Safety
- ID badge
- must have company rep with them at all times
- personal protective equipment – protective glasses must be worn in machine area, wear solid, sensible shoes, no jewellery, no shorts, hearing protection
- follow pedestrian walkways / don't leave group
- be careful of vehicles in factory / moving machinery
- don't touch any machinery/equipment
- tell them about fire procedures / what do in the event of a fire
- identify all hazards – forklift trucks, fumes from a machine, signpost warnings
- make sure they don't put hands on moving conveyor belts, etc.
- watch for hot or sharp surfaces

Group B: Security
- no videos or photos allowed
- wear visitor badge at all times
- do not take anything away from factory
- control access to confidential areas

6C Put students in pairs – one person from Group A and one from B. Point out that there are two steps. First, students present their ideas to each other. This needs to be done in the classroom. During the activity, monitor and help as necessary. Second, students write a report similar to the one in Exercise 3. If you have time, this can be done in class. Otherwise, assign it as homework.

Model answer

Introduction
We have been asked to prepare a visitor safety and security report recommending new safety and security procedures for visitors to the new premises. After completing a risk assessment, the following actions are recommended.

1 Security

1.1 Offices
Firstly, only authorised visitors can enter our premises. So security must be quick and effective. All visitors to the main reception should have their photo taken and complete a form with basic information so that a security identification badge can be made. This must be visible at all times. We also feel that mobile phones and cameras should not be used in our premises.

1.2 Factory
Access to the factory should only be given to senior staff and we should use fingerprint recognition for access to increase security. A senior staff member must be responsible for any visitors they have to the factory and they should inform reception when visitors are coming. They must also sign in their visitors at reception.

2 Safety

2.1 Offices

All visitors should be warned not to touch office equipment unless a member of staff is present.

2.2 Factory

There are more potential hazards for visitors in the factory. The person responsible for the visitor must make sure that the visitor has read the safety rules before entering the factory. Visitors should wear protective clothing at all times and not go anywhere without a member of staff.

In conclusion, we feel that these recommendations will ensure that our premises are secure and that visitors are kept safe.

MyEnglishLab: Teacher's resources: extra activities

Review ‹ 6

1 **1** pose **2** issue **3** visibility **4** masks **5** resistant
   6 defenders **7** fit **8** handle **9** hold **10** record
   11 drops **12** injures

2 **1** must **2** don't have **3** have **4** didn't have
   5 must **6** didn't need to **7** have to **8** Must we

3 **1** must **2** have/need **3** position **4** Either **5** unless
   6 relationship **7** outcome **8** see

4 **1** from both sides **2** we proceed **3** really appreciate
   4 suggestion is **5** not happy with **6** how you feel
   7 come to a compromise **8** Why don't we
   9 to an agreement

5 **1** Don't **2** Beware **3** Make **4** not allowed
   5 mustn't **6** forget **7** Watch **8** careful

7 >> Customer service

Unit overview

	CLASSWORK		FURTHER WORK
7.1 > **Airline customer service**	Lead-in	Students discuss good customer service.	**MyEnglishLab:** Teacher's resources: extra activities
	Video	Students watch a video about customer service in the airline industry.	**Teacher's book:** Resource bank Photocopiable 7.1 p.144
	Vocabulary	Students look at vocabulary related to air travel and prepositions that follow certain words.	**Workbook:** p.34 Exercises 1–3
	Project	Students design an expensive service where a high level of customer care is essential.	
7.2 > **Hanging on the telephone**	Lead-in	Students talk about how they communicate with customer service departments.	**MyEnglishLab:** Teacher's resources: extra activities; Reading bank
	Listening	Students listen to two customer service phone conversations.	**Grammar reference:** p.124 Verb + *to*-infinitive or *-ing*
	Grammar	Students learn how to form phrases with verb + *to*-infinitive or *-ing*.	**Pronunciation bank:** p.117 Unstressed syllables at the end of a sentence
	Writing	Students write a complaint on a company forum.	**Teacher's book:** Resource bank Photocopiable 7.2 p.145
			Workbook: p.35 Exercises 1–3, p.36 Exercises 1–3
7.3 > **Communication skills:** Responding to customer concerns	Lead-in	Students discuss their views on the saying 'the customer is always right'.	**MyEnglishLab:** Teacher's resources: extra activities; Interactive video activities
	Video	Students watch a video about the importance of responding well to customer concerns.	**Workbook:** p.37 Exercise 1
	Reflection	Students reflect on the conclusions from the video and discuss their own customer service skills.	
	Functional language	Students look at phrases they can use to deal with customers who are not satisfied.	
	Task	Students roleplay a scenario involving a manager and an unhappy customer.	
7.4 > **Business skills:** Generating and presenting ideas	Lead-in	Students discuss the importance of generating ideas.	**MyEnglishLab:** Teacher's resources: extra activities; Functional language bank
	Listening	Students listen to a manager giving an introduction to a staff training day.	**Pronunciation bank:** p.117 Introducing a topic
	Functional language	Students look at useful phrases for sharing and talking about ideas.	**Workbook:** p.37 Exercise 2
	Task	Students discuss ideas to solve a problem.	
7.5 > **Writing:** External 'thank you' email	Lead-in	Students read and complete a 'thank you' email.	**MyEnglishLab:** Teacher's resources: extra activities; Interactive grammar practice; Writing bank
	Functional language	Students look at the organisation of and some useful phrases for a 'thank you' email.	**Grammar reference:** p.124 *some (of), any, all (of), most (of), no, none (of)*
	Task	Students assess a 'thank you' email and then write their own.	**Workbook:** p.38 Exercises 1 and 2
Business workshop 7 > Red Cushion Furniture	Reading and Speaking	Students read and discuss case histories of how customer complaints were addressed by different companies.	**MyEnglishLab:** Teacher's resources: extra activities
	Listening	Students listen to a talk about dealing with unhappy customers.	
	Task	Students discuss, present and analyse problems with customer service and their solutions.	

Business brief

This unit looks at **customer service** – an organisation's effort before, during and after a purchase to help customers by answering their questions and listening to their complaints, giving them advice on using a particular product or service, and providing any other ongoing **product support**.

The success of any company depends on **customer satisfaction**, which is achieved when **customer expectations** are met, that is, when consumers get what they wanted. For **premium** products and services, where customers spend a lot of money, a high level of customer service is essential. In such situations, it is crucial for **customer-facing** employees to be able to create a positive experience for customers, even when dealing with a complaint. A single **customer experience** – good or bad – can deeply affect the customer's perception of the organisation.

For **budget** products and services, customer service may not be an important part of the relationship. Consumers are generally aware that a cheaper price means a more basic experience, and so expectations are lower.

A lot of customer service is carried out by telephone. This involves **customer service agents** at **call centres** – sometimes called **contact centres** – answering phones and trying to deal with questions. The global telecommunications network makes it possible for call centres to be located virtually anywhere in the world, so often customers in the UK or the USA may receive **telephone support** from India, the Philippines or Pakistan. Some companies also offer support using **live chat**, where customers type questions or comments into a **chat window**, the customer service agent responds and a conversation takes place.

Increasingly, some aspects of customer service are **automated**. Rather than a direct connection with a person, telephone customer service may consist partly or completely of menu options that can be chosen by pressing numbers on the phone's keypad. In addition, websites often provide lists of **FAQs** (frequently asked questions) and also **chatbots** – computer programs that can answer basic questions using a chat window. Chatbots are increasingly difficult to distinguish from actual people performing customer-service duties online.

In business, there is an old saying: *The customer is always right*. This attitude is intended to stress the importance of good customer service. Without happy customers, businesses will not succeed. However, it has been pointed out that this attitude can make employees unhappy when customers have unreasonable expectations or are rude, and can encourage customers to be aggressive and to take advantage. It might be more reasonable to say that customers should be treated with warmth and respect, and that their concerns should be taken seriously and dealt with quickly.

Customer service and your students

Most jobs are in some way connected to or supported by customers buying products or services. Even workers who never deal directly with the public need to remember that, ultimately, their goal is customer satisfaction. Students who are not yet working will need to develop an understanding of the importance of customer service in all fields. Working students can improve their understanding of customer service skills in order to develop their careers.

Unit lead-in

Look at the quote and ask students what it means. Elicit the idea that though a company may have a department called Customer Service, in fact, companies exist only because there are customers, so it is every worker's job to serve the customer. Look at the photograph and ask if anyone knows what it shows (an Egyptian plover cleaning the teeth of a Nile crocodile). Ask if the photograph has a message about customer service. (When customers are happy, the relationship is easy, but if the customer becomes upset, it could be very difficult for the customer service employee.)

7.1 ❯ Airline customer service

GSE learning objectives

- Can follow the main points in TV programmes on familiar topics if delivered in clear and standard speech.
- Can give or seek personal views and opinions in discussing topics of interest.
- Can use language related to complaints and resolving complaints.
- Can give a simple presentation on a work-related topic.

Warm-up

Write the following on the board: *Good customer service is about looking after the customer before, during and after the sale.* Ask students to think of examples of customer service they have experienced at each stage. Examples: Before – going into a shop and being asked if you'd like help finding anything; During – having a car salesperson talk through all of the options available for a car you have decided to buy; After – taking a faulty product back to a store to exchange it for one that works. If you would like to extend the discussion, ask students to tell stories of both good and bad customer service experiences they have had.

Lead-in

Students discuss good customer service.

1 Put students in groups and give them a minute to read the instructions. Encourage them to think of other businesses and services, e.g. a department store, clothes shop or supermarket. After students have talked for a couple of minutes, get them to share a few ideas with the class, then teach or elicit the idea of the stages of customer service (see Notes below) and how the service could be good or bad at each stage.

Video

Students watch a video about customer service in the airline industry.

2 ▶ 7.1.1 Teach or elicit the meaning of *ground staff* and *in-flight staff* (see Notes below). Give students a minute to read items a–e, then play the video. Get students to compare answers in pairs before checking with the class.

> **1** c **2** e **3** a **4** d **5** b

Notes

In aviation, ground staff (also ground crew) are the people who work for an airline in an airport rather than on an aircraft. This includes people who check tickets, people who load luggage into planes, people who direct planes, etc. The in-flight staff are the crew on the aeroplane – flight attendants who deal with passengers and pilots who fly planes.

3 ▶ 7.1.1 Give students a minute to read the notes. Then play the first part of the video again (00:00–02:23). Get students to compare answers in pairs before checking with the class. Ask if anyone understood any more details about the type of training sessions – assertiveness (taking control of situations) and interpersonal skills (communicating effectively).

> **1** queue **2** extras **3** on time **4** a hotel
> **5** training (sessions) **6** (customer service) problems

4 ▶ 7.1.1 Give students a minute to read the summary. With stronger classes, you could ask students to try to do the exercise before watching, then watch and check/complete their answers. Play the video again (2:24–4:12) and then check answers with the class.

> In the premium service segment, airline companies ~~remove~~ **add on** little extras that passengers ~~ask least~~ **pay more / are charged more** for. For example, United Airlines attracts business-class and first-class passengers with ~~its faster~~ **no** queue to check in. The company's CEO says that their research showed that a good ~~food service~~ **night's sleep** was most important for passengers. British Airways distinguishes its first-class service through an elaborate ritual on board: the British ~~breakfast~~ **afternoon tea**. For airlines, things like a ~~big lunch~~ **business lounge** and comfortable bed are ways to make passengers feel more important and better cared for.

5 Put students in pairs or small groups to discuss the questions. For question 1, make sure they understand *pros* (good points) and *cons* (bad points). For question 2, clarify that students should work individually to answer the questions, then compare answers with their partner. During the activity, monitor and help / correct students as necessary. If you want to extend the exercise, ask: *How might leisure and business passengers' needs be different?* (Leisure passengers often simply want to save money. Business passengers generally value comfort and efficiency.) *How do airlines offer a distinctive service for business travellers?* (Most airlines offer business-class seats, which are more comfortable and often come with better food service. They may also have business lounges in airports.)

Possible answers

1 Low-cost airlines

Pros: they are cheap; they get you from A to B, usually on time; they are safe

Cons: you have to pay not to queue, to board first and for everything else; they will not put you in a hotel if your flight is delayed; customers will get angry when things go wrong

Standard airlines
Pros: premium service; they handle all your bags; you get a big seat and lots of personal attention; extra and exclusive features; no queues at check-in; good food; able to sleep on board; priority baggage; distinctive customer service; cabin service; seat design; passenger feels important / better cared for
Cons: high price tag

Pros and cons not mentioned on the video
Low-cost airlines
Pros: special offers with even lower fares; mobile app for boarding pass
Cons: have to pay to check in baggage and hand baggage allowance is smaller than regular airlines; fly to secondary airports not close to city
Standard airlines
Pros: offer a wide range of international flights; strategic alliances with other airlines; fly to best airports
Cons: tendency to reduce costs and cut services (e.g. in-flight meals) in order to compete with low-cost airlines
2 Students' own answers

Extra activities 7.1

A ▶ 7.1.1 Ask students to do this individually, then play the video for them to check their answers. Check answers with the class and clarify any new vocabulary, e.g. *flag carrier* (an airline that is or used to be owned by a government, e.g. British Airways in the UK) and *priority* (most important).

> **1** elite **2** choice **3** goes wrong **4** assertiveness
> **5** body language, raise **6** price tag **7** Flag carrier
> **8** priority, on board **9** charge

Vocabulary: Customer service

Students look at vocabulary related to air travel and prepositions that follow certain words.

6A Explain that the words are from the video. Students could do this individually or in pairs, using their dictionaries to help them.

> body language, business-/first-class, exclusive features, premium service, 'no-frills' flight, personal attention, priority boarding, VIP treatment

6B Again, this exercise can be done individually or in pairs – the second option may be easier for weaker classes.

> **1** premium service / business-/first-class
> **2** exclusive features
> **3** business/first-class / premium service
> **4** VIP treatment / personal treatment
> **5** priority boarding
> **6** personal attention / VIP treatment

7 Do the first item on the board. Write *anxiety* and teach or elicit its meaning (the feeling of being very worried about something) and then teach or elicit the adjective form of the word (*anxious*). Point out that where there are two gaps, there are two or more correct answers. Get students to do the exercise. Let them use their dictionaries if they need help.

> **1** anxious **2** apology **3** assist **4** complaint
> **5** confident **6** demand **7** empathy **8** handle
> **9/10** helpful/unhelpful/helpless **11** request
> **12/13** satisfied/dissatisfied/satisfying/satisfactory/
> unsatisfactory **14** upset

8 Before students do this exercise, elicit or explain what a *dependent preposition* is (see Notes below). You could also point out some verb + noun collocations as an extension exercise, e.g. *offer assistance, make a complaint / an apology / a request*. Another option is to focus on the personal characteristics and skills needed for staff who have to handle demanding, dissatisfied or anxious customers, e.g. *assertive, calm, confident, friendly, helpful*. Also, elicit the negative characteristics they should not have, e.g. *rude, aggressive, uncaring*.

> ### Notes
>
> In English, as in other languages, many verbs, nouns and adjectives are followed by specific prepositions. These are called dependent prepositions because the preposition used depends on the particular word and its meaning. A frequent error students can make when speaking and writing in English is to transfer the dependent preposition from their native language. It is very useful to encourage students to notice the differences when they occur.

> **1** about **2** to, for/about **3** to **4** to, about
> **5** about/in **6** with

9 Put students in pairs or small groups to discuss the questions. Get a few students to share their answers with the class.

Extra activities 7.1

B This activity practises key vocabulary from the lesson. You could ask students to do it individually, as a quick vocabulary quiz, and then get them to compare answers in pairs before checking with the class. With weaker classes, you could help students by providing the last letter of each missing word.

> **1** personal **2** treatment **3** boarding **4** assistance
> **5** complaints **6** Handling **7** dissatisfied **8** helpful

Project: Design a premium service

Students design an expensive service where a high level of customer care is essential.

10A Students can do this project as a short round-up exercise at the end of class, without access to internet research. Alternatively, it can be done as an extended project, with students doing research into the latest trends in premium customer service. If you are doing it in class, put students in groups and go through the instructions. Answer any questions they may have before they begin and set a time limit. During the activity, monitor and help as necessary.

Possible answers

1 airlines – examples from video; banks – personal banking service, better rates on loans; hotels – access to VIP lounge; internet provider – higher-speed connection; restaurant – better table; online retailer – faster delivery; shop – personal shopper

2 Some more examples of companies offering premium services are: The online retailer Amazon, which has a premium faster delivery service. Cable TV channels that charge premium customers extra for exclusive access to more channels such as sports and film channels. In another example, Airbnb has introduced a premium service to compete with high-end hotels. TripAdvisor has a premium-subscriber service as well. Many professional websites, such as LinkedIn, also offer a premium service with more features.

3 Students' own answers

10B Get students to look at the box. Go over the ideas and elicit some additional ones (members-only services or products, products that include special product support, upgrades to a higher level of service, etc.). Groups choose one type of business they discussed in Exercise 10A and think about what they could offer as a premium service. During the activity, monitor and help as necessary.

10C Students present their ideas to other groups. Allow 4–6 minutes for each presentation. During the activity, monitor and help as necessary. Then give students feedback: suggest areas for improvement and highlight any errors that made communication difficult.

MyEnglishLab: Teacher's resources: extra activities
Teacher's book: Resource bank Photocopiable 7.1 p.144
Workbook: p.34 Exercises 1–3

7.2 ❯ Hanging on the telephone

GSE learning objectives

- Can extract key factual information from a phone conversation on a familiar topic.
- Can follow instructions on recorded phone menus.
- Can express how they feel in simple terms.
- Can express belief, opinion, agreement and disagreement politely.
- Can use a range of verbs taking *to* + infinitive.
- Can use a range of common verb + verb combinations using the -*ing* form.
- Can distinguish between *to* + infinitive and -*ing* after certain verbs with a change of meaning.
- Can write basic comments and complaints about products and services.

Warm-up

Ask the following questions, pausing after each one to elicit a few answers:
- *When did you last contact the customer service department of a company?*
- *Why did you contact them? A problem with a product or service? A question? Something else?*
- *How did you contact them? Phone? Internet? Visit to a shop?*

Lead-in

Students talk about how they communicate with customer service departments.

1 Teach or elicit the term *call centre* (an office where people answer customers' questions, make sales, etc. by using the telephone) and explain that *contact centre* is also popular these days. Teach or elicit the meaning of *chatbot* (a computer program designed to simulate conversation with people using artificial intelligence, especially over the internet), *live chat* (an online system where customers type questions or comments into a chat window, the customer service agent responds, and a conversation takes place) and *automated customer service systems* (see Notes below). Students answer the questions individually, then compare answers in pairs. As a round-up to students' discussions, find out who has had the worst experience(s) with customer service and what happened. Ask if they think automated customer service systems will be more common in the future.

Notes

Automated customer service systems: voice recognition and artificial intelligence (AI) applications online and on the phone, which are a growing trend. These interact with customers by responding to keywords and triggers. For example, this technology allows customers to do things like request account information or pay a bill through an automated system. More complex requests are passed to agents. Another common feature is self-service FAQs help on the website, which companies hope will reduce calls to contact centres.

1 Students' own ideas (Research shows most people prefer to phone a service agent when they have a problem or query.)
2 Students may have other experiences to add to the list, e.g.
  a An automated system does not understand your request.
  b You don't know which option to choose.
  c An automated voice tells you to call back later.
3 Students' own ideas

Listening

Students listen to two customer service phone conversations.

2A 🔊 7.01 Teach or elicit the meaning of *internet provider* (also called an internet service provider, or ISP – a company that provides the technical services that allow people to use the internet) and *phone provider* (a company that provides the service that allows you to make and receive calls on a mobile phone). Check that students understand the context for the listening (a customer is phoning her internet and phone provider). Play the recording, then check answers with the class.

Call 1: The woman called about her internet connection not working.
Call 2: She called to query her high mobile phone bill.

2B Ask: *What's a script?* (the written form of a speech, play, film, etc.) Ask: *What's the difference between a call with a script and one without a script?* (With a script, the agent will say only certain things and can't always respond to a caller's statement or question.) Discuss the question with the whole class. Also ask students if they think the mobile phone company should reduce Angela's phone bill.

In both conversations, there are elements of using a script.

3 🔊 7.02 Get students to do the exercise individually, then check answers as a class. Point out that item 8 is something the customer says in the call, although it is useful language for both callers and customer service agents. You could also refer students to the audioscript of the second phone call on page 150 to find more useful phrases for customer service agents (see Notes below).

Notes

These are useful phrases for customer service agents from audioscript 7.02:
I'm sorry, I don't understand.
Good morning, this is Judith speaking. Can I have your name, please?
I'm sorry for the long delay – we're receiving lots of calls today.
How can I help you, Angela?
Can I just ask your date of birth for verification purposes?
I'm just looking at your bill on screen.
I'm sorry, we can't do that, Angela.
We always recommend contacting customer services to check roaming charges abroad before you travel.
Next time don't forget to do that. You can also find the information on our website.
Can I help you with anything else today?
I'm afraid she will give you the same information.
OK, I'm just transferring you now.

1 busy 2 May I have 3 How can 4 account 5 just ask
6 give me 7 put you through 8 speak up 9 on hold
10 assist you with

4 🔊 7.03 Students could do this individually or in pairs. As an optional exercise, students could roleplay one or both of the phone calls using the audioscript or invent their own call centre dialogues using some of the useful phrases.

1 the phone number
2 the automated system does not understand what she wants
3 because she wants to talk to a person not a machine
4 because she went to a country (Andorra) outside the European Union and there was a roaming charge
5 to reduce the charge on her phone bill
6 to phone customer services or check the website before travelling abroad / to check roaming charges before she travels

5 Students could do this individually or in pairs. Check answers with the class.

Possible answers
1 My internet connection isn't working.
2 I'm sorry, I can't hear you very well.
3 Could you speak up, please?
4 I have a query about my mobile phone bill.
5 It's taken me fifteen minutes just to speak to a real person.
6 I want to query my mobile phone bill for last month.
7 Look, could you possibly reduce the charge?
8 Could I speak to your supervisor, please?

6 Do the exercise in small groups or as a class. Discuss the pros and cons of scripts.

Notes

Scripts and pre-designed decision trees on a call-centre agent's computer screen allow companies to provide a consistent service. However, this consistency can create interactions that may seem robotic. This can frustrate the customers and fail to result in a better customer experience, especially when the agent repeats the same script or can't deviate from the script. This feels unhelpful to customers rather than helpful.

1 Students' own answers
2 Students' own answers. There is an opportunity here to mention generational and cultural differences in communication styles in modern day 'one-size-fits-all' global customer service (see Notes below).
3 Students' own answers. Companies do this to try to increase sales.

Notes

The main issue for customer service agents using their caller's name is formality and the professional image of the company. The agent can often seem too informal if they use the caller's first name rather than *Sir* or *Madam*. Using *Mr* and *Ms* and the surname is a more universal sign of respect. Some callers may not like the fact that agents use their first names; it could seem impolite, insincere or over-familiar, especially when the caller is making a complaint. Whereas addressing people by their first name is now normal in North American business culture, it is not common in other parts of the world. Some companies tell agents to ask for their caller's full name and then ask how they prefer to be addressed to avoid offending.

Extra activities 7.2

A Students could do this exercise individually and then compare answers in pairs, using their dictionaries if necessary. Item 6, *busy*, is more common in American English. If a telephone you are calling is busy, it makes a repeated sound to tell you that the person you are calling is talking on their telephone. A synonym in British English is *engaged*.

1 screen **2** abroad **3** bill **4** turn on
5 switch off **6** busy **7** query **8** inquiry
9 put (someone) on hold **10** put (someone) through
11 roaming charge **12** account

B Again, students could do this exercise individually and then compare answers in pairs.

1 c **2** e **3** d **4** f **5** h **6** a **7** g **8** b

C Explain that each of the eight sentences in Exercise B fits into one of these four categories. Do the exercise with the class.

a 1,4,6 **b** 5 **c** 2,3 **d** 7,8

Grammar: Verb + *to*-infinitive or *-ing*

Students learn how to form phrases with verb + *to*-infinitive or *-ing*.

7A Point out that these sentences are from the listening. Get students to do the exercise individually and then to compare answers in pairs before checking with the class.

1 to add **2** switching off, turning it on **3** to come on
4 coming on **5** to get **6** to query **7** using
8 contacting **9** to look for

7B Get students to do the exercise individually and then to compare answers in pairs before checking with the class. Refer students to the Grammar reference on page 124 and clarify any points as necessary.

1 *to*-infinitive **2** *-ing* **3** both forms

8 Write on the board: *I stopped using my phone* and *I stopped to use my phone.* Point out that both are grammatical but they mean very different things. Elicit the meaning of each (*I stopped using* ... means I quit using my phone – I no longer use it. *I stopped to use* ... means I was walking or driving but stopped so that I could use my phone.). Ask students to complete the exercise individually. You could get them to compare answers in pairs before checking with the class.

1 Did you remember sending the email? (This is asking if you have a memory of it.)
   Did you remember to send the email? (This is a different meaning. It is checking if you did it.)
2 They stopped to look at the new website design. (This means they stopped another activity in order to look at the website design.)
   They stopped looking at the new website design. (This is a different meaning. It means they no longer looked at the website.)
3 We continued to argue about the charges. We continued arguing about the charges. (same meaning)
4 She went on to ask for a discount. (This is the next thing she did.)
   She went on asking for a discount. (This is a different meaning. This means she repeatedly asked for a discount.)
5 I forgot to pay the phone bill last month. (This means I didn't pay the bill.)
   I forgot paying the phone bill last month. (This is a different meaning – I paid the bill but then didn't remember the action.)
6 He began complaining about the poor service. He began to complain about the poor service. (same meaning)
7 She tried not to get angry. (This means she made a big effort to do something that was difficult for her.)
   She tried not getting angry. (This is a different meaning – she tried this approach as an experiment to see if it would work.)
8 He prefers to sit at the front in the cinema. He prefers sitting at the front in the cinema. (same meaning)

9A Teach or elicit the meaning of *forum page* (a website where people can leave comments, ask questions and have discussions, and where customer service agents sometimes reply). Check answers with the class.

1 to pay **2** to inform **3** losing **4** operating
5 to reduce **6** going **7** getting **8** to give

9B Get students to do this in pairs or, with smaller groups, do it as a class. This short discussion exercise could be followed up with an optional writing task for homework.

Extra activities 7.2

D Ask students to do this individually. Check answers with the class.

1 He avoided ~~to go~~ **going** to the meeting.
2 ✔
3 ✔
4 Have you arranged ~~visiting~~ **to visit** the customer?
5 ✔
6 ✔
7 They denied ~~to damage~~ **damaging** the passenger's luggage.
8 Did they promise ~~delivering~~ **to deliver** the order by Friday?
9 ✔
10 ✔
11 I forgot ~~locking~~ **to lock** my car door and someone stole it.
12 After three hours of negotiations they stopped ~~having~~ **to have** lunch.

❯ Pronunciation bank
p.117: Unstressed syllables at the end of a sentence

Warm-up
Write the following on the board:
A: What should we eat?
B: How about pizza?
A: Yes, I'd love pizza!
Get students to read the short conversation in pairs and ask: *Which words are stressed?* (The stressed words are most likely *eat* in the first line, *pizza* in the second and *love* in the third.) Refer students to the explanation in the box and drill the example conversation.

1 ◆ P7.01   Do the exercise as a class.

2 Get students to do the exercise in pairs. Walk round and monitor to check that students are using the correct word stress.

3 ◆ P7.02   Keep students in pairs and play the recording for them to listen and check, and then again to listen and repeat.

1 **B:** I can't <u>afford</u> to take a few days off work.
2 **B:** I <u>hate</u> phoning customer services.
3 **B:** I've already <u>agreed</u> to join the project.

Writing
Students talk about their own preferences, memories, hopes, etc.

10A Put students in pairs for this exercise. If they need help, get them started with some ideas for *bank* (see answer key). Share answers with the whole class.

Possible answers
bank – high or hidden bank charges;
internet service provider – slow connection;
insurance company – unexpected increase in car insurance;
telephone company – charges for call you did not make

10B Refer students to the complaint in Exercise 9A and remind them to include the three details mentioned in this exercise. Students can provide feedback in pairs or you can collect their work for marking and later feedback.

See model in Exercise 9A.

MyEnglishLab: Teacher's resources: extra activities; Reading bank
Grammar reference: p.124 Verb + *to*-infinitive or *-ing*
Pronunciation bank: p.117 Unstressed syllables at the end of a sentence
Teacher's book: Resource bank Photocopiable 7.2 p.145
Workbook: p.35 Exercises 1–3, p.36 Exercises 1–3

7.3 ❯ Communication skills
Responding to customer concerns

GSE learning objectives
- Can extract key details from conversations between colleagues about familiar topics.
- Can recognise that a speaker is expressing concerns in a formal discussion.
- Can give or seek personal views and opinions in discussing topics of interest.
- Can respond to customer concerns.
- Can suggest simple solutions to a customer service problem.
- Can carry out a work-related phone conversation using polite fixed expressions.
- Can give brief reasons and explanations, using simple language.

Warm-up
Say: *We talk a lot about good customer service. But what about customers? Can we talk about good customers and bad customers?* Elicit a few answers. One idea might be that good customers treat shop workers politely and with respect, and bad customers are rude. Ask: *We know customers have rights, but do they also have responsibilities?* Elicit a few answers. Following on from the previous question, we might say that customers should be honest, not steal, be polite, etc. But probably not everyone in the class will agree.

Lead-in

Students discuss their views on the saying 'the customer is always right'.

1A Put students in pairs. Give them 3–4 minutes to discuss the situations, then invite different students to share their ideas with the class.

1B Discuss the question as a class.

Video

Students watch a video about the importance of responding well to customer concerns.

2A ▶ 7.3.1 In the first sequence, we see Beata and Daniel discussing a possible problem. Their customer, Mateo, does not want to follow their recommendations for how to handle and store their product. Get students to read the questions. Then play the video. Get students to answer in pairs. Then check answers with the class.

> 1 They need to understand why Mateo does not want to refrigerate the Diabsensor.
> 2 Daniel suggests that Mateo may have other suppliers or may not have enough money to cover the costs of refrigeration.
> 3 Beata suggests that Mateo's refrigerators may be full.
> 4 Mateo responds by pointing out that the outstanding issues may not be that small.

2B Discuss the question as a class.

3A Get students to think about possible solutions to the problem. How would they handle a conversation with a customer? Explain the idea of Daniel having two options in his conversation with Mateo and go through the details of Options A and B with the class. Make it clear to students that they can choose which option they want to see first on the video. Put students in small groups and ask them to discuss the two options, giving reasons for their answers. Elicit ideas from a few groups and as a class, decide which video to watch first.

3B ▶ 7.3.2 ▶ 7.3.3 Give students a minute to read the questions for Option A or Option B, depending on their choice, and help them with any unknown words. Play the video and then check answers with the class. Do the same for the second video.

> **Option A**
> 1 His experts have told him that the Diabsensors do not need to be stored at 5°C.
> 2 He listens but offers no judgement.
> 3 He does not respond to any of the criticisms.
> 4 Daniel promises to look into the problem before the meeting in Manchester.
> 5 Daniel does not mention Beata's name except to say that she is listening in to the conversation.
>
> **Option B**
> 1 His experts have told him that the Diabsensors do not need to be stored at 5°C.
> 2 He says that Beata is correct.
> 3 He shows that he fully supports Beata.
> 4 Daniel promises to look into the problem before the meeting in Manchester.
> 5 Daniel refers to Beata six times, either to support her or to confirm that she has already informed him of something.

4 Ask students to discuss the questions in pairs or groups first, and then have a whole-class round-up.

> **Suggested answer**
> In Option A, a possible advantage is that Mateo will believe Daniel is open to new ideas or does not know the full story. A disadvantage is that Daniel might send a signal that he does not trust Beata fully.
> In Option B, the advantage is that Daniel is showing Mateo that he fully supports Beata and that the question of refrigeration is not open for discussion. A possible disadvantage, however, is that Mateo may feel that there is no flexibility in the position Daniel is taking.

5 ▶ 7.3.4 Explain that students are going to watch the last section of the video, with conclusions on and tips for responding to customers successfully. Play the video, twice if necessary. Check answers with the class, then get students to discuss the tips given in the video. This could be a class discussion or you may prefer students to discuss in pairs / small groups first.

> 1 Personal relationships are useful to help resolve difficult negotiations. While listening, appear neutral and gather information.
> 2 Showing support sends a very clear message that the customer may not be right.

Reflection

Students reflect on the conclusions from the video and discuss their own customer service skills.

6 The main aim of these questions is to help students reflect on their own natural style: How would they deal with a difficult situation involving a colleague and a customer? Put them in pairs and give them 4–6 minutes to discuss the questions, then broaden this into a class discussion.

Functional language: Responding to customer concerns

Students look at phrases they can use to deal with customers who are not satisfied.

7 Ask students why responding well to customer concerns is important (it keeps customers happy and therefore willing to continue doing business). Ask them for some examples of the sorts of things they might need to say when responding to a customer (explaining reasons, reassuring them, saying what you are going to do to address their concern, etc.). Explain that phrases a–g are useful when they need to respond to customer concerns, and ask students to complete the table.

> **1** c **2** d **3** b **4** f **5** a **6** g **7** e

8A Put students in pairs and explain the activity. Give pairs 3–5 minutes to read the scenario and note the useful phrases from Exercise 7.

8B Students stay in pairs to roleplay the phone call. Monitor and make sure they are using the phrases from Exercise 7 correctly. Get pairs to act out their dialogues for the class.

Extra activities 7.3

A Get students to do this individually and then compare answers in pairs before checking with the class. After checking answers, you could put students in pairs to practise the dialogue.

1 b **2** a **3** e **4** c **5** d

Task

Students roleplay a scenario involving a manager and an unhappy customer.

9A Start by putting students in groups of three. Refer them to page 130 and have them read through the three scenarios and choose one. Ask groups to assign roles.

9B Students read the scenario and the instructions for their role. During the activity, monitor and help as necessary.

9C Set a time limit of 4–5 minutes for the roleplay.

9D When students have finished their roleplays, allow time for peer assessment. Monitor and make note of any points to highlight during class feedback.

MyEnglishLab: Teacher's resources: extra activities; Interactive video activities
Workbook: p.37 Exercise 1

7.4 ❯ Business skills

Generating and presenting ideas

GSE learning objectives

- Can follow the main points of short talks on familiar topics if delivered in clear standard speech.
- Can use language to introduce and present ideas.
- Can give brief reasons and explanations using simple language.
- Can contribute to a group discussion if the discussion is conducted slowly and clearly.

Warm-up

Write *ideas* on the board. Ask: *When you need an idea, for example, for a school or work project, what do you do? How do you help yourself think? Where do you look for ideas?* Elicit answers or give a few of your own (e.g. go for a walk, search the internet, have a cup of coffee, start writing notes).

Lead-in

Students discuss the importance of generating ideas.

1 Put students in small groups and give them 3–4 minutes to discuss the questions. As feedback, invite a few students to share their answers with the class.

Listening

Students listen to a manager giving an introduction to a staff training day.

2A 🔊 7.04   Ask students to read the questions so they know what they are listening for. Play the recording and get them to answer the questions individually, then check answers in pairs.

1 Ideas come to us at any time.
2 They disappear, either through forgetfulness, being afraid of being laughed at or due to lack of a system for capturing them.
3 The manager wants to hear ideas about how to generate ideas, how to share ideas and how to capture those ideas.
4 The group must come up with a list of ideas of how to generate ideas and not lose them.

2B 🔊 7.04   Get students to do the exercise individually, then play the recording again for them to check their answers.

1 generate   2 share   3 enough   4 ways   5 lose

3 This activity aims to get students to practise the language of generating ideas. Put students in small groups and do the exercise.

4A 🔊 7.05   Explain the activity and play the recording, twice if necessary. Check answers with the class.

4B 🔊 7.05   Play the recording again. For weaker classes, pause after each speaker to give students time to think and tick their answers. Check answers with the class.

See the audioscript on page 150. The speakers who talk about ways to record ideas are: 1 (brainstorm using lists), 2 (use a notebook or smartphone), 3 (draw a mind map) and 5 (draw pictures). Speakers 4 and 6 do not mention recording or capturing ideas.

4C Put students in pairs. Refer them to the words and phrases on the sticky notes to the left of the exercise.

Possible answers

1 Brainstorm – write lists – as many ideas as possible; quality not quantity is the key
2 Use a notebook/smartphone to record thoughts and ideas
3 Mind mapping – start with a word or phrase, then connect ideas related to each other
4 Roleplay – use different viewpoints – take on a different role or personality
5 Visualisation – draw pictures or diagrams to summarise ideas and record creativity
6 Devil's advocate – take opposite view to others' ideas – question everything; risk of making people upset or angry

Functional language: Discussing and presenting ideas

Students look at useful phrases for sharing and talking about ideas.

5A Ask students to do the exercise individually, referring to audioscript 7.05 on page 150 if necessary. Check answers with the class.

> **1** b **2** f **3** d **4** e **5** h **6** g **7** a **8** i **9** j **10** c

5B Students could do this exercise individually and then compare answers in pairs before checking with the class.

> **Introducing the idea:** 1, 3, 7, 10
> **Adding a comment or explanation:** 2, 4, 5, 6, 8, 9

5C Refer students to the audioscript on page 150. Explain that they are looking for phrases that are used when an idea is first mentioned and phrases that are used to add a comment or explanation.

> **Introducing the idea**
> We think that the big problem is …
> We like the …
>
> **Adding a comment or explanation**
> But then we need to …
> So everyone takes on …
> For example, …
> So not just … , but …
> Basically every time …
> The risk is that … , but …
> It helps …

6 Get students to do this exercise in pairs. Explain that for each of the four statements, they should add several of their own comments. Remind them to use as much of the language from Exercise 5 as possible, and not to use one or two phrases over and over again. Get feedback by asking a few pairs to share their answers with the class.

Extra activities 7.4

A Get students to do the exercise in pairs. Go through the two example problems and point out that neither is very serious. The point of this exercise is to use the language in Exercise 5A rather than to discuss a serious problem. Encourage weaker students to discuss one of the two example problems and not to worry about coming up with their own idea.

B Students continue in their pairs. Point out that they only need to complete one of the phrases in item 1, but that they should try to use several of the phrases in item 2.

C Each pair now joins another pair to present their problem and solutions.

> ▶ **Pronunciation bank**
> **p.117: Introducing a topic**
>
> ### Warm-up
> Write *Introducing a topic* on the board. Ask students to imagine that they are introducing the topic of a meeting. Ask how they would do that, and accept any reasonable answers. (Possible answers: Today, we're going to talk about … , I'd like to discuss … , Let's talk about …) Refer students to the explanation in the box.
>
> **1** ◆ P7.03 Get students to listen and repeat. Point out the pause after the introductory phrase, before something is said about the topic.
>
> **2** Get students to do the exercise in pairs. Walk round and monitor to check that students are using the correct stress.
>
> **3** ◆ P7.04 Play the recording for students to listen and repeat.

Task

Students discuss ideas to solve a problem.

7A Go through the five problems with the class and ask them to hold up their hand if they have that problem. Ask if anyone has any other common problems to add to the list. Give students time to choose a topic.

7B Put students in small groups. Refer them to the list of techniques in Exercise 4B and get them to choose two or to use other techniques that they may know. Additional ideas might include gap filling (saying where you are and where you would like to be, then filling in what you need to do to reach your goal), SWOT analysis (thinking about your situation or problem in terms of strengths, weaknesses, opportunities and threats) or brainwriting (everyone writes an idea on a card which is then shared randomly with other participants; ideas can be discussed without anyone knowing whose idea it is).

7C Give students 4–5 minutes to do the exercise. During the activity, monitor and help as necessary. Remind them to make sure they capture their ideas so they can remember them for the next step.

7D Ask groups to present their ideas to the class. Remind them to use phrases from Exercise 5. Monitor and make notes during the presentation.

7E Get feedback by asking students to share with the class what they think went well and what could be improved. Find out if there was an idea generation technique that most of the class used and liked or if everyone used different techniques. Then highlight any points you noted while monitoring.

MyEnglishLab: Teacher's resources: extra activities; Functional language bank
Pronunciation bank: p.117 Introducing a topic
Workbook: p.37 Exercise 2

7.5 ▶ Writing

External 'thank you' email

GSE learning objectives

- Can write an email that clearly conveys information
- Can use *some* and *any* as quantifiers in negative statements and questions with mass and count nouns.
- Can use *all of, none of* and *most of* to describe subsets and proportions of groups of people and things.

Warm-up

Write the following questions on the board: *Have you ever written or read a 'thank you' email or letter? What do you think an effective 'thank you' email should include?* Get students to discuss the questions in pairs or groups first, and then as a class. You could come back to the second question at the end of the lesson, asking students to say what they have learnt about 'thank you' emails and how they would answer this question having completed today's lesson.

Lead-in

Students read and complete a 'thank you' email.

1A Before students do the exercise, ask a few questions to focus their attention on it. *Who wrote the email?* (Franz Benheim) *Who is he thanking?* (Glen and his staff) *What is he thanking them for?* (organising a trade conference) *What did they have problems with?* (the catering facilities – the food preparation and service) Get students to do the exercise individually. Do not check answers yet.

1B Put students in pairs to compare answers before checking with the class.

> 1 provided 2 event 3 express 4 handled
> 5 responded 6 deal 7 recommended 8 near

Functional language

Students look at the organisation of and some useful phrases for a 'thank you' email.

2 Students could do this individually or in pairs, using their dictionaries if necessary. Check answers with the class and clarify any vocabulary. Write *Greeting* on the board and ask: *Which part of the email is the greeting?* (Dear Glen)

> 1 writing 2 much 3 take 4 appreciated 5 wanted
> 6 smoothly 7 sorted 8 helpful 9 replaced
> 10 definitely 11 recommended 12 once

Extra activities 7.5

A This exercise practises useful phrases for 'thank you' emails. It is a consolidation exercise, so it would be better for students to do it individually. Check answers with the class.

> 1 f 2 i 3 d 4 c 5 a 6 h 7 j 8 e 9 b 10 g

Optional grammar work

The email in Exercise 1 contains examples of *some (of), any, all (of)* and *none (of)*, so you could use it for some optional grammar work. Refer students to the Grammar reference on page 124 and use the exercises in MyEnglishLab for extra grammar practice.

Task

Students assess a 'thank you' email and then write their own.

3A Put students in pairs. Refer them to page 132 and give them time to read the email and discuss how it could be improved. As feedback, elicit and discuss students' suggestions.

Model answer

We would like to take this opportunity to thank you for getting the extra supplies to us earlier than you had originally promised. Your help meant that we were able to fulfil our customer's order on time and they were extremely happy with our service.

I would therefore like to thank you once again for all your help and look forward to extending our contract with you in the future.

3B Students write their own 'thank you' email based on the notes on page 132. Remind them to use the functional language from Exercise 2 and point out the word limit. Monitor and help students as necessary.

Model answer

I am writing to thank your company for the excellent service we received when some of the computers we had bought from you did not work properly.

We contacted your help desk immediately and the person I spoke to was very friendly and obviously knew a lot about the product. He apologised for the problems we were having and suggested that he could exchange the computers or send out an engineer to solve the problems. We decided that it would be better to have new computers and they arrived the next morning.

One week later we received a phone call from your customer service department asking us if everything was now OK. We were happy to report that there were no more problems.

I would like to thank you once again for your prompt and excellent service and we will certainly use your company again.

3C Put students in pairs. Give them a couple of minutes to read each other's emails. Then have them answer the questions and suggest ways in which they could improve them.

MyEnglishLab: Teacher's resources: extra activities; Interactive grammar practice; Writing bank

Grammar reference: p.124 *some (of), any, all (of), most (of), no, none (of)*

Workbook: p.38 Exercises 1 and 2

Business workshop ❯7
Red Cushion Furniture

GSE learning objectives

- Can scan short texts to locate specific information.
- Can convey simple relevant information emphasising the most important point.
- Can contribute to a group discussion if the discussion is conducted slowly and clearly.

Background

Students read about a Mexico-based furniture maker that is dealing with some customer service issues.

1 Put students in pairs and ask them to read the background and discuss the questions. Check answers with the class.

1 It was founded by Alejandro Roja in his workshop at home.
2 It produces modern, stylish domestic and commercial furniture made from sustainable woods.
3 when the company expanded into Europe
4 not enough wood / raw materials, late orders, production line stopped due to equipment breakdowns, key staff have left / are leaving, customer services unable to deal with increased complaints
5 Students' own answers

Did customer services get it right?

Students read and discuss four customer service case studies.

2A Divide the class into two groups. Explain that each group is going to read two short case histories of customer service situations. Refer Group B to page 137. Give them 4–6 minutes to read the case histories and answer the questions.

Possible answers

Case history A – poorly; Reasons: staff not properly trained, front desk manager did not listen to the customer, manager did not have authority to make decisions = too much control from top

Case history B – well; Reason: staff listened to the customer and did whatever they could to help – well-trained staff, allowed to make decisions

Case history C – well; Reason: Executive Chef solved the problem creatively and helped the young family

Case history D – poorly; Reason: restaurant delivered poor service but blamed the customers, criticising them publicly

2B Put students in pairs, each with someone who read the other two case studies. Encourage them to explain the case study from memory, looking at the texts only if absolutely necessary.

2C Put students in small groups to discuss ways to improve each situation. During the activity, monitor and help as necessary. After 8–10 minutes, get groups to share some ideas with the class.

Extra activities Business workshop 7

A This activity provides students with extra reading practice for Case histories A and B. Students can either do just the two texts that they studied more closely or all four (see extra activity B below). During the activity, monitor and help as necessary. Get students to check answers in pairs.

1 disturb 2 cleaner 3 nothing 4 General
5 connecting 6 asked 7 arrived 8 held

B This activity provides students with extra reading practice for Case histories C and D. Students can either do just the two texts that they studied more closely or all four (see Extra activity A above). During the activity, monitor and help as necessary. Get students to check answers in pairs.

1 allergies 2 family 3 products/food
4 mother-in-law 5 anniversary 6 restaurant
7 negative 8 laugh

Dealing with angry customers

Students read and discuss emails of complaint from customers, listen to a customer services expert explain how to deal with angry customers, and respond to a customer complaint.

3A Refer students to the emails on page 135. Explain that these are complaints emailed to Red Cushion Furniture. Point out that students are to write notes, not full sentences. Get them to do this exercise individually.

Email 1
1 chairs were delivered which were not ordered and company hasn't collected them even though they said they would; now received an invoice for the unordered goods
2 customer services promises every day to collect but does nothing
3 wants the company to collect the chairs (doesn't say in email, but must also want the invoice cancelled)

Email 2
1 invoiced for order not completed
2 hasn't yet replied to customer's email sent last week
3 to complete the order or they will not pay

3B Put students in small groups to discuss their answers to Exercise 3A. Then give them a few minutes to decide on the best course of action for both situations. When they have finished, invite a few groups to share their ideas with the class.

4A 🔊 BW 7.01 Get students to read the sentences so they know what information they are listening for. Play the recording for students to complete the exercise individually. Check answers in pairs.

> 1 Act 2 facts 3 contact 4 priority 5 a solution
> 6 loyal 7 customer-facing 8 training 9 respect
> 10 records

4B Put students in pairs and get them to allocate roles. Tell them that the customer should explain the problem and the manager should respond, trying to follow the advice in Exercise 4A. Monitor and note down any points to highlight during feedback.

Task: Turn failure into success

Students come up with solutions for dealing with customer complaints.

5A Put students in small groups. Go through the instructions with them and refer them to the three complaints on page 136. Give them sufficient time to read the complaints. Point out that the complaints were made using three different types of communication: email, social media and text message. Ask students if they think any of the methods are more likely than the others to get a response. Ask if they think all three methods are appropriate. Answer any questions they may have. During the activity, monitor and help as necessary.

5B Do the exercise, with a time limit of 3–4 minutes per group. Monitor and note down any points to highlight during feedback.

5C If there is no time to do this in class, it would make a good homework assignment. Tell students that they could use some of the ideas from Exercise 4A.

Model answer

Information sheet for Customer Service staff
It is important that we deal with all problems in the same way. Therefore, we have prepared this information sheet to remind you of the key points of good customer service. You must remember to:
- act quickly (social media posts should be dealt with first as they can spread the fastest).
- treat each complaint as a priority.
- let the customer know that you care about them and understand how they feel.
- apologise for the customer being unhappy but don't admit liability until you have investigated.
- respond to all emails and posts immediately, saying you are looking into the complaint.
- investigate the facts and get back to the customer as quickly as possible with a solution.
- offer more than they expect if possible.
- keep the customer informed of progress if it takes longer than you expected.
- make sure you reassure other customers after negative social media posts by giving details of how you resolved the complaint.
- keep accurate records of the complaint and the steps taken to resolve the situation.
- contact the customer a few days / a week later to check that everything was resolved to their satisfaction.

At the same time, you need to remember not to:
- get angry or argue with a customer.
- tell the customer their problem isn't important.
- offer something you cannot deliver / make promises you cannot keep.
- take too long getting back to a customer.

MyEnglishLab: Teacher's resources: extra activities

Review ◀7

> 1 1 premium 2 priority 3 body 4 personal
>   5 satisfactory 6 demanding 7 apologetic
>   8 handling
> 2 1 about 2 with 3 to 4 about
> 3 1 waiting 2 to waste 3 making 4 to pay
>   5 signing 6 to refund 7 to tell 8 to find
>   9 ringing 10 to help
> 4 1 wanted to make sure 2 filled me 3 correct about
>   4 have to say 5 Let me speak to 6 confident we'll
> 5 1 should 2 suggest 3 Basically 4 come
>   5 What
> 6 1 writing 2 for 3 take 4 helpful 5 sorted
>   6 once 7 in

8 ▶ Communication

Unit overview

	CLASSWORK	FURTHER WORK
8.1 ▶ **Face to face?**	**Lead-in** Students discuss different types of communication. **Video** Students watch a video about how a company improved communication in the office. **Vocabulary** Students look at vocabulary related to ways of communicating in the digital world. **Project** Students do a survey to find out about different methods of communication.	**MyEnglishLab:** Teacher's resources extra activities; Reading bank **Teacher's book:** Resource bank Photocopiable 8.1 p.146 **Workbook:** p.39 Exercises 1–3
8.2 ▶ **How to communicate**	**Lead-in** Students talk about two different ways of organising offices. **Reading** Students read and discuss an article about effective workplace communication. **Grammar** Students learn how to talk about possible future outcomes. **Speaking** Students talk about communication problems and solutions.	**MyEnglishLab:** Teacher's resources: extra activities **Grammar reference:** p.125 First and second conditional **Pronunciation bank:** p.117 Conditional sentences **Teacher's book:** Resource bank Photocopiable 8.2 p.147 **Workbook:** p.40 Exercises 1–3, p.41 Exercises 1–3
8.3 ▶ **Communication skills:** Closing a deal	**Lead-in** Students discuss negotiation and some important considerations when closing a deal. **Video** Students watch a video about the importance of closing a deal by creating a win-win situation. **Reflection** Students reflect on the conclusions from the video and discuss their own negotiating skills. **Functional language** Students look at phrases they can use to finalise negotiations and come to an agreement. **Task** Students roleplay a scenario where they try to close a deal.	**MyEnglishLab:** Teacher's resources: extra activities; Interactive video activities; Functional language bank **Workbook:** p.42 Exercise 1
8.4 ▶ **Business skills:** Talking about priorities	**Lead-in** Students discuss the relative importance of issues that need to be dealt with. **Listening** Students listen to a consultant talking about setting priorities. **Functional language** Students look at useful phrases for talking about what's important and urgent. **Task** Students discuss and set priorities.	**MyEnglishLab:** Teacher's resources: extra activities; Functional language bank **Workbook:** p.42 Exercise 2
8.5 ▶ **Writing:** Short report	**Lead-in** Students read and complete a short business report. **Functional language** Students look at the organisation of and some useful phrases for a short business report. **Task** Students assess a short business report and then write their own.	**MyEnglishLab:** Teacher's resources: extra activities; Interactive grammar practice; Writing bank **Grammar reference:** p.125 Past Perfect Simple **Pronunciation bank:** p.117 Contractions in speech **Workbook:** p.43 Exercises 1 and 2
Business workshop 8 ▶ Global communication	**Listening** Students listen to two colleagues talking about communication problems. **Reading** Students read email exchanges about a problem. **Task** Students discuss and write about ways to improve cross-cultural communication.	**MyEnglishLab:** Teacher's resources: extra activities

Business brief

This unit looks at **communication** – the process by which people exchange information or express their thoughts and feelings. In business, communication occurs on many levels in a huge variety of contexts.

Office communication includes meetings, email, text messages, letters, reports, company newsletters, **social media**, formal and informal conversations with colleagues and so on. These days, one of the biggest challenges of communication in the workplace is **information overload**. Communication is so quick and convenient that often people send several emails, each about a single topic, copied to a large group of people. The result is that people spend a lot of time opening and reading emails that may not be relevant. Also, because of the convenience of smartphones and tablets, a lot of workers look at email in the evenings or at weekends. This is especially true in international companies with workers in different **time zones**, where the normal workday in one region is the evening or night in another.

Office organisation plays an important role in communication. Some view the **open-plan office** as a great way to encourage the easy flow of communication, while others consider it impossibly distracting, preferring **private offices** instead. In any case, experts agree that **informal conversations** in the workplace are as important as **formal meetings** for generating ideas and moving work forward.

The ability to discuss and set **priorities** is more important now than ever, given the speed and volume of communication that workers must deal with. The key to setting priorities is knowing the difference between what is **urgent** – needing to be dealt with immediately – and what is **important** – having a big effect, but not necessarily needing attention right now.

Negotiation – official discussions between the representatives of opposing groups who are trying to reach an agreement, especially in business or politics – is a type of communication that can be hugely important. In business, **closing a deal** – the situation where two sides agree to work together, often as buyer and seller – is at the heart of keeping the business going. The ideal outcome of a negotiation is a **win-win situation**, where both sides feel they have benefited. This is far better for a healthy **long-term business relationship** than a **win-lose situation**, where one side feels that they have been taken advantage of.

In business today, English is a global **lingua franca** – a language used between people whose main languages are different. However, the fact that everyone is speaking the same language in a business situation does not mean that it is always easy for them to understand one another. **Intercultural communication**, where people from different countries work together, is challenging because people often have **assumptions** about ways of working that they aren't even aware of. In some cultures, it is considered good practice to start talking business as soon as you meet someone from another company, whereas in other cultures, it is important to get to know someone before you start talking about work.

Psychologist Paul Watzlawick said, 'You cannot not communicate.' This means that no matter what we do or say, we are sending some kind of message. In business, sending the message you intend to send and correctly understanding the messages you receive are hugely important.

Communication and your students

Virtually all of us communicate all day, every day. In fact, in the age of information, the challenge is not so much how to communicate, but how to deal with the huge volume of communication that we are faced with each day. Both students and people in work need to develop skills in this area. Globally, about seventy-five percent of communication in English does not include a first-language user of English, which means that a great deal of English communication, both in the workplace and in education, is intercultural. Students in all walks of life will benefit from developing communication skills needed in an English-as-a-lingua-franca environment.

Unit lead-in

Ask students to look at the photo and unit title. Explain or elicit that the actor in the image is a mime artist and ask what is special about this type of actor (They do not speak – they communicate entirely by using body language.). Ask students to read the quote and to give examples of communication that does not depend on words (facial expressions, hand gestures, body language – how close we stand to others, how we move, etc.). Ask if anyone has an idea about what the actor in the photo is communicating (She is probably saying, 'I don't know,' but she might also be saying, 'Here you are,' or maybe 'Here I am.').

8.1 > Face to face?

GSE learning objectives

- Can follow the main points in TV programmes on familiar topics if delivered in clear and standard speech.
- Can give or seek personal views and opinions in discussing topics of interest.
- Can ask simple questions in a face-to-face survey.
- Can answer simple questions in a face-to-face survey.

Warm-up

Write *communication* on the board. Ask: *Every day, how many types of communication do you use?* Elicit answers (e.g. speaking in person, texting, emailing, writing a letter, looking at people – non-verbal communication, speaking on the phone). Say: *Today we're going to talk about communication.*

Lead-in

Students discuss different types of communication.

1A Teach or elicit the meaning of *time-waster* (something that you spend a lot of time doing that does not help you in any way), *interruption* (when someone is stopped from continuing what they are saying or doing by suddenly speaking to them, making a noise, etc.) and *manageable* (easy to control or deal with). Get students to do the exercise individually, then compare answers in pairs.

1B Give students time to read the example sentences. With weaker classes, complete the first example as a class (see Possible answers below). Students do the exercise in pairs. During the activity, monitor and help as necessary.

Possible answers

I use text messages with my friends to make plans. We usually text the time and place we're going to meet, and text to say exactly where we are.

I use email a lot for work. Every day, I have to write about thirty emails to clients, and I receive a similar number.

I usually carry my phone with me, but I don't use it too much. I'd rather talk to people face-to-face. I think too many people spend too much time on their phone, and I don't want to be like that.

Video

Students watch a video about how a company improved communication in the office.

2A Explain to students that they are going to watch a video about communication in the office – especially email. Teach or elicit the meaning of *tearing up the rulebook* (doing things in a completely new way), *after hours* (not during the usual work day), *dependence* (when you need something in order to exist or be successful) and *productivity* (the amount of work people are able to complete in a certain period of time). Give them a minute to read and answer the two questions, then ask them to compare answers in pairs before checking with the class.

Notes

Procure Plus is a not-for-profit company that works in the government-funded housing sector, helping to locate goods and services for the repair and maintenance of government-funded housing and for new-build social housing.

Professor Sir Cary Cooper is a Professor of Organisational Psychology and Health at Manchester Business School in England and also a visiting professor at Lancaster University Management School. He has written more than 160 books about occupational stress, organisational psychology and women in the workplace.

Possible answers

1 talking face-to-face, texting, emailing, social media, telephone, online video chat
2 people not communicating clearly or communicating enough, communication taking too much time, problems with people speaking different languages

2B ▶ 8.1.1 Play the video. Check answers with the class.

dependence on email; too many emails, and having to use time outside of work to catch up; this over-dependence can reduce productivity

3 ▶ 8.1.1 Give students a minute to read the notes. Then play the video again. Get them to compare answers in pairs before checking with the class. Ask if anyone understood any details in the video other than the ones they have already noted down – for example, that Cary Cooper is a psychologist from Lancaster University or that the workers are now servants to technology rather than its masters.

1 email
2 work outside the office, send internal emails for a week
3 face-to-face
4 a bit bored, worried, but then relaxed and happy
5 work and life – the need for technology and working more humanely with people
6 good – a buzz and a hum

4 ▶ 8.1.1 Give students a minute to read the sentences. With stronger classes, you could ask them to try to do the exercise before watching, then watch and check or complete their answers. Play the video, then check answers with the class.

> **1** F – He's concerned that they spend too much time working after hours.
> **2** T
> **3** F – He bans internal email.
> **4** F – He says that the two need to be balanced so we can be healthy.
> **5** F – They didn't work after hours.
> **6** T
> **7** T

5 Put students in small groups to discuss the questions. During the activity, monitor and help as necessary.

Extra activities 8.1

A ▶ 8.1.1 Ask students to do this individually, then play the video for them to check their answers. Check answers with the class. Point out that the words in bold will be defined in the next exercise

> **1** P **2** C **3** P **4** P **5** P **6** P **7** C **8** M

B Ask students to do this individually, then check answers in pairs. Get stronger students to try to define the words first, then do the matching.

> **1** d **2** g **3** a **4** e **5** b **6** h **7** f **8** c

Vocabulary: Digital communication

Students look at vocabulary related to ways of communicating in the digital world.

6 Explain that the words are from the video. Students could do this individually or in pairs, using their dictionaries to help them – the second option may be easier for weaker classes.

> **1** check **2** reply **3** catch **4** overloaded **5** internal
> **6** Technology **7** servant **8** master

7 Get students to do the exercise individually, then check answers in pairs before asking and answering the questions.

> **1** reply **2** check **3** master **4** catch **5** overloaded

Extra activities 8.1

C This activity practises key vocabulary from the lesson and looks at the relationship between verbs and nouns. Get students to do the exercise individually, then check answers in pairs.

> **2** communication **3** dependence **4** produce
> **5** performance **6** organisation **7** benefit

D Ask students to do the exercise individually and then get them to compare answers in pairs before checking with the class. With weaker classes, you could help students by providing the last letter of each missing word.

> **1** dependence **2** transformation **3** benefit
> **4** organisation **5** perform **6** communicate
> **7** productivity

Project: Communication survey

Students do a survey to find out about different methods of communication.

8A Get students to make their notes individually. During the activity, monitor and help as necessary. Do not get them to share answers yet, as they will use the information they have made notes about to complete the next steps in the activity.

8B Put students in pairs or small groups. Write *wh- questions* on the board and elicit the words that *wh-* refers to (*who, what, when, where, why, how*). Refer students to the example questions and get them to write more of their own. With weaker groups, who may need more support, get them to write some questions on the board for everyone to refer to. During the activity, monitor and help as necessary.

8C Ask students to get up and move around the room while asking questions. Allow 4–6 minutes to complete the activity. During the activity, monitor and help as necessary and listen out for any areas where they may need improvement. You can share this with them in the feedback part of Exercise 8D.

8D Students present their ideas to other groups or to the class. Allow 2–3 minutes for each presentation. During the activity, monitor and help as necessary. Then give feedback on the entire project: suggest areas for improvement and highlight any errors that made communication difficult.

MyEnglishLab: Teacher's resources: extra activities; Reading bank
Teacher's book: Resource bank Photocopiable 8.1 p.146
Workbook: p.39 Exercises 1–3

8.2 › How to communicate

GSE learning objectives

- Can scan short texts to locate specific information.
- Can describe hypothetical (counterfactual) results of a current action or situation using the second conditional.
- Can describe possible future outcomes of a present action or situation using the first conditional.
- Can express opinions as regards possible solutions, giving brief reasons and explanations.

Warm-up

Write the following on the board: *You cannot not communicate.* (a quotation from Paul Watzlawick, a psychologist) Ask: *What do you think this means?* Accept any reasonable answers. It means that no matter what we are doing, even if we are silent, we are communicating something. Everything we do sends some kind of message. Even when you try not to communicate, you are communicating the message that you do not want to communicate.

Lead-in

Students talk about two different ways of organising offices.

1 Refer students to the question. Make sure that everyone, especially pre-work students, understands the difference between a private office (a room where someone works alone and can close the door) and an open-plan office (a large area with a lot of workers and no walls dividing it into separate rooms). Pre-work students can think about the two situations, even if they have not experienced them, as they will already understand the concept of public and private spaces. Students answer the question individually, then compare answers in pairs. As a round-up to students' discussions, ask them to share their experiences of workplaces. If you want to extend the exercise, ask: *Which type of office do you think encourages better communication?* (Opinions vary about this. The person in a private office can more easily make and concentrate on a phone call, but the people in an open-plan office can communicate more easily with the people sitting around them.)

Private office: It's easier to concentrate. You can make phone calls in private. You can have meetings with another person privately. There is no opportunity to socialise.
Open-plan office: People will share ideas more. Small talk is easier. There are more distractions.

2 Put students in pairs or small groups. During the activity, monitor and help as necessary. Then get a few groups to share their ideas with the class.

Reading

Students read and discuss an article about effective workplace communication.

3 Teach or elicit the meaning of *skim* (to read something quickly to find the main facts or ideas in it). Suggest that to skim this text, students read the introductory paragraph and the first and last sentences of the three main paragraphs in the article. Get students to do the exercise individually, then check answers in pairs. Then check answers with the class.

> **1** b **2** a **3** d

4 Go round the class and assign each student two or three questions to find the answer to: questions 1 and 2; 3 and 4; 5–7. Then have them read the text to find the answer to their questions. Finally, get them into groups of three to share answers to all seven questions.

> **1** You lose the ability to work well in teams and also put the success of projects at risk. (He says 'lack of communication and team work can make projects fail.')
> **2** Water-cooler chat / informal office conversation. Scott Bedbury said that 'the really useful conversations between colleagues generally took place at the vending machine, in the cafeteria or in the gardens outside the office'.
> **3** Building relationships. According to the article, 'Bedbury says that a company's internal communication needs to be both formal and informal to help build the relationships necessary for success'.
> **4** Noise. The reason for this is that it makes it difficult for workers to concentrate.
> **5** A combination of public and private space – she says that companies should provide a choice, which would cause an increase in productivity and happiness.
> **6** Email. In China, social media is far more commonly used.
> **7** 24/7 communication means you are always at work, and it may seem rude not to reply to a message.

Extra activities 8.2

A Students could do this exercise individually and then compare answers in pairs, using their dictionaries if necessary.

> **1** engaged **2** jeopardise **3** 24/7 **4** background
> **5** downside **6** open-plan **7** swapped

5 Get students to do the exercise in pairs. During the activity, monitor and help as necessary. Ask a few pairs to share their answers with the class. To extend the exercise, ask: *Where do you go when you want to work on something – to concentrate rather than communicate?* Discuss answers. Ask: *When you're in a situation where you'd rather focus on your work, but people keep talking to you, what do you usually do? Stop working? Go somewhere else? Some other solution?* Discuss.

Grammar: First and second conditional

Students learn how to talk about possible future outcomes.

6 On the board, write *conditionals* and ask students what words are typically used in a conditional sentence (*if*, *when*, *then* – though *then* is often left out). Ask for a simple example (e.g. *If it rains, I'll wear my raincoat.*). Point out that the sentences in this exercise are from the reading. Get students to do the exercise individually and then to compare answers in pairs before checking with the class.

> **1 a** Present Simple **b** future **c** likely
> **2 a** Past Simple **b** No, it isn't – it's referring to the future.
> **c** less probable

7 Get students to do the exercise individually and then compare answers in pairs before checking with the class. Refer students to the Grammar reference on page 125 and clarify any points as necessary.

> **1** will be **2** won't have **3** will spend **4** would have
> **5** talked **6** would be **7** would feel **8** turned

Extra activities 8.2

B Students could do this exercise individually and then compare answers in pairs. Point out that some of the sentences could be first or second conditional, depending on whether they see the event as probable or unlikely.

> **1** If they had ten employees instead of 100, an open-plan office would work better.
> **2** It will be quieter if we have tomorrow's meeting in the conference room.
> It would be quieter if we had tomorrow's meeting in the conference room.
> **3** If you call me on my mobile at one o'clock, I'll answer right away.
> **4** If I were CEO, I'd move the offices to a bigger building.
> **5** We wouldn't communicate 24/7 if social media weren't/wasn't so popular.
> **6** If he's used to a private office, he'll find the open-plan office quite noisy.
> **7** If she didn't love her job, she'd quit.
> **8** We'll cancel tomorrow's meeting if Greg can't come.

➤ **Pronunciation bank**
p.117: Conditional sentences

Warm-up

Write the following on the board: *If it's cold, wear a coat. Take an umbrella if it's raining.* Get students to read the sentences aloud and ask: *Which words are stressed?* (The stressed words are most likely *cold*, *coat*, *umbrella* and *raining*.) Refer students to the explanation in the box and drill the example sentences.

---

1 ◀) P8.01 Put students in pairs to do the exercise.

> **1** If we give workers private <u>offices</u>, they'll be less <u>distracted</u>.
> **2** I'd stop to <u>chat</u> more often if I wasn't so <u>busy</u>.
> **3** If we encourage our employees to <u>chat</u> with each other, they'll get to <u>know</u> each other better.
> **4** I'd stop using social <u>media</u> at work if <u>I</u> were you.

2 Get students to do the exercise in pairs. During the activity, monitor to check that they are using the correct word stress.

Speaking

Students talk about communication problems and solutions.

8A Get students to do the exercise in pairs. Check answers with the class.

> **1** a,c **2** b,d **3** f,h **4** e,g

8B Get students to do this in small groups. It might be useful to have an observer in this exercise, making sure conditionals are used, and also to assess whether they're used correctly.

Possible answers

2 If we moved to a building that's three times bigger, every employee would have a private office and it would be easier to make phone calls.
People will be able to make phone calls more easily if we provide a few small, private rooms for employees to use when needed.
3 If we create a small break area near the water cooler, employees will meet there and chat informally.
If we bought the café next to the office building and turned it into a private break room, employees would meet there and chat.
4 If we bought every employee a smartphone and told them to turn it off outside of work, they would stop complaining about the constant communication.
Employees will stop complaining about constant communication if we encourage them not to respond to work texts and emails outside of office hours.

8C Get students to do this in the same small groups. Monitor and make note of any points to highlight during class feedback.

MyEnglishLab: Teacher's resources: extra activities
Grammar reference: p.125 First and second conditional
Pronunciation bank: p.117 Conditional sentences
Teacher's book: Resource bank Photocopiable 8.2 p.147
Workbook: p.40 Exercises 1–3, p.41 Exercises 1–3

8.3 ❯ Communication skills

Closing a deal

GSE learning objectives

- Can extract key details from conversations between colleagues about familiar topics.
- Can suggest pros and cons when discussing a topic, using simple language.
- Can use simple language to close a deal.
- Can summarise the position at the end of a negotiation in a simple way.

Warm-up

Write *negotiation* on the board and teach or elicit the meaning (official discussions between the representatives of opposing groups who are trying to reach an agreement, especially in business or politics). Say: *We all negotiate – with our friends, our family, our colleagues.* Give an example of negotiation from your own life, e.g. *My friends and I wanted to go to the cinema, but we wanted to see two different films. We argued a bit, then we decided to see one film on Saturday night and one film on Sunday night. Everyone was happy.* Ask students to think of situations when they negotiated with friends, family or colleagues.

Lead-in

Students discuss negotiation and some important considerations when closing a deal.

1A Put students in pairs. Give them 3–4 minutes to discuss the two points, then invite different students to share their ideas with the class.

Possible answer

Summarising is important so that both sides confirm that they are on the same page and that there have been no misunderstandings. (Note: A contract is a formal summary of what has been agreed and is, in effect, the result of the summary.) Working through the outstanding issues is important, otherwise there is no agreement and the deal cannot be closed.

1B Write *win–win* and *win–lose* on the board and teach or elicit the meaning of each (see Notes below). Students discuss the questions in pairs. Invite a few pairs to share their ideas with the class.

Notes

Although the dictionary defines *win* as *to be the best or most successful in a competition, game, election etc.,* and as the opposite of *lose*, having a winner does not always mean there is a loser. Businesspeople frequently say that the ideal outcome of a business negotiation is a win–win, as described in the instructions. The opposite of a win–win situation is a win–lose situation – one that will end well for only one side.

Possible answer

1 A win–win situation means that both sides get a good result from the negotiation, and helps to make sure that the good relationship continues between the two parties. If the deal is a one-off (e.g. the purchase of a second-hand car), a win–win is not necessary, although there is the risk that one party might decide to cancel the deal rather than close it.

2 A win–lose situation means that one side will be dissatisfied. This reduces the chances of a long-term business relationship continuing.

Video

Students watch a video about the importance of closing a deal by creating a win–win situation.

2 ▶ 8.3.1   In the first sequence, we see Beata, Daniel and their customer Mateo discussing a possible solution to a problem they're having: Mateo does not want to follow their recommendations for how to handle and store their product. Get students to read the questions, then play the video. Get them to answer in pairs. Then check answers with the class.

1 yes
2 Daniel is worried that Beata might use very technical language.
3 They talk about the weather and have a laugh together. This will help the discussion because they already know and trust each other.
4 He first wants to summarise what has been agreed, to make sure that he and Mateo have the same understanding of the situation, and then he wants to discuss outstanding issues.

3A Explain the idea of Daniel and Beata having two options in their conversation with Mateo and go through the details of Options A and B with the class. Make it clear to students that they can choose which option they want to see first on the video. Put students in small groups and ask them to discuss the two options, giving reasons for their answers. Elicit ideas from a few groups and as a class, decide which video to watch first.

3B ▶ 8.3.2 ▶ 8.3.3   Give students a minute to read the questions for Option A or Option B, depending on their choice, and help them with any unknown words. Play the video and then check answers with the class. Do the same for the second video.

Option A

1
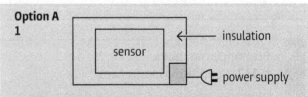

2 Daniel: Mateo does not have to pay extra for the portable units, but only for the power supply. Beata: Portable refrigerators are supplied with the Diabsensors.

Option B

1 Students' own answers
2 Daniel: Mateo does not have to pay extra for the portable units, but only for the power supply. Mateo can reuse the refrigeration units once the Diabsensors have been used. This is a 'great deal' for Mateo.
Beata: Portable refrigerators are supplied with the Diabsensors. The diabetes teams will be very happy.

4 Ask students to discuss the questions in pairs and then have a whole-class round-up.

> The key lessons learnt should include (a) the importance of summarising what has been agreed and what still needs to be discussed, and (b) two possible approaches which can be used to 'sell' an idea or solution.

5 ▶ 8.3.4 Explain that students are going to watch the last section of the video, with conclusions on and tips for closing a deal. Play the video, twice if necessary. Check answers with the class, then get students to discuss the tips given in the video. This could be a class discussion or you may prefer students to discuss in pairs / small groups first.

> **Possible answers**
> It's always good to summarise what has been agreed and what hasn't. The video showed two common ways of selling an idea: focusing on a technical solution and emphasising benefits rather than technical details. Both styles can be effective.

Reflection

Students reflect on the conclusions from the video and discuss their own negotiating skills.

6 The main aim of these questions is to help students reflect on their own natural style: how would they negotiate and close a deal? Put them in pairs and give them 4–6 minutes to discuss the questions, then broaden this into a class discussion.

Functional language: Closing a deal

Students look at phrases they can use to finalise negotiations and come to an agreement.

7A Explain to students that phrases 1–6 are useful when they are negotiating to close a deal. Get them to do the exercise individually, then check answers in pairs.

> **1** sums **2** agreed **3** leaves **4** sum **5** mean **6** return

7B Make sure that students understand *summarising* (making a short statement giving only the main information and not the details of a plan, event, report, etc.), *clarifying* (making sure you have understood something correctly) and *referring to outstanding issues* (mentioning or speaking about matters that are not yet decided). Get them to do the exercise individually, then check answers with the whole class.

> **a** 1,2 **b** 4,5 **c** 3,6

7C Do this as a quick whole-class activity.

> **1** a **2** c **3** b **4** c **5** c/b **6** a

8 Get students to do the exercise individually, then check answers in pairs. Ask them to practise the conversation. After they have practised it once, encourage them to do it again, but saying it from memory rather than reading it. If they forget what they need to say, they should stop speaking, look at the book and read silently, then look up again and continue speaking.

> **1** As I understand it **2** That leaves
> **3** So what you mean is **4** If you agree **5** to sum up

> ### Extra activities 8.3
>
> **A** This exercise gives students more practice of the language of closing a deal. Get them to do it individually and then compare answers in pairs before checking with the class.
>
> > **1** e **2** d **3** c **4** f **5** g **6** a **7** b

Task

Students roleplay a scenario where they try to close a deal.

9A Get students to read about the three items. Teach or elicit the meaning of *kayak* (a type of light boat, usually for one person, that is moved using a paddle) and *worn* (a worn object is old and damaged, especially because it has been used a lot). Ask each pair to choose an item to negotiate the sale of.

9B Students read the seven steps. During the activity, monitor and help as necessary. Set a time limit of 4–5 minutes for the roleplay.

9C When students have finished their roleplays, allow time for peer assessment. Monitor and make a note of any points to highlight during class feedback.

MyEnglishLab: Teacher's resources: extra activities; Interactive video activities; Functional language bank

Workbook: p.42 Exercise 1

8.4 ❯ Business skills

Talking about priorities

> ### GSE learning objectives
>
> - Can follow the main points of short talks on familiar topics if delivered in clear standard speech.
> - Can use language to talk about priorities.
> - Can contribute to a group discussion if the discussion is conducted slowly and clearly.

> ### Warm-up
>
> Write *priorities* on the board. Say (e.g.): *My priorities for today are to teach this class, have lunch and prepare for the next class. I'd like to go for a walk, but I may not have time.* Ask: *What are your priorities today?* Get a few students to answer.

Lead-in

Students discuss the relative importance of issues that need to be dealt with.

1 Teach or elicit the meaning of *urgent* (very important and needing to be dealt with immediately). Get students to do the exercise individually, then compare answers in pairs.

2 Write *staying healthy* on the board and ask: *What are the tasks you need to do to stay healthy?* Elicit a few answers (e.g. eat well, exercise, stop smoking). Put students in pairs to do the exercise.

Listening

Students listen to a consultant talking about setting priorities.

3A 🔊 8.01   Ask students to read the questions so they know what they are listening for. Play the recording and get them to complete the matrix individually, then check answers in pairs.

> **1** Make a list of the tasks. Compare the tasks and decide which are important and which are urgent.
> **2** Important tasks have to be done because they matter to your business; urgent tasks have to be done now, even if they are not important.
> **3** **1** important and urgent   **2** important but not urgent
> **3** urgent but not important   **4** not important or urgent

3B 🔊 8.02   Explain that the speaker talks only about *task 1*, *task 2* and so on, but not about actual specific tasks. Get students to do the exercise individually, then check answers in pairs.

> **1** important and urgent: 3, 6
> **2** important but not urgent: 2
> **3** urgent but not important: 4
> **4** not important or urgent: 1, 5, 7

3C This activity aims to get students to think about how the matrix works by using it to prioritise tasks. Put students in pairs and do the exercise.

> **Task 1** – 7   **Task 2** – 4   **Task 3** – 1   **Task 4** – 3   **Task 5** – 6
> **Task 6** – 2   **Task 7** – 5

3D 🔊 8.03   Get students to read the question before listening. If necessary, teach the meaning of *distraction* (something that stops you paying attention to what you are doing) and *discipline* (the ability to control your own behaviour, so that you do what you are expected to do).

> Be disciplined and don't put things off.

Functional language: Talking about priorities

Students look at useful phrases for talking about what's important and urgent.

4A Ask students to do the exercise individually. With weaker classes, do the first two or three as a class. Check answers in pairs.

> **1** utmost   **2** low   **3** high   **4** really   **5** quite
> **6** extremely

4B Students could do this exercise individually and then compare answers in pairs before checking with the class.

> **1** g   **2** a   **3** b   **4** f   **5** j   **6** h   **7** i   **8** e   **9** d   **10** c

5 Get students to do this exercise in pairs. During the activity, monitor and help as necessary. Get feedback by asking a few pairs to share their answers with the class.

Extra activities 8.4

A Get students to do the exercise individually. Check answers in pairs.

> **1** waste   **2** one   **3** time   **4** distraction   **5** bottom
> **6** while   **7** things

B Students continue in their pairs, then share their ideas with another pair.

> **1** urgent = must be done quickly; important = of value or significance
> **2** high priority = must be done as soon as possible; low priority = not important or urgent
> **3** to put something on a list = to write it down; to put something off = to delay doing something

Task

Students discuss and set priorities.

6A Students do the exercise individually.

6B Put students in pairs. Refer them to the matrix in Exercise 3A and the phrases in Exercise 4. Give them 3–4 minutes to do the exercise.

6C Put students in new pairs and give them another 3–4 minutes. During the activity, monitor and help as necessary.

6D Ask groups to present their ideas to the class. Remind them to use phrases from Exercise 4. Monitor and make notes during the presentation. Get feedback by asking students to share with the class what they think went well and what could be improved. Did they think the matrix was useful? Or was it too complicated? Then highlight any points you noted while monitoring.

MyEnglishLab: Teacher's resources: extra activities; Functional language bank
Workbook: p.42 Exercise 2

8.5 ❯ Writing
Short report

- Can write a short report on a work-related task or event.
- Can use the Past Perfect in a range of common situations.

Warm-up

Write *report* on the board and ask: *What is a report? What does a report contain?* If students struggle to answer, ask: *Do we expect to find jokes in a report? Poems? Stories? Is it a type of email?* (A report is a written description of a situation or event, giving people the information they need, and in business, an official document that carefully considers a particular subject.) Ask if anyone has ever written a report (not necessarily in English) and to say briefly what it was about. This could include any simple report written for school or something for work. You might like to give an example of a report you have written to get them started. If no one has ever written a report, tell them that they will write one in this lesson.

Lead-in
Students read and complete a short business report.

1A Before students do the exercise, focus their attention on the headings in the report. Teach or elicit the meanings of *findings* and *recommendations* (see Notes below). Ask: *What problem is the report about?* (communication between departments) *What solution does the report suggest?* (managers monitor and report problems) Get students to do the exercise individually.

Notes

Short reports usually have three mains sections:
Introduction: A couple of sentences that explain the main topic of the report, often a problem that needs to be investigated and solved.
Findings: The information that has been discovered as a result of study or investigation.
Recommendations: Advice or suggestions about what to do next.

1 policy 2 reasons 3 issues 4 orders 5 department
6 stock 7 updates 8 technology 9 systems 10 heads

1B Students compare answers in pairs before checking with the class.

Functional language
Students look at the organisation of and some useful phrases for a short business report.

2 Students could do this individually or in pairs, using their dictionaries if necessary. Check answers with the class and clarify any vocabulary if necessary.

1 looks 2 purpose 3 asked 4 aims 5 make 6 key
7 thing 8 found 9 seems 10 recommended
11 should 12 aims 13 might

Extra activities 8.5

A This exercise gives another example of a short business report. Get students to do it individually, then check answers with the class.

1 aims 2 reasons 3 recommendations 4 at
5 problems 6 found 7 recommended 8 might

Optional grammar work

The report in Exercise 1 contains examples of the Past Perfect Simple, so you could use it for some optional grammar work. Refer students to the Grammar reference on page 125 and use the exercises in MyEnglishLab for extra grammar practice.

❯ ### Pronunciation bank
p.117: Contractions in speech

Warm-up
Write *did not* on the board. Ask students to say it. If no one mentions the contraction *didn't*, prompt them to do so by asking: *Is there another way of saying it?* Refer students to the explanation in the box.

1 Teach or elicit the meaning of *contraction* (a shorter form of a word or words) and elicit a few examples (*do not – don't, they have – they've, we are – we're*). Ask: *Are contractions generally more formal or less formal?* (less formal) Explain that reports often contain fewer contractions than less formal types of writing such as emails between colleagues. Get students to do the exercise individually, then check answer in pairs.

1 The sales department **hadn't** checked stocks before accepting the order.
2 Staff **won't** talk to each other.
3 Stock updates ought to happen automatically, but they **don't**.
4 The economic situation **hasn't** helped.
5 When I contacted the warehouse, **they'd** ordered more stock.
6 **It's** been decided that we should make our brand more attractive to younger customers.
7 **There've** been a few problems.
8 Problems should be reported immediately, so that **everyone's** aware of them.

2 🔊 P8.02 Play the recording for students to listen and check. Then play it again for them to listen and repeat.

Task

Students assess a short business report and then write their own.

3A Put students in pairs. Refer them to page 131 and give them time to read the report and discuss how it could be improved. As feedback, elicit and discuss students' suggestions.

Possible answers

1 This report aims to / The boss has asked me to write this report in order to find out how staff feel …
2 This report looks at …
3 One of the key problems is / The first thing I noticed was that …
4 It was also found / Another factor is …
5 It also seems …
6 It is therefore recommended that we tell / My recommendations are to tell…
7 We should do this / This should be done …

3B Students write their own report based on the notes on page 132. Remind them to use the functional language from Exercise 2, and point out the word limit. Monitor and help students as necessary.

Model answer

The HR Manager asked me to write this report because too many staff are leaving the company after only one year. This report looks at the reasons why staff are leaving and offers recommendations.

One of the key problems seems to be pay. Employees say they can earn more money in other companies, so they leave here and go to our competitors. It was also found that staff feel that communication within the company is not very effective and that it is difficult to get the information they need. Another factor is that there seems to be too much work for everyone, which means staff are stressed and often have to work late.

It is therefore recommended that the company reviews staff salaries to make them more competitive. We should also look more closely at improving company communication and train staff to communicate more effectively. Finally, we should review our staffing levels and the way in which work is delegated.

3C Put students in pairs. Give them a couple of minutes to read each other's reports. Then get them to answer the questions and suggest ways in which they could improve their reports.

MyEnglishLab: Teacher's resources: extra activities; Interactive grammar practice; Writing bank
Grammar reference: p.125 Past Perfect Simple
Pronunciation bank: p.117 Contractions in speech
Workbook: p.43 Exercises 1 and 2

Business workshop > 8
Global communication

GSE learning objectives

- Can extract key details from conversations between colleagues about familiar topics.
- Can express opinions as regards possible solutions, giving brief reasons and explanations.
- Can write an email making a recommendation, given a model.
- Can make simple recommendations on a work-related situation.

Background

Students read about an aviation navigation equipment maker that is dealing with some communication issues.

1 Put students in pairs and ask them to read the background and discuss the questions. Check answers with the class.

1 They manufacture aviation navigation equipment.
2 English
3 communication problems
4 Students' own answers
5 Possible answers: ask questions, repeat information using different words if possible, don't rush

Identifying communication problems

Students listen to two DaneAv employees talking about communication issues.

2A ▶ BW 8.01 Get students to read the instructions so they know what they are listening for. Teach or elicit the meaning of *cultural approaches to communication* (see Notes below). Play the recording. Get students to check answers in pairs.

Notes

People in different countries and cultures often have different ideas about what is normal. In some cultures, businesspeople feel that their job is to do business, and so when they meet people from other companies to talk about business, they immediately start talking about work. Other cultures, however, feel that it is important to socialise first and to get to know one another. When people from two different places with very different ideas of 'normal' get together, they can often feel confused or upset because they feel the other person is behaving strangely or rudely.

1 b 2 d

2B ▶ BW 8.01 Ask students to read the questions so they know what they're listening for. Then play the recording again. Check answers with the whole class. Point out the meaning of *outstanding* in this use (extremely good) as opposed to its other meaning (not yet done, solved or paid).

> 1 a South African, Vietnamese
>   b He expected to discuss business.
>   c That in Vietnam, people like to get to know each other before discussing business. Also, they rarely discuss work at dinner.
> 2 a weekly
>   b monthly
>   c outstanding

2C Put students in small groups to discuss the questions. During the activity, monitor and help as necessary. After 2–3 minutes, get groups to share some ideas with the class.

Possible answers

> 1 A Vietnamese businessperson would probably expect to spend some time getting to know people he/she's doing business with before talking about business. However, he/she would probably find that South Africans tend to talk about business straightaway – over meals, for example. The Vietnamese businessperson would probably feel that South Africans are very direct, which might feel strange and uncomfortable.
> 2 Students' own answers

Extra activities Business workshop 8

A ▶ BW 8.01 This activity provides students with revision of the main ideas they have been working on and with extra listening practice. Get students to do the exercise individually, then play the recording while they check answers in pairs.

> 1 cross-cultural 2 expected 3 confused
> 4 direct 5 performance 6 pain 7 outstanding
> 8 communication

3A Refer students to the emails on page 138. Explain that these are emails between Mr Lau and Frederik, about Frederik's upcoming trip to Paris.

> The plans for Frederik's trip are going well. Mr Lau will be able to supply the new design model by the Saturday before Frederik's Monday meeting.

3B Refer students to the emails on page 136. Explain that they continue the discussion between Frederik and Mr Lau. Put students in pairs to discuss the questions. When they have finished, invite a few pairs to share their ideas with the class.

> 1 There's a problem with the design model.
> 2 No he won't, because the design model will arrive just in time.

4A ▶ BW 8.02 Tell students that they are going to hear Frederik's side of the story. Get them to read the sentences so they know what information they are listening for. Play the recording for students to complete the exercise individually. Check answers in pairs.

> 1 T 2 F 3 T

4B ▶ BW 8.03 Tell students that they are now going to hear Mr Lau's side of the story. Get them to read the sentences so they know what information they are listening for. With more advanced groups, see if they can guess the correct answers, then listen to check.

> 1 knew 2 to show respect
> 3 his own cultural understanding

4C Get students to do this exercise in small groups.

Possible answers

> Frederik feels frustrated with the situation and confused. He thinks Mr Lau should have sent the design model back to manufacturing as soon as he realised there was a problem. He thinks Mr Lau shouldn't have waited to ask.
>
> Mr Lau feels that the team is working as it should and that the job will get done just in time.
>
> Both Mr Lau and Frederik have worked hard to make sure the presentation will go well, and both want the company to succeed.
>
> Neither is aware of how the other person thinks and feels.

Solving problems

Students analyse a problem and possible solution.

5 Get students to read the email and two questions. Check answers with the whole class.

Possible answers

> The email discusses the problem of communication among the offices globally. It offers cross-cultural communication training as a solution.

Extra activities Business workshop 8

B This activity provides students with extra reading practice. During the activity, monitor and help as necessary. Get students to check answers in pairs.

> 1 a 2 c 3 b 4 b 5 c

Task: Recommend ways to improve communication

Students write an email suggesting ways to improve communication.

6A Put students in small groups. Go through the instructions with them and get them to read the three bullet points. Explain that these are all possible solutions to cross-cultural communication issues. Answer any questions they may have. During the activity, monitor and help as necessary.

6B This exercise could be assigned as homework. Point out that the email in Exercise 5 is a model and remind students to use the checklist.

Model answers

To all employees,
We are aware that recently many of you have felt that communication among the offices globally has at times been difficult. We would like to address the issue by gathering key employees from all offices for a formal meeting to discuss ways to improve communication. We think this will give everyone a chance to explain the things that aren't working, and to work together to find solutions.

We will be in touch again soon with more information about the time and location of the meeting.

We will review the situation again after six months.

If you have any questions, please don't hesitate to get in touch.

To all employees,
We are aware that recently many of you have felt that communication among the offices globally has at times been difficult. We would like to address the issue by arranging an informal weekend away for all employees at a beach resort, so people can get to know one another. We think this will allow everyone to develop a better understanding of their co-workers and of the places we all come from.

We will be in touch again soon with more information about the time and location of the weekend away.

We will review the situation again after six months.

If you have any questions, please don't hesitate to get in touch.

To all employees,
We are aware that recently many of you have felt that communication among the offices globally has at times been difficult. We would like to address the issue by offering employees more opportunities to work in offices outside their own country for two or three months at a time. We feel that this will give employees an opportunity to see first-hand how other parts of the business work.

We will be in touch again soon with more information about how the programme will work.

We will review the situation again after six months.

If you have any questions, please don't hesitate to get in touch.

6C Put students in pairs, making sure that they work with someone from another group. During the activity, monitor and help as necessary. As a follow-up, with the class, talk through the benefits and any possible drawbacks of all of the solutions that have been discussed. Finally, ask the class to vote on which of the solutions they think would be the most effective.

MyEnglishLab: Teacher's resources: extra activities

Review ◀ 8

1 1 overloaded 2 checking 3 master 4 reply 5 catch
2 1 productivity 2 organise 3 performance 4 benefits
   5 transformation
3 1 will be 2 were 3 would think 4 wouldn't spend
   5 will have 6 does 7 would see 8 had
   9 wouldn't do 10 will be
4 1 sums 2 leaves 3 understand 4 return 5 sum up
5 1 utmost 2 make 3 priority 4 off 5 schedule
6 1 This report aims to 2 It looks at why 3 it will make
   recommendations 4 One of the key problems
   5 It was found 6 It also seems that 7 It is
   recommended

Resource bank

Reading bank

Writing bank

Functional language bank

1.1 > Vocabulary

1 Work in pairs. Look at the list of transferable skills (a–h) and then read your partner's profile below. Which of the skills do you think your partner might have? Choose at least four that you can support with clear reasons. You can also add ideas of your own.

a	can-do attitude	**e**	integrity
b	communication skills	**f**	can set goals
c	critical thinking	**g**	team player
d	determination	**h**	can think outside the box

Student A

Profile
- has a degree in business management
- worked for two years in customer service; received an award for excellence
- switched to a job in project management last year
- volunteers at a local citizens' advice centre
- hobbies include kite-surfing and basketball

Student B

Profile
- is just about to graduate as a graphic designer
- hasn't started a permanent job yet, but has waited tables at a restaurant for years
- loves the arts, and regularly volunteers at a local arts venue
- contributes expertise when friends and family have difficulty with technology
- enjoys sports and plays on the university football team

2 With your partner, take turns to share your ideas from Exercise 1. Discuss the skills you selected for each other and your reasons for choosing them.

3 Read the job advert for your partner. Then identify at least four of the transferable skills from Exercise 1 required for this job.

Student A

HUMAN RESOURCES ASSISTANT

We are looking for someone to join our busy Human Resources department. The perfect person for this job will be calm and organised. You must have confidence in your ability to finish tasks quickly and with enthusiasm. You will need to deal with unexpected problems and be resourceful in finding solutions. As the files about our workers are private, you must be reliable and very honest.

Student B

ARTS FESTIVAL COORDINATOR

Are you someone who thinks in a creative and original way? Can you give very clear written and spoken information? Are you good at working closely with others, and working together to get things done? If so, join our team and make the next arts festival our best one yet. This role is exciting, but sometimes challenging. If you're someone who doesn't give up easily, who continues trying when things get difficult, then contact us today.

4 Discuss the job and the skills it requires. Point out the transferable skills from Exercise 1 that make your partner suitable for this role. Discuss at least four transferable skills.

1.2 > Grammar

1 Choose the correct option to complete the suggestions and advice.

1 Why don't you ____ a promotion?

   a requesting   **b** request   **c** to request

2 You could ____ with an employment agency.

   a signs up   **b** signing up   **c** sign up

3 You shouldn't ____ so much!

   a worry   **b** worried   **c** worries

4 What about ____ for a different job?

   a to apply   **b** apply   **c** applying

5 You ought ____ your CV.

   a update   **b** to update   **c** updating

6 How about ____ for a raise?

   a asking   **b** ask   **c** to ask

7 Why not try ____ to your manager?

   a to speak   **b** speak   **c** speaking

8 You should ____ a job you love.

   a doing   **b** to do   **c** do

2 Complete the suggestions and advice with the phrases in the box. Use each phrase only once.

> how about   what about   why don't you   why not try   you could   you ought to
> you should   you shouldn't

1 _____ sign up for an evening course.

2 _____ thinking outside the box?

3 _____ use every opportunity to network.

4 _____ going to a trade fair?

5 _____ work during the weekends!

6 _____ transferring to another department?

7 _____ develop new skills.

8 _____ research other career options?

3 Work in pairs. Read the information for your partner and take turns to roleplay a conversation. Use the phrases from the box in Exercise 2 to give your partner advice and make suggestions. You can use one idea from the box below and two other ideas of your own.

Student A

- studied history at university
- wants to work in marketing
- has no marketing experience

Student B

- is a qualified teacher
- would like to work in banking
- has no experience in finance

> do an internship   go to a networking event   speak to someone in the industry

2.1 ❭ Vocabulary

Student A　Look at your three job cards. Your partner also has three job cards. Take turns to ask and answer the questions below to find out your partner's jobs. Keep asking *yes/no* questions of your own until you guess the job title. Then say which sector the job is in and explain why.

A1	A2	A3
bus driver	**farmer (crops only)**	**car factory worker**

Questions for Student B

B1
1 Do you make a product? ☐
2 Are you a furniture maker? ☐
3 Do you use raw materials? ☐
4 Are you in the electronics industry? ☐
5 Do you mainly work outside? ☐
6 Are you in the construction industry? ☐
7 Do you build factories? ☐

Sector: _____　Reason: _____

B2
1 Do you work for a private company? ☐
2 Do you manufacture something? ☐
3 Do you work in an office? ☐
4 Do you work in the retail industry? ☐
5 Are you a salesperson? ☐
6 Do you sell clothes? ☐
7 Do you sell electronics? ☐

Sector: _____　Reason: _____

B3
1 Do you work in a factory? ☐
2 Do you work in a service industry? ☐
3 Is your job based at sea? ☐
4 Do you work in fishing? ☐
5 Do you extract something? ☐
6 Are you in the energy industry? ☐
7 Is your job in gas extraction? ☐

Sector: _____　Reason: _____

✂ -

Student B　Look at your three job cards. Your partner also has three job cards. Take turns to ask and answer the questions below to find out your partner's jobs. Keep asking *yes/no* questions of your own until you guess the job title. Then say which sector the job is in and explain why.

B1	B2	B3
house builder	**salesperson in phone shop**	**worker on an oil rig**

Questions for Student A

A1
1 Do you work in the finance industry? ☐
2 Do you provide a service? ☐
3 Do you work in health care? ☐
4 Is your job in entertainment? ☐
5 Do you work in transportation? ☐
6 Are you a manager? ☐
7 Are you a pilot for an airline? ☐

Sector: _____　Reason: _____

A2
1 Do you work in education? ☐
2 Is your job a traditional one? ☐
3 Do you work for a private company? ☐
4 Do you produce something? ☐
5 Do you make wine? ☐
6 Is your job in agriculture? ☐
7 Are you an animal farmer? ☐

Sector: _____　Reason: _____

A3
1 Do you extract raw materials? ☐
2 Do you work in tourism? ☐
3 Do you manufacture something? ☐
4 Is it textile manufacturing? ☐
5 Do you work in a factory? ☐
6 Is it a robotics factory? ☐
7 Are you in the automotive industry? ☐

Sector: _____　Reason: _____

2.2 ❭ Grammar

Student A

1 Choose the correct option in italics to complete the text.

> In 2017 I ¹*visited / was visiting* an interesting British company for the first time. It's called The Big Lemon, a community interest company (CIC), which means they work for the benefit of the public. I'd heard they ²*run / were running* a number of buses without using any fossil fuels, so I decided to go and see them. At the time, I ³*researched / was researching* the energy industry and I ⁴*wanted / was wanting* to find out how different companies ⁵*used / were using* renewable energy sources. For example, The Big Lemon provides public transport on buses that use recycled cooking oil as their fuel. But then they tried something else.
>
> When I ⁶*arrived / was arriving*, there was a great deal of excitement. I was thrilled to discover that The Big Lemon ⁷*launched / was launching* an excellent new product that day: a bus powered by solar panels! I immediately ⁸*saw / was seeing* the bright yellow bus, which can drive for 100 miles without being recharged, and is the first of its kind in the UK. Exciting times for the future of sustainable energy!

2 Read the text again carefully and make sure you understand all the main points.

3 Work in pairs. Tell your partner about your text in your own words. Do not show him/her your text. Then ask him/her the following questions.

    1 What type of company is The Big Lemon?

    2 What type of fuel were they using in their buses?

    3 What were they launching in 2017?

4 Share your worksheet with your partner and discuss the two projects. Do you think they're good ideas? Do you think they'll be successful in the long term? Why / Why not?

Student B

1 Choose the correct option in italics to complete the text.

> In 2010 my brother Pete and I moved to Detroit in the USA, where we both had places at university. Pete was doing a science degree. I ¹*studied / was studying* environmental engineering and really enjoying the course. I ²*watched / was watching* the news on TV one night when I ³*heard / was hearing* about Highland Park, a poor area in Detroit which ⁴*struggled / was struggling* to pay for its street lighting at the time. They didn't manage to pay the bill so, one day, the local energy company ⁵*arrived / was arriving* and took all the street lights away. Highland Park was in the dark! Fortunately, however, a local community group called Soulardarity ⁶*worked / was working* on a solution. It successfully ⁷*installed / was installing* the first solar street light in Highland Park in 2012. From then on, many people began to help Soulardarity and by 2016 the area ⁸*had / was having* five more solar street lights. A success story!

2 Read the text again carefully and make sure you understand all the main points.

3 Work in pairs. Tell your partner about your text in your own words. Do not show him/her your text. Then ask him/her the following questions.

    1 What was the problem in Highland Park?

    2 Who was helping?

    3 How did the situation improve?

4 Share your worksheet with your partner and discuss the two projects. Do you think they're good ideas? Do you think they'll be successful in the long term? Why / Why not?

3.1 > Vocabulary

Student A

1 Read Henry's paragraph. Then read the questions below and make notes with your ideas.

> ### Henry
>
> My whole family is going on holiday to Thailand in two years' time: brothers, sisters, parents, aunts, uncles, cousins ... everyone! Altogether, there will be fourteen of us, but I suppose some people might decide not to travel. Uncle Felix and Aunt Jane are in charge of all the details. They've arranged some family meetings so we can discuss our ideas. At the last meeting my cousins suggested travelling in February, but Uncle Felix thinks that strikes in the UK might cause flight delays. We've agreed to travel in June. Flights and accommodation will be around £2,000 per person. We don't have to pay that all at once; we can divide it into a few separate payments. Uncle Felix has just called another family meeting. He says there might be an issue, but we don't know what it is yet.

1 What is the project?
2 When is it taking place?
3 What is Henry anticipating?
4 Who are the project managers?
5 What did Uncle Felix predict?

6 Are they doing anything to reduce risk?
7 Do you think they have a risk register?
8 What kind of milestones are in place?
9 What is the budget?
10 What do you think the setback might be?

2 Work in pairs. Show your partner your paragraph, but not your notes. Then discuss the project and the questions.

3 If you were the project manager, would you organise things differently? How?

Student B

1 Read Sue's paragraph. Then read the questions below and make notes with your ideas.

> ### Sue
>
> I'm in my second year of university, studying history. My classmate, Amina, is my best friend, and we have a business idea. In our spare time we're going to design and sell T-shirts. I think they'll be popular because we've already done a few designs, just for ourselves, and everyone loves them. We only have £200 to buy the materials we need, but Amina feels that's enough to get started. She's offered to manage all the details. For maximum profit, I thought we should make as many T-shirts as possible, but Amina wants to begin with a smaller number. She wants to sell the T-shirts at festivals and outdoor markets every weekend, but I prefer online sales. My brother can build a website for us. I'm worried because I'm starting my exams soon, and I need to study at the weekends.

1 What is the project?
2 Who is involved?
3 What is Sue anticipating?
4 Who is the project manager?
5 What is the budget?

6 Are they doing anything to reduce risk?
7 Do you think they have a risk register?
8 Do they have any milestones in place?
9 Is the plan clearly established?
10 What setback might there be?

2 Work in pairs. Show your partner your paragraph, but not your notes. Then discuss the project and the questions.

3 If you were the project manager, would you organise things differently? How?

3.2 ❭ Grammar

1 **tall** *(superlative)* building world	**2** **cheap** *(comparative)* materials other buildings	**3** **famous** *(superlative)* city canals	**4** **early** *(comparative)* project expected
5 **profitable** *(comparative)* summer winter	**6** **high** *(superlative)* deaths Panama Canal	**7** **hard** *(comparative)* steel iron	**8** **long** *(superlative)* Grand Canal China
9 **famous** *(superlative)* the Sagrada Família Barcelona	**10** **modern** *(comparative)* metal stone	**11** **quick** *(superlative)* gondola ferry Grand Canal, Venice	**12** **strong** *(comparative)* new team previous team
13 **interesting** *(comparative)* participate watch	**14** **big** *(superlative)* challenge budget	**15** **easy** *(comparative)* dig cool weather	**16** **early** *(superlative)* constructions simple
17 **new** *(superlative)* design exciting	**18** **old** *(comparative)* wood plastic	**19** **unusual** *(superlative)* feature door	**20** **short** *(comparative)* Panama Canal Suez Canal
21 **popular** *(comparative)* canals Europe	**22** **difficult** *(superlative)* bridge beautiful	**23** **profitable** *(comparative)* housing sectors	**24** **dangerous** *(superlative)* Panama Canal world

Possible answers

1 The tallest building in the world is in Dubai.
2 They used cheaper materials than in the other buildings.
3 The most famous city for canals is Venice.
4 The project finished earlier than expected.
5 It's more profitable in summer than in winter.
6 The highest number of deaths occurred during the building of the Panama Canal.
7 Steel is a harder metal than iron.
8 The world's longest canal is the Grand Canal in China.
9 The Sagrada Família is the most famous building in Barcelona.
10 Metal is more modern than stone.
11 A gondola ferry is the quickest way to cross the Grand Canal in Venice.
12 The new team is stronger than the previous team.
13 It's more interesting to participate in building something than to watch.
14 The biggest challenge was the budget.
15 It's easier to dig in cool weather.
16 The earliest constructions were very simple.
17 The newest design is very exciting.
18 Wood is older than plastic.
19 The most unusual feature of the building is the door.
20 The Panama Canal is shorter than the Suez Canal.
21 Canals are more popular in Europe than in the United States.
22 This beautiful bridge was the most difficult to build.
23 Housing is more profitable than other sectors in construction.
24 The Panama Canal was one of the world's most dangerous construction projects.

4.1 > Vocabulary

1 Complete the collocations for global markets with the words in the box.

| brands   local   luxury   product   strategy   territories |

1 _____ goods
2 marketing _____
3 _____ preferences
4 target _____
5 _____ customisation
6 consumer _____

2 Match the collocations from Exercise 1 (1–6) with the definitions (a–f).

a ____ a company's plan for advertising and selling the goods they make
b ____ adapting goods to suit a particular purpose
c ____ the specific areas where a company wants to sell their goods
d ____ well-known goods that are bought by the public rather than by businesses
e ____ what the people in a specific area or region particularly like
f ____ expensive things that are not necessary but are nice to own

3 Work in pairs. Discuss real-life examples of all six phrases from Exercise 1, naming specific companies and products. Make notes with your ideas.

1 _____
_____
2 _____
_____
3 _____
_____
4 _____
_____
5 _____
_____
6 _____
_____

4 Work with another pair. Using your notes from Exercise 3, compare and contrast your examples. Are they similar or very different?

4.2 > Grammar

Student A

		NAME	often	sometimes	never
1	In the past month, did you buy clothes online?				
2	Do you pay for access to any news websites?				
3	In the past week, did you order takeaway food online?				
4	Do you ever sell items online?				
5	Do you expect free shipping when you shop online?				
6	In the past year, did you provide customer reviews online?				
7	Did you buy books online recently?				
8	Do you request online recommendations for services or goods you want to buy?				
9	Does social media influence the online purchases you make?				
10	Did you leave without buying anything from online sites that didn't have a clear layout?				

Student B

		NAME	often	sometimes	never
1	In the past six months, did you buy shoes online?				
2	Do you use a credit card when you shop online?				
3	In the past month, did you order groceries online?				
4	Do you use your phone to shop online?				
5	If you see something you like in a shop, do you try to find it cheaper online?				
6	Do you prefer online shopping to retail shopping?				
7	Did you make a complaint about an online purchase last year?				
8	In the past year, did you buy electronics online?				
9	Do you read online reviews before you make a purchase?				
10	Did you use any 'click and collect' services recently?				

5.1 ❯ Vocabulary

1 Match sentences 1–9 with sentences a–i to complete the descriptions.

1 This camera is great because the instructions are very easy to understand. ____

2 I love this jacket because there isn't another one like it. ____

3 That e-reader is the very best one you can buy. ____

4 It's the most reliable car I've ever had – it never breaks down! ____

5 The design of these headphones is really unusual and clever. ____

6 It's such a fashionable laptop! It looks so cool. ____

7 I used to have a basic printer but the one I have now is a much higher standard. ____

8 My brother's jacket is the latest fashion, but mine is more traditional. ____

9 They carefully planned every detail when they made this phone. ____

a It's really **stylish**.

b It's completely **dependable**.

c It's a **classic** design.

d It's completely **unique**.

e It's so i**nnovative**.

f It's very **well designed**.

g It's totally **user-friendly**.

h It's the **advanced** model.

i It's **top-of-the-range**.

2 Work in pairs. You are going to create and present an advert for an innovative product of your choice. Decide what product you will talk about. Add your own ideas to each section. Then agree on a product to advertise.

Product ideas	
electronic item	*tablet, MP3 player,*
lifestyle item	*fitness tracker, e-reader,*
household item	*digital radio, electric toothbrush,*
other ideas	

3 For your chosen product, pick <u>four</u> of the adjectives in bold from Exercise 1 and use them in your advert. Make sure you explain how these adjectives are suitable for this product. Your advert should be 30 seconds long. Make notes with your ideas.

Advert points	Advert notes
Name of product:	
Type of product:	
People should buy it because it's: adjective 1 _____ adjective 2 _____ adjective 3 _____ adjective 4 _____	
Other selling points:	

4 With your partner, present your advert to the class. Share the speaking time equally.

5.2 ❯ Grammar

1 Read the scenarios and choose the correct options.

1 Bruno invited Nina to the cinema to see a science fiction film he was interested in. Nina didn't go with him because she'd seen the film with her sister.

a Nina has already seen the film.   b Nina hasn't seen the film yet.

2 Greg wants to buy a new tablet but he doesn't have enough money for it.

a Greg hasn't saved the money yet.   b Greg has already saved the money.

3 I got a text from my brother asking me to phone our dad. But two minutes before I received the text, I was speaking to my dad on the phone!

a I've just spoken to my dad.   b I haven't spoken to my dad yet.

4 The assistant is offering us coffee but we'd both had one on our way to the meeting.

a We haven't had coffee yet.   b We've just had coffee.

5 Zoe got a new smartphone but it's still in the box. She says she'll open it tomorrow.

a Zoe has already used her new phone.   b Zoe hasn't used her new phone yet.

6 Liam ordered a new camera online. A week later he changed his mind and tried to cancel the order, but the company said it had been shipped a few days before.

a The camera has already been shipped.   b The camera has just been shipped.

Student A

2 Look at your work diary for today and note which items have (✓) and haven't (✗) been done so far. Pay attention to the times.

10.00 a.m.	work on product report	✗
11.00 a.m.	product testing meeting	✓
12.30 p.m.	lunch with marketing team	✓
1.50 p.m.	email sales figures	✓
2.00 p.m.	**It's 2.00 p.m. now.**	
2.30 p.m.	contact product testers	✗
3.00 p.m.	conference call	✗
4.00 p.m.	planning meeting	✗

3 Work in pairs and roleplay a meeting. Take turns to be the manager. Look at each item in the list and ask your partner if he/she has done it. Put a tick (✓) for the items that he/she has done and a cross (✗) for those he/she hasn't done.

Have you:	
design meeting / yet?	
product presentation / already?	
email / sales report / yet ?	
lunch with Sales Manager / already?	
send out / launch invitations / yet?	
product launch meeting / already?	
conference call / yet?	

Student B

2 Look at your work diary for today and note which items have (✓) and haven't (✗) been done so far. Pay attention to the times.

9.00 a.m.	design meeting	✓
10.30 a.m.	product presentation	✓
11.30 p.m.	email sales report	✗
12.45 p.m.	lunch with Sales Manager	✓
3.55 p.m.	send out launch invitations	✓
4.00 p.m.	**It's 4.00 p.m. now.**	
4.30 p.m.	product launch meeting	✗
5.00 p.m.	conference call	✗

3 Work in pairs and roleplay a meeting. Take turns to be the manager. Look at each item in the list and ask your partner if he/she has done it. Put a tick (✓) for the items that he/she has done and a cross (✗) for those he/she hasn't done

Have you:	
work on / product report / already?	
product testing meeting / yet?	
lunch with marketing team / already?	
email / sales figures / yet?	
contact / product testers / already?	
conference call / yet?	
planning meeting / already?	

6.1 ❭ Vocabulary

1 Read the two situations on your worksheet. What do you think happened next? Work in pairs and make notes with your ideas. Then, for each situation, write your answers to these two questions. Use at least four words/phrases from the box below.

1 Who do you think was affected by the incident? Why? How?

2 What health and safety rules do you suggest?

> bleed   break   cut   damage   fall   fit cameras and sensors   handle sharp debris   hit
> hold training programmes   hurt   injure   issue personal safety equipment
> pose a risk of injury   record an accident   slip

2 Work with a pair from the other group. Take turns to present your situations to each other. Discuss each story. Ask for the other pair's ideas about what happened next. Then share your own answers with them and compare your ideas.

Group 1

A

It was a very busy day at the office. Ramiro didn't have time to eat lunch, and he had a planning meeting at 2.30. He decided to bring some food into the meeting, so he went to the office cafeteria and bought some soup. Ramiro was late, so he hurried. In the hall outside the meeting room, he didn't notice that he'd spilled some soup. His colleague, Olga, was running to the same meeting.

B

Early one morning, there was a delivery of heavy boxes at a warehouse. Two workers, Boris and Franz, were asked to put the boxes away. Boris and Franz chatted while they moved the boxes to a high shelf. But they weren't paying attention to their work and they didn't put the boxes safely on the shelf. Later that day, their colleague, Jack, was standing near the same shelf. Jack wasn't wearing any protective clothing.

Group 2

C

Melanie Kane got a new job at her local supermarket in London. On her first day, she finished work at 2 p.m. Before she cycled home, Melanie decided to do some shopping. It was close to her mother's birthday and she wanted to buy some presents. When Melanie finished shopping, it was after 3 p.m., and beginning to get dark. It was very cold, but her long black coat kept her warm as she cycled. Suddenly, a car came round the corner at very high speed.

D

Elena Fusco, a college student, was at home studying for her exams. She left her bedroom to get a glass of water from the kitchen. Suddenly, the glass slipped from her hands and fell on the floor. There was broken glass everywhere! Elena started to pick it up, but the phone rang, so she left the kitchen to answer it. Unfortunately, she forgot about the broken glass. A few minutes later, her brother Dino came downstairs for a snack. Dino wasn't wearing any shoes.

6.2 ❱ Grammar

Read the information in italics. Then choose the correct option to complete each sentence.

1　*It isn't necessary to do this at all.*
　You ____ switch off your mobile phone on the train.
　a must　　　　**b** don't have to　　**c** have to

2　*It's OK to do this, but it's not really necessary.*
　You ____ shut down your laptop at night.
　a have to　　　**b** must　　　　**c** don't need to

3　*Doing this is not allowed.*
　You ____ read text messages while driving a car.
　a mustn't　　　**b** have to　　　**c** need to

4　*It wasn't necessary to do this.*
　In the past, people ____ wear protective clothing at work.
　a need to　　　**b** mustn't　　　**c** didn't have to

5　*It's absolutely necessary to do this.*
　In the workplace, accidents ____ be recorded and investigated.
　a don't need to　**b** must　　　　**c** mustn't

Everyone **has to**	You **don't need to**	We **must**
You **had to**	People **didn't have to**	Everyone **needed to**
We **need to**	They **mustn't**	We **didn't need to**
carry an ID badge.	have security doors in all buildings.	keep your passwords safe.
have CCTV on buses.	keep meat in the fridge.	smoke inside the hospital.
use metal detectors in airports.	wear a seat belt on flights.	have security cameras in schools.

7.1 › Vocabulary

1 Work in pairs. Read and discuss the customer needs (1–4) and match them with the most suitable airline (a–e). There is one extra airline you don't need to use.

1 **Customer 1: Airline _____**

   I'm working on a project in another European country for the next three months. I need to take the 90-minute flight there every Monday morning, and fly back on Friday evenings to see my family. I have to use a pretty basic airline, as I can't afford expensive fares, but I don't want to wait in long queues every time.

2 **Customer 2: Airline _____**

   We are a couple celebrating our tenth wedding anniversary, and we're planning a fantastic holiday abroad. For us, it's a big occasion, obviously, and we want it to be unforgettable. We're looking for an airline that will treat us like we're celebrities and make us feel really important and special!

3 **Customer 3: Airline _____**

   I'm the personal assistant to the president of a major company in the UK. She has to travel to Japan for a big meeting next month and I want to make sure that the long journey is as comfortable as possible for her. I'm looking for an airline that offers a higher standard of travel and extra things that are only available to certain passengers.

4 **Customer 4: Airline _____**

   I need to book a flight for my elderly mother. I usually accompany her but, unfortunately, I can't travel with her this time. My mother is very nervous about air travel, so I want to feel completely confident that the cabin crew will be empathetic and take good care of her. I don't mind what it costs.

Airlines

a This airline offers business-class fares for a higher price, which include many exclusive features that keep our customers satisfied.

b This is a 'no-frills' airline that understands the importance of low-cost fares as well as other customer needs, such as priority boarding.

c This airline really gives personal attention. And the staff get special training in body language so that they can recognise and support anxious passengers.

d This is one of the world's most popular 'no-frills' airlines. Personal service and priority boarding are not offered, but it's perfect when low fares are all that matters.

e This airline has many qualities, but it is best known for offering premium service and VIP treatment.

2 Roleplay a conversation between a travel agent and each customer from Exercise 1. Take turns to be the travel agent and the customer. Use these notes to help you.

> **Travel agent**
> - Ask who the flight is for.
> - Ask what two things are most important to the customer.
> - Suggest an airline, saying why it's suitable.

> **Customer**
> - Explain who the flight is for.
> - Describe the two things that are most important to the customer.
> - Say whether this airline sounds suitable.

7.2 > Grammar

1 Complete the extracts from four customer service calls with the correct form of the verbs in brackets.

Call A

A: I'm afraid I forgot ¹_____ (pay) my credit card bill last month.

B: Oh, I'm sorry to hear that. Have you tried ²_____ (create) an alarm on your phone? It will help ³_____ (remind) you about the bill every month.

A: Thanks. That's a good suggestion. But would you mind ⁴_____ (cancel) the late fee this time? I'm a good customer and I usually pay on time.

Call B

A: I'm not satisfied with this phone. It keeps ¹_____ (drop) calls and I'm having other problems with it, too.

B: Oh, I am sorry; that's disappointing. If you want ²_____ (return) it, I suggest ³_____ (send) it back by special delivery. We can offer you a refund.

A: OK, but I don't want ⁴_____ (pay) the shipping costs. After all, it's not my fault the quality of the phone is poor.

Call C

A: I'm sorry to hear the item hasn't arrived yet. Would you like ¹_____ (speak) to someone in customer service?

B: No, I'd prefer ²_____ (get) a call back from them. I really don't enjoy ³_____ (wait) on hold. It always takes ages!

A: I'm so sorry, our agents can't make calls. If you don't have time right now, I recommend ⁴_____ (try) early in the morning. It's usually quiet then.

Call D

A: I regret ¹_____ (order) this item in the summer. It isn't suitable, and I'd like ²_____ (request) a full refund.

B: I'm afraid items need ³_____ (be) returned within thirty days for refunds. You've had this item for three months.

A: Yes, but as I've just finished ⁴_____ (explain) to your colleague, I've been ill.

2 Work in pairs. Look at the extracts in Exercise 1 again. We don't know whether the customers got what they wanted. What do you think the companies decided to do? Discuss each call with your partner and make notes. Remember to use the *to*-infinitive or *-ing* with the correct verbs.

A _____

_____

B _____

_____

C _____

_____

D _____

_____

3 Use your notes from Exercise 2 to continue each call from Exercise 1. Decide what the customer and the customer service agent said next. Read the example for Call A and then roleplay at least two new lines of dialogue for Calls B, C and D. Take turns to be the customer and customer service agent.

Call A, continued

B: Yes, I can see that you're a very good customer. Let me try to get rid of this fee for you … OK, I've managed to cancel it.

A: Thank you so much for agreeing to do that! I'll try setting a reminder on my phone now.

8.1 › Vocabulary

Student A

Digital communication in the workplace			
Questions	Name	True	False
1 Technology helps me to do my job (or study) in a very efficient way.			
Notes:			
2 Internal emails make it easier to keep up-to-date with important developments.			
Notes:			
3 The best approach is to answer all emails in the same order that you received them.			
Notes:			
4 People who feel overloaded by emails are not using digital communication properly.			
Notes:			
5 The internet is amazing, but it's not the master. We could still work and manage successfully without it.			
Notes:			

✂ -

Student B

Digital communication at home			
Questions	Name	True	False
1 My friends and I would never manage to organise our social events without technology.			
Notes:			
2 Digital communication is used too much. My family members expect me to check my phone all the time.			
Notes:			
3 Social media lets me catch up on my family and friends' news when I have time.			
Notes:			
4 I'm not a servant to technology because I carefully choose the blogs, sites, etc. that I want to look at.			
Notes:			
5 Too many people are overloaded by digital communication. If I could delete the internet from the world, I would.			
Notes:			

8.2 > Grammar

Read the sentences. Are they in the first conditional (F) or the second conditional (S)?

1 If she concentrated more, she'd understand the issue.   ____
2 You'll save a lot of time if you use this app.   ____
3 We'll fix the computers if they break.   ____
4 I'd send him an email if I had his email address.   ____
5 If you didn't look at your phone all the time, you wouldn't be so stressed.   ____
6 If you reply to her email, she'll explain everything.   ____

---

1 First if we / not be / satisfied, we / complain / social media	**2 Second** they / not care / if you / ignore / their calls	**3 First** if you / want / more money, they / give / you extra work	**4 Second** if she / organise / her emails, she / not be / overloaded
5 Second you / not have to / worry / if you / protect / your passwords	**6 First** we / work / harder / if you / give / us nicer offices	**7 Second** he / fix / your phone / if you / ask / him nicely	**8 First** if you / listen / carefully, you / understand / how they feel
9 First they / not like / it / if you / charge / money for wifi	**10 Second** you / have / more free time / if you / stay / off social media	**11 First** she / lose / the document / if she / not save / it	**12 Second** I / start / my own blog / if I / have / the time
13 Second we / feel / happier / if they / encourage / us	**14 First** if you / not speak / clearly, no one / understand / you	**15 Second** if everyone / help, we / finish / the project on time	**16 First** they / enjoy / social media more / if they / not rely / on it so much
17 First I / open / an account if they / give / me a discount	**18 Second** we / not succeed / if we / not have / this technology	**19 First** if he / send / another text, I / just / delete / it	**20 Second** if they / speak / clearly, there / not be / problems

1.1 ❯ Vocabulary

- Tell students that they are going to practise using vocabulary related to transferable skills and personal qualities.
- Put students in pairs, A and B. Hand everyone their copy of the worksheet.
- Give students a moment to look at the transferable skills. Check that everyone understands the phrases. Review any definitions if necessary.
- Explain that each student has a profile with five bullet points each. Give them a few minutes to read through the points and, again, check understanding before moving on.
- Students should link at least four transferable skills from the list to their partner's profile based on the bullet points provided. Emphasise that students work on their partner's profile, not their own. Start the activity, and remind students that they should be able to support their choices with reasons.
- Get students to discuss answers in pairs, then check as a class.
- Point out the two job adverts in Exercise 3. Again, remind students that they will work with the advert that interests their partner. Give the class a moment or two to read through the adverts. Make sure everyone understands the language.
- Explain that students should look for four skills or personal qualities that the job requires. Encourage students to underline words or phrases in the advert that help them to identify specific skills and qualities.
- Next, they should see if their partner is suitable for this job by cross-checking their skills from Exercise 1.
- When they have finished, get students to take turns to roleplay a conversation about the job advert and the required skills. They should point out which transferable skills make their partner suitable for the job and why.
- Ask pairs to share their ideas with the class.

---

1 Possible answers
Student A
(c) critical thinking: customer service award / obviously found ways to keep customers satisfied; (a) can-do attitude: kite-surfing and professional achievements require courage; (f) can set goals: experience in project management; (e) integrity: citizens' advice / helping others and caring about people

Student B
(h) can think outside the box: designer which involves creativity/originality; (b) communication skills: being a waiter requires excellent communication skills; (g) team player: sports interest + part-time job involve working as a team; (d) determination: helping others with tech problems

3
Student A
can-do attitude (calm/organised/confident); can set goals (finish tasks on time); critical thinking (deal with unexpected problems); integrity (reliable and honest)

Student B
can think outside the box (creative and original thinker); communication skills (give clear information in writing and speaking); team player (work closely with others to get things done); determination (doesn't give up easily)

1.2 ❯ Grammar

- Tell students that they are going to practise giving advice and making suggestions about careers.
- Put students in pairs and give everyone their own copy of the worksheet.
- Point out that they will practise the language from Lesson 2 in the first two activities. Then they will use the key phrases, and some of their own ideas, in a roleplay exercise with their partner.
- Get students to work individually on Exercise 1. Ask them to check their answers with their partner. Then check answers as a class by getting volunteers to read each sentence aloud.
- Move on to Exercise 2. Point out that more than one answer may be possible and remind students to ensure that their answers are grammatically correct. Advise them to pay attention to the punctuation at the end of each sentence. Give students a few minutes to complete the exercise individually.
- Get different students to call out their answers, confirming or correcting them as necessary. Ask whether others used different options from the box, and get them to call out their answers, too.
- Move on to Exercise 3 and go through the instructions with students. Do a brief demonstration with the class first, e.g. say: *I really want to work in the tourism industry, but I have no previous experience.* You could write this on the board. As different students call out their suggestions and advice, respond with phrases such as *Really? Do you think that would work? / Good idea, but how would you do that? / That's a great suggestion. What else could you do?* You might like to write these on the board as well.
- Get students to do the roleplay. Encourage them to come up with interesting advice and suggestions of their own. At the end, invite pairs to perform their roleplays for the class.

1
1 b **2** c **3** a **4** c **5** b **6** a **7** c **8** c
2 Possible answers
1 You could / You ought to / You should
2 How about / What about / Why not try
3 You could / You should / You ought to
4 How about / What about / Why not try
5 You shouldn't / You could / You ought to / You should
6 How about / What about / Why not try
7 You could / You ought to / You should
8 Why don't you

2.1 ❯ Vocabulary

- Tell students that they are going to talk about sectors and industries, and practise vocabulary from Lesson 2.1.
- Put students in pairs, A and B. Give each student their half of the worksheet so they each have a set of cards and questions. Tell them not to show these to their partner.
- Explain that both students have three cards with a different job written on each one. It is their partner's task to figure out what each job is by asking a series of questions. Point out that all questions can only be answered with *yes* or *no*. Anyone unsure of the correct answer should make their best guess.
- Give students a few minutes to read through their three job titles and their three sets of questions. They may use a dictionary if necessary to check any vocabulary they do not know.

- If necessary, do a quick review of Lesson 1 to ensure that everyone understands the key vocabulary.
- Start the activity with Student A asking Student B questions about job B1. Get students to take turns, alternating as follows: B1; A1; B2; A2; B3; A3.
- Draw students' attention to the tick boxes. As the questions are being answered, students should mark the boxes with a tick for *yes* and a cross for *no*.
- To establish the correct job, students should ask one final question, e.g. for job B1: *Do you build houses?* Once they know the job, the student asking the questions has to say which sector this job belongs in, and to explain the reason why. For example, if the job were 'supermarket worker', then the sector would be tertiary because this is a commercial service that connects consumers with products.
- At the end, check answers as a class. If some students had difficulties with any *yes/no* questions, spend some time confirming the information. Do the same with the sectors.

Student A
B1 Tick: 1, 3, 5, 6; Cross: 2, 4, 7
Final question: Do you build houses? (yes)
Secondary sector because you use raw materials to develop and build products.
B2 Tick: 1, 4, 5, 7; Cross: 2, 3, 6
Final question: Do you sell phones? (yes)
Tertiary sector because you provide a commercial service connecting products with consumers.
B3 Tick: 3, 5, 6; Cross: 1, 2, 4, 7
Final question: Do you work on an oil rig? (yes)
Primary sector because you extract basic raw materials.

Student B
A1 Tick: 2, 5; Cross: 1, 3, 4, 6, 7
Final question: Do you drive a bus? (yes)
Tertiary sector because you provide a service to the public.
A2 Tick: 2, 4, 6; Cross: 1, 3, 5, 7
Final question: Do you grow crops? (yes)
Primary sector because you are a farmer who works with basic materials.
A3 Tick: 3, 5, 7; Cross: 1, 2, 4, 6
Final question: Do you work in a car factory? (yes)
Secondary sector because you use raw materials to develop and build a product.

2.2 ❯ Grammar

- Tell students that they are going to practise using the Past Simple and Past Continuous by discussing two interesting solar-energy projects.
- Put students in pairs, A and B. Give each student their half of the worksheet. Ask them not to show their worksheets to each other.
- Ask students to complete Exercise 1 individually. Remind them to pay attention to the context, as well as any clues in the sentences, such as *when* or *while* as they decide whether the Past Simple or Past Continuous is more appropriate.
- Walk around the room as students are working on this. Offer support if any students have questions.
- When they have finished, do not check answers yet. In their pairs, tell students to take turns to tell each other about the project from their text. Emphasise that they should not share the worksheet or simply read the paragraph to their partner. The student listening can ask questions and, if he/she wishes, take brief notes, too.

- Next tell students to ask their partner the three questions on their worksheet. When all questions have been answered, ask students to share their worksheets and check that they both answered everything correctly.
- Finally, give them a few minutes to discuss both projects, sharing their opinions on each one.
- Now check all answers as a class. Open a class discussion based on the questions in Exercise 4. Also ask whether students know of any other interesting solar-energy projects.

Student A
1
1 visited **2** were running **3** was researching **4** wanted
5 were using **6** arrived **7** was launching **8** saw
3
1 It's a community interest company; it helps the public.
2 They were using recycled cooking oil to run their environmentally friendly buses.
3 They were launching their new solar-powered bus.

Student B
1
1 was studying **2** was watching **3** heard
4 was struggling **5** arrived **6** was working
7 installed **8** had
3
1 The Highland Park area was poor and the community couldn't afford its street lighting bill.
2 A local community group called Soulardarity was helping by working on a solution.
3 Soulardarity installed solar street lights.

3.1 ❯ Vocabulary

- Tell students that they are going to discuss project management and practise the vocabulary from Lesson 3.1.
- Put students in pairs, A and B. Give each student their half of the worksheet and get them to complete Exercise 1 individually. Point out that some of the answers can be found in the paragraph. For others, they may need to use their imagination and make their best guesses. Emphasise that they should jot their answers down in note form only.
- When they have finished, ask pairs to work on Exercise 2. Allow a couple of minutes for them to read each other's paragraph, but ask them not to share their notes yet.
- Beginning with Student A's paragraph, tell them to discuss the project and the questions. Encourage them to keep the discussion going, supporting their ideas with reasons and/or examples.
- Move around the classroom and try to spend a little time with each pair. Ensure that they are using the target vocabulary.
- When they have finished, check answers as a class and move on to Exercise 3. Ask the pairs to try to reach consensus on how they would handle each project, as if they were joint project managers.
- Invite some volunteers to present their ideas to the class. You could take a class vote on the best ideas.
- After a few minutes, put students in new pairs and get them to discuss five different questions.
- Students share one answer they found interesting or surprising with the class.

Possible answers
Student A
1
1 a family holiday **2** in two years' time **3** that some people will change their mind and not travel after all **4** Uncle Felix and Aunt Jane **5** that the strikes in February might cause travel problems **6** Yes, because they are considering the best time to travel so that they won't have delays. **7** It doesn't seem that they do. **8** They're having regular meetings, and the cost of the holiday will be split into smaller payments. **9** £2,000 per person **10** We don't know what the setback is. One possibility is that it's weather-related (June is the rainy season in Thailand).

Student B
1
1 designing and selling T-shirts **2** Sue and Amina **3** that the T-shirts will be popular **4** Amina **5** £200 **6** Yes, because Amina doesn't want to make all of the T-shirts at once. **7** It's not clear, but Amina seems to be identifying risks. **8** It doesn't seem that they do as yet. **9** No, they still haven't agreed on some key details. **10** The setback is probably related to exams and the fact that there may not be much spare time.

3.2 > Grammar

- Tell students that they are going to practise comparatives and superlatives in a game on the theme of building and construction.

- Do an example. Write *large* on the board. Then write *comparative* in brackets. Underneath that, write *company* and *contract*. Tell students their task is to use the comparative form of *large* in a sentence, which should link to the themes of building or construction. Point to the two nouns and explain that they must feature in the sentence. These nouns should help students to come up with a topically relevant sentence more quickly. Remind students that their sentence must be grammatically correct and have some kind of building context. Invite volunteers to suggest sentences. Answers will vary but one possibility is: *The **larger** company got the construction contract.*

- Put students in pairs and give each pair their set of cards, making sure all cards are face down on the desk.

- Tell students to take turns to choose a card. Once they see their card, they should write down the number of the card and the required comparative or superlative, which they then use in a sentence, saying it out loud to their partner. (They do not need to write the sentence down, just the comparative or superlative.)

- Encourage them not to think about it too long and to play quickly, adding that the student with the most correct sentences at the end is the winner.

- You might want to put a limit on the time students have to come up with each sentence, e.g. 40 seconds. They forfeit a turn to their partner if they have not supplied a complete sentence in that time.

- Students play the game. At the end, hand out the answer key and get students to check the correct answers against the comparatives and superlatives they have written down.

- Ask them to tally their score and see who has the most points. If you have time, you could go through all the squares asking different students to call out their sentences.

4.1 > Vocabulary

- Tell students that they are going to practise using collocations related to global markets.

- Put students in pairs and give each student their copy of the worksheet. Ask them to work individually on Exercises 1 and 2. Do not allow too long for this. Check answers as a class.

- In their pairs, students discuss the six collocations. Tell them to think carefully about the phrases and work together to come up with a real-life example that demonstrates each one. The idea is to give context to the six collocations and to get students thinking about everyday examples of how they apply to global companies. Ask students not to reuse any of the examples from the Student's Book.

- You might like to do the first collocation as an example. Number 1 is *luxury goods*. Write it on the board and invite volunteers to call out companies and products that fit into this category. If students are slow to suggest their ideas, offer one or two (e.g. Porsche sports cars, Gucci handbags). List all other ideas on the board as students call them out.

- Point out that some of the collocations will require students to provide more detail, e.g. to describe a specific marketing strategy in item 2 or how companies cater to local preferences in item 3.

- Walk around the room as students are working on this. If any pairs are struggling to think of a particular example, help them with a prompt or hint.

- When they have finished, join pairs together into groups of four. Ask them to compare the answers and examples they came up with in Exercise 3: have they named any of the same companies or given the same examples? They should comment on each other's ideas and make sure the examples are appropriate for each phrase.

- When they have finished, check answers by calling on various pairs to share their examples, writing them on the board as they are given.

1
1 luxury goods **2** marketing strategy
3 local preferences **4** target territories
5 product customisation **6** consumer brands
2
a 2 **b** 5 **c** 4 **d** 6 **e** 3 **f** 1
3 Possible answers
1 luxury goods: Porsche sports cars; Gucci handbags
2 marketing strategy: Nike linking their products with the idea of success
3 local preferences: To cater to local tastes, restaurants and pubs are more likely to offer fish and chips in the UK than in other countries.
4 target territories: Dividing up the regions where you want to sell, e.g. LATAM (Latin America), EMEA (Europe, the Middle East, and Africa), APAC (Asia-Pacific).
5 product customisation: Adapting packaging in Japan so that items are not sold in packs of four, as the word for 'four' in Japanese sounds similar to the word for 'death' and is considered unlucky.
6 consumer brands: Penguin (books), L'Oréal (beauty products), Levi's (clothing)

4.2 ⟩ Grammar

- Tell students that they are going to practise using the present and past passive by conducting a survey and then writing a report on online shopping habits.

- Split the class into two halves, A and B.

- Hand all the Student As and Student Bs their respective surveys. Give them a moment to look it over and to ask about any items they do not understand. Question 8 in the Student A survey might require some clarification. If necessary, explain to students that it refers to checking consumer reports or customer reviews before buying.

- Explain that all Student As are going to survey four to six Student Bs, and vice versa. Tell them that when they ask each question, they should write the student's name down and tick the appropriate column: *often*, *sometimes* or *never*.

- When they have completed their survey, ask them to write all the results in the passive. They should have ten sentences. Point out that some of the questions are in the past tense and some are in the present, and ask students to use the same tenses in the passive.

- Put students in pairs, A and B, and ask them to present their reports to each other.

- Invite some students to present their reports to the class. Check that everyone is clear on the correct passive forms.

Possible answers

Student A

1 Clothes were bought online by __ students in the past month.
2 Access to news websites is paid for by __ students.
3 Takeaway food was ordered by __ students in the past week.
4 Items are sold online by __ students.
5 Free shipping is expected by __ students when they shop online.
6 Online customer reviews were provided by __ students in the past year.
7 Books were bought online by __ students recently.
8 Online recommendations are requested by __ students.
9 __ students' online purchases are influenced by social media.
10 Sites with unclear layouts were left by __ students.

Student B

1 Shoes were bought online by __ students in the past six months.
2 A credit card is used by __ students when they shop online.
3 Groceries were ordered by __ students in the past month.
4 A phone is used by __ students to shop online.
5 Cheaper goods are searched for online by __ students.
6 Online shopping is preferred to retail shopping by __ students.
7 Complaints about online purchases were made by __ students last year.
8 Electronics were bought online by __ students in the past year.
9 Online reviews are read by __ students before making a purchase.
10 'Click and collect' services were used by __ students recently.

5.1 ⟩ Vocabulary

- Tell students that they are going to practise describing innovative products.

- Give each student a copy of the worksheet and draw their attention to Exercise 1. Explain the task, point out the adjectives in bold and tell students to look for clues that fit with each one.

- Students work individually on Exercise 1. Then check answers as a class by asking volunteers to call out the matching sentences, confirming or correcting them as necessary. Ask them to say what clues in sentences 1–9 helped them to decide on their answers.

- Put students in pairs. Read the Exercise 2 instructions aloud. Add that they should think of a product they will be able to describe using some of the adjectives from Exercise 1.

- Point to the table and explain that some product ideas have been supplied. Check that everyone understands what these products are.

- Point out that pairs should brainstorm additional ideas of their own until they both agree on the product they are going to advertise. Do not allow too much time for this – set a time limit, e.g. 3 minutes.

- When the time is up, move on to Exercise 3. Tell students they can use the table to make notes with their ideas, and explain the task, emphasising that it is not enough to just list the adjectives. They must explain how this product is *unique*, *user-friendly*, *dependable*, etc. Remind them that they need to speak for 30 seconds.

- Tell the pairs to practise presenting their adverts, and to ensure that they divide the speaking time equally. Keep the focus of the activity on speaking rather than writing. Dissuade students from writing out full scripts and have them rely on their notes instead.

- When the planning and rehearsal time is up, have all pairs present their adverts to the class. Tell them not to read directly from their notes, but to speak as naturally as possible.

- At the end, take a class vote in a number of categories: the most stylish produc, the most innovative product, etc.

1
1 g **2** d **3** i **4** b **5** e **6** a **7** h **8** c **9** f

5.2 ⟩ Grammar

- Tell students that they are going to practise using the Present Perfect with *just*, *already* and *yet*.

- Give every student a copy of Exercise 1. Get them to do the activity, then check answers as a class. If you notice that some students are getting the answers wrong, review the grammar rules.

- Put students in pairs and tell them they are going to do a roleplay. Explain that they will take turns to play a manager and an employee having a meeting. Give Student As and Student Bs their part of the worksheet. Tell them to look at Exercise 2 and their work diary and ask them not to show their respective calendars to each other. Give them a moment to read through the entries. Point out that a tick means that the task has been done, and a cross means it hasn't.

- Tell students to read the instructions in Exercise 3. Point out that the questions relate to the jobs their partner has in their diary. Tell them to start the roleplay. Stress that they must use the Present Perfect throughout this activity. If necessary, review how to form questions in the Present Perfect. Point out that they should use *already* or *yet* as shown, and that they may need to add a verb.

- Remind the student playing the employee to also use the Present Perfect. Tell them to pay attention to the times on the card to ensure they are using *just, already* or *yet* appropriately.

- As the manager hears the answers, he/she should put a tick or a cross in the column. When students have finished both roleplays, ask them to compare the manager's checklist with the employee's calendar and see if all the items tally.

1
1 a **2** a **3** a **4** b **5** b **6** a
3
Student A questions
Have you had the design meeting yet?
Have you already done/given the product presentation?
Have you emailed the sales report yet?
Have you already had lunch with the Sales Manager?
Have you sent out the launch invitations yet?
Have you already had the product launch meeting?
Have you had the conference call yet?

Student B questions
Have you already worked on the product report?
Have you had the product testing meeting yet?
Have you already had lunch with the marketing team?
Have you emailed the sales figures yet?
Have you already contacted the product testers?
Have you had the conference call yet?
Have you already had the planning meeting?

6.1 ⟩ Vocabulary

- Tell students that they are going to practise using vocabulary about health and safety.

- Divide the glass into two groups, Group 1 and Group 2. Within each group, put students in pairs.

- Give each pair the top section of the worksheet, Exercises 1 and 2. Then give the pairs in Group 1 situations A and B, and the pairs in Group 2 situations C and D.

- Read the instructions for Exercise 1 out loud, and call on two students to read out questions 1 and 2. Explain that the two paragraphs describe a different situation where safety was an issue.

- Give the class a moment to read through their two situations and check if there are any words or phrases they do not understand.

- Emphasise that they should discuss each situation with their partner and, together, decide what happened next. As they answer questions 1 and 2 for each situation, remind them that they should just jot down their ideas in note form rather than write lengthy sentences.

- Draw students' attention to the word box and remind them that they should use at least four words and phrases from this box for each situation. Point out that they may need to change the tense of some of the verbs.

- When students have finished Exercise 1, put them with a pair from the other group. Read the Exercise 2 instructions out loud.

- Tell students to take turns to present their two situations to each other. Explain that the 'new' pair should say what they think happened next, and what safety rules they suggest. The original pair should then share the answers they came up with, and see if both pairs' ideas are similar or different.

- As students are working, draw four columns on the board: A, B, C and D, subdivided into halves, 1 and 2.

- Discuss the situations as a class. Invite volunteers to call out their ideas about question 1 for each situation, and also their safety recommendations (question 2). Write them on the board as they are given.

Possible answers
1
A 1 We think Olga was injured. Because of the spilled soup, we think she slipped. She probably fell and hit her knees hard. We think she hurt her hands, too.
2 First, management needs to record the accident. Second, we suggest a new rule not allowing food outside the cafeteria because it poses a risk of injury.
B 1 We think Jack was hurt. Because the heavy boxes were not put carefully on the shelf, we think they fell and hit Jack on the head. He probably doesn't have any broken bones, but may have damaged his back or neck.
2 First, management needs to hold training programmes for Boris and Franz. Second, everyone needs to wear a hard hat in the warehouse. Jack should have been issued with personal safety equipment.
C 1 We think Melanie was injured. Because she was wearing a black coat and it was getting dark, the driver of the car probably couldn't see her. We think the car hit her. She fell off her bike and broke her leg. She probably cut her face and arms, too.
2 First, Melanie has to wear high-visibility clothing when she cycles, especially in the dark. And we think the town council should fit cameras and sensors to stop cars driving too fast.
D 1 We think Dino was hurt. He stood on the broken glass and cut his feet because he wasn't wearing shoes. We think his feet were badly injured and bleeding a lot.
2 First, picking up sharp debris is extremely important and the task should not be stopped until it is finished. Second, family members should always wear something on their feet when they walk around the house.

6.2 ⟩ Grammar

- Tell students that they are going to practise using modal verbs of prohibition, obligation and no obligation.

- Put students in pairs and give each pair a copy of the multiple-choice exercise. Explain the task, making sure everyone understands that the sentences in italics are paraphrased versions of the correct modal. Pairs work together to complete the activity. Check answers as a class.

- If the exercise indicates that students are having problems, do a quick review of each modal verb to reinforce understanding. Then move on to the game.

- Divide students into groups of three or four, depending on class size. Tell them they are going to play a game using the modals they have been practising.

- Give each group their two sets of cards (plain cards and shaded cards) in two separate receptacles such as jars, boxes, bags or hats. It is important to keep the two sets of cards separate.

- Explain that the cards in the first set feature modals, and those in the second set feature various safety instructions. Groups play against each other, taking it in turns to draw one card from each set. They must use that information to form a sentence that is both grammatically correct **and** a correct safety rule. They get one point when they do this, and those two cards are then removed from the game.

- The game is partly based on luck. If two cards cannot successfully be matched, they must be returned to their respective jars, and that group skips a turn.

- The opposing group can challenge any sentence that they believe is incorrect, e.g. *Everyone has to smoke inside the hospital*. Groups should be able to resolve any disputes among themselves, but be available to arbitrate if necessary. The winning group is the one with the most points at the end.

- You could extend the activity by calling out some of the sentence stems from the first set of cards and asking volunteers to suggest new answers of their own.

1 b **2** c **3** a **4** c **5** b

(Answers for the game will vary. These are just some possibilities).
Everyone has to carry an ID badge.
You don't need to have security doors in all buildings.
We must use metal detectors in airports.
You had to keep your passwords safe.
People didn't have to wear a seat belt on flights.
Everyone needed to keep meat in the fridge.
We need to have CCTV on buses.
They mustn't smoke inside the hospital.
We didn't need to have security cameras in schools.

7.1 ➤ Vocabulary

- Tell students that they are going to practise using vocabulary about airline customer service.

- Put students in pairs and hand out the worksheets. Explain that, in their pairs students should discuss each set of customer needs and match them with the most suitable airline. Remind them that one of the airlines is not suitable for any of the customers listed. Ask students to ensure they identify *how* the airline can provide what each customer needs.

- Get students to do the activity. Walk around the room making sure they are really discussing each item and making their decisions together.

- Move on to Exercise 2 without checking the answers to Exercise 1 (this will be done at the end of the worksheet).

- Tell students they are now going to do face-to-face roleplays based on the information in Exercise 1. Point out the notes. Tell students that the travel agent will always start the conversation. Ask them to alternate roles so that each student plays the travel agent twice, and the customer twice. Emphasise that they should try to make the roleplays sound natural. They should use their own words as much as possible, and not just read out the text from Exercise 1.

- When students have finished, check which airlines were matched to which customers and find out if there is consensus. As students volunteer their answers, ask them to say what it is about that airline that meets the customer's particular needs. Ask why Airline d is not suitable for any of the customers (no one wants to pay less without also having another customer service feature such as priority boarding or personal attention).

- Invite different pairs to act out their conversations for the class.

1
1 b **2** e **3** a **4** c

7.2 ➤ Grammar

- Tell students they are going to look at some customer service calls and practise using verbs + *to*-infinitive or *-ing*.

- Put students in pairs and give each pair a copy of the worksheet. Read the instructions for Exercise 1 aloud. Explain or elicit what *extract* means.

- Students work in pairs to complete the extracts. Remind them to pay attention to the verb that comes before the gap. Then check answers as a class.

- For Exercise 2, read the instructions aloud. Ask students to discuss the calls and to decide whether the company agreed to give the customer what he/she asked for.

- Move on to Exercise 3 and explain that students should use the decisions they agreed on in Exercise 2 to continue each phone call by at least two lines, and to practise roleplaying them. Point out the example for Call A and get two students to roleplay it for the class.

- At the end, invite volunteers to share the decisions they made for each situation, writing them on the board as they are given. If there is time, ask some pairs to act out their extended dialogues for the class.

1
Call A **1** to pay **2** creating **3** to remind **4** cancelling
Call B **1** dropping **2** to return **3** sending **4** to pay
Call C **1** to speak **2** to get **3** waiting **4** trying
Call D **1** ordering **2** to request **3** to be **4** explaining
2 **Possible answers**
A Agree to cancel the fee for customers who are never or very rarely late.
B Apologise and offer to pay for returns if there were problems with a product the customer ordered.
C Suggest calling at a different time if customers don't want to wait on hold for an agent. But, if they really insist, offer to connect them with a manager.
D Try repeating the thirty-day return policy to the customer. Continue to explain it calmly and politely, even if the customer gets angry.

8.1 ⟩ Vocabulary

- Tell students they are going to practise using vocabulary about digital communication.

- Put students in pairs, A and B, and tell them they will interview each other about a specific aspect of digital communication.

- Hand out the first survey to Student As and the second to Student Bs. Draw their attention to the title of their respective surveys. Give students a moment to read through all the statements, and provide an opportunity for them to ask questions about any items they do not understand.

- Do a demonstration so that everyone is clear on how to carry out the survey. On the board, replicate the first item in the Student A survey. Create the four headings and label them *Questions, Name, True, False*. Underneath it, create a section for *Notes*.

- In the *Questions* section, write the first statement from the survey: *Technology helps me to study/do my job in a very efficient way.* Read the statement aloud and call on a student by name, asking: *Is this true or false for you?* Write that student's name in the *Name* section. When he/she answers, tick the appropriate box, *True* or *False*.

- Now ask this student a follow-up question, e.g. *Can you explain why that is?* or *Can you give me an example?* You could write this on the board, too. In the *Notes* section, write the student's answer.

- Check that students are clear on how to carry out the survey. If necessary, do another demonstration or two.

- Remind students to ask for more information for the *Notes* section each time. Emphasise that their completed surveys should not simply be a series of true or false ticks, but answers should be supported with reasons and examples.

- Allow around 15 minutes for the surveys. Then put all the Student As and all the Student Bs into separate groups. Ask them to collate the information they gathered. They should count up the number of true or false ticks for each statement and share the different examples and reasons that were provided.

- Now invite various students from each group to share their findings with the class. Find out whether there are consistent trends or a broader variety in how people feel about digital communication in the workplace and in their personal lives.

8.2 ⟩ Grammar

- Tell students that they are going to practise using the first and second conditionals.

- Give each student their own copy of the first exercise and ask them to complete it individually. Then check answers as a class. If necessary, review how both conditionals are formed.

- Put students in pairs and tell them they are going to play a game and compete against each other.

- Before handing out the cut-up cards to each pair, do a demonstration. On the board write: **First:** *I / be / tired / if I / stay up / late* and **Second:** *if he / have / a better salary / he / buy / a house*. Tell students they will get prompts like this and their task is to form a correct sentence with the information in the first or second conditional as indicated in bold. Invite volunteers to do the examples on the board (*I'll be tired if I stay up late. If he had a better salary, he'd buy a house.*). Encourage students to use contractions where possible.

- Give each pair their set of cut-up cards, ideally placed in a jar or other receptacle.

- Explain that students take turns to pick a card and form a sentence using the information shown. Pairs should be able to agree on whether or not the sentences are grammatically correct, but be available to arbitrate if a pair cannot agree.

- When a student forms a sentence correctly, he/she gets a point, and the card is set aside. If he/she is not correct, his/her opponent gets an opportunity to form the sentence and win the point. The winner is the student with the most points.

- You might want to set a time limit. You could have students forfeit their turn if they have not submitted an answer within 15 or 20 seconds.

- At the end, go through the cards one by one, checking answers as a class.

1
1 S **2** F **3** F **4** S **5** S **6** F
Game
1   If we're not satisfied, we'll complain on social media.
2   They wouldn't care if you ignored their calls.
3   If you want more money, they'll give you extra work.
4   If she organised her emails, she wouldn't be overloaded.
5   You wouldn't have to worry if you protected your passwords.
6   We'll work harder if you give us nicer offices.
7   He'd fix your phone if you asked him nicely.
8   If you listen carefully, you'll understand how they feel.
9   They won't like it if you charge money for wifi.
10   You'd have more free time if you stayed off social media.
11   She'll lose the document if she doesn't save it.
12   I'd start my own blog if I had the time.
13   We'd feel happier if they encouraged us.
14   If you don't speak clearly, no one will understand you.
15   If everyone helped, we'd finish the project on time.
16   They'll enjoy social media more if they don't rely on it so much.
17   I'll open an account if they give me a discount.
18   We wouldn't succeed if we didn't have this technology.
19   If he sends another text, I'll just delete it.
20   If they spoke clearly, there wouldn't be problems.

Unit 1 >

1 Read the article quickly and choose the statement that sums up the main idea.

  1 More companies plan to increase the number of female managers aged between thirty and fifty-four over the next three years.

  2 Multinational companies in twenty-six countries start programmes to encourage workers to take career breaks in order to gain more skills.

  3 A telecoms company plans to help people return to work after they have had years away from their job.

2 Complete the definitions with the words/phrases in bold in the article.

  1 People considered for a job or training programme are _____ .

  2 A period of ten years is a _____ .

  3 _____ is when you meet people involved in the same kind of work to share information and support.

  4 *Recruit* and _____ are verbs that mean 'employ'.

  5 A _____ is a period of time when people take time away from their job, for example to look after their children or family.

  6 When a woman spends time away from work after she has a baby, it's called _____ .

  7 _____ are in charge of small groups of people, but do not take important decisions that affect the whole organisation.

  8 People working for a company for a short time without pay are on _____ .

3 Find the numbers (1–5) in the article and match them with the information they refer to (a–e).

  1 1,000   **a** countries where the scheme will operate

  2 96 million   **b** number of weeks that new mothers can have paid leave

  3 26   **c** number of people Vodafone wants to employ over three years

  4 7,500   **d** approximate number of women around the world on a career break

  5 16   **e** number of management jobs at Vodafone

4 Decide if the statements are *true* (T) or *false* (F).

  1 The ReConnect programme wants to help people return to work after up to five years out of a job.

  2 Vodafone is not the only company encouraging workers to return to the workplace.

  3 Studies show that most women want more support when they return to work after a career break.

  4 Only people who worked for Vodafone can join the ReConnect programme.

  5 Men cannot apply to join the ReConnect programme.

  6 Vodafone hopes that the programme will increase the number of women in management in the company.

5 Without looking at the article, choose the option which best completes each sentence. Then read the article again to check.

1 Half of Vodafone's new employees will be in managerial positions and the other half will work in jobs such as

   a call centres and shops.

   b catering and restaurants.

   c factories and delivery.

2 Some companies offer programmes that include networking opportunities and

   a study skills.

   b coaching.

   c interviews.

3 The Vodafone scheme plans to extend to twenty-six countries and will offer

   a paid holiday.

   b regular training courses.

   c flexible working options.

4 The pilot ReConnect programme was successful and the candidates were aged between

   a eighteen and twenty-four.

   b thirty and forty-five.

   c twenty-eight and fifty-eight.

5 Vodafone allows new mothers to work fewer hours for six months on

   a full pay.

   b eighty percent pay.

   c fifty percent pay.

Vodafone starts programme to recruit career-break women
By Andrew Hill

Vodafone is starting a programme to recruit women who have taken a **career break.** The telecoms company aims to **hire** 1,000 people worldwide over three years. Half will be in roles such as call centres and shops, and the other half in managerial positions. It hopes to attract skilled workers who are trying to return to a job after up to a **decade** out of the workplace.

5 Vodafone's ReConnect programme is the latest in a number of initiatives aimed at encouraging workers to restart their careers after a break.

Royal Bank of Scotland's Comeback Programme provides 'returnships' of 12–16 weeks, including **work placements**, coaching and **networking** opportunities.

A study prepared for Vodafone estimates that 96 million skilled women aged between 30 and
10 54 are on career breaks worldwide. This includes 55 million who have experience as **middle managers** or in more senior roles. Another survey showed that eight out of ten believed that more support is needed for women who want to return to work.

Vodafone's programme is not restricted to former Vodafone staff and is open to men as well as women. However, the group expects most of the **candidates** to be women, many of whom will
15 have stepped off the career ladder to have children. The scheme will extend to 26 countries. Participants will have the opportunity to refresh skills and will be offered flexible working options. An early ReConnect programme in eleven countries recruited 50 people, aged between 28 and 58, who had been out of the workplace for between 1 and 10 years.

ReConnect candidates will account for 10 percent of all Vodafone's external management
20 recruitment. Those taking part will have the chance to apply for permanent new jobs or to replace staff who leave. Vodafone believes the programme will help it meet its target of increasing the proportion of women in its 7,500 managerial roles from 27 percent to 30 percent.

In 2015, Vodafone became one of the first multinational companies to offer new mothers equal minimum **maternity leave** – set at 16 weeks – around the globe. It also offers full pay for new
25 mothers for a reduced 30-hour week during their first 6 months back at work.

Unit 2 >

1 Before you read, check that you know the words in the box. Match them with their definitions.

> assembly   reputation   revenue   testing   weld

1 the income of a company: _____
2 putting different parts of a product together: _____
3 join two parts together using heat: _____
4 checking that everything works correctly: _____
5 the opinion that people have about a brand or company: _____

2 Read the article quickly and find the following. Use a dictionary to check any words you don't know.

1 two things the factory robots do: _____ , _____
2 two factory actions carried out by humans: _____ , _____
3 the year the first Royal Enfield was produced: _____
4 the year production of Royal Enfield motorbikes stopped in the UK: _____
5 the price of a Classic 350 in rand and dollars: _____ , _____

3 Decide if the statements are *true* (T) or *false* (F).

1 Six times more cars than motorbikes were sold in India in the financial year.
2 Companies such as TVS help promote India's reputation as a key manufacturing centre.
3 The only vehicle manufactured by TVS is motorbikes.
4 Eighty percent of the revenue of TVS comes from the home market.
5 Global companies recognise that manufacturing in India is better now than in the past.
6 Royal Enfield's bikes are popular because they are less expensive than their competitors.
7 Wages in the Indian IT industry started to increase after 2010.

4 Which text summarises the main information in the article?

1 Global companies are now moving their production bases to India due to the huge market for luxury motorcycles and scooters. Industry leaders in the automotive sector are sending their top engineers to factories around the country in order to test quality control and use of robotics in assembly.

2 The government and business leaders in India are keen for the country to be known around the world as a base for high-quality manufacturing. They are promoting key transport industries such as scooter and motorcycle production. Human expertise and robot technology are used in factories to make vehicles both for the large home market and also to export abroad.

3 The automotive industry in India is experiencing slower growth compared to other sectors. The number of motorcycles produced each year will soon overtake the number of cars being sold. The most popular classic motorcycles such as Royal Enfields are finding new markets in Egypt and Indonesia amongst young professionals.

5 Match 1–5 with a–e to make collocations used in the article. Which pair is written as one word?

1 joint   a leader
2 production   b room
3 manufacturing   c venture
4 show   d line
5 market   e centre

6 Complete the sentences with collocations from Exercise 5.

1 The factory workers assemble the product on the _____ and it's then tested and sent to the customer.

2 Our company worked closely with an organisation in Warsaw on a _____ to produce a new self-drive vehicle for the automotive sector.

3 The new _____ in Milan will contain a range of luxury bikes and sports cars.

4 Bangladesh is a major _____ for the textile industry.

5 They are currently the _____ in this sector but sales have fallen this year.

India's motorcycle manufacturers
Simon Mundy in Mumbai

More than 16 million motorcycles and scooters were sold in India during the financial year, far more than in any other country and nearly six times the number of passenger cars sold. Exports in that same period reached 2.5 million, up from 1.5 million five years before.

5 The TVS Apache is a lightweight Indian motorcycle. At a time when the government is trying to promote India as a manufacturing centre, TVS and its peers provide encouraging examples.

The Apache can be purchased in showrooms from Bogotá to Jakarta, while TVS' three-wheeled autorickshaws are on the streets of Cairo and Addis Ababa. 'We're hoping that within the next three years, exports should be thirty-five to forty percent of our sales,' says Venu Srinivasan, chairman of TVS, which currently generates about twenty percent of its revenue abroad.

10 In a nearby building at TVS' plant at Hosur in southern India, robots weld and seal motorcycle parts while human workers perform testing and assembly.

On one production line, two visiting engineers from Germany inspect motorcycles made for BMW. The European company's decision last year to move production for the global market to an Indian partner reflects an improved reputation for manufacturing quality in India.

15 Siddartha Lal is the chairman of Eicher Motors, the company which owns the motorbike producer Royal Enfield. The first Royal Enfield is the world's oldest surviving motorcycle brand. It started in the UK in 1901, but production in the UK stopped in 1970. It now continues to be produced in India as a joint venture.

Royal Enfield has experienced increasing sales at home for its relatively expensive bikes.
20 The popular Classic 350 retails for about Rs130,000 ($2,000), compared with less than Rs50,000 for Hero Motocorp's Splendor, the Indian market leader. Royal Enfield sold 60,113 motorcycles last month, compared with fewer than 52,000 in the whole of 2009.

Mr Lal points to the emergence of prosperous young consumers over the past decade. 'By 2010, the IT and consumer goods companies in India were more mature, and starting
25 salaries, which had been absolutely awful, started looking up. So now there are more single young men willing to spend a bit more on themselves,' he says.

Unit 3 >

1 Read the article quickly. Match the names (1–3) with the information (a–c).

1 Kristine Van Cleve   **a** creators of Scrum

2 Ken Schwaber and Jeff Sutherland   **b** a business academic

3 Hirotaka Takeuchi   **c** head of a dental lab in the USA

2A Complete the diagrams about the project management process with *Agile* or *Waterfall*.

---

1 _____ : each department works in sequence

department 1 completes part of task and sends product/documents to department 2
↓
department 2 completes task and sends to department 3
↓
send final product to customer

---

2 _____ : teams from various departments work together

daily update meeting
↓
develop first stage in period of less than one month
↓
send latest version of product to customer
↓
customer gives feedback
↓
work on product continues
↓
daily update meetings
↓
send to customer again

B Read the article again and answer the questions.

1 Which project management method was used first?

_____

2 Which method does the article suggest is more successful? What factual information helped you to decide on your answer?

_____

3 Which method takes less time between the start of making a product and when it is delivered to the customer?

_____

3 Complete the table with the words in the box.

budget collaborate done individual progress retrospectives stand-up users

A successful Waterfall project is completed:	Scrum stages on Post-it notes:
• in a reasonable time period. • within [1]_____ . • to the satisfaction of [2]_____ .	• To do • In [3]_____ • [4]_____
Three types of Scrum/Agile meeting: • [5]_____ • planning (before Sprint) • [6]_____	Reasons some team members resist: • they don't like to [7]_____ • they like to be the stars • less room for [8]_____ heroics and rewards

4 Match the words from the article (1–5) with their definitions (a–e).

1 signed off		**a**	things that make progress difficult
2 top-down		**b**	make something better
3 obstacles		**c**	manager says what to do and team follows orders
4 improve		**d**	work closely together
5 collaboration		**e**	officially approved

5 Complete the summary with words from Exercise 4.

> Some company managers prefer a ¹_____ approach to project management, where team members take orders from the project leader and give progress reports at each stage of the project. With this method, every stage of a project needs to be ²_____ as each department completes their part of a task. More modern methods of project management encourage regular meetings that help the group to discuss their work on the project and explain any ³_____ that could delay deadlines. Rather than wait for a finished product, the teams work in ⁴_____ with customers and clients. They share the work while it is in progress and discuss developments with the client and use their feedback to ⁵_____ the product before it is finalised.

How project management turned into a Scrum

By Lisa Pollack

The performance gap between the newer Agile ways of working and more traditional styles of top-down, plan-driven project management is huge.

The most commonly used old approach, Waterfall, has a success rate of just eleven percent. A successful project is defined as one completed in a reasonable period, within budget and to the satisfaction of users.

5   Waterfall involves a lengthy process of gathering and documenting all aspects of the new product. The documents are passed through assorted departments to be signed off.

In 1986 two professors, Hirotaka Takeuchi and Ikujiro Nonaka, wrote a paper in the *Harvard Business Review* which declared that 'the old, sequential approach to developing new products simply won't get the job done'. The 'relay race' wasn't working – this is where departments completed their part of a task

10   and then handed over the project to the next department. Instead, they recommended that people from different parts of a company work together like a team in sport.

Jeff Sutherland and Ken Schwaber are the co-creators of Scrum, an Agile approach to project management. According to research, projects that use Scrum or other Agile approaches have a thirty-nine percent success rate.

15   The term *Agile* came from seventeen software engineers who got together to write down their ideas in a ski resort in Utah in 2001. They highlighted the need for close collaboration with customers and responsiveness to change. Sometimes it could take months between the start of a project and product delivery. Instead, they suggested that teams from different departments worked on the product together for short periods. The aim was to be able to quickly show the unfinished product to the customer, who

20   could make suggestions. The team would use the comments to improve the product for the next stage.

Scrum calls its development cycles 'sprints'. These often last less than a month. Instead of detailed requirements, there are very brief descriptions of what a user wants from a feature and why. This information can be shown on Post-it notes arranged on a board in columns labelled *To do*, *In progress* and *Done*.

25   There are daily 'stand-up' meetings where members give updates, including any obstacles others might help with. There are also planning meetings before a sprint, and 'retrospectives' afterwards to discuss process improvements for the next sprint.

An example of a company which uses Scrum is DPS Dental, a small dental lab in Iowa. Kristine Van Cleve, the lab's president, says it was difficult at first. 'We have pockets of resistance,' she says. 'Some

30   don't like to collaborate. They like to be the stars.' With the focus on the team, there is less room for individual heroics and rewards. Nonetheless, Ms Van Cleve thinks Scrum will be useful for her business.

Unit 4 ❯

1 Before you read, choose the correct definition (a or b) for the words in bold in these sentences. Then read the article to check your answers.

1 The company made alterations in order to **tailor** the product to the target market.

  a make changes to something to fit different requirements

  b use material to increase the size of a product

2 Hershey and Mars Inc. are examples of global companies that make **confectionery** products such as Reece's Pieces, M&Ms and Mars bars.

  a sweets and chocolates

  b fruit and vegetables

3 There were **fluctuations** in the market, which meant that profits rose and then fell.

  a things remaining steady for a long time

  b unexpected increases and decreases

4 This is a **universal** product which is suitable for global markets.

  a designed for a range of different countries and situations

  b designed for a specific market

5 Some customers prefer to buy from **homegrown** companies rather than global organisations.

  a from a range of countries

  b from own country

6 At the moment, the best-selling items in our eye range are **mascara** and eyeliner.

  a cream for the face

  b colour for eyelashes

7 We are offering regular clients a **makeover** to demonstrate our new range of cosmetics.

  a change of style for hair and make-up

  b new health and fitness exercises

2 Which summary matches the content of the article?

1 Large companies agree that marketing campaigns should be adapted to local markets. Some companies have found that cosmetics are more difficult to promote than other products.

2 Some global companies are making changes to their product range to reflect what local customers prefer. They are also considering the differing requirements of individual geographic areas.

3 Universal products are generally cheaper to produce compared to adapting goods to a specific market. Many Western brands will only adapt their range to local needs if research shows that they will be guaranteed to make a profit.

3 Match the information (1–5) with the paragraph it appears in (A–E).

1 company extends product range _____

2 what's happening as a result of competition _____

3 examples of changes to marketing message _____

4 strategy company used to demonstrate product _____

5 three types of products changed _____

4 Decide if the statements are *true* (T) or *false* (F).

1 Companies are starting to use models and music from the local area in their marketing.

2 Quiet stereos were introduced to one African market.

3 In some areas, products need to adapt to power supplies that are not always steady.

4 In the past, poor research meant that products were not adapted for the local market.

5 Oriflame introduced everything in its product range to the African market.

6 Local supermarket chains are in competition with Western cosmetic brands.

5 Choose a word in italics from the article to complete the sentences.

1 Consumers in local markets have different *tastes / results* in terms of flavours.

2 As well as confectionery, the company also produces *sweeten / soft* drinks.

3 They didn't do enough market *competition / research* on the product range.

4 The organisation set *out / up* branches in China and Brazil last year.

5 The new online marketing campaign encourages customers to spread the *word / brand* to their friends and family.

Companies adapt to local African markets

By Katrina Manson in Nairobi

A Big companies are beginning to tailor their marketing messages for global contexts. As a result, they are increasingly choosing local models, languages, music and food to reach target audiences. In addition, some companies are beginning to adapt their products to the tastes of local markets.

5 **B** This can be seen in Africa, where manufacturers of soft drinks and confectionery typically sweeten products aimed at home markets, while South Korea's Samsung recently brought out extra-loud stereos to appeal to Nigerian consumers. Other examples include fridges that can be used where electricity is unreliable due to power cuts and fluctuations in the electricity supply.

10 **C** One European corporate executive remarks that in the past, companies had a habit of introducing universal products to the African market as they had not bothered to do market research. But that is changing now with the arrival of competition, particularly from homegrown African companies.

D Swedish beauty company Oriflame set up in East Africa last year, but could only
15 introduce 300 products from its full range of 1,500. Some of its make-up was developed for the Indian market, but the company plans to introduce darker shades of foundation for an African range soon.

E Often, the cosmetic products are so entirely new to local markets that customers are confused. 'Some of our customers try to put black mascara on their lips – they don't
20 know what it's for,' says Tracy Wanjiru, at East Africa's largest supermarket chain Nakumatt.

The company set up free nail bars and makeovers to spread the word and tempt new custom for more expensive Western brands entering the market, including Revlon and L'Oréal's Maybelline.

Unit 5 ⟩

1 Before you read, choose the correct definition (a or b) for the words/phrases in bold in these sentences. Then read the article to check your answers.

1 Design and innovation are **intrinsically linked** and often work together.
   a completely different
   b very closely connected

2 Design companies don't always have the **resources** to spend on developing their ideas.
   a finance
   b employees

3 Not all suggestions **make the grade**, but the team knows that we listen to their ideas.
   a are tested
   b are successful

4 The engineers made a model of the design but we needed to produce 1,000 for our customer and it was too expensive **scaling up** production.
   a increasing the amount of materials required to produce a larger number of products
   b saving money by using more than one manufacturer to produce products

5 Small companies can save money if they work **collaboratively**, for example by sharing ideas or equipment.
   a together
   b in competition

2 Complete the sentences with words/phrases from Exercise 1.

1 Some of the best designs are a result of the team working _____ and sharing ideas.

2 We researched the equipment and _____ that we needed to complete the project and then we agreed a budget.

3 Good looks and usefulness are _____ when designing products for the home.

4 Eduardo didn't _____ in his exams last term but his latest work shows significant improvement.

3 Read the article quickly and match the sub-headings (1–5) with the sections of the article (A–D). There is one extra sub-heading which you don't need to use.

1 What challenges do small design firms face? ____

2 What are design skills used for? ____

3 How do small design companies work together? ____

4 How much finance is required? ____

5 What should good design and innovation do? ____

4 Read the summaries of sections A–D. Replace the words in italics with the words in the box.

> critical   distribution   visionary   work spaces

A There are many *imaginative* design companies that create interesting products for their customers by using existing or future trends. _____

B Production and *delivery* to customers and retail outlets is expensive for small companies. _____

C Finance is *essential* to help small design companies to grow. _____

D Some companies work together by sharing *offices or design studios*. _____

5 Decide if the statements are *true* (T) or *false* (F).

1 The design sector doesn't have enough companies with interesting ideas.

2 For small companies, investment is particularly important during the later stages of development.

3 Innovation requires time and money to experiment on ideas that work and also on ideas that don't work.

4 William Mitchell believes that finance for small design companies is essential to help them develop and have future success.

5 4C Design think that if a product looks good then it doesn't always need to be useful.

6 The main reason that designers and engineers need more funding is to spend time creating effective marketing campaigns.

The funding dilemma for small design firms

By Steve Hemsley

A Design and innovation are intrinsically linked, with both able to significantly improve business performance.

The design sector is full of visionary companies and individuals using their skills to develop products and services for their clients, solving problems or connecting with consumers in a particularly effective way. Great designers could be tapping into a trend or predicting a new demand from customers.

B However, design companies face unusual challenges, particularly when they are small businesses. Anything new requires investment at an early stage of its development, and smaller design businesses can struggle to support their R&D strategy and facilities. Without the resources to spend on great new ideas – and on ideas that never make the grade – it's easy for innovation to stagnate as a business struggles to juggle the demands of sustaining existing client work with developing their product range or breaking new markets.

Often, an SME* in the design or engineering sector will produce an innovative idea which proves incredibly popular. However, scaling up production or distribution can be a real challenge or even impossible without adequate funding.

C 4C Design are successful innovators who understand how important future investment will be if they are to reach their full potential. 4C Design's founder, William Mitchell, says funding is critical to continue expanding. He believes that no product design or engineering company can survive without innovation, but he stresses that any invention or creative advance must solve a real problem.

'I have always been excited by design and I appreciate products that work well, look good and have been put together well,' he says. 'But we do have a natural filter within the consultancy to only work on projects that use innovation to create something new and useful. It essentially has to solve a problem and not just clog up your life.'

D Many SME design companies are keen to work more collaboratively with similar businesses. There is a trend, for example, for designers to support each other by sharing ideas and even work spaces. But smaller design and engineering firms need investment to enable them to devote their time and expertise to doing what they do best creating great products.

*Small or Medium Enterprise

Unit 6 ›

1 Before you read, check that you know words 1–7. Match them with their definitions (a–g). Use a dictionary to help you if necessary. Then read the article to check your answers.

1 hacking		**a**	sending emails designed to gain secret information such as computer passwords
2 firewall			
3 phishing		**b**	a range of dishonest schemes
4 cyber		**c**	related to computing, information technology and the internet
5 scams		**d**	gaining unauthorised access to data in a computer system
6 breach		**e**	a network security system to prevent unauthorised access to computer data
7 watchdog			
		f	an organisation or person that makes sure rules are followed
		g	a breakdown in security

2 Read the article again quickly and match the sub-headings (1–4) with the sections of the article (A–D).

1 Tips to help a company prepare for a cyber attack ____

2 A comparison of employee and computer safety ____

3 A car company experiencing many cyber incidents ____

4 Examples of two types of computer attack ____

3 Choose the correct option (a, b or c) to answer the questions.

1 How many days does it take most companies to realise that a security problem has occurred?

a almost 100   **b** fewer than 60   **c** about 7

2 Who disapproved of the way Yahoo! handled the security problem?

a investors   **b** customers   **c** both

3 Why is it a danger to trust the security controls set by the company that supplies the computer network?

a They could already have a virus.   **b** They might not be secure enough.   **c** They don't have firewalls.

4 What did the hacking of San Francisco's public transit system affect?

a safety   **b** health   **c** payments

4 Find words/phrases in the article with a similar meaning to the following.

A 1 criminal _____

    2 move money from one bank account to another _____

    3 too trusting _____

B 4 unfriendly _____

    5 main objectives _____

C 6 tidy up _____

    7 paying attention and being interested _____

D 8 at the centre _____

5 Complete the sentences with words/phrases from Exercise 4.

1 The customer realised that he had been _____ when he gave his password and card number to a stranger, but explained that he thought that the email was from his credit card provider.

2 As a result of the security breach, the bank advised customers not to _____ money to unknown accounts.

3 Trust is _____ of a company's relationship with its clients, which is why the company must communicate quickly when data is hacked.

4 A successful business needs teams that are _____ and motivated.

5 In the meeting, we decided that the two main _____ are to review cyber security and check our staff guidelines.

How to turn cyber attacks to your advantage
By Andrew Hill

A When handling hacking, the main weaknesses in most organisations are not technological – firewalls, software – but human. Since a villain pressed 'send' on the first phishing email, the human factor has played a part in cyber plots.

For example, scams where the widow of a general promises you money to help transfer their fortune – gullible people who believe the first sentence are most likely to trust the rest of the tale.

More recently, criminals have started making attacks to demand money from a company or threaten to create problems with its share price. Again, the approach uses basic human weaknesses. As a senior executive, you may well not know whether the hack is real or not – it still takes at least ninety-nine days for companies to discover a security breach, says consultancy Mandiant. So, are you prepared to risk saying that the news is fake?

B Big companies are under hostile cyber fire all the time – Volkswagen said it was facing 6,000 attacks a week – so it would be better to start thinking of the threat as an opportunity. As Amitava Dutta and Kevin McCrohan of George Mason University wrote in the early days of cyber risk, 'information security is not a technical issue; it is a management issue'. Leadership, culture and structure (or lack of them) have a 'significant impact' on what happens in an attack. So check your company's priorities.

C Spring-clean your structure. Organise files and throw out what you don't need. Find out what information you hold and where.

Update lines of communication, internal and external, and reexamine what your response will say about your attitude to different interests. For two years, Yahoo! failed to reveal a huge security breach as it tried to sell its core business, inviting criticism from customers, investors and watchdogs.

Make sure your staff are engaged. Carelessness about security may suggest reduced loyalty, risk taking, or worse, potential attacks from inside your own organisation.

Review your network. The computer security controls set by the supplier may not be secure. This could allow a virus to find a way in and infect the computers in your company.

Finally, be prepared. Executives' first reaction to a breach is often to spend time asking 'Who did this to me?', followed by a search for the 'guilty'. By contrast, when San Francisco's public transit system was held hostage by cyber attackers, managers were prepared and were able to decide quickly to open the gates and allow free travel. But if hackers had attacked safety rather than payments, the correct decision would have been to close the network.

D Good cyber security, like worker health and safety, is becoming obligatory, said Elizabeth Corley, vice-chair of Allianz Global Investors.

Hackers may be inadvertently performing a useful service: prompting executives to fix the human weaknesses at the heart of their organisations.

Unit 7 ❯

1 Read the title of the article and choose the option (a, b or c) which best explains its meaning.

    a The customer services department of a company makes a complaint.

    b A new company plans to make it less difficult to complain.

    c A company complains about start-ups' customer services.

2 Read the article quickly. Then read these sentences and choose the correct definition (a or b) for the words/phrases in bold.

    1 If you are **waiting on hold**, you are likely to be on the

        a phone.   **b** internet.

    2 If you **rip off** someone, you _____ their time, money or ideas.

        a buy   **b** take

    3 When a person is **matter-of-fact**, they are calm and

        a unemotional.   **b** bored.

    4 The **lion's share** of something is the _____ part.

        a largest   **b** smallest

    5 **Twitter storm** and **the one-star TripAdvisor review** both refer to _____ feedback online.

        a positive   **b** negative

    6 When someone **vents their rage**, they express a strong or _____ emotion and say or write what they are thinking at that moment.

        a angry   **b** excited

    7 People or software that get **smarter** become more

        a enthusiastic.   **b** intelligent.

3 Read the article again and complete the gaps (1–5) with these phrases (a–f). There is one extra phrase you don't need to use.

    a social media sites

    b saving your branding

    c cancellations and lost bags

    d during the holiday period

    e before making a complaint

    f fill in a form

4 Decide if the statements about Michael Schneider and Service are *true* (T) or *false* (F).

    1 Michael Schneider had the idea for the company after personal experience of waiting for his complaints to be dealt with by customer services.

    2 He thinks that customers usually explain the problem well when they deal directly with customer services.

    3 Service charges customers $300 to help with their complaint.

    4 Complaints about travel make up about fifty percent of Service's business.

    5 Start-ups which have not succeeded gave customers a place to complain about service but did not try to solve the problem.

    6 Service aims to have a large workforce in the future.

    7 As Service gains more experience, it learns to solve complaints more quickly.

    8 So far, all of the problems have been difficult to solve.

5 Put the steps in the correct order (1–4) to make a complaint using Service.

    a Service explains the problem to the company.

    b The customer gets the money.

    c The customer completes a form online.

    d Service and the company negotiate and agree an amount.

Customer service start-up aims to take pain out of complaints

By Malcolm Moore

A Los Angeles start-up wants to save people from waiting on hold on customer service helplines by resolving their complaints for them.

'The idea for the company was me wasting too much of my time dealing with customer service,' said Michael Schneider, the founder of Service. 'If you deal with it yourself, you feel you are losing your
5   time. If you do not do anything, you feel like you have been ripped off.'

Service, which has raised almost $4 million in seed funding, asks customers to ¹_____
on its website or app. It then tries to negotiate a settlement with the poorly performing company.

'We are more efficient. Customers are often not the most articulate and can often be emotional. That makes the job more difficult at the other end. We are not emotional; we are matter-of-fact,' said
10 Mr Schneider.

Service processes more than 100 requests a day and recovers just under $300 on average for customers. 'The biggest area is travel, with the lion's share being airline delays and
²_____ ,' he said. 'Travel makes up half our cases. Then there is retail: Amazon, Home Depot and Best Buy and telecoms companies, with queries over cable and mobile phone bills.'

15 Mr Schneider said Service planned eventually to make money by charging either consumers or the offending companies. 'My goal is to go to these companies and say not only are we saving you money by having people not call your call centre but we are ³_____ by preventing the angry Twitter storm or the one-star TripAdvisor review.'

A number of failed technology start-ups have in the past attempted to name and shame bad
20 customer service by giving consumers a place to vent their rage online. In recent years, several companies have focused on using ⁴_____ such as Twitter to respond to unhappy customers.

Service only employs eleven staff but said it would take on another person ⁵_____ .
'Our eventual goal is to have the software do most of the work,' said Mr Schneider. 'Every time we solve
25 a case, the software gets a bit smarter. The first time we called British Airways we had no idea what we were doing,' he said. 'Now we have mapped most large companies so we know the quickest way to resolve problems. Some companies are easy, some are more difficult.'

Unit 8 ❯

1 Read the title of the article and choose the option (a, b or c) which best explains its meaning.

   a how to make your computer more secure and safe for the future

   b ways to avoid competitors stealing your ideas for new technology

   c how to make things better, not worse, when you make mistakes using electronic communication

2 Read the article quickly and match the sub-headings (1–5) with the sections of the article (A–E).

   1 A banking mistake   ____

   2 I make mistakes too   ____

   3 What not to do   ____

   4 Errors in emails sent to me   ____

   5 Why mistakes are made   ____

3 Read the article again. Then read these sentences and choose the correct definition (a or b) for the words/phrases in bold.

   1 Karl has made another **blunder** on the invoices. He doesn't pay attention to his work.

     a request   **b** mistake

   2 Experts advise that workers who **juggle** tasks are less likely to do a good job.

     a do more than one thing at time   **b** take frequent breaks

   3 When I watch TV while messaging and writing a report, I can suffer from **digital overload**.

     a the effect of using too many devices at the same time   **b** the result of forgetting to turn off devices

   4 As requested, the customer **transferred** €2,500 and it arrived in our account this morning.

     a sent the money by electronic banking   **b** made a credit card payment

   5 Is it better to **recall** an email when you make a mistake or simply apologise?

     a request delivery confirmation   **b** retrieve an email that has not yet been opened

4 Which statements describe the writer's attitude to mistakes? Is the information *true* (T), *false* (F) or *not given* (NG)?

   1 She gives examples of errors made by three colleagues.

   2 She thinks we are making more mistakes than in the past.

   3 She always checks her emails and never makes mistakes herself.

   4 Sometimes she suffers from digital overload.

   5 She is surprised that big mistakes don't happen more frequently.

   6 She thinks the bank worker should have been fired for his mistake.

   7 When you make a mistake, say 'sorry' and carry on.

   8 She has never searched for a recalled email to read the message.

5 Match the email extracts (1–4) with the people who are likely to have made the mistakes (a–d).

   1 I'm afraid the money was sent in error and needs to be returned immediately.

   2 Congratulations on your promotion – well done!

   3 Pieter worked in Hong Kong for six months. After that Peter moved to Shanghai.

   4 Your work will be more productive if you concentrate on one task at a time.

   a the writer

   b the PR woman

   c a researcher

   d a bank worker

6 Complete the communication tips with the words/phrases in the box.

> correct   hasty   inbox   mis-typed   pay attention   spelt

It's important to ¹_____ when writing because if you concentrate, you will make fewer mistakes. If you do make an error in your communication, make sure that you ²_____ it quickly. Careful checking will help to avoid most mistakes. Before you hit 'Send' are you sure that you haven't ³_____ an email address or ⁴_____ a word incorrectly? Simple details are sometimes the easiest things to get wrong, especially when writing a ⁵_____ message while you are doing more than one thing at a time. When you look in your ⁶_____ , you will find plenty of examples of emails containing errors that are easy to avoid. Try to make sure that your communication doesn't contain the same mistakes.

The best way to recover from a technological bungle
By Pilita Clark

A   The other day when I got to work, I found an email from a PR woman I have never met congratulating me on my new job at City AM, a newspaper I have never worked for.

'Sorry,' she wrote in a hasty follow-up mail. 'Clearly not concentrating.' The next day I heard from two men, one from an investment bank, the other a credit-rating agency. Both had made email muck-ups they needed to correct. These people are far from alone. The idiotic mistakes we make at work are awful and getting worse.

B   I know this because I make so many myself. The other week I gave one colleague a mis-typed email address for someone she needed to contact and another the wrong date for a meeting. Then I nearly wrote a story with the name of one person spelt two different ways.

C   Researchers have been warning for years that people who constantly juggle emails, texts and messages do not memorise or manage their work as well as those who pay attention to one thing at a time. Digital overload has been estimated to cost as much as $997 billion a year in lost productivity and innovation, just in the USA. No wonder, when it is claimed we tap and swipe our phones an average of 2,617 times a day.

D   I am astonished that the levels of office bungling are not far worse. It is still quite rare to see a huge blunder, such as the $6 billion a Deutsche Bank worker accidentally transferred to a customer a couple of years ago.

E   One big lesson I have learnt is this: if you do happen to send an idiotic email at work, unless you have caused a stock market meltdown, just apologise and move on. Never try to recall it.

A look through my inbox shows there was only one month this year – August – when I did not get at least one message from someone announcing they 'would like to recall' an email. In almost every case, I did what everyone does in this situation: I tracked down the note to see what it said.

Unit 1 >

1 3

2 1 candidates
   2 decade
   3 Networking
   4 hire
   5 career break
   6 maternity leave
   7 Middle managers
   8 work placements

3 1 c 2 d 3 a 4 e 5 b

4 1 F 2 T 3 T 4 F 5 F 6 T

5 1 a 2 b 3 c 4 c 5 a

Unit 2 >

1 1 revenue
   2 assembly
   3 weld
   4 testing
   5 reputation

2 1 weld, seal
   2 testing, assembly
   3 1901
   4 1970
   5 Rs130,000 $2,000

3 1 F 2 T 3 F 4 T 5 T 6 F 7 T

4 2

5 1 c 2 d 3 e 4 b 5 a
   Showroom is written as one word.

6 1 production line
   2 joint venture
   3 showroom
   4 manufacturing centre
   5 market leader

Unit 3 >

1 1 c 2 a 3 b

2A 1 Waterfall
   2 Agile

2B 1 Waterfall
   2 Agile (39 percent success vs. 11 percent for Waterfall)
   3 Agile

3 1 budget
   2 users
   3 progress
   4 Done
   5 stand-up
   6 retrospectives
   7 collaborate
   8 individual

4 1 e 2 c 3 a 4 b 5 d

5 1 top-down
   2 signed off
   3 obstacles
   4 collaboration
   5 improve

Unit 4 >

1 1 a 2 a 3 b 4 a 5 b 6 b 7 a

2 2

3 1 D 2 C 3 A 4 E 5 B

4 1 T 2 F 3 T 4 T 5 F 6 F

5 1 tastes
   2 soft
   3 research
   4 up
   5 word

Unit 5 >

1 1 b 2 a 3 b 4 a 5 a

2 1 collaboratively
   2 resources
   3 intrinsically linked
   4 make the grade

3 1 B 2 A 3 D 4 not used 5 C

4 A visionary
   B distribution
   C critical
   D work spaces

5 1 F 2 F 3 T 4 T 5 F 6 F

Unit 6 >

1 1 d 2 e 3 a 4 c 5 b 6 g 7 f

2 1 C 2 D 3 B 4 A

3 1 a 2 c 3 b 4 c

4 1 villain
   2 transfer
   3 gullible
   4 hostile
   5 priorities
   6 spring-clean
   7 engaged
   8 at the heart

5 1 gullible
   2 transfer
   3 at the heart
   4 engaged
   5 priorities

Unit 7 >

1 b

2 1 a 2 b 3 a 4 a 5 b 6 a 7 b

3 1 f 2 c 3 b 4 a 5 d (e is not used)

4 1 T 2 F 3 F 4 T 5 T 6 F 7 T 8 F

5 1 c 2 a 3 d 4 b

Unit 8 >

1 c

2 1 D 2 B 3 E 4 A 5 C

3 1 b 2 a 3 a 4 a 5 b

4 1 F 2 T 3 F 4 NG 5 T 6 NG 7 T 8 F

5 1 d 2 b 3 a 4 c

6 1 pay attention
   2 correct
   3 mis-typed
   4 spelt
   5 hasty
   6 inbox

1 ❯ Emails

Lead-in In general, emails are either informal or formal/semi-formal. Emails to people inside your organisation may use less formal language than those sent to people outside of the company. Before writing an email, think about the level of formality needed and make sure the information you want to communicate is clear to the reader:

1 Who is the email to and what level of formality is needed?

2 Is the main information that you want to communicate clear to the reader?

Model answers

Dear Miku and Chris,

I'd like to introduce myself to you both. My name is Luiz Sousa and I am the new project leader for the Marshall account. Before joining the team, I worked in a similar role in the PR department of Kline and Marriott Associates for almost a decade.

It's a pleasure to work with you on such an exciting account. You've both worked on this project for some time and I would therefore like to discuss the background and hear your ideas.

I'd like to request a meeting on Tuesday 12th at 10 a.m. This will be both an update meeting as well as a discussion on how to proceed with this account. Could you let me know if this is convenient for you?

In the meantime, could you prepare a brief update report for me to read prior to the meeting? Chris, I'd like to know what strategy has been used in managing the Marshall account. Miku, it would also be useful to have a summary of any interaction with this client in the last six months.

I'm looking forward to meeting you both and working with you on this project.

Kind regards,
Luiz

Hi Miku and Chris,

Many thanks for attending the meeting on Tuesday and for preparing the project updates. Both were very productive and informative.

As we discussed in the meeting, strategy for managing the Marshall account hasn't changed in over two years. However, the industries and sectors that Marshall operates in have experienced many technical advances in recent years. In order to do the best for our client, we agreed that we should explore a variety of potential new directions for the account. Please find below a summary of the main action points from our meeting:

- Chris to research and share information related to technology and energy industries and automotive sector for the Marshall account. Deadline Monday 18th.
- Team meeting (Chris, Miku and Luiz) to finalise strategy and prepare presentation. Tuesday 19th.
- Miku to contact Dev Saunders and organise initial meeting to share findings and discuss expansion of the Marshall account. By Thursday 21st.
- Luiz to present new strategy to board of directors at Marshall. Arrange by w/c 25th.

Thank you again for sharing your thoughts and ideas. This is an exciting opportunity to explore new directions for this key account. Feel free to contact me if you have any questions.

Best wishes,
Luiz

Subject: Customer service feedback

Dear Sir or Madam,

I am writing to thank you for the excellent customer service which I experienced when hiring a car from your company last week.

While travelling on business with two colleagues, we hired a Hyundai Tucson to drive to a conference in Budapest. Unfortunately, on the second night of our stay the car was stolen. When we spoke to your customer care team, the response was excellent. Within two hours one of your representatives, Gergo Belov, had driven to our hotel and delivered a replacement vehicle. In addition, Mr Belov stayed with us and helped complete the insurance form. I wanted you to know how much we appreciated his assistance.

We look forward to returning to your beautiful country in the future and we would certainly use Alcan Car Hire again.

Yours faithfully,
Max Hastings (HR Director)

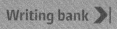

Functional language
Starting and ending an email

	Formal/Semi-formal	Informal
Greeting	Dear Sir or Madam, Dear Ms/Mrs/Miss/Mr/Dr Peck, Dear Katrin,	Hi/Hello, Anton, Good morning, Jasmine,
Closing	I'm looking forward to our meeting next week. Do let me know if you have any queries. Perhaps we could arrange a lunch meeting to discuss? It was a pleasure meeting you and thank you for choosing our company. Please do not hesitate to get in contact if you require any further information.	Looking forward to speaking on Thursday. Feel free to contact me if you have any questions. Shall we have a brief chat to discuss progress? It was great meeting you and thanks for your interest in our company. Let me know if you need anything else.
Signing off	Kind regards, Regards, Yours,	Best wishes, All best,

Main sections of an email

Linking to previous communication	Many thanks for attending the meeting. It was great to meet you last week.
Introducing yourself	I'd like to introduce myself, I'm … Can I take this opportunity to introduce myself. My name is … I've recently joined the finance team. I'm the new Sales Manager. I'm delighted to join the team in my new role as Media Coordinator. I am the HR Director at LMK. In my previous position/role I worked in the manufacturing sector.
Thanking	I am writing to thank you for your help arranging the training seminar last week. I am writing to say thank you for the excellent service that we received at your hotel during our visit. Thank you very much for your help with our order. We really appreciate all your hard work on this project. I would like to take this opportunity to thank you for your help. We appreciated your assistance with the presentation. Your team was most helpful and the event was a great success. We would recommend your products and excellent service. We would certainly use your company again.
Requesting an update	Could you prepare a brief report to update us? Can you let me know where we are with the Andrews project? Would you talk me through the stages of the process? I'd like to request a meeting to discuss how the project is progressing.

Action points

These list points where action is required and add the name of the person who will do the task.
Note: Bullet points and numbered lists are often used to summarise action points. For more information, see Instructions and warnings, in section 4 of this Writing bank.

As we discussed in the meeting, the date of the office move is now 26th April.

The aim of the meeting was to discuss important changes in the pharmaceutical industry.

Here is a summary of the main action points from the meeting:

Please find below a list of the key points from the meeting:

Here are some phrases and acronyms that are used when discussing dates and deadlines:

* *w/c* – week commencing (the date at the start of the week)   *We'll finalise the brochure **w/c** 24th May.*
* *EOD* – end of day   *I'll send you the update by **EOD** Monday.*
* *latest* – the final date/time that something is needed   *The team will need the marketing data my Friday morning **latest**.*

2 ❯ Letters

Lead-in Letters usually have a more formal style than emails and do not usually use contractions. The greeting and ending of a letter changes when you know the name of the person that you are writing to.

Model answers **Letter confirming an order**

Natalia Bray
Kendal House
Westfield Business Park
Newmarket
NM82 SJP

Marcus Dale
Sales Manager
Bloom Floristry Supplies
22 Lark Avenue
Ashford
Kent
KH12 0PA

Wednesday 4th October

Dear Ms Bray,

Re: Order 245192/DS

Further to our telephone conversation on Monday, I am writing to confirm your order for plants and flowers for the new headquarters in Kendal House.

As discussed, twelve large houseplants will be delivered and installed in your reception area on Thursday 12th November. The upkeep of all plants will be arranged by members of the Bloom Floristry team. In addition, we will supply fresh, seasonal flowers twice a week in the boardroom.

As agreed, payment terms are monthly and you will receive the first invoice thirty days after the plants have been installed. Thank you for the deposit, which we received yesterday, and a receipt for this is enclosed.

Please also find enclosed an order confirmation which includes a list of plants selected and a current price list. If you would like to amend or add to your order, please do not hesitate to contact me.

It was a pleasure speaking to you about your requirements and sincere thanks for choosing Bloom Floristry Supplies.

Yours sincerely,
Marcus Dale

Enclosed: order confirmation, price list, receipt

Functional language
Opening and closing a letter

	Name of person is known	Name of person is not known
Opening	Dear Ms/Mrs/Miss/Mr Peck,	Dear Sir or Madam,
Ending	We look forward to working with you. If you have any queries, please do not hesitate to contact us. Do let me know if you need any further information.	Looking forward to seeing you at the conference. Let me know if you have any questions. If you need anything else on this, just let me know.
Closing **Note: Only the first word uses capital letters.**	Yours sincerely, Sincerely, (U.S.)	Yours faithfully, Yours truly, (U.S.)

Subject line and enclosing documents

Subject line	Re:
Referring to documents	Please find enclosed (a copy of the invoice). The enclosed (documents) …

Details

Referring to past contact	Further to our meeting last week, … It was a pleasure meeting you and your colleagues at the conference in Basel.
Saying why you are writing	I am writing to confirm your order. We are pleased to confirm your order. I would like to request a copy of your latest price list. I have an enquiry regarding order number DET/34P.
Terms and conditions	Payment terms are €2,500 per month. Goods will be delivered within five working days. Please arrange payment within twenty-one days of receiving the invoice.

3 ❯ Product reviews

Lead-in

Product reviews can be brief, informal comments on a website or longer, more formal reviews in a blog or magazine. A balanced review will highlight both positive and negative aspects of a product or service and include details to support opinions. Online reviews are increasingly important to businesses. If a company responds to a review online, the language should remain neutral and try to encourage a solution to any problems.

Model answers   **Brief review**

Attractive design, bad fit   ★★☆☆☆

Comment

This smart cover looks great but doesn't fit my device. Product details are wrong. Wouldn't buy again – very disappointed.

Reply

We are very sorry to hear that you have experienced this problem with our product. Customer satisfaction is very important to us and we will be in contact to arrange a suitable replacement or offer a full refund.

Longer review

SmarTech Interior Systems   Rating ★★★☆☆   RRP €2,700

After a lot of research I selected SmarTech Interior Systems to fit smart technology in our house. I sometimes work from home but also frequently travel on business, so I needed a system which was flexible and reliable and could also be fitted quickly.

I approached two other companies for quotations, but they were both more expensive and also took a minimum of six weeks to complete the task. In contrast, the online reviews and testimonials on the SmarTech website said that they offered quick, dependable service and worked closely with customers. I was impressed by the expertise and experience they displayed in our initial consultation and opted for the silver package. This package included fitting smart technology to my home office, kitchen and living areas.

The technology I purchased in the silver package included:
- smart lighting, where lamps turn on and off automatically when a person enters or leaves the room in the evening.
- device-connected technology in the kitchen (so that appliances can be checked and controlled from my phone when I am out of the house).
- multiple screens so that video conferences can be held in different rooms.

The company fitted the technology within the agreed deadline and were friendly and helpful. They have a great deal of experience in fitting this home technology, which helped me feel confident.

At first, I was delighted with the work they carried out. They fitted the items within the agreed deadline and offered advice on use. Unfortunately, despite this positive experience, the customer service stops this from being a five-star review. I have needed to contact the company three times with queries and problems with the technology. Each time I have had to wait several days to receive a response from an engineer. This can lead to frustration and delays in solving simple technological issues.

So, in summary, I would certainly recommend the products that the company uses and also their expertise and their excellent, speedy fitting service. However, the poor after-sales care makes it impossible to give a full recommendation. My advice to SmarTech is improve your customer service and you will soon have five-star feedback.

Functional language
Brief review

Section	Information	Examples
Headings	Some website reviews have headings. They can be used to summarise opinion but usually don't repeat the exact words used in the review.	Great performance Excellent value for money Unhelpful customer service Good idea, poor design
Identify positive or negative	Brief reviews often use short sentences, cutting out unnecessary words.	~~This machine makes great bread.~~ Makes great bread! ~~The service is very slow and too expensive.~~ Slow and expensive service. ~~The design is beautiful and I would recommend the product.~~ Beautiful design – would recommend.
Responses	An online response from the supplier should be polite, use neutral language and a more formal, professional style.	Thank you for taking the time to leave a review. We are delighted that you had such a positive experience – customer satisfaction is very important to us. We are very sorry that you experienced this problem with our service. We will be in contact soon to discuss the issue and offer a solution.

Longer review

Introduction	After a lot of research, I chose the updated model. I opted for the premium package. I selected model X145.
Describing the product or service	The website says that the products are high quality. The package includes consultation, fitting and repairs. The specifications include additional memory and storage. The product features a front- and back-facing camera.
Good points	I was impressed by the quick delivery. The product matched the online description. It has an attractive and stylish design.
Support with detail	The goods arrived on time and in excellent condition. This machine cleans perfectly every time.
Bad points	Unfortunately, the product stopped working after three days. The product did not match the description. It has a lot of features but the results are not always reliable. The main downside is the cost. One thing I didn't like was the colour.
Support with detail	The quality was poor. Each time I turn on the device, it makes a noise. I rang the company twice but received no response. For example, the plug gets very hot when the printer is in use.
Compare or contrast	In contrast, the previous model, Zi24, was much slower. The software update is an attractive design, but it has fewer features compared to the original version. Despite the fact that it is less expensive than most of its competitors, it is a better design.
Conclusion	To summarise, I would recommend this product for quality, price and reliability. In summary, the design is innovative but not all the features work effectively.

4 ❯ Instructions and warnings

Lead-in   Instructions, warnings and guidelines are all used to communicate key information to employees clearly and contain important information.

- A warning is usually a brief notice (e.g. to alert staff about potential dangers when using equipment or machinery).
- Instructions or guidelines provide more detailed information about how something works or how to carry out a task.
- Any important notes and warnings go at the start of the instructions or guidelines.
- For clarity, instructions should be organised with headings to summarise each new part of the task and numbered lists or bullet points to list information step by step.
- It should be clear to the reader what to do when the task is complete.
- Instructions and warnings use clear language and contain only essential information.
- Sentences are often short and direct to prioritise key information.

Model answers   Notice

Stop!
Safety helmets must be worn on site at all times.

Guidelines

Sample tests for drinking water

Follow the instructions to take samples of drinking water. Warning! All samples must be sent to the laboratory within 24 hours of collection.

Collection

1 Collect sample from a cold water tap.
2 Do not take samples from drinking water fountains or garden taps.
3 Let the water run for one minute before taking the sample.
4 Remove the cap from the sample bottle.
5 Avoid touching the top of the bottle or inside the bottle with fingers.
6 Fill the bottle to the 100 ml line. Do not overfill.
7 Replace the cap on the bottle.
8 Store sample in refrigerator.

Testing

1 Deliver the water sample within 24 hours to laboratory 315.
2 Leave samples in laboratory during opening hours only:
   9 a.m.–4 p.m, Monday–Friday.
3 Complete form 12AEW with name and the location where the sample was taken.
4 Keep one copy of form 12AEW and attach the other copy to the sample.
5 Samples must not be left at reception.

Test results

1 Results are available within 48 hours.
2 Collect results online using website password shown on form 12AEW.
3 Contact laboratory reception with any queries about test results.

Functional language

Imperatives	~~You use the green button to switch on the machine and the red button to switch off.~~ **Switch on** the machine using the green button. **Switch off** the machine using the red button.
Sequencing	**Beginning** Firstly ... First ... To start with ... **Continuing** Secondly ... Second ... Then ... Next ... **Ending** Finally ...
Linking words for time	Before ... After ... As soon as ... While ... During ... At the same time ... To finish ... At the end ...
Adverbs of frequency	**Always** tell a member of staff if you feel unwell. **Never** open the door while the kiln is in use.
Modals	Visitors **must** sign in at reception. Floors **should** be cleaned every day. Windows **must** not be opened.

Organising information

There are different ways to help the reader follow instructions. These include:

Headings	Use headings to break the information into sections to make it easy to read. *On arrival* *Safety checks* *In the building* *Before leaving*
Bullet points and lists	Use **numbered lists** when the order of information is important and put the most important information first. *In the event of a fire:* *1 Leave the area by the nearest exit.* *2 Do not stop to take bags or coats.* *3 Once away from the fire, phone emergency services.* Use **bullet points** when the order of information is not essential. The reader can choose which points are most useful. • *Leave work boots and hard hats in the staff room.* • *Report any loss of equipment to a supervisor.* • *Give the team leader the time sheet before leaving the building.*

5 ❯ Short reports

Lead-in

The content and style of reports may differ from company to company. Consider these points when writing a report:

- A short report might be sent in an email or as a separate document.
- Headings and bullet points are used to organise information.
- Sections of a report may include an introduction, findings, recommendations and a conclusion (the recommendations may sometimes function as a conclusion).
- Edit your report to check punctuation, spelling and grammar.

Model answer

Introduction

The purpose of this report is to investigate a recent communication problem between the sales department and the warehouse, which led to significant delays in fulfilling orders to some of our key customers. We looked into some of the issues which contributed to the problem and then made recommendations to avoid any reoccurrence for future orders.

Findings

Firstly, we interviewed members of staff in both the sales department and the warehouse in order to clarify details and explore why the problem occurred. We then spoke to the customer service department to understand what impact this had on customers.

Until recently, the sales department sent orders to the warehouse using a computer system which automatically raised the order and also sent an email confirmation to the warehouse. The email confirmation was used by both departments to show any urgent orders and also included information about any special requirements connected to the order.

We discovered that the sales department recently updated their computer software. The sales team received full training in the new system but the warehouse team did not. One of the main issues with the new software is that the warehouse no longer receives additional notes with orders. As a result, the most recent communication from the sales department did not inform the warehouse which orders were a priority.

We found that the warehouse administration team arranged a delivery schedule in the sequence that each order arrived. Unfortunately, they did not check the delivery schedule with the sales department. As a consequence, Customer Services received five complaints from clients because their goods were received after the agreed date. Two of the complaints were from major customers.

Recommendations

We recommend the following suggestions for consideration:

- Provide training for all departments when new computer software in installed.
- Carry out a risk assessment to identify potential issues before software is updated.
- The sales team need to inform the warehouse about urgent orders.
- The warehouse administration team should check final delivery schedules with the sales department.
- A weekly briefing meeting between the Sales Manager and the Warehouse Manager would be useful in order to improve communication between the departments.
- Send a letter of apology and a credit note to customers who experienced late delivery.

Conclusion

In summary, the findings show that good communication is essential between all departments. This is especially important when there are changes in one department which might have an impact on another, such as technological improvements. It is also vital that we communicate with our customers and are open when problems occur. The main conclusion is that all teams need to learn from any communication issues so that we can continue to improve and find solutions, not only within our company but also for our clients.

Functional language

Section	Function	Examples
Introduction	It states the purpose of the report.	The purpose of this report is to identify ways to reduce costs. The aim of the report is to communicate the main findings from our recent research trip.
Findings	A summary of key findings, e.g. results of experiments, research or surveys.	We found that less than half of those questioned would buy the product again. A small number of those interviewed disliked the material. The results of the research show that fresh vegetables contain more vitamins. We discovered that the majority of those tested preferred bottled water.
Recommendations	Bullet points or numbered lists may be used to highlight key information. For more information on bullet points and lists, see Instructions and warnings, in section 4 of this Writing bank.	The main recommendations are as follows: • It is recommended that all employees undergo safety training. • The kitchen area should be cleaned every day. • The teams need to identify solutions. • We might consider contacting suppliers to discuss possible price reductions.
Conclusion	It summarises the main message of the report.	In summary, the sales promotion was a success. The main conclusion is that objectives need to be clearly communicated to the teams. In conclusion, there will be major changes to company strategy.

Language and register

Sequencing	Firstly, the calculations were checked. Then the findings were compared with the same sales figures from the last financial year. After that, the data was put into the computer system. Finally, we looked at strategies which could improve the process.
Communicating findings	We discovered that the security system had not worked. One of the key issues is the location of the business. As a result, the team was able to improve the design. As a consequence, the wrong goods were delivered.
Personal or impersonal?	*We* can be used to indicate that more than one person was involved in gathering the information included in a report. It can also be used to deliver the information in the report in a more formal and less personal style. *I researched ways that new technology could improve communication.* *We looked into ways to improve customer experience in our stores.* Information can also be made more impersonal through the use of grammar. Compare: *I asked the sales team to prepare a report.* (Past Simple) *The sales team was asked to prepare a report.* (Past Simple passive)

1 ❯ Conversational skills

Lead-in Some business practices may differ from country to country. Here are some questions to research before you meet new business contacts:

1 In conversations, is it usual for the person who isn't speaking to remain silent or to comment on the conversation?

2 When you meet someone when networking, is it usual to exchange business cards and to send an email after the event?

3 What greetings are most appropriate (e.g. shaking hands, bowing)?

Introductions

Introducing yourself	Responding to an introduction
Hi/Hello, my name's Toby. Can I introduce myself? I'm Chris.	It's a pleasure to meet you. Good to meet you.

Participating in a conversation

	Formal	Informal
Starting or joining a conversation	What do you think of the conference? Do you mind if I join you? Do you have a moment to discuss your company? Would it be possible to talk about your training programme?	Hi, are you enjoying the conference? Is it OK if I join you? Do you have time for a quick chat? Is now a good time to talk about your training programme?
Closing	I really appreciate your time. Thank you. Would it be possible to contact you to discuss this further? Thank you so much, that was very informative. Can I give you my business card? May I have your business card?	Thanks for taking the time to talk to me. Can I get in touch next week to talk about this in more detail? It was great speaking to you. Here's my card. Do you have a business card?

Showing interest

There are different strategies for showing interest during a conversation. It is polite to keep your attention focused on the speaker and to use body language as well as words to show that you are paying attention (e.g. looking at the person speaking, nodding, smiling).

Commenting	Really? That's interesting! Right. OK. I see. Ah! Uh-huh.
Asking questions	Can you tell me more about the recruitment process? Who is the best person to contact about applications?
Clarifying	Did you say that you employ 3,000 people worldwide? So is it better to contact you by phone or email?
Showing your research	I noticed on your website that you employ interns. Your company brochure was very informative.
Repeating back	So you have a graduate training programme. It's interesting to hear that you have apprenticeships in computing.

2 › Telephone skills

Lead-in

Some business practices may differ from country to country. Here are some questions to research before you make telephone calls:

1 Are calls usually short and to the point or is some small talk expected?
2 How quickly are phone messages returned?
3 When you take or leave a message, what key information would you expect to exchange?
4 How are numbers grouped when saying a telephone number?
5 What details would be expected when recording a message on the telephone?
6 Is it acceptable to cut a conversation short when you are busy or will the person you are speaking to be offended?

Making contact

	Formal/Semi-formal	Less formal
Starting a call	Hello, my name is Claudia Peck from Tevo Industries. Can I speak to the Sales Director, please? Good morning, my name is Cara Madaki. We met at the computer security seminar last week.	Hi, Fabio. It's Susan here. This is Monika from accounts.
Receptionist	Cranfield Computing, how can I help? Could you hold the line, please? I'm putting you through now.	Hi, Kendle Electronics. One moment. I'll put you through now.
Receiving a call	Hello, Tang Ka-yee speaking. You're through to the Customer Services Manager.	Hi, James Glover. Speaking.
Stating the reason for your call	Would it be possible to arrange a meeting to present our new product range? I have a quick query about your latest expenses claim. You suggested that I call to discuss my internship application. Hi Lars, this is Charlotte. I received your message about the brochures.	It's about the presentation. I'm calling with a quick question. You said I should call to discuss the internship. Hi, Gina. I'm calling about your voicemail message. Hi, I got your message.

Ending the call

Cutting short a call	Can I call you back? I'm in the middle of something. I'll take your details and call you back. Can I call you later? I'll get back to you later today.
Confirming action	So, I'll see you on Thursday at 3 p.m. I'll call you back as soon as I have the figures. I'll call tomorrow to confirm details.
Ending the call	Thanks for calling, bye. Thank you for your help. It was nice speaking to you, bye.

Leaving a message

Leaving a message	Can I leave a message, please? Could you tell Lisa that Judith called about the catering order?
Checking understanding	Could you read that back, please? Would you like me to repeat the number?
Requesting action	Do you know when she will be back? Can you ask him to call me back this afternoon? Could you tell Tomas that it's urgent, please? Is there anyone else who could help?

Taking a message

Taking a message	Sorry, Louis isn't in the office today. Can I take a message?
	Katrin isn't here at the moment. Would you like to leave a message?
Checking understanding	So that's 738 562 991?
	Can I read that back?
	Did you say fifteen or fifty?
Confirming action	I'll give him your message as soon as he returns.
	She won't be back in the office until Monday. Would you like to speak to someone else about this?

Voicemail messages

Identifying yourself	Hi, this is Lars Jansen from Lumiglow.
Giving a reason for your call	I'm calling about your order for the new brochures.
Giving key information	There is a problem with the delivery date.
	Could you call me back on 0998 639 232?
	I'll be in the office until 6 p.m.
	Could you contact me by tomorrow morning, please?
Repeating or spelling information	That's oh_double nine_eight, six_three_nine, two_three_two.
	That's spelt L_U_M_I_G_L_O_W.

3 ❯ Meeting skills

Lead-in Some business practices may differ from country to country. Here are some questions to research before you prepare for a meeting:

1 Is the meeting formal or informal? What is the aim?

2 Are there likely to be different opinions? What are the main arguments for and against the topic being discussed?

3 What outcome do you want from the meeting? How will you record action points?

Introductions and opening

Welcoming people	Thank you all for coming today.
Introducing participants	I think we all know each other, don't we?
	Could we all say our name and role?
Clarifying aims	The aim of this meeting is to agree the new budget.
	You'll see from the agenda that we are here to discuss three main points.
	We need to agree on who is working on each project.
Opening a meeting	OK, let's begin by looking at the first point on the agenda.
	Shall we start by discussing the schedule?

Participating

Asking for opinions	What are your thoughts on this?
	What do you think, Natalia?
	Any ideas?
Giving an opinion	In my opinion, we should look for a new supplier.
	I think this would help our clients.
Agreeing/ Disagreeing	That's a good point.
	I agree with Jean Luc.
	That's a really good idea.
	That would work.
	I can see your point but I can't agree.
	I'm afraid I don't agree.
Clarifying	What I meant to say was (the figures aren't reliable).
	To put it another way (we need to spend less on marketing).
	Can I check what you mean by (cost cutting)?

Updates and action

Asking for an update	How are we doing with the new factory plans? Can you give me a quick update on your current projects? Have you updated the team on the new schedule? Where are we with the new price list? What's happening with the new computer software? Can you bring me up to speed on the Ferguson contract?
Giving an update	
Talking about past action Talking about current action Talking about planned action	I completed the sales figures on Monday. The delivery was late so we missed the deadline. The design is in progress at the moment. I'm currently finalising the report I'm expecting the order confirmation this afternoon. We'll sign the contract tomorrow.
Giving an update on problems and solutions	The only problem is the currency rates, which might affect the budget. There was a problem with the menu, but we spoke to the caterers and found a solution. We're working on it at the moment and should have a solution by the end of the day.
Action points	Can you call the supplier by the end of today and change the quantity? We need a response by the end of this week. Get back to me on Thursday with an update, please. Justin will speak to sales and Monika can talk to the client. Does everyone know what they need to do?

Talking about priorities

Important	It is of the utmost importance that we come to a decision. This should be our number one priority. This issue is high priority. This is extremely important. We really need to decide on the deadline. The main issue is how much this will cost.
Less important	This is a low priority for our department. It's quite important but we don't need an immediate decision. It's not urgent. This isn't currently a priority. That isn't so important for us. We'd prefer to focus on the budget.
Postponing	We can put off the decision until we have more facts. Can we delay the deadline until next week? Let's explore some solutions and then come to a decision. We can talk about this later.

Reaching agreement

When discussing problems and issues, consider the following:

1 Understand and communicate the main priority of the discussion.
2 Talk about facts and issues rather than personal comments. Try to use *we* statements rather than *you* statements.
3 If it is not possible to come to agreement, arrange another discussion at a later date.

Agreeing	Yes, I agree with Anton. I see what you mean. I completely agree. Exactly!
Disagreeing	I'm afraid I disagree. Sorry, I don't agree. I'm not sure I agree with that.
Agreement not reached	We may have to agree to disagree. I don't think we can reach agreement today but we'll discuss this again later.
Making suggestions / Stating preferences	I think we should (have an international team). How about (changing the logo)? Why don't we (ask our customers)? We could (hire some short-term staff for the project). Have you considered (replacing the old equipment)?
Reacting to suggestions	That's a good point. That's a good idea. That could work. I think you're right. It's a nice idea, but I don't think it will work.

Resolving conflict

Explaining problems	The main problem is that (the supplier can't deliver the order). The issue is that (we don't have enough staff). The thing is that (the equipment is broken) and so (we won't be able to finish the task).
Outlining solutions	It might be a good idea to have weekly meetings. There are two possible solutions. What do you suggest? Let's try to find a solution together. What would you like to happen?
Inviting consensus	Can we come to an agreement? Would that work? Are we all agreed? Can we all agree on that?

Closing a meeting

Thank you for coming today. It was a very useful meeting. We'll meet again next week to discuss next steps.

4 ❯ Presentation skills

Lead-in

Some business practices may differ from country to country. Here are some questions to research before you prepare presentations for different audiences:

1 How formal or informal is the presentation?

2 Are you presenting as an individual or as a group? If presenting as a group, how have tasks been allocated? Is everyone clear what they need to do?

3 How much detail do you need? What does your audience already know about the topic?

4 What information is better spoken and what information would be clearer presented as slides or pictures?

Presenting ideas (informal presentation)

Generating ideas	Shall we brainstorm some ideas? I want to hear your ideas about how to improve customer service. What are your thoughts on the new marketing campaign?
Discussing ideas	What we need to do is identify our key market. Basically, sales and marketing should share an office. Why don't we work in small groups?
Presenting ideas	Our team came up with a new idea for the marketing campaign. We suggest that Spain would be the best location for the team-building weekend. Our idea is to completely change the logo. Another way is to increase our online profile.

Getting started

	Formal/Semi-formal	Less formal
Opening and welcome	Thank you for inviting me to speak to you today. I'm here to talk about our new product range.	It's great to be here today. I'd like to show you our latest exciting product.
Providing a brief outline of the talk	The talk consists of three main parts. I'd like to start by giving an outline of the talk. I will be focusing on three main areas. These are ...	I'm going to talk about three things. First ... I've split the talk into three sections. First ...
Telling the audience when they can ask questions	I will be happy to answer any questions during the presentation. Please don't hesitate to ask questions at any point. I welcome questions, but could you please keep them to the end of the presentation? There will be an opportunity to ask questions after the presentation.	Feel free to ask questions during the presentation. Just ask questions as we go along. You don't need to wait till the end. Let's keep questions till the end of the presentation. You'll have time at the end of the presentation to ask any questions.

Moving from point to point

Signposting	Let's start by looking at ... Firstly ... Secondly ... And that leads me on to my next point. OK, let's move on. And finally ...
Referring to earlier points	Remember that at the start of the presentation we said that good staff are key to a successful business? As we already mentioned, good customer service is essential.

Features and benefits

Features	Available in various colours. It can be used at home or in the office. An award-winning design. Made from 100 percent recycled materials. Our most popular model.
Benefits	It's strong/lightweight/stylish/modern/practical/easy to clean/reliable/popular. This means that you can use it at home or in the office. This makes it easier to clean.
Specifications	It weighs 2 kilos / 12 grammes. It's 1 metre long and 3 metres wide. It's made from wood/metal/leather/plastic/glass. It has 250 gigabytes of memory.
Giving examples	For example, the new model is faster. For instance, it allows you to work while commuting. Let me give you an example …
Adding information	In addition … Also … Another important point is …
Emphasising	The most important thing to remember is that … This is important because … This is a key point …

Presenting visual information

Drawing attention to visuals	As you can see from this slide, (the product is small and stylish). Let's move on to the next slide. Let's look at the sales figures shown in this chart. Now, I'd like to show you the results of our research.

Closing

Summing up	To sum up …
Closing	We've reached the end of the presentation. We've come to the end of the talk. Let me end by saying … In conclusion …
Thanking the audience	Thank you for listening. Thank you for your attention. It's been a pleasure speaking to you today.
Inviting questions	Does anyone have any questions? Are there any questions? I'm happy to answer any questions.

Videoscripts

1.1.1 P = Presenter   YB = Yvonne Buysman
AH = Ashley Hayward   RB = Ruth Badger
LS = Lord Sugar   RF = Richard Farleigh

P: The twenty-first century workplace is constantly changing. In many countries, the idea of a career for life is long gone. What employers want are skills that can be applied to a range of tasks and roles. As a result, they look for flexible people who can demonstrate transferable professional skills as well as personal qualities that will benefit the company. Here's an insider's guide to the skills and qualities that will get you hired and also help you survive in today's job market.
A large part of the academic experience is based around individual performance.
In business, however, things are quite different. You need to develop a range of transferable skills. And one thing that many recruiters put at the top of their list is the ability to work in teams.

YB: I would look at ... can this candidate fit into the team well, do they work well with people, are they passionate about the topic, do they think outside of the box?

AH: Employers value teamworking skills very highly indeed, so if you're studying, it's really important you try and get some experience. Now, obviously, an internship's an ideal way to do this but you can also do it through part-time jobs, through vacation work, through voluntary work, or helping with societies and clubs while you're at university.

RB: Your experience at school is really, really important. So, if you played in a team – guess what? You're a team player – you set goals, you achieve.

P: Twenty-first century careers involve a lot of movement, not just between jobs, but also between industries and countries. It's no good if your skillset locks you into one industry or even into one company, and this is where flexibility is important.

AH: Be prepared to develop attributes that are transferable across sectors so you can make the best moves for your career. I'm talking about things like critical thinking, which means analysing information very carefully, communication skills, problem solving, being able to influence people. Make sure you work on your communication skills – in person, on paper, face to face, in small groups, in large groups – you'll need to do this wherever you work, whatever job it is, across all sectors – communication skills are absolutely key.
Employers are not just hiring a package of skills, they're hiring a person, and it's personal qualities that are of key importance: honesty, flexibility, enthusiasm – these things matter a lot.

YB: Be passionate – if you're really going to apply to a company that you're interested in, make sure your passion comes through and be genuine and authentic about that passion. You're going to work hard, you're going to play hard but you have to be passionate to be successful.

LS: It's their own determination that's gonna get them a job, right? Employers, you know, are gonna look at them not necessarily for the skills that they may have, but for the passion that they may, you know, express.

RF: Convince them that you have integrity. You know, integrity is very important, obviously. And convince them that you have ability, that you'll do everything you can to make that job work.

RB: If you are motivated and have a can-do attitude, you will get wherever you want.

P: So to sum up our insider's guide ... You need professional skills that can transfer from one job to another, especially the ability to be a good team player. And don't forget that employers look at the person behind the CV or résumé to identify the personal qualities they value in the workplace.

1.3.1 D = Daniel   A = Alex   J = Jessica
B = Beata

D: Hi, I'm Daniel Smith. I'm heading up the Diabsenor project here at Evromed. It's a new treatment for type 1 diabetes.
There's a lot of excitement about it, which I love. There's also a lot of work to do, which means a lot of stress. So I'm putting together a small team of our trainee graduates. Hopefully, none of them will be as nervous on their first day as Alex was

A: I heard that!
Is that Beeta? Batta? Barta?

D: Beata. She's Polish. I spoke to her on the phone. Great CV. Very promising. Business school in Krakow, five years' experience in Japan. Confident ... but not *too* confident.

A: Ah. Good. Hopefully she'll get on with Jessica then.

J: I'm Jessica Scott. Evromed is a small family-owned business dealing in the pharmaceutical sector. As CEO, I'm looking for the right attitude in an employee. Confident, but not arrogant. And sometimes I feel that overconfidence can come across as arrogance.

B: Hello. Daniel, isn't it?

D: That's me. And this is Alex. He's been here just over a year.

A: A year already? That's hard to believe. Twelve months in this crazy place!

B: Sorry?

D: Don't worry, Beata. Alex is just a bit of a joker, that's all.

1.3.2 B = Beata   A = Alex   D = Daniel
J = Jessica

B: That's OK. I was just confused for a moment. Nice to meet you.

A: You, too. I hear you lived in Tokyo. Where exactly did you live?

B: Suidobashi. Do you know it?

A: Ah, yes, near the baseball park. I lived there myself for a while. Loved it. How long were you in Japan for?

B: Five years. When were you in Tokyo?

A: 2013 to 2015. About eighteen months.

B: What did you do there?

A: Teaching English, mainly.

B: Teaching. Interesting. What did you like best about it?

A: Mainly the food!

D: This is Jessica Scott. She's our CEO.

B: Hello, Ms Scott. Beata Kowalska. Nice to meet you.

J: Please, call me Jessica. I hear you worked with one of our main competitors in Tokyo?

B: You mean MEDilink?

J: You must have learnt a lot while you were there.

B: Absolutely. But I'm very keen to learn even more here.

J: Well, you're going to be working with a great team. Daniel and Alex really know their stuff. How about we chat in a couple of weeks' time?

B: Sounds great. Thank you, Jessica.

J: Nice to have you on board.
I was very impressed with Beata. Confident but not arrogant. Just the right balance.

D: Beata made a great first impression. I'm sure she and Alex will have lots of Tokyo stories to share. And even Jessica liked her!

1.3.3 B = Beata   J = Jessica   D = Daniel

B: Oh. Right. So I'm working on the Diabsensor project, yes? What will I be doing exactly?
Hello, Ms Scott. Beata Kowalska. Very nice to meet you. Let me tell you about myself. I have lots of experience working in project management, and have recently completed an internship in another medical supplies company in Japan. MEDilink. I'm sure you know it?

J: I'm aware of our biggest competitor, yes.

B: How is the Diabsensor project coming along? I'd like to discuss my ideas, if possible.

J: Well ... it's probably best if you get to know the product and the company first. Daniel and Alex will look after you for the next few days.

B: Yes. Of course.

J: Welcome to Evromed.
Beata? Hmm. Honestly, I'm not sure. I love her enthusiasm, but ... she seemed a little arrogant with it.

D: Beata meant well, I'm sure. But Jessica didn't respond well to her, which is a shame. Perhaps she needs to work on her communication skills a little more.

1.3.4

Basically building rapport is about getting on well with people, individually or in a group. Once you build rapport, you generally find communication flows more easily and it's usually more effective too. Sometimes rapport just happens naturally, but other times you need to use simple techniques to develop a link with the other person.
If we observe Beata in Option A, she doesn't have any problems building rapport with Alex. They both have an interest in Japan and rapport seems to come naturally. It's not the same with Jessica. In Option A Beata comes across as confident, which Jessica seems to appreciate, and this way the two create a bond. It's quite different in Option B, where Beata tries too hard to show how much she knows. There are different ways of building rapport. One way is to find out what you have in common with the other person. It's not difficult – start by asking simple questions; business travel is often a good place to start. There are also simple non-verbal techniques you can use. Try to keep an open posture when you're speaking and smile. And eye contact will help you develop rapport in most cultural contexts, but make sure it's not too intense.

2.1.1 P = Presenter   CG = Carlos Ghosn

P: Different countries often dominate in different industries. When we think of luxury goods, we think of France and Italy, and we associate internet technology with the USA. Japan is well known for its strong consumer electronics and car-making industries. Let's take a closer look at the country's economic development over the past decades.
Japan's industrialised, free-market economy is the third largest in the world. In the past, the country's been seen as a mystical land of cherry blossoms and samurai. Nowadays, it's better known as one of the world's leading high-tech economies.
Japan enjoyed rapid expansion after World War Two. It recovered from devastation to become the world's second-largest economy by the 1960s. Japan's service sector, which includes finance, trade, entertainment, tourism, retail and transportation, accounts for a massive three-quarters of Japan's total economic output. It isn't surprising therefore that within the financial world, the Nikkei is one of the most important markets, and that many Japanese banks are global players. But it has been Japan's manufacturing industries that have made the most global impact.
The automotive industry has been particularly successful. Japanese car manufacturers enjoy a reputation for producing reliable, high-quality and innovative vehicles. They pioneered technological advancements in the use of robots, which enabled the Japanese auto industry to produce cars to a high standard and very efficiently.
In the 1970s Japanese car makers became aggressive and successful exporters. The cars were cheap, reliable and popular with consumers. This meant domestic car makers in the USA and Europe lost market share.

Japanese vehicles' continuing popularity enabled Japan to become the largest car-producing nation in the world in 2000.

Despite increasing competition, Japanese automakers continue to innovate – the Toyota Prius was the first, and is still one of the best-selling, mass-produced hybrid cars. In 2010, Nissan released the world's first all-electric car: the Leaf.

CG: This car represents a real breakthrough. For the first time in our industry history a car manufacturer will mass-market a zero-emission car, the ultimate solution for sustainable mobility.

P: It isn't only the automotive industry, however, that provides world-beating products.

Japanese electronics companies are known for producing small, well-designed and often innovative products. Some of these have been so original that they have changed the way we live, work and play.

In 1979, Sony released the Walkman, a small and portable cassette player allowing consumers to listen to music while on the go – a concept that was revolutionary back then.

In the realm of video game technology, Japanese company Nintendo is credited with producing the best-selling handheld console in history – the DS, while electronics giant Sony claims the highest selling console of all time in the Playstation 2.

As we've seen, in the twentieth century Japan was very successful in using technology to innovate in areas like the automotive and electronics industries. Will it be able to use twenty-first century technologies as effectively? That is the challenge.

2.3.1 B = Beata   J = Jessica

B: The CEO is holding an induction meeting today so I thought I'd prepare a little over my morning coffee. Evromed … family-owned business … 145 employees … main market share in Europe … And suppliers based in China … in Shenzhen … newer projects in South America … New contract in Rio to supply hospital with device for diabetes patients. A trip to Rio would be very nice at this time of year … or any time of year …

J: Please feel free to ask questions as we go along.

2.3.2 J = Jessica   B = Beata   G1 = Graduate 1

J: Please feel free to ask questions as we go along.

B: How does the new product work, Jessica?

J: Good question. Who hates the sight of blood? Wow. It's not often meetings come to a consensus so quickly. Now, imagine you have to prick your finger several times a day just to check your blood sugar levels. With the Diabsensor, you don't have to. It's a real breakthrough.

B: Sorry, Jessica, when you say 'blood sugar', do you mean 'glucose'?

J: Yes, that's right.

B: And how does it work?

J: It analyses the patient's glucose level. A sensor collects the data through a patch on the skin and then sends it to a remote monitor. Basically it's a reliable and pain-free way to manage diabetes. Does anyone have any other questions …

B: How big is it?

J: Small. It fits in the palm of your hand, weighs about 35 grams. I actually have a prototype handy. Would anyone like to see it?

B: And the assembly process? I understand it's made in China?

J: The components come from China, yes. But we assemble the product at our plant here in Manchester. Just across there, in fact.

G1: Sorry, Jessica, if I could just …

B: Why don't you assemble the product in China? Isn't it cheaper?

J: Beata, I like your enthusiasm. But maybe someone else has a question? Please, yes, go ahead.

G1: What was the reaction to the product?

J: Very good initially …

B: I probably asked too many questions, I think. But to be honest no one else seemed very interested, which is a shame because it's a really innovative product. My mum has type 1 diabetes and this device would make her life so much easier. It's also one of the reasons I wanted to do this graduate programme. But yes … Jessica was getting a little irritated by my interruptions. I should be more careful about that next time.

2.3.3 G1 = Graduate 1   J = Jessica   B = Beata
G2 = Graduate 2   G3 = Graduate 3

J: Please feel free to ask questions as we go along.

G1: What can you tell us about the product? It sounds very innovative.

J: Good question. And it is very innovative. But here's a quick question for you first. Who hates the sight of blood? I bet we're all scared of spiders, too. Anyway. Imagine you hate the sight of blood, but you have to prick your finger several times a day just to check your blood sugar levels. Yes?

B: Sorry to interrupt, Jessica.

J: That's OK. Please go ahead.

B: When you say 'blood sugar', do you mean 'glucose'?

J: Glucose. Exactly. Yes.

G2: Ah, good, thanks. I was wondering about that, too.

J: So, as I was saying … no more pricking of fingers. The Diabsensor uses a sensor to read the patient's glucose level. It collects the data through a patch on the skin and then sends it to a remote monitor. Basically it's a reliable and pain-free way to manage diabetes.

G2: How big is it?

J: Small. Handheld. It weighs about 35 grams. How about I pass round a prototype for you to have a look?

B: Excuse me, Jessica, can I just ask … ? I understand the components are made in China. Is that right?

J: Yes, they *are* made in China … but we assemble the product here in our Manchester plant. Just across there, in fact. Any more questions?

B: I'd like …

G3: Yes, please can …

J: Yes, please, go ahead.

G3: Thanks. What was the reaction to the product?

J: Very positive, actually. There are several articles in medical journals. I can send you some links.

G3: That would be great. Thanks.

J: So … no more questions? Alright, then. My assistant Carol will be here soon and she'll take you to meet the production team.

B: That went really well. I had so many things I wanted to ask – but it was important to let others speak, too. Such a relaxed, friendly atmosphere. I think I'm really going to enjoy working with these guys.

2.3.4

It's clear Beata is highly motivated, not only by the programme, but also by the product.

In Option A, we see how she dominates the meeting; she interrupts continuously and even criticises the production process. She's clearly focused on getting answers to her questions. As a result, she gets information on the product but she makes a bad impression.

In Option B we see her using a more balanced approach. She's much more respectful, not just to the speaker but to the other participants as well. This time, she makes a better impression.

So here's my advice. We all have our own agenda when we attend a meeting. The important point is to respect the other participants, and that includes the presenter. Two things: first, this means knowing

---

when to listen. And second, we should remember to watch the other participants so we know when to interrupt.

3.1.1 P = Presenter   M1 = Man 1
W1 = Woman 1   NR = News Reporter
PH = Phineas Harper

P: In business, as in life, things can and do go wrong. Imagine this situation: you are responsible for a major construction project that, after years of planning and careful project management, appears to fail in front of the world's media. A Project Manager's worst nightmare. In the case of London's Millennium Bridge, it was a nightmare come true.

The Millennium Bridge hit the headlines for all the worst reasons. As people walked across the bridge, it started to move from side to side.

M1: Bit surprised by the degree of sway.

W1: I feel very seasick, yes. But it's not too much further and we can get off the other end.

NR: The architects say that as a suspension bridge it was always intended to move, although not quite as much as it has been over the last few days.

P: What was making the bridge wobble? Was it safe? It wasn't a big movement, but people could feel it and were worried about the safety of the bridge.

PH: The Millennium Bridge opened in the year 2000, on the millennium, but that was actually slightly behind schedule and slightly over-budget, but in a project of that complexity, that's not so unusual. What was unusual; was that when people started to walk across the bridge, it began to sway, quite dramatically, from side to side.

P: The engineers were sure that the bridge was safe, but the team closed the bridge while they investigated the problem.

PH: One of the central parts of a project manager's job is risk management, so that's anticipating all the things that could possibly go wrong, and having a plan in place to reduce those risks. And in the case of the Millennium Bridge, they just didn't see the wobble coming at all.

P: While engineers investigated the mysterious wobble, the project managers also had a busy time.

PH: After a setback like this, the project manager's highest priority is to manage all the different specialist teams who are working on the bridge, but also to facilitate good communication between those teams. Together, they're going to have to come up with a new plan of what to do, which is going to involve setting new budgets, coming up with new schedules and agreeing new milestones; but the most important thing, immediately, is to figure out what the problem was and to find a solution.

P: The investigation was complicated and took a long time. The engineers found that the cause of the problem was the way people's bodies reacted to the very small movement of the bridge. The bridge's slight movement caused people to walk differently, and the change in their walking made the bridge move more. Engineers came up with the solution of attaching additional parts to the bridge to stop the movement. The work resulted in even greater budget and schedule over-runs.

PH: I don't think it's fair to blame the project managers on the Millennium Bridge for the wobble, because although we've known that lightweight bridges are prone to lateral motion, that phenomenon of thousands of people synchronising their steps had never been seen before. So, it's not the kind of risk you can just predict easily. However, from now on, you can be sure that at the top of every project manager's risk register, 'bridge wobble' will appear.

P: Two years after the initial problems, the bridge finally reopened, and it remains a popular London attraction. It has not suffered from any further severe movement. Despite that, it is still known in popular culture as the 'Wobbly Bridge'.

3.3.1 D = Daniel B = Beata C = Clarice

D: The thing is, I'm going to be really busy on Jessica's new project for the next few weeks. So I need Beata to do the day-to-day work on the Diabsensor.
I'm sure she'll be able to stand her ground and deal with the various issues. But, if she does have problems, I'm still the project manager, and she knows that my door is always open – apart from when I'm having my lunch break. That's my time.
B: Daniel mentioned that he would like me to speak to Clarice about the new requirements. I'm sure I can handle it. I've worked with sub-suppliers and clients on many other projects. And Daniel is always close by, in case I need him.
D: Clarice. Good to see you. This is Beata. She'll be taking over from me as your main contact on the Diabsensor. As you know, Clarice is our main sub-supplier on the project. Her company will be sending us almost all the components. She's almost as vital to the project as I am.
C: No one could be as vital as you, Dan. Very pleased to meet you, Beata.
B: Likewise. I'm looking forward to working with you.
D: I have a meeting room booked. Shall we … ? So, that's the tech side covered. There's just the details of the shipment deadlines to sort out. We need to make some changes. Beata, I'm already late for another meeting. Can you bring Clarice up to speed?
B: No problem, leave it with me.
D: Great.
B: He's so busy today. Well, we all are.
C: It looks that way.
B: Anyway as Daniel said, I think there is a problem with one of our shipment dates … Here we are. April 17th. That's when the delivery is supposed to leave your factory, isn't it?
C: Yes. Four weeks from now.
B: And the container will arrive on the 28th of May?
C: That's the plan.
B: The trouble is that one of our deadlines has been moved forward so we need at least some of the components by the 10th of May. I should have the details here … ah. Yes. These ones. The new schedule would mean we need at least one shipment early, probably by air.
C: Hmmm. Difficult. That will put a real strain on the budget. We planned to ship everything by sea. It was going to be part of a consignment for the UK.
B: There's no flexibility, I'm afraid. We really need the components earlier. Two weeks earlier, in fact.
C: OK. I understand your position. I think we can do it. Just let me recalculate the budget. There'll be additional costs.
B: But … is that really our responsibility? The original shipment was due in by the 9th of May. You changed it to the 28th.
C: That was all cleared with Daniel. Arrangements have been made. If we had known otherwise, we would have shipped earlier.

3.3.2 B = Beata C = Clarice

B: But things have changed now. You need to meet this new deadline. I'm afraid I can't compromise on this.
C: So there's no flexibility at all? How about a few days later?
B: I'm afraid I'm just not that flexible. My hands are tied. We need that shipment by the 10th.

C: Alright. Let's be clear here. You now need me to get these components to the UK by the 10th, and I have to cover all the costs myself?
B: Exactly, yes.
C: Seriously, Beata – there's nothing you can do here? No flexibility? Fine. Leave it with me. I'll call the factory in Shenzhen and get back to you.
B: Excellent. Thank you.
I got what I wanted, which is good. And she knows that I am the boss, which is also good. I don't think I'm going to have too many problems with Clarice in the future.

3.3.3 B = Beata C = Clarice

B: Yes, I know that Daniel cleared the existing schedule, but it doesn't change anything. We still need the shipment by the 10th. As I said earlier, I have no room for manoeuvre on this.
C: It's a pity we don't have another container leaving this week. We could have sent them straightaway. As I say, they're ready to go.
B: So it seems to me we have two problems here. I need the components to arrive by the 10th. You need to be able to cover additional costs. How about this? I could speak to one of our other suppliers. We have another container leaving China this week. Maybe they'll have some space?
C: That could work. We're talking two cubic metres, maximum.
B: Let me make some calls.
C: I'll see if we can get the components down to the docks in time. Pretty sure we can. Do you know where the container is right now?
B: Probably still in the factory.
C: Where's that?
B: I couldn't point it out on a map … but I know it's in Guangzhou. That's near Shenzhen, right? Looks like this could be a win for both of us.
C: A big win. And all before lunchtime, too.
B: I'm very happy with how that meeting went. I got what I wanted, and I think that listening to Clarice and trying to solve her problem, made our working relationship stronger. That will help me in the future.

3.3.4

We all have times when people tell us what to do. We all have times when we need to tell other people what to do. In the clip we see two ways of doing this.
In Option A, we see how Beata chooses to use her authority to get the job done – she's in charge and she knows that Clarice will do what she wants.
In Option B, we see Beata and Clarice working together to find a solution to the problem. So here she also achieves what she wants, but the outcome seems to be better for Clarice. I think in this option their relationship improves, too.
Of course, every situation is different, and it is impossible to say what always works best. But there is an English proverb which might help: 'to put yourself in the other person's shoes'. How would you feel if someone didn't treat you in the way that you treated them? Would you still respect them and work hard for them? This is a question every person in authority has to think about.

4.1.1 P = Presenter ST = Susanne Taylor
BL = Betty Liu LM = Lawrence Maltz

P: Whilst markets may be global, not all products are universal. Multinationals need to analyse their target territories, adjust their marketing strategy and adapt their products to meet local preferences. China is a vast country with a rich elite and the world's largest middle class. This makes it a highly attractive market to multinational companies. There's a strong appetite for Western goods and brands. Chinese consumers have their own preferences. Therefore, product customisation is an

important consideration for selling into China. This can affect both high-end luxury goods as well as mass-market consumer brands.
Cars are one example at the luxury end of the scale. Volvo launched a new high-end sedan in Shanghai. It is customised for the Chinese market. They have removed the front passenger seat to make more room in the back and added a host of luxury features. Why? Because wealthy Chinese have drivers and won't ever need the front passenger seat. They want more room in the back.
Jaguar adopted a similar approach for their new sedan. They didn't go as far as removing a seat, but they packed the rear with luxury features.
ST: The focus is on chauffeur-driven. There's a lot of chauffeur-driven cars within Hong Kong and mainland China. It's a very unique product that we think really appeals to premium customers who want a good experience in one of our cars.
P: But it's not just the richer consumers in China who are spending money on Western goods. China's huge middle class is a good opportunity for mass-market consumer brands.
But those global brands also have to adapt – even if only slightly.
For example, at the opening of Starbucks' flagship store in China, we could see that the Starbucks branding – known all over the world – was different. The words weren't there. This made it clearer for consumers used to the Chinese alphabet.
The rest of the world associates Starbucks with coffee. China, however, is the home of tea. So in China, Starbucks has adapted the brand to specialise in selling a range of premium teas, whilst still offering the same 'Starbucks experience' to consumers.
BL: Some of the teas that they're going to sell in China: black tea with ruby grapefruit and honey. And then there's a green tea with aloe … so you know that … that … continues to … um … reinforce that premium feel of Starbucks, right? That you're drinking something a little bit different.
P: And, of course, Starbucks also hopes to convert the Chinese to coffee.
LM: You know people say why … why … go to China, because they drink tea and not coffee? And I'm saying, what an opportunity. You know … We believe that the coffee consumption will continue to grow here, and we want to set a standard for that growth.
P: China will continue to grow as a market for multinational companies wishing to appeal to the middle class and the wealthy. And while the market continues to exist, so will novel adaptations of Western products in the Asian market.

4.3.1 A = Alex B = Beata

A: So, will it be your first time in Rio?
B: Yes, first time. I feel worried. But I know I shouldn't be. I don't really know why. I was in Japan for five years. I'm used to travelling.
A: Don't worry. You'll love Rio. I've been there twice. I guess you'll be meeting Mateo, right?
B: Mm.
A: Daniel's probably explained by now. Mateo is a nice guy but he can be very domineering. Likes the sound of his own voice. It's difficult to stay on track sometimes.
B: I'll bear that in mind. Here is my main worry, Alex. I think I'm well prepared. I bought a book about Brazil: history, customs and so on. But I have a feeling it's going to be really difficult. I'm only there a couple of days. Will that be enough time to get to know Mateo? What about the local market? Or how we can adapt the Diabsensor to its needs.
A: Seriously? Don't worry. You'll be fine. Just remember Mateo likes to multitask. Just go with the flow.

4.3.2 M = Mateo B = Beata

M: ... on a vacation last year. Great memories. What about your family? Are your parents in the same field as you, the healthcare business?

B: Ah, no. Dad's a professor. Mum worked various jobs but she's basically retired now. Can we move to the Diabsensor?

M: Which university?

B: Excuse me?

M: Your father, the professor. Which university is he at?

B: Erm ... Warsaw. The Chopin University of Music.

M: Ah, the Chopin University. That's not too far from the National Museum. I know Warsaw well. It's one of the world's great capital cities.

B: I'm very fond of the place, too. Anyway, the Diabsensor ...

M: There will be plenty of time for that later. Remind me. What's the name of that really tall building in the middle of Warsaw? I went to a trade fair there once, many years ago.

Alô!

Tchau. Tchau. Obrigado novamente. Tchau.

B: Is this a good moment to start talking about the Diabsensor?

M: Relax. We'll come to that later. Back to the tall building. Do you know the one I mean?

B: The Palace of Culture and Science?

M: The Palace! That's it. That reminds me. I met Jessica Scott there for the first time. What was the event again? I think I still have a programme somewhere around here. Do you want to see it? Don't worry. We'll get to the Diabsensor in a moment.

B: Mateo, I really think we should get to the Diabsensor now. We don't have long to talk.

M: If you insist. Fine. I just thought you would be interested in the programme. That's all. Before I forget, tell me again why Daniel couldn't come.

B: Wow. We certainly have very different approaches. In the end Mateo seemed a little unhappy when I took control of the conversation. I tried again and again to bring him back to the Diabsensor. But he wanted to talk about other subjects. I see what Alex meant about multitasking.

4.3.3 M = Mateo B = Beata

M: ... on a vacation last year. Great memories. What about your family? Are your parents in the same field as you, the healthcare business?

B: My parents?

M: Yes, are they in the healthcare business?

B: No, not at all. Mum had various jobs, but she's basically retired now and dad's a professor.

M: Oh yes? Whereabouts?

B: Warsaw. The Chopin University of Music. He's a bit of a musical mastermind.

M: Ah, the Chopin University. That's not too far from the National Museum.

B: You sound like you know Warsaw well.

M: I adore Warsaw. It's one of the world's great cities. I've been there twice. Remind me, what's the name of the really tall building in the middle of the city? I went to a trade fair there once. Many years ago. *Alô! OK. Tchau. Tchau. Obrigado novamente. Tchau.* Now, where were we?

B: I think you were talking about the Palace of Culture and Science?

M: The Palace! That's it. That reminds me. I met Jessica Scott there for the first time. What was the event again? I think I still have a programme somewhere around here. Want to see it?

B: Of course.

M: Great. And don't worry. We'll get to the Diabsensor in a moment.

B: He liked to talk a lot! But, as Alex said, it really was best to go with the flow. I didn't want to seem rude or uninterested even though I really wanted to discuss the Diabsensor. Mateo has a very different way of handling meetings to me and I had to respect that.

4.3.4

Mateo and Beata are different in terms of nationality, age, experience, status and personality. In this case Mateo seems very comfortable with the situation and is in control. He decides the topic of conversation. Beata can do little to change Mateo's more dominant style.

So, she has two choices. She can try to get Mateo to follow her agenda and talk about the Diabsensor, or she can simply go with the flow and see what happens.

If she tries to push her own agenda, she might save time, but she might also affect the business relationship. On the other hand, if she goes with the flow, she might build up the business relationship, but she could also end up losing control of the situation.

5.1.1 P = Presenter SD = Scott Drummond
M1 = Man 1 M2 = Man 2 MP = Mike Peng

P: These lunchtime diners in San Francisco are intrigued by a fully automated restaurant that looks more like a computer store with touch-screen ordering and freshly made meals, delivered in a box.

SD: Technology is allowing us to provide a product at an unprecedented speed, so the time-pressed consumer in the financial district really doesn't have the patience for the old ways of going out and buying food, interacting with somebody who might not hear your order correctly.
We've addressed that by creating a process that's incredibly fast, incredibly precise and ultimately gives the customer much more control about what they want for lunch.

P: I had to try it for myself. Much like any other touch-screen menu, it starts with the swipe of your credit card. You can customise the menu. The food here is all vegetarian. Once your order is placed, it's prepared at lightning speed by chefs working behind the scenes.
So here it is, that was less than two minutes, the food has been delivered, it says here tap twice, the door opens and here's lunch, with my name on it, my balsamic beet salad. Looks good.

M1: Usually we only have half an hour, 45 minutes for lunch, so it's nice to be able to come out during actual lunch hour and get a quick healthy lunch. This is the first time I've seen anything this automated and this high quality coming out of a machine. I've seen, you know, they have similar things in Amsterdam, but the quality of the food isn't half as good.

M2: I think that we're moving away from social interaction and this is just completely facilitating that. We didn't have to talk to anyone to get our, to get, uh, food made for us, which I don't necessarily think is the best thing, but it's certainly, um, I think the direction where we're all going.

SD: We've just taken the model and figured out how to interact with the customer differently, it's a completely different way of uh, assisting the customer in making the choices that are best for them.

P: Other restaurant chains have embraced touch-screen technology to replace humans. It's a trend in the business, fewer staff and a more automated approach to ordering food.

SD: What we're doing is changing the way that the workforce is contributing to the preparation of food. So instead of having, you know, a cashier, or five cashiers, um, we've created other opportunities for those, those workers, both in terms of being involved in the technology that's supporting the restaurant, um, having opportunities to interact with customers in a different and more personal way.
And in the process, not dissimilar to any innovation where technology comes in, changes the ball game, we believe that other jobs and other types of jobs will be created, they just won't be minimum-wage traditional restaurant jobs.

MP: Well, a lot of what we do is bring our clients out here to be inspired by, sort of, either new technologies or new services, new platforms, and so we had heard about Eatsa, and so we wanted to drop by and, kind of experience it ourselves.

P: But in Japan you have similar restaurants to this, don't you?

MP: Yeah, there's a lot of vending machine-type restaurants, so meaning, like, you would order your food via vending machine and you get a ticket and you hand the ticket over and you get your meal automatically, but nothing as, sort of, designed, I think, as this and so I think that's why we wanted to experience the sort of, there's so many different magical moments uh that are just, kind of, uh, really fun.
And so once they introduce the app and you can order it and just go pick up your food, I think that's really gonna disrupt the current food business today.

5.3.1

I'm so glad that's over. Mateo wasn't focused at all ... lots of questions about my family, non-stop talk about his trip to Warsaw. I suppose it was all good experience though.
I'll be talking to Daniel soon. But what should I tell him? If I go into detail on all the difficulties ... he might think that I can't handle things. I think I'll just give him an overview. If he wants to know more ... well, I'll just play that by ear.
OK. Let's do this. Sightseeing later.

5.3.2 D = Daniel B = Beata C = Clarice

D: So, Beata ... tell us about your meeting with Mateo. Then you can go and enjoy some sunshine. You've earned it.

B: Well, he talked a lot about the colour of the product. His team carried out some market research last month ... interviewed patients, healthcare professionals, pharmacists ...

C: Wait, wait, wait. Did you say pharmacists?

B: Yes. They did some focus groups ... sent out a really detailed questionnaire ...

C: And *that's* what he asked them about? The colour? Seriously? What's wrong with the colour? Why did they spend so much time on this?

B: Sorry. I didn't really have a chance to ask.

C: You didn't?

D: Mateo can be a little domineering, Clarice. Have you ever met him?

C: No, no I haven't. Sorry. Please go on, Beata.

B: Well ... according to their focus group results – I have them here if you want to see them – people prefer the darker shade of ....

D: Beata, ... what does Mateo want us to change, exactly?

B: The colour of the Diabsensor. But I told Mateo I'd get back to him. I hope that was OK.

D: Of course. You did the right thing. Clarice, what do you think? Can we change the colour?

C: I'm sorry, no. It's really not possible at this stage of the production schedule.

D: Right. I thought so. Anyway, Beata, tell us about the rest of the discussion.

B: There's possibly some problem with storage, but we can come to that later. And ... ah, yes, the packaging. There's a problem with the design.

D: What do you mean, a problem with the design of the packaging ?

B: Mateo doesn't think it's very practical.

D: So, what does he want exactly? Does he want us to change the design?

B: Well ... yes.

D: Are you sure?

B: Erm ... yeah ... I guess so ...

D: Next he'll be asking for a whole new product altogether. Clarice? Is it possible to change the packaging design?

C: Maybe. I'll have to check with our product manager, but at this stage … it's a long shot.
D: It's a very long shot, I know. How long will it take for you to confirm this?
C: I'm not sure. We're closed tomorrow for a public holiday.
D: Can you get back to us by Monday?
C: Monday? Yes, no problem.
D: Beata, do you have any other news for us?
B: Um, no … That went well. I wasn't totally sure Daniel wanted to know all the little details … but I'd rather he knew everything.
Anyway. Sightseeing time!

5.3.3 D = Daniel B = Beata C = Clarice

D: So, Beata, over to you. Tell us about your meeting with Mateo. And once you're done, you can go and enjoy some sunshine.
B: Of course. There's not much to tell really. Mateo wants to change the colour of the product to a darker shade of blue.
D: The colour of the Diabsensor itself or the packaging?
B: The colour of the Diabsensor. I told him I'd get back to him. I hope that was OK.
D: Of course. Clarice?
C: I'm sorry, it's not possible at this stage of the production schedule.
D: Yes, I thought so. So, tell us about the rest of the discussion.
B: There's possibly some problem with storage, but we can come to that later. And … um, yes … they wanted to change the design of the packaging, but I told them that wasn't possible. That's about it, I think.
D: Really? Nothing else? Mateo must not have been in a talkative mood. For the first time in his life …
B: Yes. That's everything.
That went well. There was no point in boring them with all the little details – we would have been here all day. And if Daniel wanted to know more information, he would've asked more questions.
Anyway. Time to join the tourists!

5.3.4

This clip is about managing information. In both options, Beata talks about the same meeting but, as we see, the information that comes across is quite different. There's a lot of detail in option A. In Option B, some things are left out. We can see how important it is for all participants to ask the right sorts of questions to get the information they need. A meeting is productive when it ends with everyone knowing what actions are required.
In Option A, Clarice and Daniel ask a lot of questions. They agree on one action point for Clarice: she needs to check if changing the design is possible. Beata mentions the storage problem, but it is not discussed.
In Option B, Clarice and Daniel don't ask as many questions about packaging and colour because Beata gives them all the information at the beginning. The meeting in Option B is shorter but key information is still communicated.

6.1.1 P = Presenter PN = Paul Neal

P: Safety is an important issue for all businesses. Companies must ensure that their operations are safe not only for their own employees but also for the public. Safety procedures are often regulated by law.
O'Donovan is a waste disposal company in London. I went along to find out how they manage safety across their operations.
Tell me who you are and what O'Donovan does.
PN: My name is Paul Neal. I'm the Logistics Supervisor here at O'Donovan Waste. O'Donovan Waste is a skip company where we collect waste from around London and recycle it.

P: The company's trucks operate on busy roads. Safety procedures that include measures for protecting the public are a priority for the company.
PN: We identified at an early stage there were too many cyclists being killed on London's roads, so we try to do as much as we can to reduce that. We initiated a programme where we tried to get the vehicle lower, so the driver can actually see more around the cab. And what we did was we fitted side guards to the vehicles just to see how low we could actually get them before they hit the ground.
P: And I also understand that you've fitted cameras and electronic sensors to all your vehicles.
PN: That's right. We have spent up to a quarter of a million pounds fitting these cameras and a system to the vehicle which tells us back at the head office how the vehicle is actually being driven. If we have any problems on the road, we can review the footage that the cameras take. They are 360 degrees, so we can see what's happening in front, to the rear and to the sides.
P: At O'Donovan's recycling centre, workers handle a wide variety of waste materials that do pose a risk of injury. Paul is responsible for maintaining a safe working environment for staff. This begins with suitable protective clothing for everyone.
How do you make sure your staff are safe both on and off site?
PN: Everyone is issued with the correct clothing to work in these environments. Also every couple of months at our head office in Tottenham we hold training programmes.
P: Tell me more about the personal safety equipment that your staff have to wear.
PN: Well, it starts from the top with the hard hat. We wear a hard hat. Firstly, anything could fall on top of your head, but what we find more often is, as people are walking around, they could hit something with their head. High-visibility clothing. With movement of vehicles we want everyone to know where everyone is. We have cut-resistant gloves. The employees are sometimes handling sharp debris. Also a mask. In the shed it can be quite dusty, so we have a mask to protect the breathing. Also steel toe-cap boots, just in case anything drops on the foot.
P: What happens if there is an accident on one of the O'Donovan sites?
PN: Well, unfortunately, accidents do occur, and if they do, we have trained staff on site, first aiders – that's the first port of call. After that, once the injured party is OK, we'll record everything. We have an accident book which we fill in and then, after that, we would try to learn what happened exactly and how we can go forward to make sure this doesn't happen again.
P: How much does all this investment in safety actually cost your business?
PN: Well, as a company, we don't see it as a cost, we see it more as an asset. We understand that by becoming a safer company, it's going to benefit us in the long run.
P: Paul, thank you very much for your time.
PN: My pleasure.
P: Nice to meet you.
There's no doubt that the safety culture at O'Donovan Waste Disposal is strong. They don't see it just as an issue of compliance with regulation, but as a core part of what they do and who they are.

6.3.1

I've got a really tough meeting with Mateo tomorrow. How will he react? Your guess is as good as mine.
I'm finding him more and more difficult to work with. He doesn't want to follow our regulations on storage procedures. So I'm going to have to

negotiate with him and … I'm not sure 'negotiation' and 'Mateo' go together well. Here's the big question: can I keep things professional and positive with Mateo while also *insisting* he accepts our storage regulations? We can't compromise on safety. But if I mess this up, that might make a bad impression with Daniel.

6.3.2 M = Mateo B = Beata

M: Let me get this straight. The Diabsensor needs storing at around five degrees Celsius?
B: Yes. It must be refrigerated, otherwise it's unsafe.
M: Sorry, but I disagree. Our storage team say there's no problem storing it at room temperature.
B: That may be the case, but …
M: Beata, I like you. You're good at what you do. I just don't think you quite understand – regulations are different here in Brazil.
B: I understand. Really. Nonetheless, perhaps we can talk about …
M: You don't have to worry about all those EU rules. We have our own safety regulations and we are very strict about them. We can store this product, no problem. Would you like to see the certificates?
B: We really appreciate all the work you're doing. But unfortunately …
M: I've told you, Beata. The plan is to launch the Diabsensor as soon as possible. Do you have any idea how much pressure that puts me under? We carried out a successful campaign at our diabetes clinic last week. My team has received all the necessary training. Look, I can assure you – we're all excited about this new product. It's going to change lives.
B: It's great that you've already done so much to promote the product. I'm sure Daniel is going to really appreciate this.
M: So am I. *Very* sure. Daniel and I have always worked very well together. I'll even speak to him myself and explain the situation. How does that sound?
B: Sounds good. I'll get him to call you.
Not the outcome I wanted … but at least Mateo seemed pleased. He'd rather speak to Daniel than me, that's pretty clear. I was able to keep things professional … even if I'm starting to think Mateo doesn't respect me. At all.

6.3.3 M = Mateo B = Beata

M: Let me get this straight. The Diabsensor needs storing at around five degrees Celsius?
B: Yes. It must be refrigerated, otherwise it's unsafe.
M: Sorry, but I disagree. Our storage team say there's no problem storing it at room temperature.
B: As I explained, Mateo … it's a question of safety. The product must be refrigerated. If we store it at room temperature, we can no longer guarantee that it *will* be safe.
M: Beata, I like you. You're good at what you do. I just don't think you quite understand – regulations are different here in Brazil.
B: I can assure you …
M: You don't need to worry about all those EU rules. We have our own safety regulations and we are very strict about them. We can store this product, no problem.
B: Yes, but unfortunately …
M: We are under a lot of pressure. Some of us more than most, perhaps.
B: Please. If I could just finish my point …
M: The plan is to launch the Diabsensor as soon as possible. My team has received all the necessary training. Look, I can assure you – we're all excited about this new product. It's going to change lives.
B: And *I* can assure *you* … the product needs to be refrigerated. I want you to understand, Mateo. *This* is a question of patient safety.

M: And, as I said earlier, I disagree. Storage is not a problem. We have the capacity, the staffing. Everything is in place. No cause for concern.

B: I understand that this is difficult for you. And you've already done so much to help promote the product. But my position is clear. We can't go ahead with the delivery unless the necessary storage measures are in place.

M: Fine. Let's see what Daniel has to say, shall we?

B: I have no doubt that Daniel will say the same thing. I'm sure we want the same outcome, Mateo. But either you find a compromise, or I can't approve the delivery.

M: You're being difficult, Beata. I don't like it. To be frank … I'm not sure I can work with you. OK. I'm going to speak to Daniel. You've left me no other choice.

B: I'm sorry you feel that way. I'm not comfortable agreeing to the delivery without the correct storage measures in place. And if you want to speak to Daniel, fine. I'll ask him to call you. Well … he's not happy. And neither am I. Still, what can I do? We can't compromise on safety. And I know for a fact Daniel is going to say the same thing. I just hope he's not annoyed with the way I handled this.

6.3.4

Beata uses quite different approaches with Mateo in this clip. In Option A, she focuses on maintaining a good professional relationship. She wants to avoid arguing with him, and succeeds. Mateo is still able to dominate the conversation and by the end, he thinks he has what he wants.

In Option B, she's more forceful and shows more confidence in her communication style. Her voice is slightly lower and she uses pauses to indicate important information. Her body language shows she's feeling much more confident and this gives the impression of more authority.

My suggestion is: if we need to explain rules and requirements, then we'll be more successful if we try to build or maintain a good professional relationship with the other person. One way to do this is to show we understand the other person's situation. But we still need to maintain our authority.

7.1.1 P = Presenter SC = Siobhán Creaton
C = Customer A = Agent LN = Lisa Francesca Nand
OM = Oscar Munoz BA = British Airways employee

P: In the early days of air travel, flying was an elite experience. All passengers got VIP treatment. Today, everyone flies. The airline industry gives passengers a choice of different levels of customer service. You can choose between classes and carriers offering a premium service – where they handle all your bags, you get a big seat and lots of personal attention – or you can go for a low-cost service. There are plenty of them: take AirAsia, Jetstar, Peach, for example. They just get you there cheaply.

Ryanair is a pioneer of low-cost, 'no-frills' flight. With flights often costing as little as the price of a good dinner, you're going to queue, and if you don't like that, you can pay for priority boarding and any other extras.

Journalist Siobhán Creaton has written about the airline and its CEO, Michael O'Leary.

SC: They offer you a cheap flight, it brings you from A to B, it gets you there safely and usually on time. That's his definition of customer service. He's always made it clear that they're not going to put you up in a hotel if your flight is delayed, that that's not part of the package.

P: The 'no-frills' model is popular worldwide. But it has a problem. There's a good chance customers will get angry when something goes wrong. Low-cost airline, Easyjet, approaches the challenge of dissatisfied passengers with training sessions

in assertiveness and interpersonal skills. These Easyjet trainees are roleplaying typical customer service problems.

C: Right, I've got … my husband's on his way. So if you could just check us in, that'd be great.

A: Where he actually is he? Is he parking the car or … ?

C: He's parking the car, yeah, he'll be … I don't know how long he is going to be …

A: I can't physically check him in without actually seeing him; well, passport-wise I have seen him. I have got to make sure he is, you know, is the same person. Yours is OK, you're fine.

C: Yeah, I know but I can't travel without him. We're going on holiday.

A: I'm sorry but I can't actually check you and your husband in without actually seeing your husband.

P: When confronting upset customers, employees are trained to use body language but not raise their voice.

C: He handled me perfectly, he brought … I was … I could have been quite anxious or angry and he brought me right down. So, James was fantastic.

LN: In the premium service segment, companies add on those little extras, those exclusive features that they feel help them justify asking a higher price tag. Each of the airlines in this segment work really hard to try and find that distinctive customer service experience so they can then charge more for it.

P: United Airlines, for example, works hard to attract business-class and first-class passengers with features like no queue to check in. The company likes to speak up about developing its customer service.

OM: We spent thousands of hours, thousands of hours, meeting with not only customers but with employees and doing a lot of extensive research … and as you might expect, the VIP treatment, the food, all of those things came into place. But interesting, our research showed that a good night's sleep was by far the most important.

P: Flag carrier British Airways distinguishes its high-price, first-class service not just in practical ways like priority baggage, but also through an elaborate ritual on board: afternoon tea.

BA: A lot of our customers from around the world will book a British Airways ticket … um … for the afternoon tea … because they like the Britishness of us.

LN: It's typical of a premium approach to customer service that businesses want to make people feel important and to focus on those things. So for the airlines, for example, it's providing things like a nice business lounge for them to relax in; it's providing them with a comfortable bed to sleep on when they're in the air. For a business like banking, it's something completely different, like increased levels of flexibility, but it all boils down to the same business issue: you can charge more if you make people feel better cared for.

7.3.1 D = Daniel B = Beata M = Mateo

D: This must be a let-down after all that gourmet coffee at the hotel in Rio.

B: I wish!

D: So take me through the main issues. How can I put Mateo's mind at ease?

B: He won't follow our recommendations and refrigerate the sensors. I was very clear: if there's no safe storage, there's no guarantee he'll get the product. He didn't like that. He kept saying I was overcautious.

D: And that's how you left it?

B: Pretty much, yes.

D: Strange. I wonder if something else is going on. Does he have other possible suppliers, perhaps? Or does he have budget issues?

B: There's one thing I did notice. All of the refrigerators were really full at Mateo's facility. Maybe he just had a big delivery.

D: Or maybe they have a shortage of refrigerators and no money to buy new ones? Only one way to find out.

M: Hello?

D: Hi, Mateo. It's Daniel. How are things?

M: Daniel, nice to hear from you. All good here, thank you.

D: Likewise. Anyway, Beata has filled me in on all of the details. It seems to me that we've got almost everything we need, except for one or two small things. I just want to hear your side of things before we have our meeting next week. I just want to make sure everything is OK for the contract signing.

M: Everything is fine, overall. But those small things you mention … Maybe some of them aren't so small after all.

D: Go on. By the way, just so you know, Beata is in the room with me. You're on speakerphone.

B: Hi, Mateo.

M: Beata, how are you?

B: Fine, thanks.

D: So, shall we get started?

7.3.2 M = Mateo D = Daniel B = Beata

M: It's nothing personal but Beata is new, so maybe there are some things that she doesn't understand. My experts assure me that there is no problem storing the sensor at room temperature, whereas Beata insists that it must be stored at five degrees.

D: Of course. Let's get back to that in a moment if we may. What about all the other issues? Delivery dates, colour, quantities, price?

M: All fine. The colour isn't right for me but I understand nothing can be done at this stage. As for everything else … Well … Storage is the only issue, really. I tried and tried to explain to Beata: things are different here in Brazil. And it goes without saying, really, no guarantee – no sale.

D: Absolutely. You've made that very clear.

M: I hope so. I'm not happy, Daniel. I'm not happy at all.

D: Mateo, may I ask a direct question?

M: Daniel, you know me. No need to ask.

D: What's your refrigeration capacity at the moment? Do you have enough storage space?

M: I'll be honest. Storage space is a problem here. But that doesn't really matter. The issue is whether or not we have to refrigerate the Diabsensors. And believe me – we don't.

D: OK, look, don't worry Mateo. I'm sure we'll come up with a solution. Let me do some calculations and speak to my people. And when you come over to Manchester next week , we'll talk some more and I'm confident we'll come up with a solution. How does that sound?

M: That sounds good. Just one thing, though.

D: Yes?

M: Please make sure it's not raining.

D: I'll see if I can schedule some sunshine. No promises, though. Speak to you soon.

M: Bye, my friend.

D: What's wrong?

B: It sounded like you agreed with Mateo. That you think I don't know what I am doing.

D: What? No, no. You're completely in the right. I wanted to give Mateo the impression that I was neutral, just to see what he would say. It's a tactic, that's all. Don't worry, I'm 100 percent on your side.

7.3.3 M = Mateo D = Daniel B = Beata

M: It's nothing personal but Beata is new, so maybe there are some things she doesn't understand. My experts tell me that there is no problem storing the sensor at room temperature, whereas Beata insists it must be stored at 5 degrees. I tried and tried to explain to Beata: things are different here in Brazil.

D: Well, I have to say that she's right, I'm afraid. Five degrees is the required temperature.

M: So Beata said. And I'll tell you exactly what I told her. No. We just don't see the need.

D: Yes, she told me about that. OK, Mateo, let's get back to that in a minute. What about all the other issues? Delivery dates, colour, quantities, price?

M: All fine. The colour isn't right for me, but I understand nothing can be done at this stage. According to Beata, at least.

D: Yes, Beata is correct about that.

M: Fine, no big deal. The only other thing is this storage nonsense. Beata says she can't guarantee us the product if we store it at room temperature. And it goes without saying, really: no guarantee – no sale.

D: Hmm. Yes, I have to say Beata is absolutely right on this. But please understand I see your point. Your positions are both very clear.

M: I'm not happy Daniel. And neither are my diabetes teams.

D: Yes, I understand that. Beata told me about your teams. Mateo, may I ask a direct question?

M: You can always be direct with me, Daniel. You know that.

D: What's your refrigeration capacity at the moment? Do you have enough storage space?

M: I'll be honest. Storage space is a problem here, but that doesn't really matter. The issue is whether or not we have to refrigerate the Diabsensors. And believe me: we don't!

D: OK, look, don't worry Mateo. I'm sure we'll come up with a solution. Let me do some calculations and speak to my people. I'll go through all the details again with Beata, too. And when you come over to Manchester next week I'm confident we'll come up with a solution. How does that sound?

M: Perfect. See you next week. And please a little less rain this time.

D: I'll see what our Sunshine Department can do. Bye.

B: Thanks for supporting me.

D: No problem. You're completely in the right. And I wanted Mateo to know that.

7.3.4

As we see in this clip, the customer is not always right. Daniel has to find a way to make Mateo understand that the sensor cannot be stored at room temperature.

This type of situation can be very difficult to deal with.

As we also see in the clip, there are different approaches. In Option A, we see Daniel simply listening and not making any comments. Basically the idea is to appear neutral and gather information. Mateo has no idea if Daniel agrees with Beata. In Option B, Daniel also listens, but shows clearly that he agrees with Beata, and will support her. In this way, Daniel shows that there is a red line which cannot be crossed.

8.1.1 P = Presenter CC = Professor Cary Cooper
**MB = Mike Brogan E1 = employee 1
E2 = employee 2 E3 = employee 3
E4 = employee 4 E5 = employee 5**

P: In the last thirty years digital technology has transformed the way we communicate in the workplace. A British company, Procure Plus, is tearing up the communications rule book. Let's see their story.

This is Mike Brogan. He and his team rely on digital technology for business. But Mike worries about their dependence on email to communicate with each other. And he's also concerned that his team spends too long working online after hours.

E1: Do I check my emails outside of work hours? Yes. Do I do it while I'm on holiday? Yes. Do I do it at the weekend? Yes. And I think that, worse than that, I tend to use the evening to try and catch up on emails. But because everybody else is doing that, it's a bit of a negative because people keep replying.

P: Professor Cary Cooper reckons this dependence could be harming the business's productivity. But, he has a plan.

CC: We have to find a better balance. Not only for our health, and the health of our families, and our relationships outside. But, actually, for the productivity and performance of our businesses.

MB: We're here today actually to conduct an experiment and we're very fortunate to have Cary Cooper here, Psychologist from Lancaster University, who's going to tell you a little bit more about what we're doing today.

CC: Thanks, Mike. We have a number of rules. From noon today, all internal emails will be banned for the rest of the week. So, you'll have to communicate eyeball to eyeball, face to face with all your colleagues. No texts, calls, emails, anything at all to do with work after hours. This should be a fun week, let's try to get our life back.

We're currently the servant to the technology. We have to take over and become the master, and if we do that properly, then I think we'll get the benefits of better work–life balance, more team building, a better culture in the organisation, much more of a buzz and better morale.

P: So, for the next five days internal emails are banned, and there's a curfew on working outside of the office.

E2: I don't quite know how I am going to get all my work done between the normal working hours and not using the email or phone before work or after work because I am naughty at doing both.

P: High noon. The last email is sent and the new regime begins. We'll catch up on these gadget junkies later in the week.

MB: Last night, when I got home, I certainly felt a little bit bored at first. But then I started to feel more and more relaxed because I had nothing to think about, I suppose.

E1: I'm still a bit concerned about not replying to some emails last night, but I'll get over it.

P: The professor behind it all is back to see how they've got on.

CC: Well, the week's over and I just want to really thank you for getting involved in this. We've suspended technology a bit, haven't we? We've tried to control technology. We have become the masters rather than the slaves of it.

So, Mike. The week is up. How have you found it?

MB: There's a buzz about the place. Now we're seeing people moving about. There's a hum around the office that wasn't there before.

CC: It's kind of a balance, isn't it? Between the need for technology and working more humanly with the people you're working with.

P: But it's not just Mike who's excited about the changes.

E3: There's been a good atmosphere this week. People have talked to each other more.

E4: Actually, I've come in on a couple of days and had no emails. No new emails!

E5: It has really helped me get to know my colleagues a lot more.

CC: All the technology interference - the emails within the business - I think has overloaded people and actually reducing that has produced, I think, really positive results, in this work environment.

P: So that experiment suggests that when it comes to communication, less is sometimes more. Perhaps, especially, where technology is involved.

8.3.1 D = Daniel B = Beata M = Mateo
D: Feeling optimistic?

B: Yes, actually. I think we've got the perfect solution for Mateo. It's a win-win.

D: Me too. Just don't get too technical. We need to focus on the benefits. I really want to close this deal today.

B: I'll try to keep things simple.

M: Hello, everybody. It's like a cinema in here. Any popcorn?

D: We're all out of popcorn, I'm afraid. Welcome, Mateo. Really good to have you here in Manchester.

M: It's good to be here. And it's not even raining this time.

D: Well, I can't take credit for that, much as I'd like to. So, shall we get started? We've come up with some ideas that will hopefully solve the refrigeration problem we discussed, or at least put us on the right track.

M: Excellent.

D: I'd first like to review where we are, just to make sure that we're all on the same page, so to speak. Then we'll discuss outstanding issues. Hope that's OK? I've put a summary on these slides.

8.3.2 D = Daniel M = Mateo B = Beata
D: So that just about sums it up. We've agreed on the delivery dates, quantities, colour …

M: Yes, yes. That only leaves the same point as before. The refrigeration issue. It's still outstanding.

D: I think we may have a way around that problem. As I understand it, your, erm, local rules do not require the sensors to be refrigerated. But we feel that we simply can't guarantee the performance of the product without that refrigeration. Does that sum up the situation as you see it?

M: Exactly.

D: Beata has an idea. Beata.

B: Thanks, Daniel. So, I was doing some research into the packaging options. At the moment we plan to send you the sensors in insulated containers that keep the sensors below five degrees during transport. Now, these containers will keep the temperature stable for the journey to Brazil, but once they are opened the sensors need to go into a refrigerator.

M: Beata, I've told you countless times …

B: Hear me out. I've found a supplier that produces portable refrigeration units. These can be connected to an exterior power source at a reasonable price. So in other words these containers are more than insulated coolers. They can also be connected to a power supply. Then they act as refrigerators.

M: So what you mean is that I don't need to put the sensors into refrigerators? They already come in refrigerators?

B: Correct.

M: But if we use these portable refrigerators won't the cost go up? Let me tell you: refrigerators are not cheap.

D: True. And yes, the containers are a little more expensive, however we are prepared to cover that extra cost providing you buy enough sensors. We are confident that you will be happy with the product and will continue buying from us.

B: In return we would need you to provide the power supply when the containers arrive. You would need to plug the boxes into your power supply on arrival. And they don't use much energy, so I don't think this will be a problem for you. Here are the specifications.

M: This is a perfect solution. You're both geniuses. Move over, Einstein. To sum up, you provide the containers, and I provide the power supply. Great. Here's what I'll do. I'll take a longer look at the specifications and chat to my technical team, and if it is as you say it is, we will be able to go ahead.

D: You were a bit too heavy on the technical details, Beata.

B: Oh, I'm sorry.

D: Don't worry. I think he actually appreciated it in the end. Great work.

8.3.3 D = Daniel M = Mateo B = Beata

D: So that just about sums it up. We've agreed on the delivery dates, quantities, colour ...

M: Yes, that only leaves the same point as before. The refrigeration issue. It's still outstanding.

D: Right, it is. But I think we may have a way around that problem. As I understand it, your, erm, local rules don't require the sensors to be refrigerated. But we just can't guarantee the performance of the product without refrigeration. Does that sum up the situation as you see it?

M: Absolutely.

D: OK. Well, Beata has an idea I think you might be interested in. Beata.

B: Thanks, Daniel. Mateo, I think you're really going to like this solution. Not to mention the hidden benefits it provides. I was doing some research into the packaging options and I figured out that we can change the type of package we use. As you know, the plan right now is to use insulated containers to keep the sensors cool, but you would need to put the sensors into a refrigerator after the journey ...

M: Beata, we've been through this over and over ...

B: ... which is why we have a new package now. One which also acts as a refrigerator. After they arrive, you simply plug in the containers into your power supply and the sensors remain cooled.

M: So what you mean is that I don't need to put the sensors into refrigerators? They already come in refrigerators?

B: Yes.

M: But if we use these portable refrigerators, won't the cost go up? If there is one thing I know about refrigerators, it's that they're expensive.

D: That's true. And yes, the containers are a little more expensive, but this supplier that Beata found is using quite interesting technology to keep the costs low. We are prepared to cover the extra cost providing you buy enough sensors. We are confident you will be happy with the product and will continue buying from us.

B: In return we would need you to provide the power supply when the containers arrive. I think your diabetes teams will be very happy.

D: And there's another benefit, too. Once the sensors have been used you end up with empty refrigeration units, which you can use for other things. You know, like keeping your drinks nice and cold.

M: If you keep my drinks cool, you're guaranteed to keep me happy. Great solution, my friends. To sum up, you provide the containers, and I provide the power supply. Let me speak to my technical team, and if it is as you say it is, we will be able to go ahead.

Do you have any information about how much power we would need?

B: Right here.

M: Thank you. Excellent. Excellent.

D: Nice work. Light on the tech stuff. Just like I asked.

B: We make a good team.

D: We certainly do.

8.3.4

One key skill to end a negotiation is to summarise what has happened so far, so that everybody understands what still needs to be done. Daniel does this very well.

Daniel also has to persuade Mateo that he has a good solution.

The refrigeration problem has not yet been sorted out. In this clip, we see two possible ways of doing this.

In Option A, Beata presents a technical solution, which she explains in some detail. In Option B, she focuses less on the technical aspects and more on the benefits. As we see, both these approaches work.

As always, what we decide to do depends on lots of factors – the issues, the personalities involved, the relationships and so on. At the end of the day, the skill is in finding ways to communicate well with your business partner.

1.01

A: Hello, caller …
B: Hello?
A: Yes, hi. Welcome to the show. What can I help you with today?
B: Hi, Jenny. I'm a recent graduate – I have a good degree. The problem is, I'm finding it hard to get a job interview. I mean, forget getting a job … I can't even get an interview.
A: OK …
B: I'm using social media – a professional-networking website – and I have a few contacts in the industry I want to work in …
A: That sounds good so far … using these sites is a great idea.
B: But honestly, I don't think there's anything on my profile that's special. I mean – I use all the right words – I'm creative, I'm good at problem-solving, I'm hard-working …
A: … but everyone says that.
B: Exactly. Everyone says employers want those things, so everyone uses the same description of themselves! So my question is: How can I make myself stand out from the crowd on social media?
A: That's a great question, caller, and I'm here to help. So first, why not try deleting everything you've written about yourself?
B: Delete everything?
A: Yep. And after that, why don't you take your description of yourself – creative, good at problem-solving and so on, and for each word, think of an example from your own experience that *shows* who you are?
B: Er … OK, like …
A: You said you're creative. How about telling me about something creative that you've done?
B: Sure, OK. Er … when I did my degree, I created a website for one of my projects. I designed it and took the photographs for it and everything.
A: That's great! So you really should put that on your social media profile – you designed and built a website. What's next? Did you say you're good at problem solving?
B: Yeah …
A: So how can you show me that?
B: Problem solving?
A: Right.
B: Well, this isn't related to school or work, but I do a lot of hiking and camping. A few times, I've had serious issues with weather or broken equipment, and I've had to figure out what to do.
A: OK, you could consider putting something about that on your profile. Explain your love of the outdoors and how you deal with the challenges in your hiking and camping.
B: I've never thought of putting that on my profile …
A: Well, you ought to think outside the box – and you need to *show* employers who you are instead of just *saying* who you are.
B: Yeah, I understand – I get it. That's really helpful. Thank you so much.
A: No problem. Good luck with your new profile and with getting some job interviews!
B: Thanks!

1.02

A: Hello, caller …
B: Hello?
A: Yes, hi. Welcome to the show. What can I help you with today?
B: Hi, Jenny. We spoke a few weeks ago …
A: OK …
B: And I just wanted to let you know … I still have a problem.
A: Really? So can you remind me – what was your problem?
B: My professional networking profile – it wasn't working.
A: Oh, sure, OK, I remember. So … my advice wasn't useful?
B: Well, not exactly. I mean it *was* useful … Maybe a bit *too* useful.
A: Ha, ha – OK, I see. So what's the problem now?

B: Too many choices! I followed your advice, and soon after, when I applied for six jobs, I got four interviews.
A: Well, congratulations!
B: And after four interviews, I got two job offers. And my problem now is that I can't decide which job to take.
A: OK, well, why don't you tell me about the two jobs?
B: Basically, one looks very interesting but not very well paid. The other, honestly, is probably a bit boring, but the money is good.
A: And you're a recent graduate, right?
B: Yes, that's right.
A: And you're single – no kids?
B: Yep, that's me.
A: OK, I think you should follow your heart. Why not try asking yourself which is more important: money or excitement?
B: That's the problem, Jenny – I really can't decide! University cost a lot of money, and I want to pay back my loans. That will take a lot longer with a low-paying job.
A: Yes, I see what you mean. OK, well, let me ask you a few more questions. What …

1.03

My first piece of advice is, be prepared. Find out which companies will be attending the careers event, choose five or six that might be interested in your profile and research them online. Visit their careers pages and find out which ones are hiring or offering internship programmes.
Update your CV and make several copies. Then, prepare an 'elevator pitch', or brief introduction – let's say 30 seconds – to talk about yourself: who you are, what you do and your past experiences. Be prepared to explain how your skills can be useful to their company. Also, think of questions to ask such as: What is the training programme for new recruits? What do you look for in a candidate?
On the day of the careers event, make sure you dress as you would for an interview – look professional. Choose your company, then network, don't interview; your aim is not to get a job interview immediately – in fact this rarely happens. Instead, introduce yourself, shake hands and make good eye contact. First impressions are important, so speak clearly and confidently and demonstrate your ability to interact professionally. Recruiters are looking for people who are adaptable and resourceful, but also ambitious and passionate. Be honest. If you don't know something, say you don't know, but show the recruiter you can learn and learn quickly. Most importantly, don't forget to get the recruiter's contact details so you can follow up afterwards.
After the event, email the recruiters or company reps you met and thank them for their time. Remind them of the conversation you had and repeat your interest in their company. Send an updated CV if necessary. Ideally, you should do this within five days after the event.

1.04

1
E = Ella   R = Recruiter
E: Hi, I'm Ella, I'd like to ask you a few questions, if possible.
R: Yes, of course. How can I help you today?
E: I heard you were taking on new recruits. Can I give you my CV?
R: Yes, of course. Which department are you interested in, Ella?
E: Oh, anything in marketing, I don't really mind. I've just always wanted to work in the tourism industry. I have a degree in marketing and I enjoy travelling.
R: Well, OK, that's a good start.
E: Can I take a brochure? I'd like to learn more about what you do.
R: Sure. Here you are. And here's my card. If you have any questions, I'd be happy to answer them.

E: That's great. Thanks for your help. Sorry, what was your name?
R: Ben Richardson. I'm the Assistant Recruitment Manager.
2
R = Recruiter   J = Jamie
R: Good morning. How are you enjoying the fair?
J: I've only just arrived to be honest, but there are a lot of very interesting companies present though. Sorry, could I just ask you a few questions about Travelogue?
R: Yes, of course. Have a seat. What's your name? I'm Ben Richardson and I'm the Assistant Recruitment Manager.
J: My name's Jamie, Jamie Mitchell.
R: Good to meet you, Jamie. So, what can I do for you?
J: I've just graduated from the University of Manchester with a marketing degree, specialising in tourism. I know you're busy, but I'd like to talk to you about my skills. I think they might be useful to your company.
R: Congratulations on getting your degree.
J: Thank you. I understand you're looking for Junior Marketing Associates.
R: We are, Jamie, that's right. What kind of practical experience do you have?
J: Well, I did my internship with a team that developed a marketing plan to promote UK tourism for a small village in Spain.
R: That sounds interesting. Can you tell me more about that?
J: It was for a small village in the south of the country. As I said, we created this marketing plan and then presented it to the local tourist board and it was adopted.
R: I see, wonderful. It sounds impressive. As you probably know we do a lot of work in Italy.
J: Oh, really? I speak a little Italian.
R: OK, that might be useful. Do you have a CV?
J: Sorry, I just gave away my last one, but I've got a business card. There's a link on there to the village website that I helped create.
R: Thank you very much. And here's my card.
J: I'd like to know more about the work you do in Italy. Can you put me in touch with the person in charge of your marketing projects? I'd like to ask them some questions if possible.
R: If you send me an email, I'll do that.
J: Can I take a brochure?
R: Here you are. It's been nice talking to you. Enjoy the rest of the event.
J: Thank you for your time, Ben. I really appreciate it.

2.01

Message 1
Hello, this is a message for Emma Newman in HR. My name's Mark Thomas, T-H-O-M-A-S and I'm calling about the logistics position you interviewed me for last Thursday. I'd like to discuss the financial package in more detail if possible. Could you call me back please on my mobile – that's 0044-7623-911-129. That's 0044-7623-911-129. I'm available until 4 p.m. today. If not, then you can send me an email so we can we fix a time to speak. I look forward to hearing from you. Thanks. Goodbye.
Message 2
Hi, it's Carla again. Erm, I hope I've got the right number. Erm, my message got cut off last time so I'm calling you back just in case. Er, erm, yeah, I've got wall-to-wall meetings all afternoon and then I have to leave early so erm I don't really have time to send an email, but the internet was down yesterday, anyway, so, er. Anyway, erm, I'm super busy as you can imagine. I wanted to speak to you about the candidates we interviewed last week for the logistics job. Er, what did you think? Not bad, erm…
Message 3
Good morning. This is Zhanna Petrovna in Logistics. Could you ask Emma to call me back? We have a bit of a problem with the references for one of the shortlisted candidates. If she can call me back on extension 4385. It's pretty urgent now, so I'll expect her call by the end of the day.

2.03
Message 4
Good morning. I want to leave a message for Emma Newman. This is Daniella Rossi, R-O-S-S-I, returning her call. Emma asked me to contact her to discuss the terms of my new consultant contract. I'm available to talk until 2 p.m. today but then I'm in meetings all afternoon. In case she doesn't have my mobile number, I'm on 07654 322 187. Otherwise, maybe she can leave a message with my assistant, Elliot Barber. Elliot is on extension 5283, that's 5-2-8-3. Sorry, can she also re-send a copy of my new contract? I can't open the document. I hope to hear from you soon. Many thanks.

2.04
A = Alice   M = Matthew   S = Stanley
A: Morning, Matthew. I'd like you to meet Stanley Dongoran, our Indonesian business partner, who's helping us set up the factory in Indonesia.
M: Hi Stanley, nice to meet you.
S: Nice to meet you, too.
A: So, Stanley what do we need to do now?
S: Well, the first thing is to get the licence from the Indonesian Investment Board. I've already submitted everything for that and it'll be ready next week.
M: That's great, so we'll be able to visit Indonesia then?
S: Yes, I think next month would be a good time to go.
A: What will we have to do first when we get there?
S: We'll need to open a bank account and then we've got to think about the factory – those are the priorities.
M: You mean we need to find one or the land for one?
S: The land. I've found a couple of suitable locations and we're going to visit them to make a final decision. Then we can arrange all the documents we need to register the business premises. All these things take time but we can get the process started.
M: How long exactly?
S: Here's the time schedule for each element.
A: Thanks.
S: Then we've got to organise all the other permissions we need. That's all on the schedule, too.
M: Right. Are we going to interview some local people for jobs while we're there?
S: I've found three great candidates to be the Site Manager for you to interview. We're going to meet them and have formal interviews so you can choose someone.
A: Thanks. Matthew, can you organise the flights and accommodation for the trip tomorrow?
M: Of course.

Ext2.01
N = Nikolay   A = Aiko   G = Genna   P = Philip   S = Sam
N: Good morning, everyone! We're going to discuss what we need to do about the problems we had last week.
A: Well, I think we should look for new suppliers. Our current supplier is always late and deliveries have been incomplete.
N: That's true, but their materials are excellent quality.
P: Yes, but we can't afford to lose any more production time because we don't have supplies.
N: OK, Aiko, can you look for alternative suppliers and give us the details at next week's meeting?
A: Sure. I'll get onto it straight after this meeting.
P: We also need to employ more factory staff. We can't produce the quantities on time even when we have the supplies. Two people left last month and we haven't replaced them, have we, Genna?
G: That's true. Nobody asked me to replace them. You said you thought you could manage.
N: I think you'd better advertise for new staff this week and ideally have some candidates ready

to interview sometime next week. What about Wednesday?
G: Certainly.
P: I'm sorry, but even if we have the staff and the supplies, we've got problems with the equipment, which keeps breaking down. We really need to buy some new equipment. Is that possible?
N: It might be. Philip, can you let Aiko know by tomorrow what you want?
P: Absolutely. That'd be great.
N: Now, I understand we've had a lot of complaints from customers this month. We need to do something about that quickly or we'll lose customers. Sam, can you write a report for me about the problems and your strategy for dealing with it? I'd like it by Thursday this week if possible.
S: Yes, of course. I'll get onto it immediately.

2.05
K = Kenzo   S = Susan
K: We need to discuss how we're going to keep everyone informed about the potential takeover of the company by Bines plc. Firstly, I think we should send a letter to all employees about the situation guaranteeing that no jobs will be lost if Bines takes over.
S: Why don't you meet the staff and explain it to face first? I think they'd appreciate that.
K: Yes, but not yet. Email all staff inviting them to a meeting on Friday 15th in the staff room. I'll tell them then.
S: I'll email them straight after this meeting.
K: We can send them a letter with all the details after we've told them face to face.
S: OK. Good idea. And what about our customers? We don't want them to hear about this from the newspapers. Shouldn't we let them know that it's business as usual?
K: Yes, I agree. We can do that after we've signed the contract on Wednesday 20th. How do you think they'll respond?
S: I think they'll be concerned about quality. Bines are not known for their quality and customer service, as we are.
K: They'll still get the best customer service we've always offered and we'll make sure the quality doesn't suffer. Bines don't want us to lose that.
S: Do you think it would be better to speak to our biggest customers individually?
K: I think that'd be a good idea, actually – before we announce it to the world.
S: Exactly. So we won't send out a press release until we've spoken to our biggest customers then.
K: Exactly.

3.01
China's Grand Canal, which connects the cities of Beijing and Hangzhou is 1,700 kilometres long. It's the longest artificial waterway in the world, and an important shipping route through the years. But what's more amazing than the length of the canal is its age. Work on the project began in the fifth century BC – more than 2,500 years ago. There was never a plan or budget for the whole project. A series of Chinese governments built and extended the canal in sections over a period of 1,700 years, finally finishing it in the 1280s. When they were working the hardest on the project, five million men and women were involved in the construction – mostly labourers, but also engineers. Today, only the section between the cities of Hangzhou and Jining– about 500 kilometres – is open for shipping. It is about 100 metres wide at its narrowest point. In some places, the canal is less than a metre deep. The Suez Canal in Egypt connects the Mediterranean Sea and the Red Sea. Work started in 1859. They thought the project would take six years, but they finished later than planned, in 1869 – four years behind schedule. At one point five million people worked on the project – mostly labourers, but also engineers, accountants and project managers. Some sources say that at least 30,000 people were working on the canal at all times during its

construction. The project ran 1,900 percent over budget. The total cost was $100 million. But it is still one of the most important shipping routes in the world. With a length of about 190 kilometres, the canal makes the journey between the North Atlantic and the Indian Ocean much shorter than going around Africa. It reduces the trip by 7,000 kilometres, making the journey less difficult and time-consuming. At its shallowest point, the canal is about twelve metres deep and fifty-five metres wide.
The Panama Canal, in Central America, connects the Atlantic and Pacific Oceans. In 1881, a team from France started work on the project after seeing the success of the Suez Canal. However, the Panama team had to work a lot harder than the Suez team. Construction in the jungles of Panama wasn't as straightforward as digging in Egypt's dry, sandy desert. In fact the digging itself was the least challenging part of the job. Dealing with the heavy rains made work impossible at times. The team missed target after target, soon falling behind schedule. They finally gave up in 1889, when they ran out of money. Fifteen years later, an American team took over the project. Work on the canal began again in 1904. It took 75,000 workers ten years to build the seventy-seven-kilometre canal – four years longer than the original estimate of six years. The team included engineers, specialised machine operators and of course labourers. Finally, in August 1914, the first ship passed through the canal. Amazingly, although the canal cost $375 million to build, the project came in $23 million under budget. At its narrowest point, the canal is about thirty-three metres wide and twelve metres deep.

3.02
1 It's the longest artificial waterway in the world.
2 But what's more amazing than the length of the canal is its age.
3 When they were working the hardest on the project, five million men and women were involved in the construction.
4 They finished later than planned.
5 It is still one of the most important shipping routes in the world.
6 The canal makes the journey between the North Atlantic and the Indian Ocean much shorter than going around Africa.
7 It reduces the trip by 7,000 kilometres, making the journey less difficult and time-consuming.
8 The Panama team had to work a lot harder than the Suez team.
9 Construction in the jungles of Panama wasn't as straightforward as digging in Egypt's dry, sandy desert.
10 In fact the digging itself was the least challenging part of the job.

3.03
Bid A
We can start the installation two weeks from now, on February twentieth. It will take our two technicians five days, but you can continue working in the office the whole time, so it's convenient. Our price doesn't include product support – we can provide a separate bid for that. But we do guarantee the hardware and the installation for three years. We can do the job for 13,000 euros.
Bid B
We can do the job next week, on February the thirteenth. We can send ten technicians and finish the job in one day, but you'll need to leave the office completely empty for us, so we can work. The price includes full product support and training, if you need it. This also includes the hardware manufacturer's standard one-year guarantee. It will be 17,000 euros for everything.
Bid C
We need to order the hardware from our supplier, and it will take three weeks to deliver. That means I can start the job one month from today – on the

sixth of March. I'll do the installation myself, over three weekends – so it will take three weeks to finish, but you won't see me. It won't interrupt your work at all. I'm happy to give full product support, and I guarantee the entire installation for two years. The whole package is 11,000 euros.

3.04
Part 1
Welcome to our first stand-up meeting. No sitting down. The idea is that these meetings will be over very fast, not more than fifteen minutes, and the aim is to bring us all up to date about what is going on in the team. This is very important. It is for all of us, not just for management.
From today these take place every morning at 9 a.m. This is a new type of meeting for most of us, so I will just explain what we plan to do.
It's very simple. I will start by throwing this ball to a person. The person with the ball then gives the rest of us three pieces of information. One: What they did yesterday. Two: What they plan for today. Three: Any problems or impediments that they see. That's it. No discussion. They then throw the ball to another person, who answers the same three questions. We go on until everyone has spoken. After the meeting I will then follow up and speak to individuals about any action items. Any questions? No? Good. OK. Let's start with Jack. Catch!

3.05
Part 2
J = Jack S = Sal T = Tom TL = team leader
J: OK. Yesterday I worked on the new contract for the China project. Today I have a meeting with the lawyers to clarify some of the questions I have. So the draft contract is in progress, and I expect to complete it today. The only impediment I see is time – the lawyers say they can only give me one hour, and it may not be enough.
S: Hi, everybody. So ... I had a meeting with a sub-supplier in the morning, where we agreed some new deadlines. We followed up the meeting with a nice lunch. And then in the afternoon I went to the dentist. Today my plan is to finish writing a summary of yesterday's meeting, and then I'll be briefing the production team leader. I don't see any impediments at the moment.
T: OK, I'm planning to work on the designs for the new logo for the rest of today. Oh sorry ... Yesterday I spent most of the day discussing ideas for the new logo ... with different departments. That was difficult because I didn't have any fixed appointments with anybody so it was really a matter of luck. ... So today, as I said, I'll be working on the designs and then I'll be discussing them with the people I missed yesterday. Hopefully. If they are available. Oh, I nearly forgot. Yesterday I also met with one of the new designers who will be working on this project until the end. Thank you.
TL: Thank you, everybody. That's great. My turn now. I've been working on the schedule for the factory shut down in November. Nothing to report. I'll be spending most of today working on the plans and I hope to finish them this afternoon. I'll then be discussing them with the boss before they go public, so I won't be answering any questions at this stage.

3.06
Part 3
B = boss TL = team leader
B: How are we doing with the redrafting of the China contract?
TL: Jack is handling that. He's meeting with the lawyers today, and is hoping to finish the draft today, too.
B: That's good. What about Sal's meeting with the sub-suppliers yesterday? I saw her in the canteen. What's happening with the deadlines?
TL: Well, they did agree some new deadlines, but I haven't seen them yet. I'm sure they'll be OK.
B: And where are we with the logo?

TL: Tom's working hard on that. He's going round the departments getting feedback, and he's meeting with the designers. It's all in hand.
B: Can you bring me up to date on the programme for today?
TL: Well, let's see, Jack is doing the contract, Sal is writing up yesterday's meeting and doing some briefings, and Tom is working on the logos. I'll be focusing on the new schedule and the factory shut down.
B: Ah, yes. What's the latest on the new schedule? Let's see ... Can you give me an update on the plans?
TL: Yes, I can do that now, if you like.
B: Fine. When will you be able to bring me up to speed on the factory shut down?
TL: I should be in a position to do that this afternoon. Can I come round your office, say four-ish?
B: Sounds good. Thanks.

4.01
Part 1
OK, so what I want to do today is focus on ways of building consensus. Building consensus is all about finding what the group wants to do, not what each individual wants to do. It's about group needs, not individual needs. Sometimes we need to meet halfway, to find the middle ground. And sometimes we will be persuaded that one way is best. We will do some practice activities later on, but first I want to remind everybody of two basic principles we all need to follow. First, if we want to build consensus, we must make sure that everybody is involved in the conversation. Everybody must have the chance to speak. And second, everybody's opinion is of equal weight and is to be respected. No one in the group is more important than anyone else. OK? Got it? Good, so now here's what we are going to do.

4.02
Part 2
M = Manager J = Jose T = Tanya S = Sam D = Dorothy
M: So the first thing we are going to do is decide as a group how we want to proceed. We have three options. We can stay as one large group, we can break into smaller groups, or we can work in pairs. Any thoughts? Remember, everybody must be involved in the discussion, and everybody's opinion is to be respected. Yes, Jose? What do you think?
J: So I think we should stay as one big group. There are not so many of us, and it will be easy for everyone to be heard.
T: I'm afraid I disagree. It will be much better in smaller groups. That way everyone gets much more talking time.
S: I agree with Tanya. Much better. With a big group one or two people always dominate.
D: Yes, I agree, too. We can be much more efficient if we work in small groups.
J: Well, I don't think my idea is that bad. I agree that in a big group one or two people could dominate, but that is easy to fix. We use talking sticks.
S: What are talking sticks?
J: Each person has two sticks. This gives them the right to talk twice. Each time they say something they must give up a stick. When they have no more sticks they cannot talk. That way everyone has the same chance.
S: Actually, that's not a bad idea. But we will need more than two sticks.
J: That was just an example. Of course we need to decide how many sticks to use.
D: So we need to find consensus about the number of sticks before we can even start a real discussion?
M: That's a good point. Yes, we need to decide on the process before we can move to a discussion. So nobody is interested in working in pairs? Good, OK. So we're already narrowing down the options

and moving towards consensus. Not everybody has spoken, so I would like to hear what the rest of us have to say. Sandrine?

5.01
Kendra
Good morning. Today, I want to introduce you to the new ZX3 Hot-Seat. The ZX3 Hot-Seat is a portable, heated seat. It's designed for sitting outside, especially in cold weather, either in the park or at a music or sports event.
So first, let me talk you through the product specifications. As you can see from the slide, the ZX3 seat is made of memory foam that automatically moulds to your body shape and is designed to be extremely comfortable. It has a removable, washable cover made of a water-resistant nylon mesh that comes in a choice of three colours – red, blue and green.
The ZX3 Hot-Seat measures 940 by 480 mm, and weighs just 1,050 g. As you can see, it comes with retractable arms to provide maximum comfort. Each arm measures 300 by 125 mm, weighs 45 g, is made of lightweight plastic and comes in black or grey. As well as two USB ports, the ZX3 also has an optional plastic container used for holding hot or cold drinks. Finally, the heavy-duty rubber handles and padded straps are designed to make transportation easier ...
Paolo
So you've heard Kendra telling you about the features of the ZX3 Hot-Seat. It's a great product, but what's in it for your customers?
How many football fans in the audience today? Quite a few. You must agree nothing beats watching your favourite team play at the stadium. But when it's cold and wet, wouldn't you rather be in the warmth and comfort of your living room? Well, the ZX3 Hot-Seat is the solution. For example, its heated seat means you can combine the excitement of the stadium with the comfort of home. For added comfort, there are optional arm-rests which allow you to sit back and relax as you watch the game, while the plastic cup-holder lets you enjoy your favourite drink at the same time. The Hot-Seat has a washable cover so it's easier to clean, plus the lightweight seat with handles and straps make it easier to carry.
Kendra mentioned the Hot-Seat has two USB ports, so you can recharge your mobile devices if you need to. In today's instant world, we know how important this will be, especially for younger customers. This also lets you post pictures on social media of those all-important goals, as they happen.

6.01
Jenn
Security is a big issue in the hospitality business although it can be very different depending on the hotel category. I mean, some low-cost hotels these days don't even have an in-room safe for people to keep their valuables in, and I think that's crazy. I work in a five-star hotel and guests need to use their room key card in the lifts to get to their floor. You just touch your room key card to the pad and the lift automatically selects your floor. You also need the room key card to get from your floor back down to the lobby. I think it's becoming quite standard in newer city hotels. Not everyone likes it. Some guests complain it's annoying when they want to visit another floor. Of course, you don't have to take the lift. You can get access to other floors by the stairs, but it's like setting your house alarm or locking your doors. It's not going to make it completely impossible for someone to commit a crime, but it's an extra barrier.
Paul
You know I've never thought about it before, but security is very relaxed in the university building where I work. Students and staff are walking in and out all day long and anyone can just walk in off the street. There's only ever one receptionist

on duty and she has to answer the phones, deal with queries and work on the computer, so she can't possibly keep an eye on everyone who comes and goes. And whenever she needs to go somewhere or take a break, the reception area is completely unattended. There are signs on the walls in all the classrooms warning students to keep their valuables with them, and lecturers have to remember to lock the staffroom door, but it's not ideal and we occasionally have had problems with theft and vandalism. There aren't even CCTV cameras in the corridors.

Aisha
I've worked in a multinational IT company for almost ten years now. We need to leave our mobile phones with the guard on reception and he puts them into a locker and you mustn't bring in any pen drives or any type of USB storage devices to the office. In the past you didn't need to wear your photo ID, but now your badge must be visible on you at all times. If a manager or the security guard catches you without it, they'll say something. And you need it for everything. You see, it has a chip with radio frequency identification which you have to use for checking into and out of the building, and it opens doors based on your access to certain areas. And you have to use it to print or scan anything as well.

6.03
Part 1
A = Alex T = Tony
A: I've told you several times already about the cleaning problem on the factory floor, Tony.
T: Yes, you have, and I've told you – several times – that the ZX390 needs repairing. We had another leak yesterday. As far as I'm concerned, I've followed procedure. I reported the fault on the machine. It's over to you now.
A: I appreciate it's difficult for you, Tony, and thank you for telling us about the leak. However, it's important that your apprentices clean up as they work. The management team are worried this is a real hazard.
T: It *is* a hazard. But I'm sorry, this is *not* my responsibility. My apprentices don't have the time to clean. And what happens if someone slips and falls? We need a full-time cleaner. He only comes in the evening and that's often too late.
A: Tony, as you know we're a small business. We just can't afford a full-time cleaner.
T: I understand what you're saying, Alex, but what's the solution? We need to repair the ZX390. I reported the problem ten days ago.
A: Yes, but to repair the 390 we will have to stop production. This is impossible – we need to meet our deadline for the Japanese order.
T: I know that, but it's also important that we fix it as quickly as possible.
A: I totally agree. I can see it from both sides.

6.04
Part 2
T = Tony A = Alex
T: So how do we proceed?
A: I think we need to come to a compromise so that we can complete the Japanese order.
T: OK. So, what's your solution?
A: Well, my suggestion is to supply your team with slip-resistant footwear. That will help prevent accidents.
T: Uh-huh, sounds like a good idea. But what about repairing the machine?
A: Well, as we both agreed, we will lose time if we stop production. So, let's complete this order first and I'll request an engineer to fix the leak. Can I just check you're happy with this idea before I speak to the management team?
T: Yes, that's fine with me.
A: And then let's review this situation at the end of the week.
T: Sure, why not?
A: Great. I'll put that in an email, just to summarise what we've agreed.

7.01
1
R1 = Recorded message 1 D = David
A = Angela K = Kabir
R1: Welcome to Noderphone. This call may be recorded and monitored for training purposes. All our agents are busy right now, please hold. All our agents are busy right now. You can also visit the Noderphone.com website for customer service information.
D: Good afternoon, my name is David. May I have your name, please?
A: Yes, it's Angela Parsons.
D: How can I help you, Angela?
A: My internet connection isn't working.
D: Is the account in your name?
A: Yes, it is.
D: Can I just ask for some further identification? Can you give me the phone number for this account, Angela?
A: Yes, it's 0208 892 2149.
D: Thank you, Angela. I'll put you through to our customer service agents. Can I ask before you go, do you have any mobile phone numbers you'd like to add to your account? There is a special offer right now.
A: No thank you, David. I only have one mobile and it's already on this account.
D: OK, just transferring you now.
R1: All our agents are busy right now, please hold.
K: Hello, Angela, my name is Kabir, how can I help you?
A: I just told your colleague, my internet isn't working.
K: I see. Have you tried switching off the router and turning it on again, Angela?
A: I'm sorry, I can't hear you very well. Could you speak up, please?
K: Yes, of course. Have you tried switching off the wifi router and turning it on again?
A: Yes, I've done all that. The lights don't come on as usual though.
K: OK, I'll re-boot it from here. This will take a few seconds. I'll just put you on hold …
K: Hello Angela, can you tell me if the lights start to come on on the router?
A: Yes, something's happening. They've started coming on. There's a yellow light, and now two blue on the left, oh, and another yellow one on the right.
K: Are you in front of your computer?
A: Yes, I'm just trying to get into my email. Yes, it's working now.
K: Is there anything else I can assist you with this afternoon, Angela?
A: No, that's fine, thanks.
K: Have a nice afternoon.
2
R2 = Recorded message 2 A = Angela J = Judith
R2: Welcome to Noderphone. This call may be recorded and monitored for training purposes. Please say the phone number about which you have an issue. If it is the phone from which you are calling, say 'It's this phone.'
A: It's this phone.
R2: How can I help you today?
A: I have a query about my mobile phone bill.
R2: I'm sorry, I don't understand. For internet services, press one; for television services, press two; for … press seven; for technical support, press eight; or please hold to speak to an agent.
J: Good morning, this is Judith speaking. Can I have your name, please?
A: At last! Yes, it's Angela Parsons. It's taken me fifteen minutes just to speak to a real person.
J: I'm sorry for the long delay – we're receiving lots of calls today. How can I help you, Angela?
A: I want to query my mobile phone bill for last month. It's ninety-three euros thirty-eight cents. That's more than three times what I normally pay.
J: Can I just ask your date of birth for verification purposes?
A: Yes, it's 23rd June 1988.

J: Thank you, Angela. I'm just looking at your bill on the screen. Yes, I see you were in Andorra and there was a roaming charge of forty-six eighty-seven.
A: What? A roaming charge? Why?
J: Andorra isn't a European Union country. It falls into our Rest of the World, Zone 2.
A: But … I don't remember using the phone's data, I used the hotel's wifi connection and I only called my mum a couple of times. Look, could you possibly reduce the charge?
J: I'm sorry, we can't do that, Angela. We always recommend contacting customer services to check roaming charges abroad before you travel. Next time don't forget to do that. You can also find the information on our website.
A: Well, I'll certainly remember to look for a cheaper operator as soon as I can.
J: Can I help you with anything else today?
A: Yes, could I speak to your supervisor, please?
J: I'm afraid she'll give you the same information.
A: Well, I still want to speak to her anyway.
J: OK, I'm just transferring you now.

7.04
We all have good ideas. They come to us when we're reading or listening to music, in conversation with friends, or alone with our thoughts. But most of the time, they just disappear. I think there are many reasons for this. We may simply forget. We may be afraid of being laughed at. But I think mostly it's because we don't have a system for capturing them.
So I want to hear your ideas about how we can generate more ideas, and how we can share them with each other. But it's not enough just to have good ideas. What I want to do in this session is to brainstorm ways we can capture those ideas to make sure we don't lose them. Yes, we need to be creative, to experiment, to innovate, to explore, to imagine. But we also need to think about how we put our creativity into practice. So in your groups, in thirty minutes, I'd like you to come up with a list of ideas – not only for how to generate great ideas, but also how not to lose them.

7.05
Speaker 1
We think the first thing we need to do is to make lists. So we should brainstorm as many ideas as possible, and write them all down. Quantity not quality is the key. We can decide what we want to keep later.
Speaker 2
We think that the big problem is those ideas which come to us when we are not expecting them. How do we record them? We suggest everyone needs to get into the habit of carrying a small notebook. Another way is to use the recorders on our smartphones. The thing is, it's got to be easy, otherwise we won't do it.
Speaker 3
Our team would like to push the idea of mind mapping. Basically, starting with a word or phrase, and then simply writing down all the ideas that come from that phrase. So it's a bit like brainstorming, which the first group mentioned. But then we need to connect the ideas so that we end up with things that are related to each other.
Speaker 4
We like the idea of using different viewpoints to generate ideas. So everyone takes on a different role to normal, a different personality, and then tries to think like that person might think. For example, if you are thinking about ideas for improving customer service, you could take on the role of a customer, or one of the suppliers.
Speaker 5
Our team came up with the idea of visualisation, or of using pictures to record our creativity. So not just writing down the idea in normal words, but drawing a picture or a diagram which summarises the idea. Doing this helps to think the idea through

Speaker 6

We like the devil's advocate approach. Basically every time someone comes up with an idea or an innovation we take the opposite view and question everything about the idea. The risk is that we make people upset or angry, but what we want to do is make sure that we really think through the issues, instead of just accepting them. It helps prevent group thinking.

8.01

Part 1

Nowadays we all have too many tasks. Everything seems urgent, and nobody has time to wait. But part of the secret of success is not to get distracted, not to react to everything that comes to your desk, but instead to prioritise. Setting priorities is very easy to do. First, you make a list of the tasks that you need to do. Second, you compare these tasks and decide which ones are important and which ones are urgent. These are not the same thing. Important tasks have to be done because they matter to your business; urgent tasks have to be done now, even if they are not important.

In his book *The 7 Habits of Highly Effective People*, Stephen Covey describes a time-management matrix which helps us to visualise the relationship between important and urgent. Imagine a square divided into four quadrants. In the top left quadrant we put the tasks which are important and urgent. The top left quadrant is for high-priority tasks. In the top right quadrant we put important tasks which are not urgent. In the bottom left quadrant we put tasks which are urgent but not important. And in the bottom right quadrant we put the tasks which are neither important nor urgent. Bottom right are very low priority, and will probably never get done.

8.02

Part 2

So let's go through your list of tasks. I see you have numbered them. Good! Task one is not that urgent, and not that important. Don't waste your time on it. Task two is quite important, but not really that urgent. Put it in your schedule. Task three is really urgent. It is also of utmost importance. Make it your number one priority. Task four is not important, but extremely urgent. Do it today if you have time. Task five is really low priority. It's a bit of a distraction, to be honest. Put it at the bottom of your list of things to do. Do it when you have time. Task six is extremely urgent and important. Give it a high priority, please. Task seven has no priority whatsoever. It's information only. You can put it off for a while.

8.03

Part 3

One last tip. I have already said that part of the secret of success is not to get distracted. But that's only part of the secret. The other part of the secret, the real tip, is discipline. Don't put things off. No excuses. Once you have identified your tasks, just get on with them.

BW1.01

JN = JobNow representative M = Maria
A = Agata T = Taro

1 Maria

JN: Tell me a bit about yourself, Maria.

M: I'm forty-two years old, and I've been a doctor for about fifteen years, managing my own clinic. I feel very tired – exhausted – all the time. I think I want a completely new career. I'm considering going back to university for another degree, but I don't like the idea of being the oldest person on the course.

2 Agata

JN: Hi, Agata. Could you give me a little background information about yourself?

A: I'm twenty-two and in my final year of studying economics at university. I'd like to find a job in the finance sector, but I've never had any kind of paid job. I play football and volunteer at a hospital, but those are not related to finance.

3 Taro

JN: Thanks for coming in, Taro. Could you give me a quick summary of what you're hoping for?

T: I'm thirty-two. I've worked for ten years writing travel magazine articles as a freelance writer. I've seen the world, but I haven't made very much money. I want to continue writing, but in a secure job in a company.

BW2.01

M = Melanie F = Franco T = Toni

M: OK. Shall I start? I looked at the graphite mining industry.

F: Why that one in particular, Melanie?

M: Well, although we've used graphite in things like pencils for years, there's a very exciting new material called graphene that can be made from graphite. I think there could be some good investment opportunities with companies using graphene.

T: I read an article about it recently. Apparently, it's the new super material. But, what is *graphite* exactly? And where do you find it?

M: OK, here's the science bit. It's a metallic mineral made of carbon but there's so much more to it than just pencils, and, even better, there's lots of it all over the world!

F: Really? Is there enough to meet demand?

M: It looks like it. I think it's a great area to invest in. Graphene's 200 times stronger than steel and very lightweight and flexible. It's definitely the material of the future. And, because it conducts heat and electricity much faster than anything else, we find it in the touchscreens on our phones and tablets.

T: What about sports equipment?

M: That too. It's great for things like racing bikes and tennis rackets. And of course it's also fantastic for electric car batteries because it's much safer than anything else.

F: It sounds like a miracle material.

M: Yeah, it does, doesn't it? And I haven't even told you about other potential uses.

T: Really? Like what?

M: It could upload data at one terabit per second or charge your phone in just five minutes.

T: Wow, that would be useful!

M: And you could even use it to clear up nuclear waste, so it'd be good for the environment, too. That's why I think we should invest in the graphite mining industry.

BW2.02

T = Toni M = Melanie F = Franco

T: I looked at the tourism industry and the main thing to report is that tourism's very big business especially in some areas where it's expanding fast.

M: What, like package holidays?

T: That's not the only growth area. I've looked at online travel providers, cruise companies, hotel chains and mega-resorts, all of which could be good investments.

M: What's a mega-resort?

T: It's where companies develop all the hotels, villas, entertainment facilities, restaurants, etc. on one site so guests have everything they want in one place. You know, things like swimming pools, villas, a spa, sports facilities, a golf course.

F: I went to one in the Caribbean last year. It was amazing.

T: They are great. But I think we should invest in the cruise industry. More people than ever are going on cruises and profits are high. In fact several companies are building enormous new cruise ships, which are like mega-resorts on the ocean. That's the industry we should be putting our money into.

BW2.03

M = Melanie F = Franco T = Toni

M: OK, what about you, Franco? Where do you think our money should go?

F: Definitely the food industry. I know it's an industry with tight margins, but everyone has to eat, don't they?

T: That's true.

F: And people are buying more snacks than ever before because they don't have time to sit down and eat proper meals, so companies are now focusing on healthy snacks. That's what we should focus on because companies new to the industry are doing extremely well and making big profits.

M: So you think the healthy snack market is a good bet?

F: Yes. Everyone's health-conscious these days and looking for more *free-from* products, you know, snacks without sugar, salt, fat, gluten, milk, etc.

M: It's true. I'm always checking the packaging to see what's in a product. I love those healthy breakfast bars. They save me a lot of time in the morning.

F: Exactly. They're ideal for today's busy working person so it won't surprise you to know then that they're flying off shelves around the world. Growth in the healthy snack market is the largest in the food industry. And it's the smaller companies that are beating the big multinationals in the healthy fruit and vegetable-based snack market. That's the kind of thing we want to invest in.

BW2.04

Welcome to this month's investment club podcast which today is aimed at new members. I'm going to tell you about the things you should know about a company before you invest in it.

Investment always involves taking a risk. Therefore you have to make sure the risk is as small as possible and that means doing some research. For example what is the company history? Finding out as much company information as possible is vital for assessing risk. Find out who set the company up and when. Naturally, most investors want to look at the financial performance first. You will need to study the figures from the past three years at least. You do this by checking the financial reports. Looking at these allows you to see what the company is worth, the trend in sales and revenues and where the strengths and weaknesses of the company are. Although the financials are very important, don't forget to look at the management team running the company as, ultimately, they're key to a company's success. You want to find out as much as possible about their experience and skills as well as those of the employees. Ask yourself, is the leadership of the company effective and able to make the best use of the skills of employees? So you've looked at what exists now, but what about the future? You need to know what the company's future plans are. How are they going to move the company forward and how risky do you think their plans are?

These days another important thing to consider is how environmentally friendly a company is, and what their social responsibilities are. For example, do they help local communities?

BW3.01

L = Lily C = Carlos

L: OK, Carlos, sorry, but this has to be really quick. I have to leave for the airport in five minutes, so let's do this as quickly as possible.

C: Sure, sure.

L: Item one on the agenda is the 'Save the date' invitations. Are they ready to go?

C: Yes, they are. The email is ready, it's approved by Casa Paradiso – we just need to send it.

L: OK, then let's do that tomorrow.

C: Great. No problem. Tomorrow is fine. I'll take care of that.

L: Item two – the contract with Lana Gabler-Jones. Has that been signed yet?

C: No, it hasn't. Her agent – her name is Constance – says she's very busy.

L: We need to use her name to promote the event. We wanted that contract signed a month ago – July first.

C: I know. We're working on it.

L: Well, we need it today, so just get it done. Can you do it today?
C: Well, I can try. I can try. I'll email her agent straightaway.
L: OK, great. Now, item three. What's this about an engineer?
C: We talked about having an engineer explain how the wind turbines work. I've talked to a couple of people …
L: Listen, I don't think … I mean, an engineer? Sorry, but I'm not convinced. I think we need to focus on the fabulous hotel, and not on the engineering of the wind turbines. Can we just forget about that?
C: Yeah, sure. I mean, you're right. It's probably just a waste of time. We can cut that.
L: Now, the food order. Where is that?
C: We don't need to order the food until a couple of weeks before the event – so mid-September.
L: OK. But we've chosen the catering company, right?
C: Right. It's called Sam's Catering Company.
L: OK, then let's say we'll do the food order on September fifteenth.
C: September fifteenth? OK. No problem. I'll ask Sarah to place the order.
L: Anything else?
C: No, I think that's it.
L: OK, thanks, Carlos.
C: Yeah, thank you, Lily.

BW4.01
I = Interviewer G = Greg
I: As more and more smaller companies go global thanks to the rise of e-commerce and social media, the supply chain is more important than ever. Today I'm talking to Greg Marshall, Supply Chain Management Consultant. Welcome, Greg.
G: Thanks, Pritti. Good to be here.
I: What are the key factors that businesses moving into a global market need to be aware of?
G: Well, you really need to have an effective and efficient supply chain that you can rely upon.
I: How do you get that?
G: First of all, it's important to keep costs to a minimum when you are competing in a global market. If the supply chain is too long and outside of your control, you'll end up dealing with delays and other problems along the chain. You have to make sure that you can offer the best customer service at the best price so your supply chain has to be able to support not only existing local customers but also the new customers in other countries as well as in your own.
I: How important is it to understand the culture of the countries you are supplying or selling to?
G: Of course it's important and, if you are targeting a specific market, then the more you know about that market, the better. However, for smaller businesses, going global often happens without a planned strategy.
I: What do you mean by that exactly?
G: Well, a customer from another country makes enquiries and then places an order and suddenly the small business has taken the first steps to going global. But it can be a very steep learning curve because you haven't exported before or done any homework on that particular country.

BW4.02
I = Interviewer G = Greg
I: So what things do you need to consider?
G: For example, cost of increased production, distribution costs – that is, how are you going to transport the items to the customer – payment terms, currency, methods and the amount of stock you can keep as online orders come in quickly and customers expect their goods as fast as possible. And of course there are the different trading laws for each country and specific documentation required.
I: So, a small business could suddenly find themselves in a very different kind of business set-up when they start exporting?

G: Exactly. And the one thing that mustn't suffer during all the expansion is the product quality or you'll have a scandal on your hands. Do you remember the scandal in the UK when it was discovered that some food products had horse meat in them? Or the terrible scandal of tumble driers catching fire and burning down kitchens and houses? There are so many parts of the supply chain that could go wrong.
I: So are you saying that not everyone should go global?
G: Not at all. It's the way to succeed if you can learn fast and get organised. Many home businesses have become global phenomena. Did you know that some of the biggest companies in the world, including Google, Apple, Microsoft and Amazon, all started in a garage?
I: No, that's amazing!
G: So what I'm saying is that it doesn't matter where you start, it's where you go and how you get there that's important.

BW4.03
I = Interviewer G = Greg
I: So, if you were a small business owner moving into the global market, how would the business change?
G: Well, let's look at a simple supply chain model first. That'll explain it best. Let's imagine a company that makes organic apple juice. It started when Walter, a student, was experimenting in his kitchen. His supplier was a local farmer who let Walter have the apples for free if he collected them. Walter created the product in his kitchen and started selling it to his friends and neighbours, so he was the manufacturer and the retailer all in one. Already you've got the beginnings of a supply chain – local farmer gives apples to Walter who makes the juice in his kitchen and then sells it to customers; in this case his friends and neighbours. However, Walter's customer base is slowly expanding and then a local shop wants to sell his product but the order is too big for him to do alone in his kitchen. Suddenly his supply chain is changing. Because he can't get all the apples he needs from the local farmer, he has to look for new suppliers, who don't give him the apples for free, which of courses pushes the price up. Then he finds he hasn't got the time to produce the quantities ordered himself so he has to find a company to produce his juices, and he's no longer the manufacturer. Then he's got to stock the products, so he has to find a warehouse and organise distribution. Now he has become a wholesaler because he sells to the shops at a wholesale price, but he's still a retailer when he sells directly to consumers online. So you can see how complicated it could get if you don't plan properly.

BW5.01
R = Researcher F1 = Female 1 F2 = Female 2
M1 = Male 1 M2 = Male 2
R: I'd like to thank you all again for taking the time to help us out with our market research. We think smart fabric is going to be the next big thing in fashion, but we need your help to get it right. So, you've all been given a T-shirt to try out – everyone had a chance to wear it, at least for a few hours?
OK, you've all filled out some written feedback as well, but I'd really love to hear what you thought. So … who will start?
F1: The shirt looks absolutely amazing.
M1: Totally. My girlfriend couldn't believe it – how cool it was.
F2: That's completely true, but was I the only one who … I thought it felt like – like plastic on my skin, but kind of rough …
M2: I think that's the big disappointment. After about two hours, I had to take it off. It was actually really uncomfortable.
F1: You're right. And it smells strange, too …
F1: But, … so … I'm a keen cyclist – I go everywhere by bike. My shirt had the lighting-up option. A couple of times, I put it on over another T-shirt,

and I wore it cycling. So I think this could be a great piece of safety equipment, maybe – if it were brighter? It's good for being seen!
M1: Right, right – good for safety, but just really uncomfortable – it feels kind of horrible to touch it – and it smells really weird.
R: Right, OK. So what I hear is that nobody really wants to wear this next to their body.
F2: The other thing – what's the washing like? You told us *not* to wash the T-shirt.
M2: I wondered the same thing. Are there special washing instructions?
R: Yes, it definitely can't just go in the wash with other clothes.
F1: That's a huge problem. A T-shirt, especially, needs to be easy to wash.
M1: It's so cool, the fabric, but you want to do something with it where you don't need to wash it.
F2: Right. I'm thinking … I don't know, curtains?
M2: Curtains are a great idea. Or wallpaper?
F1: Yeah – you could change the colour of your wallpaper without changing the wallpaper. That would be so cool.
M1: Or back to the idea of clothing – could this be a good material for road workers to wear – like on a safety jacket? It would make them easy to see.
F2: And you could even have words, right? Like 'slow down' on the back of a safety jacket.
R: OK, yes, those are some great ideas. I'd like to just go back to …

BW5.02
M = Man W = Woman
M: It's obvious that the smart fabric has great potential – we just need to figure out the marketing mix.
W: OK, so the products we have on the list so far: cycling safety wear, road-worker safety wear, curtains, wallpaper. So two basic categories – safety clothing and home decoration.
M: Right. So let's look at cycling safety wear first. The product would be …
W: To begin with, it would be a cycling safety vest. This would work because it wouldn't be worn next to the skin, and because it makes great use of the smart fabric.
M: Right, OK. So it would be practical – it lights up, so it's safe – but also we could bring fashion to it, too, right?
W: Exactly. At the moment, there isn't a safety vest for cycling that's also fashionable. In the market, *safe* and *fashionable* are two very different ideas. So we could bring those together in a great new product.
M: OK, great. So who wants to buy that?
W: Well, I think this one probably isn't for serious racing cyclists, or sports cyclists – they don't usually wear safety gear like that. But people who cycle to work – commuters – who in fact are often very serious about cycling, they're out in traffic every day – they're probably the target market.
M: OK, agreed – at least to begin with. So that means we probably don't want to promote it in serious cycling magazines, but maybe we do want to push it in … I don't know, lifestyle magazines – travel, women's magazines, men's magazines … ?
W: Yeah, OK. And probably online. Social media …
M: Definitely, if we're selling online – which of course we will. But what about bike shops?
W: Distribution is expensive – shipping is getting more expensive all the time. That's a big consideration. But I think if people actually see the product in a bike shop, they'll want one.
M: That's true. So that's an obvious placement, but also a big opportunity for promotion.
So what about price?
W: It won't be easy. The smart fabric isn't cheap to produce, but a cycle safety vest isn't really a premium product.
M: Well, the usual bright orange and bright green ones aren't, but we're selling something special here. The basic ones are about five euros, and some of the nicer ones are about twenty euros. Our cost, per vest, at least at first, will be about twenty-two euros, so we're looking at a retail price of over forty euros.

W: Forty euros …
M: I know. It's high. But then … if we price it as a premium product – a fashion safety vest …
W: … we might place it in some of the more expensive department stores, not just cycle shops.
M: I like that idea! And who knows, if the vests are popular, we might develop a whole range of cycling products.

BW6.01

M = Man   W = Woman

M: Why do you have to do risk assessment for offices?
W: We do it to make sure that the work environment is safe for the employees and any visitors. In fact, in most countries you have to do it – it's the law.
M: So how does it work?
W: Firstly, you have to identify any significant hazards in the office and also who is at risk: employees, visitors, cleaners, etc.
M: What kind of things can be dangerous?
W: Well, things like wires and cords that trail across the floor, and carpet that doesn't fit properly or is torn, both of which could trip people up. Erm, dangerous machines that don't have guards on them, for example. You don't want to have any accidents.
M: Is that all you're looking at?
W: Oh, not at all. Then there are things like the heat or the noise in the workspace. Is it too hot or too cold or noisy for people to work safely and comfortably?
M: I hadn't thought of that. But I suppose if you're too hot or cold, you can't work effectively because it can make you feel ill.
W: Exactly.
M: Would you also look at things like lighting?
W: Yes, you can't expect people to work in places where there's inadequate lighting because it could damage their eyesight.
M: What about office furniture? Is it important to have good chairs for example?
W: Oh, absolutely. One of the most common causes of staff being off sick is backache, so it's a good idea to ensure that the seating is good for their posture.
M: So, once we've identified these risks, what happens next?
W: Then you need to evaluate the risks involved and put procedures in place to limit the risks and …

BW7.01

This morning I'm going to talk about dealing with unhappy customers and how to turn a bad situation around. When things go wrong, many people's first reaction is to be very angry and demand that it be dealt with immediately. So whether the complaint is on social media, the phone or in an email, act as quickly as you can to resolve the situation. However, don't go making offers without checking the facts as that can be almost as bad as not resolving it. Customers like to know that a company cares about them.
With social media and emails, respond immediately by apologising and indicating that you are looking into the complaint and will contact the person as soon as you can. But then don't fall into the trap of taking too long. It's important to treat each complaint as a priority. If necessary, imagine that if you do not solve the problem, you could lose your job. That's a good way to focus your mind. Then get back to the customer with a solution as quickly as you can. And if you can give a customer a little more than they expect, they are likely to become your most loyal customer.
Many employees in customer service are dependent on the manager to give them permission to solve problems. All customer-facing staff should be able to solve as many complaints as possible without referring back to someone who may not be available at the time. This is where a comprehensive company policy and good training can be invaluable. These can help to ensure that similar problems don't occur again. A company must create a culture of good service and respect for the customer. It should keep accurate records of every communication between the company and the customer for each complaint so that everyone knows what's happened or is happening and can use this information to either improve a service or make sure something similar doesn't happen again.

BW8.01

Speaker 1

I'm based in Durban, in South Africa, but I sometimes visit our production facility in Vietnam, near Hanoi. On my first visit there, I was introduced to the top management of our subsidiary soon after I arrived. My visit wasn't very long, and we had some important business to discuss. I expected to meet people, have a short conversation, then get down to business. On the first day, we went to the factory in the afternoon, and I had a tour. That was interesting, but not very useful to me. Then we went out for dinner. I expected this to be a business dinner, but my hosts never mentioned work, and whenever I tried to go onto that topic, they changed the subject quickly. We finally discussed business on the second day. The whole experience really confused me. It was only later that I learnt about how important it is in Vietnamese business culture to get to know people first, before talking business. Also, apparently it's OK to talk business at lunch, but almost never at dinner. Now that I understand, it makes a lot of sense. I like it, actually. I guess they think we South Africans are probably too direct!

Speaker 2

I completely understand that the management needs to know what the sales team is up to – what we're doing. The business depends on our performance. But a few months ago, they asked us to write a weekly report of our sales activities. Before that, it was a monthly report, which I liked. But a weekly report – it's too much, a real pain. I really need to focus on selling. And do the managers really want to read a weekly report from sales reps all over the world? Don't they have more important things to do? I would understand if the sales team were failing, but we aren't failing. The last couple of years have been outstanding for the business. This is a case of too much communication – too much paperwork.

BW8.02

I've scheduled a meeting with one of our biggest clients in France next Monday. China is going to supply the model for the meeting just in time, but it's stressful. If something goes wrong with the shipping, I'll have big problems. We don't have to work this way! Why didn't Mr Lau send the design model back to manufacturing as soon as he realised there was a problem? Why did he have to ask what I wanted? Why couldn't he just *do something* instead of waiting for orders from me? It doesn't make sense to me – not at all.

BW8.03

When I received the design model of the HM-02, I knew the problem was serious. However, Frederik works in Head Office in Denmark, and he's above me in the company. It's really important for employees to respect their superiors and to include them in making important decisions, so I could never have returned the design model for the correction without first asking Frederik. Teamwork is extremely important in business. It's why we are successful as a company. Also, I knew we could supply the model just in time, so there wasn't going to be a big problem.

P5.02

1   the best rest'rant in town
2   while they're deliv'ring the food
3   I've seen something sim'lar in Amsterdam
4   only because it's necess'ry

P7.02

1
A: Why don't you take a few days off work?
B: I can't a<u>fford</u> to take a few days off work.
2
A: Why don't you phone customer services?
B: I <u>hate</u> phoning customer services.
3
A: Maybe it's better not to join the project?
B: I've already a<u>greed</u> to join the project.

Pearson Education Limited
KAO Two, KAO Park, Harlow
Essex, CM17 9SR, England
and Associated Companies throughout the world

www.pearsonELT.com/businesspartner

First published 2018

Fourth impression 2023

ISBN: 978-1-2922-3718-3
Set in Burlingame Pro
Printed by CPI Group (UK) Ltd, Croydon CR0 4YY

We are grateful to the following for permission to reproduce copyright material:

Text
Article 1. from Vodafone launches programme to recruit career-break women, *FT.com*, 03/03/2017 (Hill. A), © The Financial Times Limited. All Rights Reserved; Article 2. from India's motorcycle makers burnish brand credentials, *FT.com*, 16/04/2017 (Munday. S), © The Financial Times Limited. All Rights Reserved; Article 3. from How project management turned into a Scrum, *FT.com*, 12/08/2015 (Pollack, L), © The Financial Times Limited. All Rights Reserved; Article 4. from Companies adapt to local African markets, *FT.com*, 16/03/2014 (Manson, K), © The Financial Times Limited. All Rights Reserved; Article 5. from The funding dilemma for small design firms, *http://www.telegraph.co.uk/*, 08/03/2016 (Hemsley, S), copyright © Telegraph Media Group Limited 2016; Article 6. from How to turn cyber attacks to your advantage, *FT.com*, 25/03/2017 (Hill, A), © The Financial Times Limited. All Rights Reserved; Article 7. from Customer service start-up aims to take pain out of complaints, *FT.com*, 01/01/2016 (Moore, M), © The Financial Times Limited. All Rights Reserved; Article 8. from The best way to recover from a technological bungle, *FT.com*, 15/10/2017 (Clark, P), © The Financial Times Limited. All Rights Reserved

Every effort has been made to trace the copyright holders and we apologise in advance for any unintentional omissions. We would be pleased to insert the appropriate acknowledgement in any subsequent edition of this publication.